WANTING EVERYTHING

Also by Dorothy Rowe

WANTING EVERYTHING

The Art of Happiness

Dorothy Rowe

HarperCollins*Publishers*

HarperCollins*Publishers*,
77–85 Fulham Palace Road,
Hammersmith, London W6 8JB

Published by HarperCollins*Publishers* 1991

9 8 7 6 5 4 3 2 1

A catalogue record for this book is
available from the British Library

ISBN 0 00 215548 6

Photoset in Linotron Palatino by
Rowland Phototypesetting Limited,
Bury St Edmunds, Suffolk

Printed and bound in Great Britain by
HarperCollins Manufacturing, Glasgow

To Nan and John

Contents

Acknowledgements

The author and publishers should like to thank the following for their permission to reproduce copyright material:

For the cartoons: Fiona Buckland, Cartoonists and Writers Syndicate, André Deutsch, Victor Gollancz Ltd, *Guardian*, Merillee Harpur, Intercontinental Features, *Kurrier*, Larry, Peattie and Taylor, Posie Simmonds, *Punch*, Universal Press Syndicate.

For the written excerpts: *Akron Beacon Journal*, *The Australian*, Jasper Becker, Peter Biddle, *British Journal of Psychiatry*, Victoria Brittain, Nirad C. Chaudhuri, Jillie Collins, Mark Corner, Judith Cutler, *Daily Mail*, Maureen Dowd, Harold Faulk, Helen Fielding, Michael Foot, Christopher French, Elizabeth Furness, Darian Gorman and DBA Television, Hermann Graff Hatzfeldt, *Guardian*, Hugh Herbert, Christopher Hill, Ann Hocking, Jo La Fatch, *Index on Censorship*, Ben Laurance, *New Internationalist*, *New York Times*, Richard Norton-Taylor, *Observer*, John Pilger, Haider Reeve, *Sunday Age*, Walter Swartz, *Time*, Linda Valins, Robert van de Weyer, Ed Vulliamy, Martin Walker, Lord Weidenfeld, Fay Weldon, *Yorkshire Post*;

Atlantic Monthly Press for T. D. Allman, *Miami*.

Basil Blackwell for Martin Herbert, *Caring for Your Children*.

Cambridge University Press for Michael J. Reddy, *Metaphor and Thought*, and Kenneth Baxter Wolf, *Christian Martyrs in Spain*.

Croom Helm for J. Mark, G. Williams, *The Psychological Treatment of Depression*.

J. M. Dent for David Smail, *Taking Care*.

Doubleday for Jo Brans, *Mother I Have Something to Tell You*.

Faber & Faber for T. S. Eliot, *Four Quartets*, for Vaclav Havel, *Letters to Olga*, and for George Steiner, *The Death of Tragedy*.

Fontana for Quentin Crisp, *The Naked Civil Servant*.

Steven Goodwin for BMW(GB) Limited.

William Heinemann for James Gleick, *Chaos*.

David Higham Associates for Hedrick Smith, *The Power Game*.

Edite Kroll for Robin Morgan, *The Demon Lover*.

Methuen for Tim Tate, *Child Pornography*.

Craig Newnes for K. Li in *Clinical Psychology Forum*.

Oxford University Press for G. W. Whitro, *Time in History*, for Alister Hardy, *The Spiritual Nature of Man*, for Leo Braudy, *The Frenzy of Renown*, and for J. Lovelock, *Gaia*.

Random Century for Ruth Rendell, *Make Death Love Me*.

Univ. of Queensland Press for Margaret Coombes, *Regards to the Czar*.

Virago Press for Anna Mitgutsch, *Punishment*.

A note on the notes

Some of the notes referred to by the numbering system within each chapter are source notes, and some of them are extended notes which discuss or illuminate the subject area further than can be accommodated within the chapter. To identify these extended notes, the reference number has been underlined.

Preface

Certain ancient Chinese philosophers used to say that what we needed to get right were our words. If we got our words right, then everything would be right.

Getting our words right is not just a matter of naming things, of pointing to objects and saying sounds like 'land – tree – house – politician – virus – atom'. It is a matter of putting words into sentences. Getting our sentences right is for all of us a matter of life and death.

Words simply point. Sentences create meaning, and it is in meaning that we live. (We cannot step outside our world of meaning. Even the sentence 'This is meaningless' has meaning.) The word 'land' is no more than the word 'land', but the sentence 'That land is mine' has a meaning which is significant in itself and which connects to other people's sentences. It could connect to one person's sentence 'I shall inherit that land', and thus to a life of peace and security, or to another person's sentence 'That land was stolen from me', and to a life of war and suffering.

We need to create our sentences with great care, making them as close to the truth as we can manage.

With some of our sentences we are very careful – sentences like 'Three plus three equals six', 'Two molecules of hydrogen and one of oxygen combine to form water', 'You'll need two eggs and eight ounces of flour to make that cake', 'This is the setting you need for the points to get the best performance out of your car', 'One tank division should be sufficient to hold the line'.

With other sentences, indeed most of our sentences, we have great difficulty in getting them right, so much difficulty that all too often we do not bother to try. These are the sentences about ourselves, how we think, feel, imagine and act.

We use these sentences to lie to others. We say, 'I'm so glad you phoned,' while thinking, 'Why does she always phone when we're having dinner?' We use these sentences to lie to ourselves. We say to ourselves, 'I love my family totally,' and deny the murderous rage that families, in the ways they frustrate us, can arouse in us.

It is hard to get our sentences right because we are, at every moment, in the midst of all our thoughts, feelings and actions. When we want to make sentences about how objects work (this includes people whom we treat as objects), we can separate ourselves from the objects, but we cannot separate ourselves from our thoughts, feelings and actions. Moreover, sentences about how objects work follow a

1

simple logic. Objects are *or* they aren't. A cannot be not-A. A motor car isn't an elephant. A house standing in Birmingham is not also located in Rangoon. Two plus two is four, not five or sixty-four. You can't have your cake and eat it too. This kind of logic is called Aristotelian, named after the ancient Greek philosopher who first described it.

However, sentences about ourselves follow a different logic. In this other kind of logic two opposites can merge together. We can say, 'The people I love I also hate', or, 'I want to be close but separate', or, 'I want to live forever and to die'. In Aristotelian logic two things which are similar are never regarded as being identical, but in the logic of our personal experiences similar things can be perceived as sharing an identity. We can say, 'That man is just like my father,' and behave towards that man in the way we behaved towards our father. Indeed, it is very difficult not to perceive a new experience as being the same or very similar to an old one, for all we can bring to a new experience is our old experience, and so we interpret every new experience in terms of our old experience. Similarities stated as identities are called metaphors, and such metaphors operate very powerfully in our lives. It is hard to construct sentences which merge opposites, or which use similarities as identities, which also truthfully reflect the subtleties of our experience. Such sentences connect to other sentences in all sorts of complex ways. It requires a special kind of intelligence to get these sorts of sentences right.

In using the sentences of Aristotelian logic about objects, we are remarkably intelligent. Out of these sentences we have constructed a vast science and technology. Even those of us who grew up without being educated in Western science and technology have the ability to construct such sentences and apply them successfully to our environment. Every race and culture has developed a science and technology appropriate to its situation and its needs. When we speak of ourselves as *Homo sapiens*, the 'sapiens' (the Latin means wise, sensible, prudent, judicious) actually refers to this kind of intelligence which puts us at the top of the hierarchy of all living things.

However, if anthropologists had classified us according to the second kind of sentence-making, sentences about our thoughts, feelings and actions, they would have had to call us *Homo stupidus* and put us at the bottom of the hierarchy. No other species wreaks so much death and suffering on itself and on one another as we do. In caring for ourselves we are remarkably stupid.

Science and technology, using Aristotelian logic and the associated logic of mathematics, have transformed the way most of us live. Within my lifetime I have seen enormous improvements in how we can feed, clothe and shelter ourselves, how we can travel and keep in touch with one another. Yet such improvements are enjoyed only by relatively few, and there has not been one improvement which has not brought other problems in its train. I remember how excited my family were when electricity finally reached my grandmother's home in the bush, and now I read of the damage that the manufacture of electricity has done to our planet. Forests have been drowned and razed to build hydroelectric generators, coal-fired power stations create acid rain, nuclear power stations spread radiation.

Sentences which follow the rules of Aristotelian logic have enabled us to change our world and the way we live. Sentences about ourselves have not. We go on behaving as we always did.

My first awareness of the world outside my country was of watching newsreels of French and Belgian families, looking just like my own family, being machine-gunned by the German air force. In Australia we waited for a similar fate as the Japanese army advanced towards us. At the end of that war my 'side' was supposed to have won, but in fact all that happened was that the war shifted to other places – Malaya, Korea, Vietnam, India and Pakistan, Africa and the Middle East. The wars have never ceased. It has been calculated that in the twentieth century there have been 207 wars in which 78 million people have died.[1]

Nor have the cruelties inflicted in the name of politics and power ceased. These have actually got worse, since technology can be used as torture. Electricity, which lit my grandmother's home and which now keeps me warm, is also used to reduce a human being to nothing but a blob of pain. The technology of torture has become big business from which many respectable people profit,[2] just as in past centuries respectable people profited from slavery.

Nor have the cruelties inflicted in the name of the family decreased. Despite the invention and vigorous prescribing of psychiatric drugs and the burgeoning of psychotherapy and counselling, the incidence of mental illness, suicide, addiction, child abuse, murder and violence as measured by statistics has not decreased. True, these matters are talked about more now than when I was a child, but there is still a great reluctance on the part of most people to see a connection between childhood experience and adult life. The beliefs that 'children forget' and 'I was beaten as a child and it never did me any harm' still allow adults to inflict on children the suffering that they experienced as children.

There has, in my lifetime, been a great increase in the number of people involved in helping other people. Members of the 'helping professions' (or professional 'do-gooders' as those envious of the people being helped call them) are supposed to have had special training in understanding themselves and other people. Some of them are very good at this and use the second kind of sentences very intelligently. However, such people are in the minority. The following two anecdotes are, in my experience, typical. They come from two articles printed on the same day on the Health page of the *Independent*. The then editor of this page, Oliver Gillie, was always very concerned that the page should be balanced, fair and report the facts, so these anecdotes cannot be considered to over-represent a certain point of view.

The first anecdote is from the beginning of an article by Linda Valins about how she came to understand and so deal with a particular kind of fear which quite a number of women feel and which expresses itself in a particular way. She wrote:

I was lying on the gynaecologist's examination couch. I felt terrified, even though the doctor was a woman. She told me to relax, and then produced a speculum – a shiny metal instrument which looked like a duck's beak. I was trembling and felt nauseous.

As she came towards me to introduce the speculum into my vagina I instinctively clamped my knees together and withdrew to the top of the couch. I had come to see the doctor because I had a deep fear of penetration and her answer was to attempt the very act I feared most. For a woman who suffers from the condition known as 'vaginismus' to the degree that I did, even the idea of a fingertip penetrating her vagina is unbearable.

The doctor tried to part my legs. I wanted to help her but they remained clamped tightly shut and beyond my conscious control. She became extremely irritated with me, as if I was trying to prevent her from doing her job. She had forgotten that I was the one with the problem.

Without giving me time to think she injected Valium directly into a vein, which immediately knocked me out. When I awoke she told me that she had succeeded in passing the speculum. I felt I had been raped in my sleep. Her assurance that there was no reason why I could not have intercourse was of no comfort – I had no memory of the speculum entering my body and so could not believe that she had really done what she said.[3]

The second anecdote comes from an article by Colin Wheeler about his severely handicapped daughter. He wrote:

A printed card arrived in the post one morning telling us that our daughter was severely subnormal. The only human touch was a tick in a box, and that indicated that her subnormality was graded as severe. The card told us what we were slowly beginning to realize. Our daughter, Andrée, then four, could not speak or understand speech. She would never be able to go to a normal school or live an independent life . . .

[Twenty-one years later] it is hard for us not to feel prejudiced about health, education and social services after our experiences of them. After several unhappy early incidents, we have always tried to avoid involvement with doctors, community nurses, social workers and local authority bureaucrats. We feel that most of the services they provide are organized more for the convenience of staff than for the mentally handicapped and their families.[4]

Of course, there are people who would not be so insensitive and behave so cruelly.

In every generation there are some people who do possess the second kind of intelligence. They believe that it is of prime importance that we strive to understand ourselves and other people. They see people as people; not as objects to be organized, used and abused, but as persons to be treated with respect and dignity. They see individuals as having the right to know and to express their own personal truth. They try to enlarge the ways in which each of us can increase our understanding, and explore and develop our talents and become all the person that we might be. In different times and places, these people have expressed their intelligence. In the centuries when the Church claimed domination over all, such people insisted on the right of each individual to find and express his or her own religious truth. When the State, in the guise of emperors or kings, plutocrats or dictators, or those who claim to know what is best for everyone, assumed total power, these people insisted on the right of each individual to freedom and self-determination. In this century such people have protested against war, against the destruction of the resources of the planet, against genocide, torture, starvation, poverty, homelessness, and against the cruelty inflicted on individuals by governments, institutions, and those who lack this intelligence about people.

Curiously, the activities of the possessors of this intelligence about people are not appreciated by those who lack it. With regard to intelligence about objects, those with much of this intelligence and those with a moderate amount get along reasonably well. True, the possessors of much of this intelligence and little of the intelligence about people usually seize and hold power, and feel contempt for those who do not share the same amount of intelligence about objects, while the possessors of a limited amount of intelligence about objects often denigrate and envy those whom they see as their intellectual superiors, but they do not usually persecute and seek to destroy those who possess much of the intelligence about objects.

By contrast the possessors of intelligence about people have always been persecuted by those who lack this intelligence. A history of the possessors of intelligence about people would be a history of persecution, imprisonment, torture, execution, murder, slander, censorship, hatred and contempt. Typical of the lives depicted in such a history would be that of Saint Zapata, as described by Voltaire, himself no stranger to such persecution.

> He isolated truth from falsehood and separated religion from fanaticism. He taught and practised virtue. He was gentle, benevolent and modest, and was roasted at Valladolid in the year of grace, 1631.[5]

Each of us is born with the potential to create the sentences which indicate both kinds of intelligence, but the education we receive allows each of us to develop only some parts of our potential and inhibits and destroys other parts. Thus, in using our intelligence about objects, some of us are 'good with figures' but find putting words on paper difficult, while others can handle words with ease but find machines a mystery. Similarly, in using intelligence about people, there are many people who have been allowed to understand that people who share their sex/nationality/race/class/religion are human and have feelings similar to their own, but there are some who have been allowed to understand that the people who do not share their sex/nationality/race/class/religion do not have feelings or are, indeed, not human beings at all.

We each develop a combination of both kinds of intelligence. Those of us who develop both kinds of intelligence to some degree lead lives very different from those who develop only intelligence about objects. There are a great many people who develop only intelligence about objects, and they are the ones who seek power over others and who, often in the guise of doing good, act selfishly and cruelly.[6]

The possessors of intelligence about objects have changed the world in which we live, but the possessors of intelligence about people make only modest gains, each insecurely held and needing to be fought for in every generation. The possessors of intelligence about people have survived and flourished only in very small parts of the world and for a very limited time. Yet their message, though expressed in a multitude of ways, has always been one which offers safety, happiness, courage and hope. It is, *If we respect and care for one another as equals and if we respect and care for our world, we can discover ways of living together safely, peacefully, and contentedly.*

Why has this message always been rejected by those who do not possess this kind of intelligence? Those who lack intelligence about objects do not reject what the possessors of this intelligence create. Such people happily use the radios, cars and washing machines that derive from the application of intelligence about objects. Yet, even though the failure to accept the creations of those with intelligence about people means that we are now facing the extinction of our species in the next few brief decades, the message is still rejected, still not understood.

How is it that we can all use, understand and applaud the sentences which emanate from intelligence about objects, and so many of us fail to understand and consequently denigrate the sentences which emanate from intelligence about people?

Why is it that we are so aware and intelligent using the first kind of sentences, and so unaware and stupid in using the second kind?

Often, as I listen to a client or a 'world leader' uttering sentences which can result only in pain and disaster, I feel that such stupidity is as inherent in us as our need for air to breathe, and that as our nature it is our doom. Then I remind myself about our understanding of intelligence about objects.

When I began studying psychology in the middle of this century I was taught that each of us was born with a lump of intelligence. Some of us had large lumps, some of us had small lumps, and some of us had hardly a lump at all. Psychologists could measure these lumps with tests which were made up of sentences about objects and which required the person doing the test to apply Aristotelian and mathematical logic. The score the person got on this test was called his Intelligence Quotient. Psychologists believed that a person could no more change his IQ than he could change the colour of his eyes.

However, in the sixties other psychologists began suggesting that perhaps the IQ is not immutable. Now we know that our ability to use sentences using Aristotelian and mathematical logic is connected not just to what food we eat and what homes we grow up in, but whether our family and teachers think we are intelligent. If people treat you as if you are intelligent, you will be intelligent.

So perhaps our stupidity with the second kind of sentences is not immutable either. Perhaps we can learn to construct better sentences so that we no longer cause ourselves and others so much pain and suffering.

I could say that if I did not believe that we can improve our intelligence about people I would not go on writing books about this second kind of sentence. But I *would* go on writing, because by writing I sort out and improve my own sentences. I gain greater clarity, and even if no one else shares my clarity (but I suspect there are some who do) I shall go on because I enjoy doing so.

This book, like all my previous books, is about the sentences we use about our thoughts, feelings and actions. It is about the logic that applies to such sentences, and how we get confused in our use of that logic. Especially, it is about how certain people deliberately confuse us in our use and understanding of these sentences. It is in the interests of those people in power – the people who make up the top of the hierarchy of the State, the Church, and the large financial institutions

– that we should not develop and use our intelligence about people, for then we would question and seek to change the organization of a society, whether capitalist or Communist or theocratic, which deprives most people of an adequate living and which gives to a small group of people power, wealth and prestige. So such people impose on the rest of us an education which bamboozles us, preventing us from seeing and understanding what is being done to us. But they, too, are products of such an education. They, too, are bamboozled. They are stupid and they treat us as if we are stupid, and we become stupid. But we need not remain so.

Because when we are in our mother's womb all our needs are met, we come into the world with a wordless, inchoate belief that, wanting everything, we can get everything. Our education at the hands first of our family and then of society shows us that we cannot have everything, but deliberately confuses us about the things we cannot have simply because of the way we define ourselves and our world – 'Boys who play with dolls are cissy', 'Girls who are assertive won't be loved' – and the things which we cannot have because of the nature of life – 'Time passes, there's no going back'. We grow up confused and not understanding how we think and feel, and not understanding that we do not understand; that is, we grow up lacking the intelligence to understand ourselves and other people. But our wanting everything does not dissipate. We go on trying, and failing, to get everything. Many people try to get everything by becoming powerful, and others try to get everything through greed, envy and total selfishness. Others, convinced by their education that it is wicked to want something for yourself, try to deny their wanting everything while trying to get everything by taking on responsibilities which need not be theirs, and by seeking martyrdom and revenge. However, in whichever of these ways people try to gain everything, they fail because they do not understand the terms under which we live our lives; that is, they have failed to develop their intelligence about people.

This need not happen. We can learn how to use this second kind of intelligence so as to turn our wanting everything into our getting everything.

DOROTHY ROWE
Sheffield, 1990

'I want to be rich and famous. I want to be Queen of the World.'
FAY WELDON

We all want to be famous, admired, universally loved, immensely powerful, honoured, revered, immortal and remembered forever. We want to be the most important person in the universe for all time, the admired cynosure of all eyes, the acknowledged font of all wisdom, the model of perfection for all to follow. We want to live our lives independently and freely, making our own decisions, unimpeded by others, at the same time as we are utterly dependable, unlimitedly generous, devoted to and caring for all others, while being loved, wanted, needed, cosseted and cared for by everyone we encounter. All skills, all possessions, all experiences we believe can be ours if we so desire. We want to have everything.

Our tragedy is that we can't have everything.

Or can we?

1

'I Can Have Everything'

**At the end of my long life I realize that what
I was looking for I had at the beginning.**
MARCEL PROUST, *Remembrance of Things Past*

How sad we all are! Sure, there are times when we laugh and shout
for joy, but most of the time we are so sad. Look about you on the
subway in London or New York, on the streets of Tokyo or Sydney
or Moscow, and what do you see? Silent, grim-faced people. Talk to
them, and what do they talk about? Their troubles, of course. Sometimes they talk about their pleasures and their joys, but mostly they
talk about what worries them.

Of course many people do have things to worry about – how to feed
themselves and their families, how to preserve their lives and the roof
over their heads. However, having ample to eat and a secure place to
live does not make people cheerful. Indeed, not having to worry about
basic necessities seems to free people to worry about everything else.

The word 'worry' implies some conscious thoughts. The world is
full of expert worriers, able and ready to turn every benefit and pleasure into a danger and a misery. Some people say they don't worry,
but this is chiefly because they are continually doing the things which
will stop worries from arising – working hard, being responsible,
pleasing other people. In all these people, under the worries and the
thought and the action to avoid worries is a deep rhythm of sadness.

In some people this sadness shows through as wistfulness. They
are like children for ever locked out of a secret garden, not knowing
for sure what the garden contains, but knowing that what is there
would make their heart expand in complete and absolute joy, and
knowing that what the secret garden contains can never be theirs.
They say to themselves, 'It cannot be,' and try to comfort themselves,
but the sadness remains.

In other people the sadness comes through as bitterness and resentment. They blame and they envy, and they want more. If they cannot
have more, if the fruits of their labour bring them only modest
rewards, they turn their bitterness and envy on those who might take
away what little they have. They denigrate and perhaps attack those
who are of a different race or nationality or religion or class or are not

family members. If they can have more, if they can use their wealth to create more wealth and possessions, they try to assuage their bitterness and envy by acts of conspicuous consumption, but even as they do, they discover that the hunger of sadness can never be satisfied. The more they have, they more they want.

Why Are We Sad?

Where does this sadness come from? Of course in the lives of every adult there are some things to feel sad about – opportunities lost, love denied. But the sadness we feel is more powerful and more pervasive than these events alone would provoke. Even when other events in our lives might be regarded as more than compensating for these disappointments and losses, the act of counting one's blessings does not dissipate the sadness. Nothing, it seems, can compensate for what might have been.

What has been lost? I have pondered about finding this sadness in me when I had reached a point in my life where all the disappointments and losses I had suffered had proved in fact to be very beneficial. I was now leading the kind of life I had dreamed of when I was an adolescent – writing, travelling, with family and friends, my own delightful home, a good income, and healthier than I had ever been. As well, I had been successful in excluding from my life quite a number of things which I did not want to do and which I would, when I was younger, have felt obliged to do (like being responsible for a husband, or devoting precious time to civic or charitable affairs, as many women my age, but less selfish than me, do). I had also relieved myself of the burden of worrying about whether people approved of me. I had decided that wise, perspicacious people approved of me, and anyone who didn't wasn't. Most of the time I felt extremely happy, but every now and then I would find myself feeling sad.

I thought about this, and I thought about my daydreams.

When I was young I imagined that as we get older we daydream less and less, because the alternatives open to us become less and less. (I think this idea came from a song, 'When I Grow Too Old to Dream', which my grandmother would get me to sing to her.) As adolescents we can dream of doing many things and falling in love with many different people, but with each passing year, I thought, the range of possibilities gets less and less, so that in old age there is nothing left to dream about.

I now know that this is not the case. We go on daydreaming, trying to dress up dull reality in fancy clothes. We go on telling ourselves stories to comfort ourselves and to view the future with hope. Even those last moments of thought which people in near-death experiences have reported seem to be daydreams about a heavenly future.

'I Can Have Everything'

So I still daydream a lot, and these daydreams, like the daydreams of my youth, are about wanting everything and getting everything. I want to have it all. My sadness is because I do not have it all.

When I was comparing notes with Fay Weldon about what we each do when we are not writing, I found that we are busy publicizing our books and ourselves as a means of acquiring it all. Fay flies to New York to talk on television, to Moscow, or Melbourne, or Tokyo to talk to her readers, while I speak at Mental Health Association Annual General Meetings in Harlow or Rochdale, or answer listeners' questions on local radio phone-in programmes. Fay and I do these things rather well and are helpful to the people who invite us and to some of the people who listen to us, so we can feel a glow of virtue if we wish. But we are honest enough to admit, at least to one another, that we actually do these things as a way of gaining our end, which is to have it all. Fay, I am sure, is only a few steps away from being the Queen of the World.

Fay and I are not two megalomaniac aberrations in the female sex where normal women eschew power, wealth and fame, and live lives of selfless devotion to others. Fay and I are just like all other women in wanting it all. It is just that so far we have been luckier than most. I know that women, like men, want it all because over the years so many people have talked to me about their fears and sadnesses, and there, under the sadness about all the terrible things that have happened to them, lies the sadness of wanting it all and not getting it all.

Usually, when a person first comes to see me we talk about the terrible, mysterious feelings to which he or she has fallen victim – the painful isolation of depression, or the heart-stopping panics, or the ridiculous, undisobeyable obsessions, or the irresponsible, ceaseless activity, or the strange thoughts and visions. These experiences seem to the person to have no connection with anything else in his or her life, and my first suggestion that there is a connection between the events of our childhood and ourselves as adults is usually rejected, for this would imply that the person's parents had not always acted in his or her interests. (One of the most striking examples of our capacity to believe two incompatible things at one and the same time is the way in which many people believe that if a child learns that it is pleasant to clean his teeth each day this knowledge will stay with him for the rest of his life, but that if a child learns that it is not pleasant to be beaten, humiliated, abandoned, betrayed, bereaved or used as a sexual object, this knowledge the child soon forgets.)

Once the person realizes that to understand ourselves we need to see our lives as a connected whole, we can then begin putting together a picture of his past, present and future. At first the picture is one of a small child in the hands of powerful adults who, by simple neglect, or cruelty, or, most frequently, by wanting to make the child be good, have taught him that he is bad. Later, when he realizes that he is not intrinsically and really bad but just defined as bad, and that he can just as easily define himself as good, the picture changes to something more benign. He can see the adults who so affected him in childhood, not as the large, looming, mysterious and dangerous giants of his childhood, but as ordinary, fallible, ignorant human beings. His story has changed from 'I can't understand why I am like this. I couldn't have had a better childhood', through 'If my parents had treated me better I wouldn't be like this', to 'My parents did the best they could in the circumstances. They didn't know any better. I can't change what happened, but I can change how what happened affects me'.

This progression of understanding brings enormous changes in the way people live their lives. I have now seen many people make this progression and go on to live rich and fulfilling lives. They not only do things differently but they enjoy what they do.

And yet, underneath this joy and freedom, there is still sadness.

Many depressed people believe that people who are not depressed are happy all the time. They envy people who are not depressed, and when they themselves give up being depressed they are disappointed to discover that they are not totally and completely happy. Dropping the defence of being depressed means facing up to what is actually going on in your life. As one woman said to me, 'My description of being depressed would be of a television set turned off. It is amazing how you can completely ignore quite important events by being depressed.'

Dropping the defence of being depressed also means discovering the underlying sadness.

Alice Miller has described how ceasing to be depressed requires the discovery of the ability to mourn those events of childhood for which there is no recompense or reward.[1] As children we are taught that if we are good nothing bad will happen to us, and children who are not canny enough to recognize that this is a lie grow up believing that if they work hard and give up their own selfish wishes and consider the wishes of others they will be rewarded. They manage to ignore the manifest unfairness of the world until compelled to do so by some event in their lives. It may be a sudden tragedy or the slow accumulation of misery in an unhappy marriage or an unsatisfying job. They can stave off disappointment, bitterness, sadness, and fear caused by the threatened collapse of the structure of their self[2] by clinging to the illusion that the world is just, by saying to themselves, 'I am bad and deserve such punishment.' However, defining oneself as bad leads inevitably to attitudes of fear and distrust towards other people and to life itself, attitudes which place the person in that peculiar isolation which we call depression.[3]

Horrible though depression is, there are many people who prefer to be depressed rather than confront two difficult truths.

The first of these truths is that whatever system of causality governs this universe, that goodness prevents disaster is not part of it. Being good does not necessarily either keep us safe or bring us rewards.

The second truth is that even good, kind, loving parents lie to their children. When parents say to their children, 'If you are bad you will be punished,' they are not lying, for so long as the child wants the parents' love and approval the parents have the power to punish the child. But when parents say, 'If you are good you will be rewarded and you will be safe,' they are lying. No parent can guarantee their child's safety, and while they can reward the child with their love and approval, they cannot guarantee love and approval by other people.

To recognize these truths for the first time in adult life means recognizing that we have wasted time in fruitless effort and have been betrayed by those we trusted. Lost time cannot be regained, while those who betrayed us are usually by then dead and gone, or old and frail, and while an apology from a parent might be comforting, we may not want to demand it, for such an apology requires the parent to make the painful discovery that he has erred and that his error cannot be put right. We then find that we have suffered a loss for which there is no recompense, and so we mourn.

Mourning can be a static, enduring state, or a process of feeling, thinking, discovering and learning. I have known many people who, having confronted the two truths, treated their mourning as a process through which they deepened their understanding of themselves, gained greater wisdom and drew closer to other people. Out of such a process of mourning came forgiveness. (Forgiveness is not something we can choose to do, although we often talk as if it is. It is spontaneous, like love.[4]) Such a mourning process is easier when the person's life offers new opportunities and the possibility of other rewards.

Once we have got over the shock of realizing that goodness is not necessarily rewarded, we can abandon the burden of trying to be good. Instead we can be good simply because it pleases us to be good. Elizabeth,[5] having discarded her disappointment that her efforts to be especially good as a wife and mother had not been rewarded, said to me, 'I *like* being good. I like feeling that I've got things right and I have done things well. I am a naturally good person.' Free though she is now to enjoy her natural goodness, Elizabeth does not see herself as young enough or sufficiently independent of family responsibilities to set about doing all the things she would have done had she not been so busy working hard at being good. Whereas June[6] was young enough and sufficiently free from family responsibilities to abandon her depression and her 'good' job and set off for America.

Like Elizabeth and June, many people have gained a considerable measure of wisdom and reconciliation. Yet, even so, some sadness remains.

A Sense of Loss

A sense of sadness comes from a sense of loss.

We feel a sense of loss only when we have lost something which we owned and valued, or something which, while we might not have owned it, played a valued part in our lives, or something which we believe we might have owned had we been given the opportunity.

For instance, some of my possessions I have been glad to lose, for without them my life is simpler. I treasure some ornaments for they were given to me by friends, but I am pleased when certain other ornaments are broken, for that means fewer objects to gather dust. I can read of the theft of art treasures from a private home or museum and feel no loss, but if I found that the Usher Art Gallery at Lincoln had lost a large painting called *The Return of the Prodigal Daughter* I would feel a sense of loss, for that painting has afforded me much gentle amusement.

We think of ourselves as owning time, or at least that portion of time between our birth and our death. When we engage in an activity which yields neither pleasure nor profit, we say with regret and sometimes anger, 'I have wasted my time,' or 'That person used up my time.' We think of ourselves as owning all those aspects of ourselves which never actually came into being. We can say, 'I wanted to be a ballet dancer, but my father didn't approve. He wanted me to be a teacher, and that's what I did,' and feel that 'myself as a ballet dancer' as something owned and lost.

> Time present and time past
> Are both perhaps present in time future,
> And time future contained in time past.
> If all time is eternally present
> All time is unredeemable.
> What might have been is an abstraction
> Remaining a perpetual possibility
> Only in a world of speculation.
> What might have been and what has been
> Point to one end, which is always present.
> Footfalls echo in the memory
> Down the passage we did not take
> Towards the door we never opened
> Into the rose-garden.[7]

What makes the loss of what we might have been so poignant is our knowledge that we shall die. If we did not die, if we lived for ever and had unlimited time, we could bring into being every possible aspect of ourselves. But we do die, so our time is limited, and we have to choose. We can try to extend our sense of how much time we have by believing in a life after death, but as we usually see the quality of our life after death as being dependent on our degree of goodness, a belief in a life after death is likely to reduce the range of possibilities of what we might be.[8]

For instance, if your religion teaches that you must be sexually abstinent or should marry in order to avoid burning in hell, then you have to abandon a vast range of possibilities for yourself and intimacy.

The belief in life after death is one example of how we use our imagination to escape from the petty limitations of our lives. If we had no imagination we could simply attend to our duties and, when the time came, lie down and die with as little anguish as we imagine animals feel when they die. But our imagination takes us far beyond the duties of our lives, and we can always see ourselves doing and being many more things than our lives allow.

Thus we can always feel a sense of loss for what might have been. It is this sense of loss which prevents us from making the most of what we do have and could have.

Our sense of loss is great, for what might have been is everything, because once in our lives we were sure that everything was ours.

When Everything Was Ours

We began our life in a warm, safe place where our every need was met. Our mother's body was organized to protect and support us and help us grow, and if it functioned efficiently we emerged into the world with our first impressions of life clearly fixed. We knew what it was like to be held and loved in perfect peace and security. We knew this in images of sight, sound, touch, taste and smell. We knew what it was like to have everything.

We come into the world expecting that we can have everything and seeing no reason why we should not have everything. We know nothing of the limitations of time and space, nor of death. We know nothing of the people who claim to do us good by preventing us from having what we want, nor of the hosts of envious, greedy people who will compete with us, attack us and try to take from us what little we might have.

We come into the world not knowing that we have been given all that we needed. Having no knowledge of other people, we experience the satiation of our needs as power, and for the first few weeks we experience ourselves as all-powerful. We feel the pangs of hunger and fantasize food, and food appears.

This practice of fantasizing food remains with us for the rest of our

17

lives. A starving person has visions of food which tantalize with their realistic solidity and aroma. In ordinary life we use our ability to fantasize food to help us choose what we want to eat. 'What do you fancy for lunch?' we might be asked. We pause to try out alternative fantasies of food, and answer, 'Just a salad, I think,' or, 'I could murder a steak.' As adults we know that we, perhaps with the aid of someone else, have to do something to bring our fantasy into being, but when we were babies we thought that we had created the food that appeared. As babies too we would miss the comforting support of the womb, and imagine it, or something like it, into being: we cried, and we were held.

If we are lucky enough to be born to a mother who is sensitive to our needs, we find for a few weeks or perhaps even longer that our wishes are answered so quickly and so well that we do not experience them as wishes but as successful commands. We have only to imagine something and it appears. We have everything.

But even the best of mothers make mistakes, and the most loving of mothers cannot always provide the food or the dry nappy as soon as it is needed. We wish, and the wish is not fulfilled. We give vent to our frustration and rage, and still our wish is not fulfilled.

We no longer have everything. We have discovered loss.

Now we need our imagination to save us from being engulfed and annihilated by our sense of loss.

Fantasy as a Way of Having Everything

Just as we use fantasy to conjure up the things that we want, so we use fantasy to comfort ourselves when we fail to get what we want. Long before we have words we create comfort fantasies in our play. Little games like Peek-a-Boo excite and satisfy us, for they reassure us that what is lost will be found, that Mummy might disappear, but that she will reappear.

As we get a little older, Mummy might not fail to reappear and so disappoint us, but she might still disappoint us by not being what we want her to be. Indeed, our whole family might be a disappointment to us. We puzzle over the discrepancy between the time when we were monarch of all we surveyed, with every wish fulfilled, and now, when people tell us that we are a mere child, insignificant and unimportant.

Some of us deal with this discrepancy by creating the fantasy that *a mistake has been made about us and our position in life*. Kenneth Williams, born the son of a strict Methodist who lived near Kings Cross, once said, 'But I really didn't belong in the Caledonian Road with the whelk stalls. I always used to think I was the unclaimed son of a prince.'[9] If in later years we fail to recognize such a fantasy as fantasy and instead treat it as the literal truth, we can go very much astray in our lives. John Stonehouse, the Labour Member of Parliament who faked his own drowning and who, on being discovered alive in Australia, returned to England and served a gaol sentence, said, 'During all those years as a politician, when I was striving to be successful, the opportunity of seeing myself as an ordinary human being eluded me, through my own fault.'[10] With the humour that made him a most loved and successful comic actor, Kenneth Williams remembered his childhood fantasy as a fantasy. John Stonehouse refused to see that his childhood fantasy was a fantasy, insisted on trying to make it reality, and thus, being unable to judge his actions with an adult, critical eye, wasted his talents and earned from his fellows not admiration but scorn.

Like most children who find themselves suffering at the hands of their parents, I explored the fantasy that I was not my mother's child. 'If I was her child she wouldn't treat me like this,' I thought. However, my observations of reality prevented me from holding on to this fantasy. The physical resemblance between my mother and me I could not deny. So I sought respite and comfort in fantasies about the bush. I could, physically, escape into the bush from my grandmother's home in the countryside and from my own home which was on the edge of the suburbs of Newcastle. The bush in both places was, I suppose, quite unremarkable, but I invested it with a magical beauty. Walking in it, or even just when thinking about it, I felt myself to be myself, safe and accepted, and ready to face the possibilities of exploration and adventure.

It is not always easy to recognize our childhood fantasy as fantasy, because what we construct in our own individual way is in fact a version of one of the popular fantasies in our society. What begins as a private individual fantasy becomes absorbed into and reworked by the myths of our society.

If anyone had said to me that the bush was my Garden of Eden I would have rejected this, for to me the Garden of Eden was a boring story told in Sunday School. However, now I can see the similarities between the stories I told myself about the bush and the story of the Garden of Eden. In the Bible the focus is on the expulsion from the Garden of Eden, whereas I concentrated on life in the Garden where everything that was most wonderful was there to be enjoyed.

The *Garden of Eden fantasies* which children create are both a memory of the time when wanting was the same as getting, and an escape from a reality where wanting means getting very little. Many people carry these childhood fantasies into adult life as the desire to go 'home' to die or to return to 'the good old days' when children were well-behaved, and everyone was honest, and families and neighbours helped one another. Such fantasies ignore the fact that dying is an uncomfortable and lonely business wherever we are, and that history books fail to reveal a time when people did not treat one another badly. Though I still find the bush very beautiful and am busy trying to grow eucalyptus in my north-England garden, I have abandoned my fantasy of the bush as the Garden of Eden. I should hate to die in the bush with the flies and the heat; the currently popular romantic tosh that the Aborigines lived in blissful communion with the rugged Australian terrain ignores just how harsh and difficult that life was. Women and babies suffered, for women were considered to be of lower status than the men, and babies were killed so that the tribe would not multiply beyond what the available resources could support.[11]

Of all the fantasies that children can create in order to comfort themselves, the most popular one and the one which most commonly persists into adult life is that *our parents are perfect.*

This fantasy is an outcome of the way we were taught that we cannot expect to have everything because we are not good enough to have everything. When we were babies we never questioned our right to have everything, but once we could crawl or toddle we found that when we tried to claim this right we were frustrated. If our parents understood and loved us, they accepted our wanting and tried to distract us by directing our attention elsewhere. 'No, you can't eat that, but here's an interesting toy to play with.' If they did not understand and accept us, they punished us.

Sometimes our punishment was our own distress, perhaps when we wanted our mother to be with us and instead she disappeared for aeons of time. Sometimes our punishment was humiliation, when we tried to gain what we wanted, and our parents laughed at our attempts and our frustration.[12] Sometimes our punishment was confusion and fear, when we wanted a cuddle and a kiss from Daddy, and instead we found him to have become a stranger who twisted and rent our small body. Sometimes our punishment was terror when we wanted to pursue our own desires and instead found ourselves alone, locked by our parent in some strange and seemingly dangerous place. Sometimes our punishment was vast physical pain, when our wanting, or perhaps simply being, caused our parents to rain blows upon us.

From such situations a small child cannot escape. Though he may not have the words to describe his situation to himself, he knows that he is in the greatest peril, for the very people on whom he depends are showing themselves to be wicked and dangerous. There is one way he can give himself the illusion of safety. He can redefine this perilous situation. He can change his sentence 'I am being unjustly punished by my bad parent' to 'I am bad and am being justly punished by my good parent'.[13] Most of us go through this process of defining ourselves as imperfect in order to fulfil our desire for our parents to be perfect.

Thus the child sacrifices his sense of self-worth for the illusion of security with a good parent, and with that his belief in his right to have everything. Being bad, he does not deserve everything. Indeed, many people grow up with the belief that they do not deserve anything, not even the right to exist. That they have to earn, day by day, by working hard to be good.

An essential part of this sacrifice of our sense of self-worth is to forget that we have done this.[14] All that we allow ourselves to remember is that the most sacrificing of people were our parents who brought us into the world and cared for us, and to whom we must always be grateful. Thus we become adults who cannot see a connection between our childhood experience and our adult life. Inexplicable depression and anxiety descend upon us without warning, and our children grow up to be adults we neither know nor understand. We accept without question the belief promulgated by psychiatrists that all aberrations of behaviour and experience are no more than aberrations in our body's functioning. Then we can fulminate against psychologists who, we say, 'blame the parents'. Such fulminations, however, do not prevent us from taking the credit when our children turn out well. In the logic of fantasy we can believe two opposite things at one and the same time.

In our fantasies, believing that two opposites are true is fine, so long as we do not try to connect our fantasy to our lived reality. Once reality enters our fantasy we either have to acknowledge that our fantasy is fantasy and so change it, or we have to keep piling fantasy on fantasy in a desperate attempt to deny the reality that we know.

If we know that something is absolutely true, we do not spend time thinking about it. For instance, if we believe that it is necessary for us to breathe we do not spend time wondering whether we ought to breathe. However, if we want to believe that something is absolutely true, but if there is at the back of our mind a doubt about this, we spend a good deal of time proving to ourselves that what we hope is true is actually true.

We might have gone through the process of defining ourselves as bad in order to preserve our picture of our parents as good, and we might have consigned the memory of all this to the vast black trunk of our unconscious, and would swear with our hand on our heart that we had perfect parents and a perfect childhood (a few imperfections are admitted, but these we define as 'unimportant' or 'character building'), but all the time we know that the black trunk is there and that there is something in it. As much as we try to make it so, our truth is not absolute. We have to go on working on it, creating fantasy after fantasy, and trying to prove these fantasies to be reality by putting them into practice (like visiting your mother Sunday after Sunday, hoping against hope that the next visit will be the one where she declares that she loves you more than anyone else in the world, and after each visit excusing her crabbiness with 'She's not well', and resolutely putting out of your head the thought that she is taking advantage of you and why doesn't your brother take some responsibility for your mother's care).

For many of us the fantasy of perfect parents becomes the script by which we live our lives. The ambitions we create, the choices we make, are determined by our continued working on our fantasy. Because in childhood we have created representations of our parents inside us, we can, in fantasy, be our parents and do what they did, or do what we wish they had done. Many people decide to marry and have children in order to prove to themselves that their parents are and could have been the perfect parents they desired.

Some of us in later life see clearly the pattern which our fantasy has created. Joseph Needham, whose great work *Science and Civilization in China*[15] is a bringing together of diverse ideas, as were his earlier scientific pursuits in biochemistry and embryology, told Ronald Eyre, 'My father was a physician and my mother was a composer. She had the artistic temperament and he had quite the scientific temperament, so they didn't get on at all well. I've often thought that my desire to bridge over chasms was a result of my infantile experience of two people as parents who didn't really get on.'[16]

'Did you have to mediate between them?' Ronald Eyre asked.

'I didn't do so much of that line. I did my best, of course, but it was rather alarming.' He went on, 'Bridge building is a marked feature of my intellectual career. As an undergraduate it was science and religion, and later it was the unification of morphogenesis and biochemistry, and then came China and the West, and that was the last of it.'

'Now, are you putting a left foot in one place and a right foot in another in order to take a third step?' Here Ronald Eyre was likening Joseph Needham's use of his childhood fantasy as that process of thesis, antithesis and synthesis which is part of the essence of creativity and progress. We look at two opposing things and instead of dismissing one as untrue or valueless, as uncreative scientists are prone to do, or, instead of uncritically believing that the simple juxtaposition of opposites is satisfactory and profound, as uncreative fantasists do, we can search for a new and more expansive meaning which brings together these apparent opposites into a unified whole.

Joseph Needham smiled. 'You could say that.' As an honorary Taoist, as he calls himself, he knows that the synthesis of opposites is always present in the ever-changing, ever-present Tao, and that we do not create syntheses but simply see them.[17]

'I Can Have Everything'

By being aware of how our childhood fantasies become some of the important structures with which we perceive ourselves and our world, many of us are able to make wiser and more understanding responses to what confronts us. Many parents, wanting to reassure themselves of the goodness of their parents, and being aware of this desire, are better parents to their children than their parents were to them.

People who do not become aware of the persistence of their childhood fantasy of the perfection of their parents attempt to make their fantasy into absolute reality by doing what their parents did and claiming that this is the right and proper way to bring up children. 'I was beaten as a child,' they say, 'and it never did me any harm.'

The reason that many people cannot bring themselves to see their fantasy as fantasy is because then they would have to confront the possibility that perhaps their parents did not love them. They want to cling to the fantasy that under their parents' lack of understanding, cruelty and indifference was a warm and genuine love. This is the secret of which Peter Biddle wrote:

> My mother keeps a secret
> Close to her heart.
> She will probably never speak it,
> But I knew from the start.
>
> My mother may beat me
> A hundred times a day.
> She may poke me and pinch me and make me
>   sit up straight
> And tell me I can't and tell me I may.
>
> She may slap me around the head
> And tell me to talk proper.
> She may tell me to eat nicely
> And forbid gobstoppers.
>
> She may threaten me with pokers
> Fresh from the fire,
> Or stick me down the cellar
> For as long as she requires.
>
> But beneath her empty smiles,
> And beneath her fulsome hate,
> My mother keeps a secret
> And I will just dream and wait.

> I am waiting to find that secret love
> Which is under lock and key,
> And the locks and chains are bound with ice
> And the ice has frozen me.
>
> But without love the child will die,
> And I do not wish to expire,
> So I'll remember the secret and forget the pain,
> And forget the pain, and forget the child.[18]

Their persistence in the fantasy that secretly their mother did love them, and therefore she was the perfect mother, though she never or rarely revealed it, ruins people's lives. To 'forget the child' they forget their childhood experiences, or refuse to remember them from the child's point of view, and instead look at the child they once were without sympathy. 'I was a bad child and deserved to be punished.' However, denying emotion is the most ineffective way of dealing with it. Denied emotions make themselves felt as physical pain and disability, and they return as apparently inexplicable fear, anger, envy and hate.

Such emotions can be so powerful that the person becomes unable to lead a life which is in any way ordinary, and so he (or she) may then find himself entering upon the career of a psychiatric patient from which, according to the usual run of this career, there is little chance of escape. Sometimes the person finds ways of keeping these emotions more or less under control, but the effort and attention required prevents him from paying adequate, realistic attention to the present, understanding other people, and forming good relationships with them. This way of living is the pattern of so many people's lives.

A major part of the everything that we want is the love and admiration of everyone. We might be able to come to terms with the discovery that a few insignificant people are so stupid or so envious of us that they withhold their love and admiration, but what is hard to accept is that, when the audience in the world auditorium rises to applaud us, our mother's seat in the centre front row is empty.

We are born with a sense of self-worth, but to retain it we need to see it mirrored in the looks and actions of the adults who care for us. When such mirroring simply does not occur, as will happen to babies born in the midst of war and famine, or to mothers who are depressed, or when the mirroring includes hatred and rejection, the small child has to try to survive as best he can, creating more and more fantasies of what he needs and wants. Such fantasies become the staple of his life, the only certainty in a cosmos of uncertainty. Everything that happens to him he interprets within the context of, 'I am bad, and my good mother punishes me because she loves me.'

A child in this situation has to cling to the certainty of his badness and his mother's love because the alternative explanations of his painful experiences are too terrifying. To say that these painful experiences occurred by chance only increases his sense of helplessness. If he allows himself to contemplate the possibility that his mother did not love him, he then has to say to himself, 'If she did not love you, then your sacrifice of your self-worth was useless. You thought you were giving her something of value when you said, Yes, mother, I am bad and you are right to punish me, but in fact you had nothing to give. You were and you always had been intrinsically bad, and she was right not to love you. If you had been good she would have loved you.' This is the internal conflict which besets the lives of those many people who are always engaged either in being depressed or in denying their depression.

We keep ourselves locked in this conflict over whether or not we are good, and we hang on to the fantasy of perfect parents because we have not questioned our assumption that 'My sense of self-worth is something that other people give me'. When we change our assumption to 'My sense of self-worth is something I give myself', we see that other people's good evaluation of us is the icing on the cake, not the cake itself, that the conflict over whether or not we are good is irrelevant, and that the fantasy of perfect parents is one that we have outgrown.

Those of us who had ordinary, fallible people as parents can, if we think about it, gain our freedom from the fantasy of perfect parents because we can construct a realistic belief along the lines of, 'My parents tried to do the best they could. Through their own lack of understanding and through the necessities of their lives they caused me pain. This pain then made me believe that I was not valuable and lovable, but now I know that this belief was incorrect. I was, as I am now and shall always be, valuable and lovable.'

Those of us who had as parents people who were cruel and indifferent to us have a more difficult task in gaining freedom from the fantasy of perfect parents, for we have to see that whom we are born to is just a matter of chance. Some of us are very unlucky. That is annoying, but still no reason to believe that because we were unlucky we are bad, or because we were unlucky in our parents we are going to be unlucky in everything else. The realistic belief we need to construct is along the lines of, 'No matter who my parents were or what they did, I was, as I am now and shall always be, valuable and lovable.'

When we create a fantasy to persuade ourselves that we have something which in fact we do not, we often need to call on the special illusions of *magic*.

Believing in magic is a way of trying to overcome our sense of helplessness as well as of trying to get everything we want. As small children we are often helpless, for we are small and weak and in the power of giants whom we cannot understand. We are always trying

25

to make sense of what is going on around us, but quite often the only explanation we can arrive at is that the world is full of mysterious, powerful forces to which some people have access.

One of these forces is the power of thought. In our early blissful state where to imagine something was the same as getting it, we acquired the belief that we could fulfil our wishes just by thinking. As a baby and a toddler there were many occasions when our thoughts did not produce the desired result, but there were enough occasions when our thoughts apparently did produce the desired result to allow us to maintain our belief in the magical power of our thoughts. We wished for an ice cream, and mother bought us one; we wished that our aggravating big brother would fall and hurt himself and he did. The belief that we can influence the world just by thinking is a great balm and comfort when we are weak and oppressed.

Many of us carry into adult life the belief that thought alone can influence events. Certainly our thoughts influence our bodies, for our thoughts and our bodies are one. This is no longer just a statement of belief. The connections between our thoughts and feelings and our body's response are now being mapped in scientific research.[12] What has not been demonstrated is that by thought alone we can influence events in other times and places. Nevertheless, many people believe that they can. They believe that their thoughts of ill-will towards another person have caused disasters to befall that person. They are not aided in sorting out the difference between thought and action by the Christian teaching that the thought is as sinful as the deed. This teaching prevents many people from using the one method of acknowledging and ridding ourselves of powerful feelings of frustration, anger, violence and hate which does not cause havoc in our society: that is, creating fantasies about our feelings and desires. Curiously, while I have listened to many people telling me of how they try to control their thoughts so that these thoughts will not do harm, I have never been told how to use thought to achieve positive ends. If only just thinking about going to the supermarket would bring the groceries home!

Another source of our magical fantasies is our ability to see the objects and animals in our world not as objects and animals but as people. As newborn babies we not only can distinguish a face, or even just a simple drawing of a face, from all else that is presented, but we prefer to look at faces above all else. Of course we need to be able to do this, for to survive we must have contact with other people. That is as basic a necessity as food, air and water. Since other people who will take notice of us can be in short supply, we can supplement our requirements for people by turning objects and animals into people. Small children see nothing strange in being told stories about the human activities of objects and animals, while adults see nothing strange in calling their car 'Betsy' or 'Fred', or in grieving over the death of a pet in the way they grieve over the death of a person they love.

The objects and animals we turn into people can, in fantasy, provide us with many of the things we want and which reality denies. Such a fantasy is captured brilliantly in the comic strip 'Calvin and Hobbes', where Calvin is a small boy with a very good friend, Hobbes the tiger. Whenever other people are around Hobbes pretends to be a toy tiger, but in Calvin's reality he is the very best of companions who makes up for the deficiencies of Calvin's parents, two very ordinary people.[20]

I was introduced to Calvin and Hobbes by Edward Janoff, a very aware nine-year-old, who, while enjoying 'Calvin and Hobbes' very much, told me that the comic strip was really for adults. None of us ever grows out of wanting a friend like Hobbes.

Hobbes, of course, has that additional quality we often see in the objects and animals which we have made human: magical power. If we see this magical power as possibly being directed against us, we have to appease and placate the possessor of that power, but if we believe that we could share in that magical power, we take good care of the object that possesses it. Thus some of us in adult life still fear to step on pavement cracks, while others of us take good care of certain possessions. When he had, in old age, given up going to racing circuits, Enzo Ferrari would, before he sat down to follow his cars' performances on radio and television, tie the good-luck handkerchief his mother had given him around his neck.[21] The power of his mother's scarf is of course obvious when we consider his career.

This is what our childhood fantasies are about – power. What is the use of wanting everything when you haven't got the power to get everything? But if you know that you are extraordinary and special, that you always have access to Paradise, that you can earn love and admiration from your perfect parents who will then give you everything, that you can use magic powers, then perhaps you will have the power to make the world over into what you want it to be.

Making the World into What You Want

Power is usually represented as position, wealth and military strength, but this is not what power ultimately is. Power is the right to define reality.

Reality, or any part of it, can be defined in an infinite number of ways. The question is which person's definition will prevail.

Suppose that one day the citizens of a town suddenly discover that the ground on which their town stands is moving, slipping and cracking wide open. Everyone in the town might use the word 'earthquake' to talk about this, but differ in how they define 'earthquake'.

The people who believe in science define the earthquake as being the result of the shifting of the 'tectonic plates', which are supposed to be a kind of ill-fitting wrapping about the core of the earth. (Within my lifetime the meaning of 'tectonic plates' has gone from being the fantasy of some crazy geologists to the received wisdom of science.) The people who believe in the Christian God define the earthquake as yet another of His mysterious ways of testing and instructing them. The people who believe in older gods define the earthquake as an expression of the gods' anger. The people who believe in their own wickedness and deserved ill-fortune define the earthquake as proof of this belief. The people who believe in money define the earthquake as the opportunity to make some more. And so on.

Each of these definitions has following from it some appropriate action – moving the town to a more stable spot, undertaking ceremonies of worship and propitiation, sacrificing oneself to remove the curse from the town, or setting up hot-dog stands and selling tents. In so far as these different actions are compatible, each person can hold and interpret his own definition of the reality of the earthquake, but where actions are not compatible each person has either to struggle to force other people to accept his definition or to relinquish his definition and accept someone else's. *Power is the ability to get other people to accept your definition of reality.*

The trappings of power often obscure just who actually has the right to define. The kings of England used to claim that they had the right to define the reality to be perceived by their subjects since this right had been conferred on them by God, but when their subjects ceased to believe in the divine right of kings, the king's right to define vanished. Our history books (which are one of the means by which those in power transmit their definitions of reality) tell us that the right to define the reality to be perceived by British subjects passed to a democratically elected parliament. Our members of parliament, especially those who form the government, act as if they have the right to define reality, but in fact they accept the definitions of reality made by those people whose definitions influence world economics. Thus it is that many of us define the world in which we would like to live as one where no one starves, but we find that such a definition is not accepted by those who benefit from an unequal distribution of wealth.

Similarly, in families the people who appear to have the power to define may not actually have this power. There are a great many families where the parents, while apparently acting like independent adults, are actually still children accepting without question their parents' definition of reality. With every decision, instead of asking themselves, 'What is right for me?' or 'What is right for us as a family?' ask, 'What would my parents think?' Even if the parents are dead and gone, their internalized representations can supply the answer.

It always seems so easy to hand the responsibility for defining reality over to institutions like the State and Church in the hope that the representatives of these institutions will form definitions of reality which will protect and benefit us. However, the leaders to whom we give political power always seem more interested in collecting taxes and preparing for war than in caring for their subjects, while no religious leader has yet been able to devise a system of belief which gives us complete security. Every set of religious beliefs contains some unsatisfactory implications for its believers.[22] In the end it is best to

29

retain our responsibility to create our own definitions of reality, even though this brings us into conflict with other people.

Struggles between people are struggles over whose definition of reality will be accepted. Sometimes people whose alternative definitions are unacceptable to some other people are silenced. They are killed, imprisoned or censored. Sometimes their definitions are defined as being invalid because the people making such definitions are defined by their opponents as mad or stupid. In the battle between the sexes this is a ploy much favoured by men, as Riana Duncan's cartoon shows.[23]

"WHAT YOU REALLY MEAN IS ......

Each of us tries to maintain at least some area of our life where our definitions of reality will prevail, for if we do not, if we accept other people's definitions in every aspect of our life, our very self will disappear. Thus whenever we find ourselves helpless in the power of other people, as we can be when we are children, or as adults in complete economic dependence on others, or as the subjects of a totalitarian State, we try to preserve a small area where our definitions can prevail by becoming disobedient, or crazy, or secretive. In ordinary life where we do have some power we do not usually go around proclaiming 'This is how I define reality', but instead use the well tried statements and commands of 'This is mine', 'This is the way it is (was, will be)', 'Do it my way', 'Do what I tell you', 'Do what I want'.

However, try as we may to define reality in such a way that we get what we want, none of us succeeds totally. Something is always withheld from us.

2
'What's to Stop Me?'

**Human suffering arises from our embodied
interaction with a world whose reality, though
it cannot be known, cannot be wished away.**
DAVID SMAIL[1]

'I can't change,' said Jim looking very pleased with himself. 'I'm that
kind of person. I'm a Type A personality.'

Anyone who pronounced his own death sentence in such a self-
satisfied way, I thought, must be stupid, but then I know that many
people would prefer to die rather than redefine themselves. Jim had
read about Type A people – the ones who rush around feeling very
stressed and competitive – and how Type A people are especially
prone to heart attacks. Jim had already had one such close brush with
death, yet here he was insisting that to change his way of living was
as much beyond his power as to change the colour of his eyes. He
was brown-eyed and a Type A person and that was that.

Of course, to change his whole way of life would require a great
deal of thought and planning, not just in reorganizing his finances but
in teaching himself different ways of thinking and acting. He didn't
have time to do this because he was engaged in a battle which had
begun long before and which he was determined to win, even though
his opponent had died twenty years ago.

Jim's father had been one of those men who think they can teach
their sons to be strong and manly by continually setting them chal-
lenges and then never letting them quite win. They assert their
superior strength and skill by defeating their sons, and when their
sons get old enough to win sometimes, the fathers still withhold the
prize of their praise and acceptance. They have specialized in the art
of damning with faint praise, and they practise it frequently, for it
keeps their sons cowed by and fascinated with their father.

Jim was not prepared to admit that his inability to stop striving and
competing, even though he had a secure, successful business and a
son who would carry it on, was because he was still trying to get from
his father his undiluted praise and acceptance. He did not want to feel
the pain that comes upon us when we realize that we cannot undo
what was done in the past. Neither did he wish to admit that if he

had been influenced by what his father had done to him, then his own son had been influenced by Jim's actions.

In wanting and getting everything Jim had done rather well. He was a man of position and influence in his community, wealthy and with many of the possessions that wealth can buy, and his family photographs showed a handsome and close group. But his wanting everything included something else. He wanted to go back in time and have his father say, 'Well done, son. I'm proud of you,' and he wanted to take the credit for his son's business acumen but none of the blame for the way that he and his son fought one another. Rather than admit that there were reasons why he could not gain these desires, he preferred to define himself as someone who could not change.

Jim is not alone in this way of thinking. Indeed, I have discovered over years of talking to people that many of them are unclear about what kind of reasons there are for why we do not get everything we want. These reasons can be grouped into two categories which, though distinctly separate, are often confused by us. Because we fail to distinguish these categories we also fail to devise effective ways of dealing with the implications of the two categories.

Two Categories

The categories can be defined in the following way:

Category One **is those things which we could have but which are withheld from us either by ourselves or by other people by the way we each choose to define ourselves and our world.**

Category Two **is those things which are excluded by the nature of human life.**

CATEGORY ONE

Category One includes all the things it is possible for us to have, but simply because of the way we define reality these things are withheld from us.

For instance, it would be possible for every person in the world to be adequately fed. With our present knowledge of agriculture and our means of transport it would be possible to organize a world-wide system of food manufacture and distribution which would provide adequate nourishment for everyone. Such a system would also solve the problem of the burgeoning world population, for we know now that the only effective way of persuading people not to provide for their old age by having lots of children is to provide them with a secure and adequate means of living. However, to achieve this we would all have to change how we define what food we are prepared to eat. Many of us would have to consume considerably less, and all of us would have to redefine what we consider to be palatable. We would also have to change how we define the value of other people. At present many people starve because the people who could help them to create a satisfactory means of food production do not consider them worth saving.

Robin Morgan, writing about terrorism, noted:

> FAO (the Food and Agriculture Organization) notes that hunger is increasing even though food has never before been as abundant or cheap as it is today; in parts of the developing world, food production is continuing to grow faster than the population. But, FAO points out, countries like India and Indonesia now *export* vast amounts of food, even though increasing numbers of their own people cannot afford to eat. 'Polarization in the global food system is continuing,' says FAO Director-General Edouard Saouma.[2]

Similarly, it would be possible to eradicate the world-wide misery of loneliness. The world is full of lonely people who, instead of easing one another's misery by becoming friends, remain trapped in their misery by the way they define themselves and other people. Because they define themselves as 'unacceptable', or 'bad', or 'boring', or 'inferior', or 'unlovable' they are frightened of other people and so hide themselves behind walls both real and imaginary. Since one way of trying to bolster up a faltering self-esteem is to denigrate other people, we define other people as bad, mad and dangerous, be it because of their race or religion, or simply because they speak with a different accent or behave in ways different from ours. Though it is true that we each inhabit our own little world of our thoughts and feelings, our inherent aloneness is not the reason for the prevalence of loneliness. We all want to have companionship and closeness, but we prevent ourselves from having this by the way we define ourselves and other people.[3]

There are many other ways in which we prevent ourselves from getting what we want by the way we define ourselves. If we define ourselves as 'stupid' we rule out all the possibilities that follow from education. If we define ourselves as 'ugly' we rule out all the possibilities that follow from enjoying our appearance. If we define ourselves as 'a cowardly stay-at-home' we rule out all the possibilities of exploration. If we define ourselves as 'a loser' we rule out all the possibilities of winning. Jim's definition of himself as a 'Type A personality' ruled out all the pleasures of taking life as it comes and cooperating with others in enterprises and in play.

If we accept without question the definitions that other people impose on us, then we find ourselves missing out on many of the things we want. Men who accept the traditional definition of what it is to be masculine exclude from their lives most of what it is to be human, and live within a sorry circle of work, sex, sport and violence. Women who accept the traditional definition of what is feminine may find much to explore and discover within homemaking and motherhood, but their awareness, however dim, of the possibilities beyond their home and within themselves can make their lives a misery.

If we accept without question the definitions which our society imposes on us we give up a huge range of possibilities. Since the Second World War working-class people in England have very largely given up the belief prevalent in the nineteenth century that certain things were 'not for the likes of us', and instead see as their right access to education, decent homes, and an income which secures not only the necessities of life but at least some of its luxuries. However, middle-class English people have not made many changes. To an outside observer like myself they seem like a tribe made distinctive by their dress and manner of comporting themselves, and held together by a vast array of rules and customs which lay the basis for their definitions of themselves and others. The sight of any living thing in a prison always saddens me, so I feel sad when I am with a member of the English middle class and I see that person, whom I know to be striving to be kind, caring, and willing to be open-minded on almost every issue, become upset because one of the rules of the tribe has been broken – someone has used the 'wrong' spoon, or spoken 'rudely', or worn the 'wrong' clothes. However, there is a good reason why the working class abandoned many of their rules and the middle class did not. Most working-class people came to realize that 'not for the likes of us' definitions led only to deprivation, while membership of the middle class might not give you everything you want, but it certainly gives you a great deal.

When we realize that it is the definitions we have made which prevent us from getting what we want we can then decide to change these definitions. By doing this we can gain something of what we want, but sometimes we are prevented from doing so by the Category Two reasons.

CATEGORY TWO

Category Two reasons have to do with the way we perceive time and space, the way our bodies operate, and the continuous interaction of everything that occurs. (Jim had locked himself into his battle with his father and with his son because he would not accept the passage of time and the continuous interaction of everything that occurs.)

Our perception of time is a curious paradox. Everything that happens to us happens in present time. The past and the future are no more than thoughts and feelings which we experience *in the present* as we remember or plan, desire and anticipate. Yet we perceive time as a linear progression from the beginning to the end, sunrise to sunset, birth to death. Physicists tell us that to understand the functioning of the universe we need to see time as integrally linked to space and simultaneously present, but while some of us can develop a physicist's imagination to conceptualize such things, most of us cannot. Time is to us a path on which we must travel, or a continuous force which comes towards us and passes us by, seemingly with increasing speed the older we get. We may try to stop walking along the path, or to hold up our hands to stop time passing, but to no avail.[4]

Many philosophers have spoken of the wisdom of relinquishing our thoughts of past and future and of living in the present, but even they, though they might relinquish clocks and calendars, must notice the change of seasons and how all living things die. We may live in the present, but in our present is our past and future.

Our past limits us in our efforts to have everything because we cannot change the past. What happened happened. What we missed out on, we missed out on. As much as we desire it, we cannot go back and do things differently. However, we can change how we remember the past. We can change the way we define our past. We can define our failures as successes and our losses as gains.

It is important that such redefinitions have some close relation to reality. People who remember their parents as being perfect are always likely to have their definition of the perfection of their parents disrupted by evidence of their human fallibility. A determined counting of one's blessings, past and present, brings no comfort when one's internal reality contains resentment, envy, despair and anguish. A valid redefinition of the past is possible only when many other things have changed.

I am reminded of this whenever I close one of the drawers on my large Edwardian sideboard. Each drawer has a brass handle mounted on two hinges. When the handle is released it falls down with a little rattle and click. This sound always gives me pleasure, for it reminds me of a similar sound which came from the handles on the sideboard which stood in the dining room of my childhood home. When I lived there as an adolescent, that sound encapsulated all those empty afternoons, all the boredom and the longing, and the fear of being trapped in that place for ever. I still remember how I felt and why, but it seems that after all these years of writing and talking about my poor mother (who was much put upon by her daughter) I have now traded resentment for nostalgia. I regard this as a considerable gain.

Just as past time limits us, so does present time. We cannot do two things at one and the same time. We may want to do two things, but to do one excludes the other. We cannot get a good night's sleep while at the same time enjoying a riotous party. Once we make a choice to do one thing, all other possibilities are excluded.

In making our choice we might plan that we shall pursue other possibilities in the future. For instance, if we want to explore the entire world (as I do), we can plan to visit a different country each year during our holidays. This year Yugoslavia, next year Outer Mongolia, and so on. However, our time is limited. If we lived for ever we would have time to do everything. But we do not live for ever, and so every choice limits our subsequent choices.

We are limited in our choices not only in what we want to *do* but in what kind of person we want to *be*. If we present ourselves as being bossy and self-confident we can't simultaneously present ourselves as a shrinking violet in need of support. This limitation of our choices causes problems, for while local wiseacres may be forever advising us that we can't have our cake and eat it too, our society places upon us contrary expectations as to what kind of person we should be, just as we create contrary expectations for our own self. Leo Braudy, in his study of how we try to use fame to gain much of what we want, described these contrary expectations.

In Europe individualism has generally been considered antisocial, while in America it seems encouraged by society, although subject to society's often-hidden terms. Every American therefore draws with each breath simultaneous urges to conformity and distinction. No other country in the midst of creating a modern state, has so defiantly evolved so many institutionalized differences, so many ways of being outside. No other country so enforces the character-wrenching need to be assertive but polite, prideful but humble, unique but familiar, the great star and the kid next door. To the extent that we are all stars, waiting to be discovered, no one is very surprised to discover that stardom and shyness, public assertion and private withdrawal, are the twin offspring of the desire for fame and recognition.

Growing up in America, I dimly realized that my own impulses to achievement, which if written out would appear logically contradictory, yet within me gripped me with perverse strength. I wanted to be the best, yet noted for my humility. I wanted to be individual and distinct, somewhat of a recluse, yet to be praised and applauded when I appeared and did my stuff. The more I was aware of these paradoxical urges, the less they seemed understandable. Whenever one was uppermost, the other would appear with a dark, beckoning hand to lead it astray.[5]

As much as a famous person like Michael Jackson might try to be simultaneously the cynosure of all eyes and invisible, he can no more escape the limitations of making a choice than he can escape the limitations of his body, though he has tried to do this in the reconstruction of his appearance. Athletes are endlessly endeavouring to achieve more and better, but what they achieve in speed, strength, endurance and skill proves not to be a lasting change. Our physical limitations remain. Fire burns us, heavy weights crush us, and our body cannot perform all that we can imagine. (Orgies are tiring.) Nor can we escape from the limitations that our relationship to space places on us. In my dreams I move effortlessly from one scene to another, but awake I find that distance has to be traversed and only in the ways that my body will allow.

Performers and athletes are not the only ones who try to bypass their physical limitations. An old friend of mine, Ann Hocking, who is well acquainted with despair, pointed this out to me in a recent letter. She wrote:

> What about that woman jumping off the top floor of the car park? They are trying to say it was an accident because her son-in-law is a famous footballer. Everyone knows it's pretty difficult to fall over an eight-foot wall, unless you're standing on the top of it at the time. If I did decide to end it all, that's how I'd go, off a roof or the top floor of a car park. Have you noticed how people choose to die doing something they've always wanted? Like my friend who always wanted to sleep sound. She took a load of tablets and never woke up. A boy I knew who was mad about speed stole a motor bike and crashed it. I always wanted to fly like a bird. So I might do it just the once. Some people kill themselves jogging. Just running away, that's all.[6]

Of course, trying to overcome our physical limitations has consequences. In the attempts that Ann described the consequence is death.

Of all the aspects of Category Two as to why we cannot get what we want, the one that causes the greatest confusion is that of the consequences which follow from the continuous interactions of everything that occurs. Most people are aware of their physical limitations, and they can, if they think about it, understand the limitations our perception of time places upon us. It is in the understanding of consequences that people not only have great difficulty but fail to realize that they have this difficulty. We can be aware that we are not good at arithmetic and unaware that we are not good at working out what are the consequences of our actions.

Our Failure to Understand

We fail to understand that our acts have consequences and what these consequences are because we fail to understand our own nature and the nature of our world. Our lack of understanding can be grouped under seven headings:
1. We think that the world is divided up into discrete boxes, when in fact everything that exists is continuous and flowing.

2. We think of causation as being a single line, when in fact it is a multidimensional net spreading far and wide.

3. We think of acting so as to bring about a good result, or a bad result, when in fact every action has a multitude of results, some of them good and some of them bad.

4. We overlook the fact that part of the continuous interaction of everything that occurs is the continuous construction of meaning in which every human being is engaged all the time.

5. We think that the meanings we create are discrete categories, when in fact they are linked to one another so that meanings of which we are not conscious can influence our actions.

6. We assume that other people create the same meanings as we do, and when other people fail to act in the way that our meanings lead us to expect that they should, we condemn them.

7. We overlook the fact that there are certain aspects of life which stand in complementary relationship to one another, so that the more there is of one, the less there is of the other.

Let me explain each of these more fully.

DISCRETE OR CONTINUOUS?

1. We think that the world is divided up into discrete boxes, when in fact everything that exists is continuous and flowing.

For instance, we like to think of ourselves as being separate individuals, distinct from our surroundings, when in fact we are continuous with our surroundings. Our body is in continuous interchange with the atmosphere, which is in continuous interchange with all living things and with the rest of the universe. We may be thousands of miles away from the plankton in the Pacific and the fragile ozone layer in the Antarctic, but we are linked to them nevertheless.

Similarly, we divide ourselves into 'body' and 'mind', and then have difficulty in understanding that the thoughts we think can, in their effects, be as poisonous to us as strychnine. We divide our experience of ourselves into 'thought' and 'feelings' (in psychologists' jargon, 'cognition' and 'affect') and claim that we can experience one without the other. Some of us claim that we can have thoughts without feelings ('I never get angry, no matter what happens'), and some of us claim to be awash with feelings that we cannot put into words ('I don't know why I feel upset').[7] Such divisions prevent us from understanding ourselves.

We judge other people by using discrete categories of 'good' and 'bad', and fail to see that few people, if any, are totally good or totally bad.

'Good' people we usually pop into that box labelled 'like us', a discrete category which is playing such a major part in our lemming-like rush to extinction. To return our planet to a state where we can survive, and to prevent ourselves from destroying ourselves in a nuclear war, we need to see ourselves as a species inhabiting a planet and not as distinct racial, national and religious groups divided by enmity. However, we have great difficulty in looking beyond the group with which we claim identity. We show this not just in the cruelty and injustice we inflict on those whom we have put in the box 'not like us', but in our ignorance about those who are 'not like us'. Wonderful though Americans are, whenever I visit there I have the feeling that the other countries of the world have slid off the planet.

CAUSATION

2. We think of causation as being a single line, when in fact it is a multidimensional net spreading far and wide.

Those of us who have grown up in a society which uses the scientific principles first established by Aristotle are taught to perceive causation as a single line, that is, A caused B and B caused C. When a policeman questions us as to why we crashed our car we give a simple linear causal explanation like, 'There was oil and water on the road. I braked, and the car skidded.' We do not include in our explanation of cause the multitude of events which brought us to that spot, such as the events in the past – where and when we were born, why we bought the car, and so on; nor do we include our thoughts as the crash was occurring (perhaps 'I hope this is a write-off. I need a new car', or, 'This is my punishment for leaving home in a temper'), or our anticipation of the future (perhaps 'I'm going to be late', or, 'I wish I didn't have to make this journey'). We know that the policeman, the court and the insurance company will regard such causes as irrelevant. Yet, in fact, this multitude of causes was what brought us to that spot at that particular time and led us to act in the way that we did.

The world picture which the scientists and philosophers of ancient China used encompassed the vast array of events in the past, present and future which led to one event occurring. Joseph Needham described this way of understanding the world:

> The keyword in Chinese thought is *Order* and above all *Pattern* . . . It was a universe in which organization came about, not because of fiats issued by a supreme law-giver which things must obey subject to sanction imposable by angels attendant; nor because of the physical clash of innumerable billiard balls in which the motion of one was the physical cause of the other. It was an ordered harmony of wills without an ordainer; it was like the spontaneous, yet ordered, in the sense of patterned movements, of dancers in a country dance of figures, none of whom are bound by law to do what they do, nor yet pushed by others, coming from behind, but cooperate in a voluntary harmony of wills . . .

40

In such a system causality is reticular and hierarchically fluctuating, not particulate and singly catenarian [that is, like a net and not like a chain].[8]

In medieval Europe the world picture was one of a supreme law-giver who determined all events. The explanation of 'why my hay wain toppled over' would go backward in time in a line of causes to the supreme First Cause. God ordained it, perhaps as a punishment or a warning, or perhaps just in one of His mysterious ways which are beyond human understanding. In the seventeenth century Descartes elaborated this world picture into one of a huge mechanical clockwork. In this clockwork, so Karl Popper wrote,

All causation was push. It was the first, and the clearest, theory of causation. Later, from about 1900 on, the world was regarded as an electrical clockwork. But, in both cases, it was regarded as an *ideally* precise clockwork. Either the cogwheels pushed each other, or the electromagnets attracted and repelled each other with absolute precision. There was, of course, no room for human decisions. Our feelings that we are acting, planning and understanding each other were illusory. But starting with Werner Heisenberg in 1927, a great change occurred in quantum physics. It became clear that minute processes made the clockwork imprecise: there were objective indeterminacies. Physical theory had to bring in probabilities.[9]

The discovery that, not only do atomic particles not behave like the traditional billiard balls or cogwheels, but the behaviour of the particles was intimately related to what the experimenter was doing at the time forced nuclear physicists to abandon the picture of the scientist being separate from what he studied and to realize that the experimenter is always part of the experiment. They developed a world picture which Werner Heisenberg described as 'a complicated tissue of events, in which connections of different kinds alternate or overlap or combine and thereby determine the texture of the whole'.[10]

How can probability be included in such a world picture in such a way as to aid us in our understanding of why things happen? To do this Karl Popper developed the concept of a tendency or *propensity* of a certain event to occur. For instance, we might expect that a penny thrown into the air has an equal possibility of landing on its head or its tail, but if a penny in a hundred throws shows heads ninety-five times we might feel that the penny had a certain inherent propensity to behave in that way. Similarly, we might expect that our greengrocer might possibly include by chance a bad apple in our kilo of apples, but if we find, week after week, that our bag of apples contains several bad apples, we might suspect that a certain propensity is operating in the greengrocer's behaviour.

Karl Popper wrote:

Instead of speaking of the *possibility* of an event occurring, we might speak, more precisely, of an inherent *propensity* to produce, upon repetition, a certain statistical average . . .

Propensities are invisible like Newtonian attractive forces. They act: they are *actual*, they are *real*. We are therefore compelled to attribute a kind of reality to propensities, especially to weighted propensities, even to those which are as yet unrealized, and whose fate will only be decided in the course of time, perhaps only in the distant future.

This view of propensities allows us to see in a new light the processes that make our world – the whole world process. The world is no longer a causal machine – it can now be seen to be an unfolding process, realizing possibilities and unfolding new possibilities. This is very clear in physics where we can see how new elements, new atomic nuclei, are produced under extreme physical conditions of high temperature and pressures, and they survive only if they are not too unstable. And with the new elements are created new possibilities – possibilities which previously simply did not exist: we ourselves become possible in this way.

These tendencies and propensities have led to the emergence of life. And they have led to the unfolding of life, the evolution of life. And the evolution of life has led to better conditions for life on earth, and thus to new possibilities and propensities; and to new forms of life that differ utterly. All this means that possibilities – even possibilities that have not yet realized themselves – have a kind of reality; a kind of, as yet, conditional reality. The numerical propensities that attach to the possibilities can be interpreted as a measure of this status of a not yet fully realized reality – a reality in the making. And in so far as these possibilities can, and partly will, realize themselves in time, in the future, the open future is, almost as a promise, as a temptation, as a lure, present; indeed, *actively* present, at every moment. The old world picture that puts before us a mechanism operating with causes that are all in the past – the past kicking and driving us with kicks into the future – the past that is *gone* – is no longer adequate to our indeterministic world. Causation is just a special case of propensity and a comparatively rare case: the case of a propensity equal to 1, a *determining* demand, or force, for realization. It is not the kicks from the back, from the past, that impel us, but the attraction, the lure of the future and its attractive possibilities that *entice* us: this is what keeps life – and, indeed, the world – unfolding.[11]

Even though these changes in the understanding of causality have been common knowledge amongst educated people since the thirties, this has made little impression on the way people think, not even the people who would pride themselves on being scientific. When, in the early seventies, a handful of scientists from different disciplines began to develop chaos theory in the study of the global nature of systems (what some physicists regard as the study of process rather than of state, of becoming rather than of being), these innovators were treated with great hostility.[12] The scientific community is still strongly divided on this issue.

So the notion of cause as being a simple line of events coming from the past is still alive and well and causing immense damage.

It is the notion of linear cause which lies behind the man-made ecological disasters which litter our world. Take, for example, the disaster of the Aral Sea, which was a large stretch of water in Soviet Central Asia into which two great rivers, the Amu Darya (the Oxus of ancient fame) and the Syr Darya, flowed. Thinking linearly, government officials and scientists devised a plan to take water from these rivers and use it to irrigate new cotton fields in Uzbekistan. All very laudable, but what they did not consider was the intimate relationship of these rivers to the Aral Sea and of the Aral Sea to the climate. Today a large area of Uzbekistan is a dust bowl, the Aral Sea has lost sixty percent of its water, a new salt desert has formed on the dry sea bed, and the rising salinity of the formerly pure artesian water has become a severe health hazard. Professor Erkin Yusupov, deputy head of Uzbekistan's Academy of Sciences, said:

> This is not just a regional matter for us in Soviet Central Asia. The Aral Sea is a decisive catalyst for the climate of the whole of Asia. This is going to affect the weather, the rainfall and eventually the food supply of India too. By forcing the cold northerly and north-westerly winds from Siberia and the Arctic to gain height as they cross the Aral Sea, and its own microclimatic zone, the Aral affects the snow formation on the Pamirs and Himalayas, and thus the climate of the Indian subcontinent. This catastrophe is global, and it transcends national boundaries.[13]

Professor Yusupov was speaking in 1988. Less than a year later,

> The literary journal *Novy Mir* quoted a local doctor as saying, 'Out of 1,000 new-born babies, 100 die before they are a year old. Deformed babies have begun to be born . . . without an anus, with shortened intestines, feeble-minded, without a limb or without a skull, just skin on the face.' The article explains, 'The population in the Aral area live on the lower reaches of great rivers and are forced to drink water that has absorbed pesticides, herbi-

cides and other abominable things. These are no longer rivers, these are the dumps of Central Asia.'[14]

It is the notion of linear cause which, in the name of psychiatry, has inflicted immense, largely untold, suffering on thousands of people.

Madness has always been explained in terms of linear cause by those in power. When the Church wielded immense power, madness was supposed to be caused by the devil and his henchmen. The cure was to beat out the devil and, in so doing, inflict gross physical punishments on the unfortunate person who was considered to be possessed. When the power and influence of the Church waned and that of the medical profession waxed, the explanation of the cause of madness changed from possession by the devil to possession by bad chemicals and genes.

Curiously, common-sense wisdom about how to avoid that most common form of madness, depression, uses a network form of causality. When Vicky Rippere surveyed the common-sense remedies for depression recorded since the sixteenth century, she summarized them as:

> The basic notion of circumspect, temperate living, based on knowledge of one's own individual and constitutional susceptibilities, the focus on enhancing efficient biological functioning through attention to diet, sleep and exercise, the strategy of deliberately avoiding known physiological and psychological precipitants, the notion of the individual as a member of a supportive social network, the practice of systematically preparing to face adversity, and, finally, the concept of personal responsibility and initiative in choosing to live with care.[15]

I am always glad to be able to remind myself of the intelligence of people with common sense when I observe psychiatrists at work and see how, while they have plenty of the intelligence which IQ tests measure, in understanding people most of them are immensely stupid.

Medical education trains doctors to see people as bodies (objects) and to cling to the notion that doctors as scientists are objective in their judgements and separate from their patients in that how the patient perceives and responds to the doctor is not relevant to the doctor's objective assessment of the case. Over the past ten or so years most medical schools have included courses in listening to the patient and behaving naturally, but such courses have had a very limited effect. I have met quite a number of general practitioners and a few psychiatrists who do treat their patients sensitively as fellow human beings, but still many doctors behave with all the sensitivity and awareness of a charging rhinoceros. Recently when I was quite ill with an ear infection in both ears which prevented me from hearing most of what was being said to me, the Ear, Nose and Throat specialist I saw (who must have been at least fifteen years younger than me) told me that it was not necessary for a counsellor like myself to hear what was said and that my hearing loss, though decidedly marked, was not as great as that of a man who had worked on a foundry floor for fifty years. I should, he said, go home and wait patiently for my problem to resolve itself.

I tell this anecdote so as to show that I do not reserve my criticisms solely for psychiatrists. However, while we might, when we have a physical illness, be able to laugh at the behaviour of our doctors, when we are caught up in those states of pain, despair and confusion which can lead to a meeting with psychiatrists, we lack the humour and self-confidence to withstand what can be done to us in the name of psychiatry.

In the tradition of psychiatry a patient is seen as being a single object, separate from his relationships with other people and his surrounding environment, like a billiard ball on a green baize table. The patient behaves as he does because he has been hit by a mental illness, and the mental illness hit him because it had been hit by a chemical imbalance, and the chemical imbalance hit the mental illness because it had been hit by a gene. (Whether this gene was set in motion by the Great Psychiatrist in the Sky is not usually discussed at case conferences.) The psychiatrist's theory demands that the treatment stop the chemical imbalance ball hitting the mental illness ball, and a drug ball or an electroconvulsive shock ball is sent in to do this.[16]

Sometimes an additional ball is added to this line-up, an event in the patient's past which the patient is keeping secret. This ball the psychiatrist can remove from the line of causality by getting the patient to reveal the secret, either willingly in the confessional of therapy, or unwillingly in abreaction when the patient is given a so- called 'truth drug' and questioned by the psychiatrist.

Psychiatrists who like to appear to be up to date in their thinking and practice will talk of the causes of mental illness as being 'multifactorial', with social factors playing their part. However, in actual practice, 'social factors' are simply one or two more billiard balls. Parents, as billiard balls, are seen by the psychiatrist as good or bad, either long-suffering and much put upon by the patient, or faulty, having passed on the mental illness gene or in preventing the drug ball from doing its work. Such a way of thinking about cause ignores the fact that the parent-child relationship is one of continuous interflow in which harmful activity can also support, and support can also harm.

In that confused and frightened state which brings a person into the psychiatric system, it can initially be a comfort to be told that one's

45

suffering has a simple cause and cure. However, patients soon discover that the explanation which they are given actually does not
encompass what they know about themselves and their life. While we
all like to think about ourselves and our life in as simple terms as
possible, we know how complicated it all is. We are entangled in what
we want and what we feel we ought to do and be, just as we are
entangled with our parents, our partners and our children. How wonderful it would be if by taking a pill we found that everyone was kind
and loving to us and we could love them back! What a relief it would
be if a burst of electricity put through our brain would wipe out all
the bad memories, leaving only the good, and instil in us complete
confidence in the future!

Thus are many psychiatric patients disappointed. Some, wisely,
look elsewhere for help. Others, still hoping that one day the psychiatrists' promises will come true, remain in the psychiatric system
because they, like the psychiatrist, want to believe in simple linear
cause. But the longer one stays in the psychiatric system the harder it
is to leave and re-enter normal life.

The psychiatrists' perception of confusion and fear as an illness
which is the end result of a line of physical causation harms people
because it denies their experience. Whenever other people deny our
experience we feel pain, anger and fear. If we can argue back we can
protect ourselves from the threat of being devalued, ignored, turned
into an object of no importance, annihilated as a person. However,
once you become a psychiatric patient you cannot argue back. Simply
being a psychiatric patient (that is, mad) renders the account you give
of your experience incorrect. The account of your experience as given
by the psychiatrist, assisted by his team, is the true one. If you argue
with the psychiatrist's account you are, at best, ungrateful and, at
worst, 'lacking insight', something psychiatrists consider to be a
characteristic of the very mad.

What we need when the events of our life have plunged us into
confusion and fear is people around us who do not deny our experience and who constantly reassure us of our value. This is precisely
what psychiatric patients are not given. The stone-floored dormitories
and the locked cells of the old mental hospitals may have been replaced
by less fearsome wards and clinics, and the lone autocratic consultant
psychiatrist may now be heading a 'multidisciplinary team', but the
hierarchical structure where the patient occupies the lowest rung
remains, and on that rung what the patient needs most is denied.

In the causal account which the psychiatrist gives of the patient's
mental illness, all the billiard balls of cause are in the past and, as
Popper described it, 'the past kicking and driving us with kicks into
the future'. The psychiatrist does not include 'the lure of the future',
yet it is such a lure which is present in the psychiatrist's concept of

mental illness and which plays a major part in determining what happens to the patient.

All the concepts we form contain 'the lure of the future', for every concept contains a prediction. Take a very simple concept like 'chair'. Suppose I say to you, 'You'll find a chair in the next room.' When you enter that room you do not look above your head because the concept 'chair' does not include the prediction 'floating against the ceiling'. Your concept of chair predicts 'standing on the floor or standing or stacked on something which stands on the floor'. Also, your concept 'chair' includes a prediction about shape. 'Chair shape' can be created in many ways out of different materials, but your concept 'chair' will lead you to choose one object rather than another – a chair rather than a cupboard. Thus do all the meanings we create contain certain *propensities* which are part of the causal net from which our actions develop.

The concept 'gene' contains the propensity 'cannot be changed'. We can prevent our genes being passed on to our children by not having children, while scientists working in genetic engineering are seeking ways of removing selected genes from cells, but once we have passed the cell stage we can no more remove a gene from our body than we can remove the eggs from a sponge cake. We are stuck with our genes. All we can do is try to inhibit the effects of the bad ones and elaborate the effects of the good ones.

Thus when a doctor tells you that your illness has a genetic cause, the propensity of the word 'gene' tells you that your illness cannot be cured. There may be all kinds of things you and your doctor can do to inhibit the effects of that gene, but the gene itself is there for ever. That is, if the gene is *really* there. There are illnesses like cystic fibrosis and certain kinds of muscular dystrophy where the gene which passes the illness from parent to child has been identified.[17] No such gene has been identified for any of the psychiatric mental illnesses.[18] Nevertheless, many people want to believe that mental illness is something we inherit from our parents.

We like ascribing all sorts of things about ourselves to our genes because that absolves us of having to take responsibility for our behaviour. 'I've got my father's red hair and his foul temper,' we might say so we can indulge ourselves by behaving badly towards our nearest and dearest. However, if the tables are turned on us and a psychiatrist says, 'Your violent temper and your irresponsible behaviour are the symptoms of mania,' then the psychiatrist is using concepts which have the propensity 'You have a genetic illness and so you must take drugs for the rest of your life to keep this illness under control'. The future, as the psychiatrist sees it, affects you in the present.

The idea that all we do and are is nothing more than the outcome of our genetic inheritance absolves us of all responsibility for our actions, but it also takes away hope, and we cannot live without hope. Without hope we have to give up our belief that we shall get what we want.

In a universe where everything that happens in the present is the outcome of a clockwork system of causes in the past, there is no room for hope, since hope can exist only where there is uncertainty. If everything that happens in the present is the outcome of a clockwork system of causes, there is no room for making a choice. The clockwork model says that our experience of choice and decision-making is an illusion. Everything we decide has already been determined in the past.

Hope and the freedom to choose are the things which make life worth living. If we have those we can feel that we have a chance of getting everything else that we want.

People who want to enjoy hope and the freedom to choose and who also want to see the universe as a giant clockwork mechanism have to perform that form of self-deception called 'I am the exception to the rule'. All of us go through the early part of our lives believing 'Everyone dies except me', until one day an accident or an illness robs us of this self-deceit. We realize our own mortality. However, amongst the scientific fraternity there are many people who believe 'All behaviour is determined by causes in the past. I alone am free to choose'. Such people are of course very limited and confused in their understanding of themselves and other people. As such they may be pitied, but because they regard themselves as superior,[12] when they get into positions of power they are dangerous. They find it very easy to see other people as objects to be manipulated and, where necessary, destroyed. They build cities with regard to 'traffic flow' and not with regard to the quality of life. They speak easily of 'limited radiation' and 'mega-deaths'. They use their power to limit how other people can exercise choice. As psychologists they draw up 'schedules of reinforcement' in order to produce unquestioning obedience. As psychiatrists they define their patients as having an illness which prevents them from making choices and taking responsibility for themselves.

However, it must be admitted that to use a network picture of cause, with so many events past, present and possible, requires a good deal of mental effort, not just in trying to take account of so many things, but in having to tolerate uncertainty and doubt. How much easier it is to have a simple explanation, instead of saying, 'There are many complex reasons which led me to make that decision,' saying, 'I did that because I'm a Sagittarian.' Of course, the stars in their courses are part of the same network as ourselves, but it always seems curious to me that so many people see their character and their future being directly affected by stars millions of miles away, and not being affected either directly or indirectly by the people who brought them up.

It is not just for simplicity's sake that we prefer a simple linear explanation. By using a simple linear explanation we can exclude those bits of reality that do not suit us. For instance, anyone who has been a patient in a psychiatric hospital knows that those drear surroundings actually hinder a return to hope and self-confidence, but in all the years I worked in those dreadful places I met very few doctors who took these surroundings into account when assessing the patient's progress, and most of the doctors who did take it into account did so because, as they would say, 'If you make the place too pleasant they won't want to go home.' A consultant psychiatrist, writing anonymously in the Royal College of Psychiatrists' *Psychiatric Bulletin* about his stay in a psychiatric hospital, said:

> Ward atmosphere changed according to the activities of its most vociferous patients, but it was at its most depressing whenever the doors were locked during the day. This measure was used only when absolutely necessary, but it always had an effect on morale and increased the sense of stigmatization felt by many.[20]

The same psychiatrist discovered something that had escaped him in his previous professional life.

> My in-patient stay made me realize that in my clinical practice I had been ignoring an important variable – the influence of patients on one another. Sometimes this was direct, with the formation of same-sex and opposite-sex pair bonds, and sometimes indirect, with one patient influencing the relationship another patient had with medical and nursing staff. Understanding these links was sometimes the key to explaining sudden changes in mood or acting-out behaviour. Although undoubtedly relationships between patients could be mutually supportive, they could at times go some way to explaining a perceived lack of improvement. Some patients obviously had a vested interest in prolonging their stay, and it was no surprise to find that they exaggerated their symptoms or actually lied about them. Non-compliance with medication was another area in which the actions of the patients were influenced by others, and sometimes it was done with an ostentatiousness that begged discovery.[21]

By using a simple linear explanation we can deny that our actions affect other people, or that other people affect us. A wife might phone me in great distress to tell me that her husband, my client, has suddenly become extremely depressed, but not mention that she had told him that she would not cooperate in his plans to leave a well paid job to become the musician he knew himself to be. She spoke to me of how she wanted to help him out of his depression and how she hated feeling helpless, but she did not mention how his plans to change his life threatened her with the loss of what she valued. She hoped I had a magic wand which I would wave and return her husband to what she wanted him to be. She wanted the situation to be limited to 'How to make my husband well', and not expanded to the complex of difficulties which arise when two people love one another but have not developed any skills of negotiation and compromise.

If we admit that we live in a world where every event is in moving contact with every other event, past, present and future, then we have to face a truth which many people do not wish to face, namely:

All acts have consequences.

They may not be the consequences we want, but consequences there are.

Since the consequences are complex and far-reaching, as are the events which led to the acts, we have to face another truth which many people do not wish to face, namely:

A statement of complete truth is not possible.

Try as we might to be truthful, we can never know, much less say, the complete truth, for our language cannot encompass the simultaneity and the contrasts and oppositions of all the events which led to one event.

Such an understanding of truth leads to uncertainty, and many people cannot bear uncertainty. They prefer to claim that their limited perception is the Great Complete Truth, and they deny other people's truth, for to admit it would render suspect two important concepts: what is good and what is bad.

A MIXTURE OF RESULTS

3. We think of acting so as to bring about a good result, or a bad result, when in fact every action has a multitude of results, some of them good and some of them bad.

By believing that cause is a single line of billiard-ball-like events from the past and that we can put events into discrete boxes, the contents of which have no contact with events in other boxes, we then think that we can act and produce the result we desire and that our action and its result will have no effect on anything else. How wrong we are!

Take, for example, a simple matter of housekeeping. When we feel the need to economize we often resolve not to buy quickly prepared but expensive convenience foods or steaks and chops, but instead prepare nutritious and cheap soups and stews. Such action may indeed produce the desired result. We save money, but what we save in money we spend in time. Of course, we might enjoy spending an hour soaking beans and chopping vegetables, but that hour could have been spent in planting daffodils or painting a picture.

The belief that we can act and produce the result we desire and no other is regularly presented by politicians who trot out their pro-grammes of action and assure us that such actions will produce noth-ing but good. As this is the prime public activity of all politicians, I can only conclude that politicians are either fools or liars. The fact that we allow politicians to behave in this way and still make decisions which affect our lives shows how much we want to believe that we can act and produce the result we desire and no other. Yet how often do we witness the far-reaching effects of politicians' actions!

I was working for the National Health Service when the Conserva-tive Government under Mrs Thatcher introduced large reductions in the funding of the Health Service under the banner of 'Value for Money'. There was much talk of good housekeeping, like the house-keeper who saves money by cooking her family cheap, nutritious soups and stews. Like the virtuous housekeeper, the Government's Value for Money scheme saved money, but spent not just time but many other valuable things as well. Anyone in any way connected with the NHS can tell stories of the waste that the Government's Value for Money programme created, stories which range from the ridiculous to the tragic. Most stories are both ridiculous and tragic. The following is an example.

A terminally-ill cancer patient, aged 69, had to travel 16 miles a day between hospitals to get radiotherapy treatment after a third of the radiotherapy beds were closed in the Queen Elizabeth Hos-pital, Birmingham.

Mr Howard Hadley, a retired postman who has since died, initially had his radiotherapy treatment delayed a month after cancer of the windpipe was diagnosed, his daughter said yester-day. Mrs Pamela Cooper said her father was 'breathless and quite ill'.

He was found a bed at East Birmingham Hospital, but had to make the daily 16-mile round trip for 10 days to get radiotherapy treatment at the Queen Elizabeth. He died three weeks later.

'An ambulance crew had to be tied up for one person all day,' said Mrs Cooper. It was ridiculous to delay treatment for a month and then have to be taken from one hospital to another, she said.

The number of radiotherapy beds at the Queen Elizabeth was reduced from 60 to 40 last year. Mr Chris Walliker, chairman of Central Birmingham health authority which is discussing ways to tackle a £1 million overspending across the district, said the temporary closures would be reassessed next month. 'But the funding position is still very difficult and there is no foreseeable prospect of reopening the beds.'[22]

The historian Christopher Hill observed,

Oliver Cromwell proceeded in suppressing Ireland on the basis of cost-effectiveness. 'If we should proceed by the rules of other states,' he told his government by way of explaining his massacres of civilian populations, getting towns to surrender would cost more. He hoped, 'through the blessing of God, they will come cheaper to you'.[23]

Whenever we act we hope that the result of our action will be good, at least for the people we value or for ourselves. If we hold to the view that our actions have one result only, we can fail to see that a result can be both good and bad. Digging a well and providing water in an arid part of Africa can seem like a wholly good action by an aid agency, but then soil erosion caused by the people and animals which use the well is not good. On the other hand, bad can include good. I reminded a dear friend who was telling me about how yet more selfish and thoughtless actions by her husband were causing her grief that it was out of similar actions by him years ago (a story too long and tedious to relate) that she and I first met. As my mother always said, 'It's an ill wind that blows nobody any good'.

My mother in her darkest hours saw all winds as totally ill, so in happier times she reminded us all that even the illest of winds does blow some good, and that what is good is inextricably mixed with what is bad and all the shades of grey in between.

Remembering this can be a comfort when we, as parents, worry about what we have done to our children. It is only by failing that we can succeed as parents. It is through our failures that our children can separate themselves from us and become independent adults. Parents who are always good parents prevent their children from seeing them as ordinary, fallible human beings, and so the children remain as children, ever fascinated by the god-like parent. 'A mother's place,' as a friend always reminds me, 'is in the wrong.'

But what is right and wrong, good and bad? Do they exist in reality or, like beauty, only in the eye of the beholder?

THE CONSTRUCTION OF MEANING
4. We overlook the fact that part of the continuous interaction of everything that occurs is the continuous construction of meaning in which every human being is engaged all the time.

While I am writing this, one sunny September morning, I can see from my second-storey bedroom window hundreds of fragile wisps, seed-bearing fragments from flowers and trees, gliding, floating, swooping, soaring this way and that. Most move slowly and peacefully, in no particular direction, but occasionally one dashes by with the speed of a rocket. Were I downstairs in the garden I would see little of this delicate dance, but from here I have this vision because the fragments are caught by the sunlight against the deep green background of the trees at the end of the garden.

These wisps, floating in the moving currents of air warming in the sun, are like the particles which nuclear physicists study, the insubstantial basis of everything that exists. As I sit here my room, the walls, the furniture and I seem very substantial, yet all this looks so to me, not because it actually is, but because that is the way I see it. Just as I can see the insubstantial wisps because I am in one place rather than another, so I can see other things as substantial because of where I am and how my way of perceiving operates.

Our way of perceiving ensures that the world appears to us as solid and real. It would certainly be difficult to live in a world which looked like the scene outside my window, a patternless, insubstantial phantasmagoria. Of course, if we were the same size as these wisps then we would perceive them differently. But we are not, and so we perceive our world in a way which is in accordance with our size and with the way our sense organs operate. Our ears limit the range of sounds we can hear; our eyes create the illusion that the world is a colourful place.

To give the insubstantial, continuously moving events which comprise everything some measure of solidity, we create patterns and impose them on what is essentially indivisible. These patterns are our perceptions, and our perceptions are the pattern we call *meaning*. Our perceptions are made up of the structures we can form from touch, movement, taste, smell, sight, sound and, most important, language. The sentences we form are the structures which create the world of meaning in which we live.[24]

We live in meaning like a fish lives in water. The only way we can stop creating meaning is to cease to exist. People who believe in a life after death see the afterlife as the continuing creation of meaning – perhaps in close communion with God, or in understanding what they do not understand now, or in meeting the people who preceded them into the afterlife, or in enduring the punishments of hell, or in returning to continue the creation of meaning in this life. But, whether our existence ends in bodily death or continues on indefinitely, *our existence is the continuous creation of meaning*. At times we see the meaning we create as clear and unambiguous, and at other times the meaning we create is confused and uncertain, but whether we say 'I am absolutely certain about that', or 'I don't know what to make of that', what we are making is meaning.

Everything we think, feel and do is part of the meaning we create. Some of the meanings we create we put into sentences. We might consciously say to ourselves, 'It's cold. I'll put on a sweater,' or, without bringing this meaning clearly to mind, put on a sweater while thinking about something else. Our actions create meaning (like shivering in the cold) and express the meaning we have created (like putting on a sweater).

Living is the creation of meaning. To create meaning is to be alive. Thought, which includes fantasy and all the feelings and images created by our different senses, is the creation of meaning. This understanding of what it is to be alive gives to thought in all its aspects primary importance. To understand ourselves and other people we need to understand how we each think and create meaning.

This understanding of how we create meaning applies to *all* of us. Everyone, philosophers and kings, politicians and tax collectors, television personalities and bag ladies, the Bushmen of the Kalahari and Japanese businessmen, the psychiatrist and his patient, the television presenter and her audience, are all involved continuously in the creation of meaning.

Every explanation about why we do what we do has a political aspect, and the political aspect of this explanation is that it is democratic. All people think. We can argue, as we do, over who has the best thoughts, but, in a democracy, each person's thoughts have an equal right to be taken into consideration.

Democracies are not popular institutions because they restrict people's power and stop them feeling superior. Consequently people who want to be powerful and to feel that they belong to an elite, superior to other people, espouse explanations of why we do what we do which promote their sense of power and superiority.

Thus it is that we have in psychiatry and psychology theories about why people behave as they do which regard thought, or 'internal states' and 'private events' as these theories refer to them, as mere 'epiphenomena of either primary biological processes or behavioural contingencies'.[25] My dictionary defines *epiphenomena* as 'a by-product of a basic process which exerts no appreciable influence on the subsequent development of the process'.[26]

In psychiatric theory the 'primary biological processes' are those genes and chemical changes which are supposed to cause mental illnesses. In psychological theory 'behavioural contingencies' are the rewards and punishments, called 'reinforcements', which are supposed to direct a person's behaviour. In both theories a person's thoughts and feelings are of no importance, just froth and bubble.

Such froth and bubble might reveal the symptoms which allow the psychiatrist to make his diagnosis. For instance, the froth which states 'I should have done more for my parents before they died' reveals the symptom 'Unreasonable Guilt', while the bubble which states 'I no longer enjoy sex with my husband' reveals the symptom 'Loss of Libido'. Both of these symptoms are regarded as indicative of the mental illness of depression. Since such statements have for the psychiatrist no more significance than red spots have for the doctor diagnosing measles, the psychiatrist does not waste time talking to the patient to find out what deeper meaning these statements could have. If he did he might find, for instance, that his patient's loss of enjoyment of sex with her husband is an expression of her anger with her husband for insisting that she put the welfare of him and their children ahead of the welfare of her parents. But to inquire into this would take the psychiatrist into those areas of morality where we all have opinions but no special expertise. In caring for our families, whom should we put first, our partner, our children, our parents, or ourselves?

Rather than get embroiled in these questions, the psychiatrist listens to no more of what his patient says than is necessary for him to decide which mental illness the patient has. Similarly, the behavioural psychologist will, in theory, spend no more time talking to his client than is necessary to define the 'behavioural contingencies'. Human activity is reduced to a simple A, B and C.

Martin Herbert, in his handbook for parents, defined the behaviourists' ABC:[27]

A stands for *Antecedents* or what set the stage for (what led up to) the
↓
B which stands for *Behaviour* (or what the child actually does) while
↓
C refers to the *Consequences* (or what occurred immediately after the behaviour).

What we have is a rough and ready rule of thumb:

Acceptable behaviour	+	reinforcement (reward)	= more acceptable behaviour
Acceptable behaviour	+	no reinforcement	= less acceptable behaviour
Unacceptable behaviour	+	reinforcement (a reward)	= more unacceptable behaviour
Unacceptable behaviour	+	no reinforcement	= less unacceptable behaviour

Thus parents who wish to encourage their children to behave in ways which the parents regard as acceptable should reward the children when they behave acceptably and ignore them when they don't. My father used this principle in all his interactions with other people, only he did not speak of 'behavioural contingencies', just, 'You catch more flies with honey than you do with vinegar.' He caught a lot of flies, only his friends called what he did charm, and my mother would be furious because I obeyed him and not her.

Behavioural psychologists try to hide the fact that the efficacy of rewards has been common knowledge, probably for as long as there have been people to know it. They do this by using jargon impenetrable to all but the psychologists' elite. Thus behavioural psychologists' techniques for dealing with depressed people are described as being based on the idea that depressive behaviour is 'the result of environmental contingencies, maintained by its consequences, and that changing the contingencies will change the behaviour'.[28] There is little in that definition to do with thought.

I said that *in theory* behavioural psychologists spend little time talking to their clients, since the 'private events' of thought are considered not to be of any importance in determining how a person behaves. In actual practice behavioural psychologists do have to spend time talking to their clients in order to discover what the client considers to be a reinforcement, that is, what *meaning* the client has given to whatever the psychologist proposes to use as a reinforcement. For instance, psychologists often advise parents to use 'time out' as a negative reinforcement for an unruly child. (This is just a psychologist's version of 'If you don't behave yourself you're going to bed straight away'.) Now some of us find being excluded and isolated, even for a short period, very painful and frightening, while others of us find a period of being alone very peaceful and a great chance to get on with our own thoughts. Parents who try to control their children by rewarding the child for doing what the parents want and punishing the child for disobedience, but who do not try to find out what the child thinks about this, are doomed to failure.

However, there are still many behaviourists who insist that the private events of our thoughts and feelings are of no importance, just froth and bubble. Such psychologists, like the psychiatrists who dismiss their patients' thoughts and feelings as no more than the symptoms of a mental illness, are indulging in that popular self-deceit, 'I am the exception to the rule.' They are saying, 'Your thought is merely epiphenomena, whereas my thought is Real, Important, and Right, and so I can tell you what to do.' They prefer not to be consistent and say that all thought, including their own, is without value and significance.

Some psychologists and psychiatrists, wishing to get around this awkward fact and still retain their sense of superiority and power, have developed cognitive therapy, which says thought is important, but there is 'distorted' or 'dysfunctional' thought which patients and clients have, and the correct, functional thoughts which cognitive therapists have. Thus, 'cognitive behaviour therapy was based on the rationale that depression is the result of ineffective coping techniques used to remedy situational life problems.. . . . The underlying assumption of cognitive theory of depression is that the patient's emotional disturbance follows from distortions in thinking.'[29] Hence, if a person whose life history is one of rejection and betrayal by those on whom he has depended (as is the life history of many depressed people) draws the conclusion that close relationships are dangerous, this belief can be labelled by a cognitive therapist as a distortion in thinking and not as a reasonable deduction from the evidence with which the person has been presented.

The systematic approach of a cognitive therapist in helping a person sort out complex ideas and feelings can be extremely helpful, but the division of thought into 'distorted' and 'not distorted', or 'dysfunctional' and 'functional' can overlook the fact that when we are frightened we all think in simple black and white terms, and that this simplicity of our thought in times of danger is a necessary survival technique. If you fear another betrayal and you doubt that you have the strength to survive the pain, then deciding to treat all people as dangerous is a necessary survival technique until such time as you feel strong and brave enough to risk another close relationship. Often the beneficial effect of a therapist comes not from the brilliance of the therapist's interpretations, or the efficacy of his schedule of reinforcements, or the clarity of his analysis of the client's thinking, but simply from the fact that, over time, the therapist proves to be the exception to the rule that all people are untrustworthy.

The systematic approach of the cognitive therapist can be seen in the following outline of a therapy session.

First, the therapist *establishes an agenda*. The therapist reviews with the patient the points they wish to be discussed in that session. This may take up to *10 minutes* at the outset of the session, and may include a review of the previous week's homework. Substantive issues arising from homeworks may, however, form a major part of the entire session.

Second, the therapist *structures the therapy time*. This involves covering all the issues on the agenda, and assigning time next session for the discussion of those issues not discussed. The therapist attempts to keep a balance between central and peripheral issues so that the latter don't predominate.

Third, the therapist *summarizes periodically* during the interview, and elicits the patient's reactions to the summary. The therapist deliberately seeks the patient's guidance on where he/she may have misinterpreted any aspect of the patient's problem.

Fourth, the session is dominated by a *questioning approach* by the therapist. Statements of fact or offering advice are not thought to be therapeutic.

Finally, the therapist does two things:

(a) *assigns homework* based on topics that have emerged during the session as problematic.

(b) asks patient to *sum up the session* and go over what the homework assignment is. The patient is encouraged to indicate any points at which the topics discussed had been (in)appropriate, hurtful or helpful.[30]

It can be seen from this that cognitive therapy could easily lend itself to the expression of the view that the therapist's way of thinking is different from and superior to that of the patient, which is an attractive attitude to the young and unsure as well as to those who wish to be powerful and to think well of themselves. For instance, the 'questioning approach' which is advocated includes such things as:

If the patient catastrophizes about the future, ask them to rate actual probability, e.g., if patient says, 'I'll never find another friend like him', ask them how probable that state of affairs actually is – one chance in a million, one in a hundred, 10 percent or 40 percent chance.

Throughout the interchange, emphasize that it is not a glowing positive interpretation which is being encouraged, but challenging thoughts with *reality*.

Check how much the patient *now* believes the original statement is true.[31]

I have lived long enough to know that the statement 'I'll never find another friend like him' need not be an exaggeration but can be, and often is, a truthful report of a tragedy about which the person can do nothing except bear it. To be told by your cognitive therapist that your grief is an example of 'dysfunctional thinking' would hardly be helpful, but the cognitive therapist cannot be helpful here, for such therapists' discipline, as defined by Aaron Beck, the originator of cognitive therapy,[32] excludes all discussion of death: either the deaths of the client's loved ones or the client's own death, or of the philosophical issues which arise from any contemplation of death. It is very easy to feel superior to others through the expediency of denying all those things which make us feel weak and frightened.

Of course, much of what cognitive therapists do is sensible and helpful, a systematic common sense which, if given with sympathy and awareness of the client's feelings, can be tremendously helpful. However, I cannot say that I see in the lives of all the cognitive therapists whom I know evidence that their thinking as it directs their lives and interacts with other people is any less dysfunctional than the thinking of the rest of us.

The belief that other people's thought is valueless and irrelevant or distorted and dysfunctional serves to do more than give a sense of power and superiority. It also allows the person who holds it to separate his own thoughts, especially the grand thoughts he has about his theories, from the circumstances which gave rise to the thoughts. This way many people, including psychiatrists, behavioural psychologists and cognitive therapists, deny the importance of the meaning they have given to their past, present and future.

If all of us are busy creating meaning, and if this is what we all do all the time, it follows that the meanings that each of us create grow out of and are related to the meanings that other people create. What I think about and write about has arisen from my experiences of the world I live in and the people I have met, both personally and through books and the media. If I had lived in another time and place I would have created other kinds of meaning and, had I written books, they would have been different from the books I write now. Stated like this it seems self-evident, but another form of self-deceit, especially common among intellectuals, is that theories are separate from the place where they are created and the people who created them.

So popular is this idea that we can separate our thoughts from the circumstances that gave rise to them that J.K. Galbraith found it necessary to state on the opening page of his *History of Economics* that, 'Economic ideas are always and intimately a product of their own time and place; they cannot be seen apart from the world they interpret.'[33] Psychologists and psychiatrists, I have found, generally dislike viewing their theories in the context of the time and place in which they were created since such a perspective prevents the theories from being seen as some Great Truth which stands outside time and place. Unfortunately, such theories do belong to their time and place. The psychiatric theory of mental illness was developed by doctors in the nineteenth century when they needed a rationale for taking over the care of the insane,[34] while psychologists' theories have always been particularly responsive to political need.[35] Meanwhile, in university departments of English, students are instructed that proper literary criticism is concerned only with the meaning of the poem, play or novel, and not with what was happening to the author at the time.

The reason that people prefer to believe that they arrived at their theories, opinions and beliefs through 'intelligence' or 'faith' or 'reason' or 'instinct' or 'intuition' rather than through the continual process of trying to make sense of what happens to them is that these concepts seem so much grander and more important and more a source of personal pride than the confusing, unseemly and often shame-making events which constitute much of our life. How much better to say, 'I was drawn to mathematics by its purity of thought,' rather than, 'When I was a boy I was scared all the time of my parents and teachers, and I found doing maths an escape to something where

I wasn't weak and frightened.' How much better to say to a depressed woman, 'Your depressive illness is hormonal,' rather than confront the misery that marriage can be, especially your own marriage. How much better to see a client's fear of loss and death as an emotional disturbance following from distortions in thinking, rather than contemplate what loss and death lies ahead for you.

Our refusal to see that our theories, opinions and beliefs are an outcome of the meaning we have created from what has happened to us may support our vanity, but it prevents us from understanding just how we create meaning, and this particular lack of understanding is one of the main reasons why we fail to achieve what we want to achieve and to get what we want to get.

Yet it is very simple. We all know what it is to draw a conclusion and how to use that conclusion to guide us in the future. For instance, you go to a new restaurant. You give your experience there a meaning. It might be 'This is a great place', or it might be 'It's expensive and the food's awful'. The meaning you create is the conclusion you draw. If you drew the first conclusion, you go to the restaurant again. If you drew the second conclusion, you don't.

Everybody knows about drawing conclusions, but where most of us get into difficulties is that we forget that *everyone is drawing conclusions and acting on them all the time.*

Because we forget that everyone draws conclusions we think that our actions do not have consequences. How often we excuse our outburst of bad temper on the grounds that in our family 'no one takes any notice'. On those grounds we can feel that we are being treated unfairly when someone in our family is distressed by our outburst or gets angry back at us.

If we do remember that other people draw conclusions, we can save ourselves the bother of trying to work out what these conclusions are by deciding that everyone must draw the same conclusions that we do.

This is where the way of raising children advocated by behavioural psychologists goes wrong. Parents may reward, ignore and punish their children in what they see as a very sensible and fair way, and their children's behaviour show none of the improvements which the parents desire, for the child draws conclusions about their behaviour very different from those they expect. For instance, a child who is given money when what he wanted was a share of the parents' time and attention does not regard the money as a reward. Having a parent ignore his bad behaviour may be seen by the child as evidence that the parent does not care about the child, and so he increases his bad behaviour in the hope that he will provoke his parent into giving him attention, albeit angry attention. Punishments that parents can give may lead the child to draw the conclusion that the parent is dangerous,

whereupon fear drives out the child's love for the parent, or the conclusion that the parent is unjust, whereupon resentment smothers
love, or the conclusion that the parent is in a power struggle with the
child, whereupon the child determines to defeat the parent, even if it
takes the rest of his life.

The failure to appreciate that those we punish may draw conclusions
which are not in our favour is one of the reasons why wars continue.
The other reason is that some people make vast amounts of money
out of war, but even if armament manufacturers became altruistic and
took to making environment-friendly refrigerators instead, murder
and fighting would continue because we cling to the notion that the
punisher and the punished give the same meaning to the punishment.
Of course they do not.

An example of this is what happened in South Africa. Despite the
South African Government's attempts to control news from that country, we heard reports of the beatings and torture black children
received when they were arrested and imprisoned.[37] The aim of this
punishment, as the punishers saw it, was to teach the children that
they should not rebel against the white Government.

This is precisely what beatings and torture will not do. When these
children were taken into custody they found themselves completely
powerless, helpless in the power of those who hated them and wished
to destroy them. Whenever any one of us finds ourself in such a
situation, we are facing the greatest threat of all, not just pain and
death, but the threat that our very self will be annihilated. In that state
of helplessness and terror there is only one way we can save our self
and hold ourselves together as a person. It is to vow revenge. By saying to ourself, 'I shall revenge myself on my enemies,' we affirm our
pride in I as I.

Certainly some of the children who emerged from the South African
prisons were broken by the experience, will never able to overcome
their fear and create a coherent sense of self, but others, probably most
of them, will grow to adulthood with a sense of self built around the
conclusions they drew from their experience, conclusions which relate
to hatred and revenge. Unless they are given what they see as a just
system of government, in adulthood they will put these conclusions
into action, just as generations of Irish people punished by the English
continue to put their conclusions into action.

Because we punish one another so much, especially adults punishing children, most of us carry inside us imperatives to ourselves to
have revenge. Since the original object of this vow of revenge is usually not available (how can we revenge ourselves on our parents, who
punished us only for our own good?) we deflect our need for vengeance on to the people we see as bad – members of the younger
generation, people of different class, race, religion, nationality or poli-

tics. Often we have to dress up our revenge in the clothes of virtue and self-righteousness, and pretend that we are doing what we are doing only for the other person's good, in order to persuade ourselves that we are good. Our need for enemies is so great and so devious that it prevents us from seeing that those we seek to punish do not give to our actions the meaning which we give to them, and so do not learn from their punishment what we intended them to learn.

The belief that other people are not continuously engaged in creating meaning and that, if they are, they create the same meaning that we do is extremely popular. Journalists often phone me for a quick quote for articles they are writing on topics like 'Do Children Today Watch Too Much Television?' or 'Do Children Today Get Too Much Pocket Money?' or 'How Can Teachers Cope with the Increasing Numbers of Delinquent Children?' (The underlying theme of these articles is usually that children should be given less and punished more.) Every time I have to explain to the journalist that children are always engaged in giving meaning to what is done to them and acting on the conclusions they draw, and that these meanings and conclusions are not necessarily the same as their parents and teachers. To most journalists this is a novel point of view and needs much explanation. It is also not a popular point of view, for it complicates matters. Our press much prefers the simple cause and effect explanation which allows each generation to deplore the behaviour of younger generations.

To live in a world of seamless movement where every event in some way affects every other event is very complicated. Nevertheless, because we are always engaged in creating meaning and drawing conclusions from the meaning we create,

We are always affected by what people do to us, but not always in the way that other people intend.

It is not enough just to understand that we are continuously engaged in constructing meaning. We need to understand how the different meanings we each create link with one another.

THE CONNECTIONS BETWEEN MEANINGS
5. We think that the meanings we create are discrete categories, when in fact they are linked to one another so that meanings of which we are not conscious can influence our actions.

The first conclusion we draw when we begin to exist is that we can have everything. Of course we do not put this conclusion into words, for a babe in the womb does not have language, but that belief in the form of images becomes the basis of the structure of meaning which each of us creates. We could speculate – and some therapists do – about the conclusions we draw from our experience of birth, whether we slipped easily down a dark tunnel into the light, or were squeezed and pushed and pulled, or were lifted suddenly from darkness into light, but, whatever, draw conclusions we did from our experience of birth and what followed immediately after.

Whatever these early conclusions were, they were not discrete ideas or images, existing separately from one another. They merged together into a complex of ideas, and every new conclusion merged into the whole.

Just how this merging operates is not yet understood. Research on sleep and dreaming suggests that sorting out and filing the day's conclusions is one of the dream's main functions. This filing process is not like office filing when discrete pieces of paper are put into separate folders and drawers. If, as the psychoneuroimmunologists suggest,[38] our mind is the software which runs the hardware of the brain, I can imagine the sorting out and filing system as being something like the word processing software I use, Wordstar 2000. Here, when I 'create a file' I set the limits of the file, that is, how many lines there will be on a page of print and how large the margins will be. Within those limits, all the words I put into that file, all the words I take out, all the spelling and punctuation corrections I make are assimilated into the file, and the necessary accommodations are made by the software programme so that each line and paragraph takes a predetermined shape. No matter how many words I put into that file – and as my computer has a large memory a file can contain a great many words – every letter, every item of punctuation, every space is related to every other one, and any change to one affects the rest of the contents of the file. Such changes may not show up on the screen, but under the 'consciousness' of the screen is the large 'unconscious' of the computer's memory.

Any analogy between the operation of our mind and any three-dimensional system is necessarily limited, for our mind in its operations is not bound by the dimensions of space, nor is it bound by the Aristotelian logic which computers use and which makes computers at times so very stupid because they do not think metaphorically as we do all the time.

Nevertheless, when we try to think about how we think and try to explain our ideas to other people, we have to use some sort of three-dimensional model. Thanks to our experience of television pictures, nowadays it is much easier to describe models in moving, three-dimensional pictures than it was when most models were reduced to the static two dimensions of a page.

If I could create on a television screen a model of how we create and develop our system of meaning from the conclusions we draw, I would begin with some small, cell-like structure and show two things happening. One would be where a new cell or conclusion appears, attaching itself to the already present cells, and all the cells rearranging their positions in relation to one another. The other would be where a new cell enters an existing cell and breaks it up into smaller cells, whereupon all the cells rearrange themselves. The first kind of change represents learning something totally new, like discovering for the first time that some things when dropped bounce and others break. The second kind of change represents learning something which makes us modify a conclusion we have already drawn, like discovering that while warm is pleasant, there is such a thing as too warm – hot.

I would show this structure as constantly growing and changing, and every change affecting every part of the structure to some greater or lesser degree, so that even the most peripheral of changes ripple through to the centre. Also, I would want to show this structure as being not isolated but in constant contact, in some kind of interflow, with everything around it.

Although the structure is in constant change and interflow, it does not break up into pieces or change its structure in any vague, amorphous way. For all its changes, it has some overall principle, a kind of dimension, which holds the structure together and on which the whole structure depends.

I call this overall principle or dimension our sense of existence. We each experience our sense of existence, and we each have our own way of experiencing it. Because whenever we know something we also know its opposite (I am cold/I am not cold), we know how we experience our sense of existence and how we would experience our not existing. It is our experience of our sense of existence and non-existence that underlies and informs every conclusion we draw and every decision we make.

To illustrate this I need to change the spatial metaphor by taking a radial slice out of the changing structure on the screen and turning this slice into a ladder. The periphery of that bit of the structure becomes the foot of the ladder, and we can go up that ladder in a process of questioning called *laddering*.[39]

Suppose someone says to me, 'My family are so untidy. I'm always having to clean and tidy our home.'

This statement forms the foot of the ladder.

I ask, 'Why is it important to you to have a clean and tidy home?'

To answer this question the person has to give an answer which relates to beliefs, wishes, needs, attitudes and opinions, that is, a more abstract idea than the original statement. This is one step up the ladder.

The person might say, 'I like my friends to see my home clean and tidy. It is welcoming. If it was a mess they might not want to have anything to do with me.'

There are two statements here which can be investigated.

First I might ask, 'Why is it important to you that you welcome your friends?'

The answer would be something along the lines of 'Well, that's what life is about, isn't it? Being close to other people.' The person would be saying, 'This is how I experience my sense of existence – being in relationship to other people.'

Second I might ask, 'What would happen to you if every person in the entire world refused to have anything to do with you?'

The answer would be something along the lines of 'That would be the end of me. I would disappear, wither away, fade to nothing.'

And so we would have reached the top of the person's ladder with a statement of how that person experiences his or her sense of existence and non-existence or annihilation.

Not all people would proceed in the same way up their ladder from the first statement about the necessity for keeping their home clean and tidy.

Some would say, in answer to the question, 'Why is it important to you to keep your home clean and tidy?', 'It is more efficient to keep my home clean and tidy. Having everything in a mess makes me nervous'.

To the question, 'Why is it important to you to be efficient?' the person would answer in terms of efficiency leading to good organization, control, clarity, personal development and achievement, and say, 'That's what life is about, isn't it?', thus describing how that person experiences his or her sense of existence.

To the question, 'What would happen to you if you could not be efficient and organized and everything fell into total chaos?' the person would answer, not in terms of disappearing but of shattering, fragmenting, crumbling to dust.

All of us, of course, want to have close relationships with other people *and* to achieve, but life often forces us to choose, usually between family and career, so we each have a priority, and if we make the wrong choice we suffer. So we each need to make very clear to ourselves what is at the top of our ladder.

How we experience our sense of existence and how we experience ourselves are identical and inextricably linked with how we experience our two realities, the reality which lies around us, our external reality, and the reality which lies inside us, our thoughts, feelings and images. Those people who experience their sense of reality as a relationship with other people (a 'people person') find their external reality more real than their internal reality, and so I call them *extraverts* (turning outwards). Those people who experience their sense of existence as the development of individual achievement, clarity and authenticity (a 'what have I achieved today?' person) find their internal reality more real than their external reality, and so I call them *introverts* (turning inwards).

Because our experience of our sense of existence and non-existence is the overall principle or dimension of the world of meaning we each create and inhabit, we take it for granted. When life is going along well for us and we are full of self-confidence, we are not very aware of the threat of annihilation of our self. It is only when we lose self-confidence that the threat presses itself upon us. Barbara, who experienced her sense of existence as the development of her individuality, and who had all her life been competent and successful, became aware of the threat when several of the people close to her died suddenly. She said to me, 'I used to think that inside I was stainless steel, but now I feel that inside I'm a meringue and I'm crumbling to pieces.' Another woman, Sylvia, who experienced her sense of existence as being a member of a group, found that as she got older it was harder to hold on to what little self-confidence she had brought from a childhood where she was always nervous and shy. She described to me how, when she was alone, she would feel that she had disappeared and that she was frightened to look in the mirror lest she see no reflection. Her sense of emptiness was not peaceful. She spoke of being racked by painful emotions. 'I've got the devil inside me, only the devil is emptiness.'

All the time, as we draw conclusions and create meanings, as we predict, decide and act, we are in the business of elaborating our sense of existence and warding off the threat of annihilation. There is an infinite multitude of ways in which we can elaborate our sense of existence, either by securing our membership of groups, or by developing our individuality. In warding off the threat of annihilation there are many things we can do, but the more frightened we become, the fewer defences we can use, until we are reduced to using those desperate defences which psychiatrists call the symptoms of mental illness.[40]

Because the way we each experience our sense of existence and the threat of annihilation is always present, we take it for granted and do not think about it. We assume that all people experience their sense of existence and the threat of annihilation in the same way as we do, just as we assume that all people breathe air and eat food. But of course they do not.

OUR DIFFERENT WORLDS OF MEANING
6. We assume that other people create the same meanings as we do, and when other people fail to act in the way that our meanings lead us to expect that they should, we condemn them.

'All the world's mad except me and thee, and even thee's a little mad.' This old saying encapsulates the way many of us feel when we are shocked and amazed at what other people say and do. Often we discuss our shock and amazement with someone whom we think shares our point of view. Such a conversation contains many sentences which begin with a version of 'Wouldn't you think s/he . . . ?', as in 'Wouldn't you think she'd look after her children better?' or 'Wouldn't you think he'd leave her after all that?', and all such questions require the answer 'Yes'. When our companion fails to give the required answer we feel even more shocked and amazed, and, if we know the old saying, we might repeat it to ourselves. One tremendously important social skill is to be able to identify accurately those people who will answer 'Yes' to our 'Wouldn't you think . . . ?' questions.

'Wouldn't you think . . . ?' conversations can be immensely satisfying for they lend themselves to much condemnation of others and justification of ourselves, and when our companion agrees with us there can be that marvellous feeling of solidarity, especially when we agree that the person whom we are condemning is treating us badly. How can we give up the great satisfaction of regarding those who differ in their views from us as mad or, even better, bad, and instead take the very unsatisfying view that other people are neither mad nor bad when they see things differently from us, but simply behaving as all human beings do: creating their own world of meaning?

So passionately do we not want to yield to others the right, much less the necessity, of seeing things differently, that when people like myself attempt to explain how another person thinks, my *explanation* is taken as an *excuse*. I might say that a certain man as a child was sexually abused, and he defended himself from being annihilated as a person by this experience by drawing the conclusion that nothing bad had happened to him. Such a conclusion shielded him from further hurt, but, as he did not revise this conclusion in adult life, he saw no reason why he should not abuse children in the way that he had been abused. Since in every conclusion we draw we are exercising choice, an explanation of the series of conclusions we drew, that is, the choices we made, does not necessarily *excuse* our behaviour. I certainly disapprove of many of the series of conclusions which are made by people and which I endeavour to explain.

As much as we like the idea of being free to choose, there are many times when we want to excuse our behaviour by claiming, 'I had no choice.' In such situations it is not that we had no choice but that, to all but one of the alternative courses of action open to us, we gave the meaning 'totally unacceptable'.

If we believe that our own way of seeing things is the only way we can see things, and that our way of seeing things is the only correct way of seeing things, then we create for ourselves a world of meaning which is fixed and inflexible. Thus we rob ourselves of freedom, and we make our relationships with other people impossibly difficult.

It is bad enough being continually shocked and amazed that people far removed from us in place and relationships think differently from us, but it is even worse when we discover that our nearest and dearest have created a world of meaning very different from our own.

I am forever explaining to parents and to journalists inquiring on behalf of their readers, many of whom are parents, that different generations see things differently. Currently, the parents of teenagers are likely to have been teenagers in the sixties, a time of considerable opportunity and optimism for young people. The present generation of teenagers, however, are well aware that their future is uncertain.

The simple adage 'Work hard at school and you'll get a good job' no longer applies for, while a government strives to gain and maintain economic stability, every country's economy is at the mercy of the multinational industrial complexes and the money markets of Tokyo and New York. No one can predict the course and outcome of the potential changes in Eastern Europe and the USSR, and in the Middle East, while the dire predictions of ecological change come thick and fast. Thus all teenagers today need greater courage in living than has ever been required from previous generations. They cannot, as millions of young people have done in the past, accept unquestioningly that they should sacrifice their lives while believing their elders' promises that such a sacrifice is for the greater glory of their nation. Uneducated young people in the Middle East may still do this, but not those who have access to the Western media. It is not surprising that such young people draw conclusions very different from their parents' about how they should live their lives. It is not surprising to me that many young people prefer to fulfil short-term goals than make long-term plans, but I know that there are many people of older generations who refuse to understand the young people's point of view but enjoy deploring it.

I have often been the instigator of a conversation which led to a married couple discovering that they differ completely on the basic purpose of their lives. It is, I recognize, a very dangerous undertaking, but I do it because the couple have asked me to help them sort out their mutual difficulties.

We talk about their arguments, and all sorts of things that sound very petty come up – like arguments about holidays. Perhaps she likes holidays because then they can do things 'as a family', and he is against holidays: 'They're a waste of money. At the end you've got nothing to show for them.' So I start asking the kind of questions which seek out the conclusions behind their conclusions about holidays, until each of them arrives at their basic principle, and, lo, there is she saying in effect, 'The purpose of life is relationships with other people,' while he is saying, 'The purpose of life is individual achievement.' While he might be aware that 'She always puts the family first', and she might be aware that 'He's always trying to better himself', neither might be aware of the profound differences in their beliefs about the purpose of life.

The sexes are equally divided in their views about the purpose of life. In another couple the wife can be the one concerned about individual achievement and the husband the one insisting on the importance of the group. This difference in views no doubt underlies the principle of 'opposites attract', and I have yet to find a couple not made up of a 'people person' and a 'what have I achieved today?' person. (Couples who feel that they are both extraverts or both introverts and want to examine my finding should look, not at what they each *do*, but *why* they do it. Unfortunately, some people cannot distinguish their own reasons, their own truth, from the reasons they believe they ought to hold.) Such opposite views certainly create complementary and pleasant contrasts, but they also lay the basis for arguments, all the worse when neither partner acknowledges the other person's point of view, much less allows that both points of view have equal rights and validity. We have a long tradition of men regarding women as stupidly emotional and women regarding men as insensitive and childish.

Even when two people share the same basic principle about the sense of existence and the threat of annihilation, no two people experience and use these in exactly the same way. I find tremendous variety in the images people give of their sense of existence and the threat of annihilation, images sometimes described in pictures like those given by Barbara and Sylvia and sometimes contained in the words people use, words like 'disappear', 'fade', 'dissolve', 'wither', 'shatter', 'crumble', 'fragment', 'collapse into a shambles'.

From differing images of the sense of existence come many different ways of elaborating that sense of existence. Some 'people persons' gather a family around them, or become a member of a team, or, as an entertainer, keep an audience engaged. Some 'people persons' see the relationship with others as one of love, while others interpret it as needing to be needed. 'What have I achieved today?' persons can seek their individual development in fame, prizes, and great discoveries, or simply in the satisfaction of a job well done. They can seek clarity in the pursuit of personal truth, or scientific theory, or metaphysical wisdom, or of an ordinary life well lived. It took me one long book, *The Successful Self*, to outline the different ways in which 'people persons' (or extraverts) and 'what have I achieved today?' persons (or introverts) elaborate their experience of the sense of existence and defend against the threat of annihilation, but no one book can capture the immense variety of individual experiences of the sense of existence and the fear of annihilation.

To understand how we each create a structure of meaning which is in effect our self and the world we live in, it is sometimes helpful to use the image of a computer, where we could think of our physical equipment – our body and all it contains – as the hardware, and our structure of meaning as the software. Doing this we can perhaps more clearly perceive that if the software does not contain a particular instruction then the computer cannot compute any information which relates to that missing instruction.

For instance, in the late seventies the information coming from satellite pictures of the atmosphere showed a fifty percent depletion of ozone over Antarctica. The computers in England and the United States which were collating the satellite reports could not accept and deal with this information because their software contained the instruction that the loss of ozone was uniform and worldwide. Only when the scientists used some software which did have an instruction allowing for the possibility of an uneven distribution of the loss of ozone – that is, they did the calculations themselves – did they perceive the meaning of the messages from the satellites.[41]

Often, when we wrongly assume that other people create the same meanings as we do, we fail to perceive that their particular software does not contain the same set of software instructions as ours does. If their software contains the instruction, 'Failure to attend mass every Sunday is a mortal sin,' they cannot accept our message that church is boring and swimming fun. If our software contains the instruction, 'All Russians are treacherous enemies,' we cannot perceive, much less accept, the friendly messages which the Russians send us. The structure of meaning we create *is* ourself, so if the basic ideas on which we build our structure are challenged, we feel our very self to be in danger. When the Russians became the good guys, Doonesbury's B.D. was thus threatened.[42]

Doonesbury

BY GARRY TRUDEAU

Thus it is that one awkward truth which we must recognize and learn to live with if we are to live intelligently is

We each create our own world of meaning, and no two people create the same world.

There is another awkward truth with which we have to live.

COMPLEMENTARY OPPOSITES

7. We overlook the fact that there are certain aspects of life which stand in complementary relationship to one another, so that the more there is of one, the less there is of the other.

In wanting everything it often happens that we want two opposite things. When the opposition of these things is clear as, say, when we want to live in the city and in the country, we see the difficulty of gaining both wishes and either give one up or organize our life so we can have a bit of both. We might live in the city and buy a weekend country retreat, or we might live in the country and take our holidays in the city. But when the opposition is composed of abstractions like 'freedom' and 'security', and what these abstractions represent are not two mutually exclusive things but things which stand in relationship to one another, so that the more there is of one the less there is of the other, the difficulty in our gaining opposite wishes is not so clear.

What we all want is to be free and secure. What we find hard to accept is that *it is impossible to be totally free and totally secure.*

We see this at a political level where governments which try to give their subjects the security of work and a fair income for all do this by restricting their subjects' freedom to make their own choices about what they believe and what they do, and governments which try to give their subjects the freedom to believe what they want to believe and to do what they want to do provide little security for their subjects. Under a socialist government we can have the security of a permanent job but little freedom of self-expression, while under a capitalist government we can have freedom of speech but no job security.

At a practical level, if we want our home and our possessions to be secure from thieves, we have to lock ourselves and our possessions up, either by living far away from other people or by securing the doors and windows of our home. I remember staying at a friend's home in Cincinnati and, early one morning, wanting to go into the garden but being unable to do so because I did not know the combination of their door lock. Suddenly their beautiful home seemed like a prison.

Even though we know the relationship between freedom and security at the political and practical level, we very often forget that the same relationship applies at a personal level. There are many men who believe that they can enjoy both the security of a home and family and the freedom of a single man, and who are surprised to discover that their home life becomes most insecure, either because it vanishes altogether or because their wife and children cease to love them. There are many women who fall in love with exciting, unpredictable men and, forgetting that excitement and unpredictability can exist only in freedom and uncertainty, mistakenly expect that such men will become secure, reliable husbands.

'What's to Stop Me?'

Many people, I have found, while living lives of considerable pain and unhappiness, will not change the way they live until they can find a way of changing which is totally secure. From the security of their prison of depression they say to me, 'All right, I'll try being kind to myself and going out and meeting people, but I want you to promise me that it'll turn out exactly as I want it to be.' Then I have to explain that to change they have first to see that they are free to change, and that freedom means risk, and risk means unpredictability. Many such people, having decided to choose freedom rather than security, have found security again in a new way of life which, from the old vantage point, looked most insecure. Jeannie, who, when she first came to see me seven years ago, was depressed and totally unable to cope as the wife of a college lecturer and mother of one, was recently telling me, when I visited her in her isolated Highland cottage, of her latest adventures as a single parent of two and therapist in training. She said, just as an aside in passing, 'My ex knows I can cope, and of course I shall.'

Jeannie, who still occasionally remarks, 'All I ever wanted was to marry and have a family,' faced up to the implications of the complementary nature of freedom and security. She also faced up to another contrast most difficult to accept, that of wanting to be an individual and a member of a group.

A friend and I were waiting to cross a busy road in Jerusalem one evening when we were approached by an American woman who asked us where she could find a café. We were planning to have coffee, so we asked her to join us. She said that her name was Lois and that she was with a tour party but stayed at cheaper hotels than the rest of the party and had to find inexpensive places to eat.

Over a meal of felafel Lois told us how excited and impressed she was with what she had seen of Israel, especially the kibbutzim with their sense of cooperation and devotion to hard work. 'What this place needs,' she said, 'is people.' All that she had seen confirmed her belief that 'Israel is where we ought to be'. At first I thought she was including me in this, but then realized that she meant the Jews.

So she was seriously considering leaving New York, where she was born and had lived all her life, to start afresh in Israel. What came through in what she said was not simply a fervent patriotism but a longing to belong. New York can be a lonely city for a single woman approaching forty whose only son is going his own way, careless of his mother. How lovely it would be to sink into the bosom of a kibbutz, to be surrounded by like-minded people who would love and support her!

Lois talked on, with my friend and I saying little. She was really thinking aloud, trying to put together two pieces of a jigsaw which refused to fit.

Lois was a New Yorker, sharp, wary, friendly only up to a point, and, as she said of herself, independent. 'I was the eldest child,' she said, 'I was never any good at doing what I was told.'

I had stayed briefly on a kibbutz as the guest of Smarda, a psychologist who had joined the kibbutz only when she married a man who lived there. She looked at it with an outsider's eye, and described to me appreciatively the security of physical care it gave (every working mother would envy the kibbutz's child care and laundry arrangements), but pointed out the lack of personal privacy. There was strong pressure to obey the rules and to conform in every way, and the chief hobby was gossiping about one another. I knew without thinking about it that I could never live happily in a kibbutz. I had already worked out that loneliness was part of the price I had to pay for being myself.

Lois was still struggling with this. She wanted to have everything in the form of being an independent individual while at the same time being an integral member of a group.

While some of us are more drawn to being an individual and the rest of us are more drawn to being a member of a group, we all want both, and wanting both underlies all our difficulties in trying to get everything that we want.

Wanting and Not Getting

The original sense of 'having everything' is one of a blissful union with everything that is. There is no clear distinction between self and other, for everything is felt as self. The distinction between self and other begins to emerge only when the other fails to respond as the self desires.

We never lose our desire to return again to the first state of bliss when everything was one. We feel it approaching as we sink into deep, dreamless sleep. We hope to find it in sex, not just in ecstasy but in a blissful union with another-become-self. We locate the sense of oneness not in our past but in our future, and work with prayer and meditation to find a oneness with God or with all that there is. We try to lose ourselves in drink or drugs, the more persistently the less we like ourselves.

But even as we long for blissful union, we reject it, for in finding it we lose that which marks us out as a person, and knowing ourselves to be a person is our most precious possession. Only when we feel secure in our knowledge of ourselves as a person can we risk relinquishing our sense of self. We can sink into sleep knowing that we shall wake as ourselves. We can join another person, knowing that we can uncouple and be ourselves. We can lose ourselves in prayer or meditation or alcohol, for we know that the period of prayer or meditation will end or that we shall become sober. What we fear is a merging from which we shall not emerge – of sinking not into sleep but into death, of becoming helpless in the power of another person or potency, or becoming incapable of controlling our own thoughts and feelings.

So our desire for having everything in a blissful union is always at odds with our desire to be ourselves.

Because we do not recognize the basis of our desire to have everything, we fail to take this desire and turn it into a striving to enjoy, experience and achieve all that is possible in our lives. Because we do not recognize that we can be prevented from enjoying, experiencing and achieving in two different ways, by the way we have chosen to define ourselves and by the nature of life, we fail to act intelligently in changing our definitions and in adapting ourselves profitably to life's conditions.

Failing to act intelligently in these ways, we find ourselves feeling not just frustration, anger, resentment and helplessness at our failure to get what we want, but shame. In terms of possessions and wealth, the have-nots not only have to suffer deprivation but as well feel shame and suffer humiliation at the hands of the haves. Posy Simmonds' cartoon illustrates how such shame is displayed in Britain.[43]

The fact that we don't recognize that we hold the belief that we can have everything, while at the same time we strive to fulfil it and consequently feel frustrated, resentful, shamed and envious when we fail, causes us endless misery. We can avoid such misery by recognizing our belief and the two categories of reasons why we do not fulfil our expectations.

Distinguishing between the two categories allows us to determine where we might usefully fight for our rights and ambitions, and where we might usefully resign ourselves gracefully to life's course.

Distinguishing between the two categories enables us to work out clearly our priorities and to make more informed choices, and thus achieve a much wiser and more gratifying level of enlightened self--interest.

Distinguishing between the two categories allows us to free ourselves from the pain of loss, mourning, resentment, envy and greed.

Distinguishing between the two categories enables us to perceive more clearly when we are the object of murderous envy and to protect ourselves more effectively. (Because we do not wish to recognize our own envy of what we see as other people's success compared with our failure to fulfil our belief that we could have everything, we do not always perceive that other people envy us.)

Distinguishing between the two categories enables us to live in the present, enjoying what we have, instead of living in the future and being for ever unsatisfied.

Experiencing our desire to possess everything as hunger traps us in

a miserable prison. Experiencing our desire to possess everything as an amusing and enlivening response to life makes everything that we have feel like everything that we want.

Why, when we have used our intelligence to work out so many extremely complicated things and so make life easier for ourselves, do we not use our intelligence to understand how we each create our own world of meaning and so make life easier for ourselves? Why enjoy, say, the benefits of electricity and not the benefits of living peacefully and cooperatively?

The answer comes back to wanting everything where the wanting is expressed in gaining power over other people. For as long as we have existed as a species, the people in power have striven to keep those whom they wish to subjugate ignorant and confused. They have withheld information, told lies, and prevented their subjects from gaining information and knowing the truth. When people in power do impart information, they do so in ways which serve to promote obedience and create confusion in their subjects' minds. It is not in the interests of those in power that their subjects be able to think clearly and be well-informed. People who think clearly and are well-informed are not likely to be unthinkingly obedient.

By people in power I mean those people who comprise the State[44] and its systems of organization and control, the Church as an instrument of obedience and control, the wealthy and their systems of gaining and maintaining wealth, the professions, and, at every level of society, parents. These are the people who tell us that we cannot have everything. The reasons they give are usually spurious and are intended to bamboozle. So we are bamboozled, and then we go on to bamboozle others.

3

'You Can't Have Everything' – Society

To understand how children are educated by
their families we need to understand how the
State educates its people. The two are
indivisible.

Our Subjective Truth

When we are born we look about us in wonder and immediately set
about trying to establish *what is*. This is a never-ending quest, for the
bodily form with which we are equipped forever excludes us from
knowing directly *what is*. But there is one part of *what is* about which
we can be absolutely certain, and that is what goes on inside ourselves
– our thoughts, feelings, images and intuitions from which we create
our structure of meaning, its overall dimension or principle being our
sense of existence. This part of *what is* is, in our early years, the rock
from which we can spring into the vast, shifting ocean of *what is*
outside us, an ocean in which we can swim, making discoveries, coming back to our rock of *what is* inside us, using it as a point of reference,
a solid base from which the ocean of uncertainty which surrounds us
seems, at least in certain parts, more understandable. Using our rock
of certainty we can explore. As babies we explore with our mouths,
examining *what is* around us by discovering how it feels in our mouth.
Once our hand can grasp we can explore with that, and all the time
we are watching and listening, trying to make sense of what is going
on around us.

As small children we can know that this way of knowing is limited
but reliable. If we are allowed to grow up still using our knowledge
of *what is* inside us as a rock in an ocean of uncertainty, or as a beacon
of light piercing an infinite blackness, we have access to our inner
truth, a sense of self, a sense of self-worth. But we are rarely allowed
to do this.

The process of bamboozlement which is called education teaches us
to regard *what is* inside us as, at best, illogical and unreliable and, at
worst, evil. Our subjective truth is no truth at all. Believing this, we
can no longer think intelligently about ourselves and other people. In
fact, we lose the ability to understand how we think.

Not Understanding How We Create Meaning

Ask anyone how to operate a familiar piece of machinery – how to drive a car or use a washing machine – and the person can give you a straightforward and correct explanation. But ask that same person to describe the process of thinking, something each one of us does continuously for every moment of our lives, and no precise and ordered answer is forthcoming. Indeed, the person may resent the question, for we do not like to think about how we think.

Of course, thinking about thought and language is very difficult because we cannot get outside thought and language to look at them. It is much easier to watch yourself driving a car than to watch yourself thinking. While we can listen to how another person uses language, we cannot observe that person thinking. This is why psychiatrists prefer to study bodies and psychologists prefer to study behaviour, rather than to take on the more difficult task of studying thought and language. Having been taught, as children, to despise their own internal reality of thoughts, feelings and intuitions, psychiatrists, psychologists, biologists and geneticists create theories about human behaviour which ignore the fact that whatever we do originates and operates within the framework of the meaning which we have created.

Explaining human behaviour while ignoring how we create meaning is as sensible as explaining the ecology of the earth while ignoring the presence of air. Because we are not taught how to understand how we think and create meaning, we are often unaware that what we are thinking is based on assumptions, which we do not make explicit when we argue about certain issues.

To understand a new experience we can use nothing but our past experience, the structure of meaning which we have created. We look at something new and ask ourselves, 'What is this like?' We see a woman we have just met as being like our mother, a new work situation reminds us of a situation at school. Our past experience provides the *metaphors* by which we comprehend something new.

Thus the general assumption on which our argument is based is a metaphor which links something we are trying to understand to something we already know.

Our Concept of the Person as a Container

Very early in our life we discover the concept of a container, an object which has something inside it. Also, very early in life we discover that what is inside the container can be good for us (say, milk) or bad for us (say, kerosene). Later in life we use this concept of a container as a way of structuring our attempts to understand things far more complex than a cup of milk. In trying to understand the immensely complex question of why people behave as they do, we reduce our awareness of the complexity by using the concept of a container. Human beings, we say, are containers. What they contain might be good, or it might be bad.

For instance, Christianity teaches that human beings are containers of something bad, namely, original sin.

> Augustine taught that everyone deserved, through original sin, to go to hell; and that Christ's death enabled a small number, chosen in advance by God, to be saved. Pelagius rejected the idea of original sin, and taught that each individual can choose freely between good and evil. To this day, young men and women are taught to see Pelagianism as a dangerous distortion of Christianity.[1]

There are many people who believe that they are Christians but who hold the heretical idea that what we contain within ourselves is good.

When we argue about education, we rarely make explicit the assumption about the nature of children on which our argument is based. Neither do we make explicit the general assumption which underlies this assumption, which is that everything we encounter which in any way affects us we construe as either good or bad. Events far off from us which we see as playing no part in our lives we can see as simply happening, but events which we see as influencing our lives we construe as either good for us or bad for us.

Thus some of us would argue that the aim of education should be to enable children to make the most of their individual talents and self-expression, while others of us would argue that all children should study a set syllabus and learn to be obedient and respectful.

The first argument is based on the assumption that the child is the container of some special force or power which should be encouraged to blossom forth. The second argument is based on the assumption that the child is the container of something bad which must be eradicated or controlled. The container itself must be moulded into a shape which will not allow this inherent badness to burst forth. The supporters of the first argument would regard the assumption that the child is a container of forces which can blossom forth in an acceptable and beneficial way as a good assumption, and the assumption that the child contains evil forces as a bad assumption, while the supporters of the second assumption would regard the first assumption as bad and the second good.

This difference in perception arises from the difference in the way we can think of ourselves as human beings. We can think of ourselves as being basically good or being basically bad. If we think of ourselves as being basically good, then if we let what is inside us out there will be no danger to ourselves or other people. But if we think of ourselves as being basically bad, then what is inside us must be kept under control, for if it escapes we put ourselves and other people in danger.

Hence all our ideas about education fall into two groups, those which see the aim of education as bringing out what is good (the Latin root of 'education' is *educere*, from *ex* meaning 'out' and *ducere* meaning 'to lead'), and those which see the aim of education as to contain and mould. In Russia the most commonly used word for education, образование (phonetically *obrazovanyi*), has its root in образ (*obraz*) meaning shape, form, appearance. Russian does have another word for education, просвещение, (*prosveshchenyi*), meaning literally 'into the lightness' or 'enlightenment'.

Those people who see education as a process of enlightenment not only believe in the basic goodness of individuals, they are also able to tolerate uncertainty. Encouraging people to pursue their own goals and make their own discoveries leads to many unpredictable results and into areas where the teacher will have to admit ignorance. Those people who see education as a process of containing and moulding prefer security to freedom. They try to leave nothing to chance. They claim to know what people ought to be and how to mould children into an ideal shape. They are sure that if people are allowed to think for themselves they will never reach the ideal, predetermined shape, and that the best way of stopping people from thinking for themselves is to bamboozle them.

The idea of education as a containment and moulding is extremely popular, first because many people believe that human beings are basically bad and, second, because it gives many advantages to the person doing the containing and moulding.

The Advantages of Education as Moulding

People who regard children as being intrinsically bad always know what children must be taught to be, and that is obedient, compliant, respectful, clean, tidy and hard working. Children should never be aggressive, except on the sports field, where they play for the glory of their team, and, later, as soldiers, when they fight and die for their country. Trusting their elders, they should never question orders, answer back or assert their own point of view. Indeed, they should not have an individual point of view, just the views which their elders have taught them to hold.

Children who meet these requirements never make their elders feel nervous. Such children are predictable and the elders feel safe.

Obedient children give their elders an easy life. Their elders do not have to expend much effort in seeing that their orders are obeyed. Obedient children do not feel that they have the choice of being disobedient. Disobedience is unthinkable. One woman told me, 'When I think of my mother I think of her with a fishing line and me at the end of it. She holds my right to exist, and she reels me out and then she reels me in.'

Obedient children can not only be relied on to do as they are told, they can be relied on to keep one another in order. Obedient children, like obedient citizens, exert pressure on their peers to obey and conform. They report their disobedient peers to the authorities for chastisement. Obedient children 'tell on' their naughty classmates and siblings. Obedient citizens report malefactors to the police.

How do parents and teachers instil obedience in children and the State instil obedience in its subjects?

Creating Obedient Children and Citizens

As small children trying to understand the world we live in, we need the adults around us to explain it to us. When the adults give us such explanations they are not merely giving us information. They are trying to persuade us to hold certain beliefs which will then guide our future behaviour. If these adults are trying to get us to be obedient, conforming and compliant, they will select the beliefs they wish us to hold very carefully and teach them to us in particular ways. They will teach us that we are part of a great and glorious whole, that if we are bad we will be punished and if we are good we will be rewarded, that we live in a Just World, that certain things are rewards which will make us happy, and that curiosity and intellect should be circumspect, and that we should not question the limited information which the representatives of God and the State give us. Failure to behave as desired will be punished with humiliation and ridicule.

In teaching us that *we are part of a great and glorious whole*, they will tell us that we are privileged to be a member of a certain family and a citizen of the most great and glorious country. No matter that our family and the State treat us badly, we are honoured to be accepted, however unworthy we are, as a member of these precious and splendid institutions. No matter how unworthy and valueless we feel in ourselves, we can partake of the virtue of the family and the power and glory of the State. The family, like the State, is a hierarchy, and we, as children, are at the bottom, but we are promised that if we are good we can advance up the hierarchy and one day share in the power and the glory of the family and the State.

Of course, we might not advance very far up the hierarchy. Such hierarchies are usually patriarchies. Since most societies believe that a proper family consists of a husband, wife and children, a woman cannot head a family. (In Western societies, a family where the head is a woman is not considered to be a proper family. Note the criticism which one-parent families receive from our society.) Nor can women, with very few exceptions, fill the important posts in the State hierarchy. Most people, men and particularly women, remain poor and powerless.

Why do so many people accept this state of affairs?

Because they are taught to believe that if they are bad they will be punished.

For the first few weeks of our lives we can do what we like and get away with it. We can yell our anger, sob our needs, expel from our bodies what we do not want, and demand and expect that our needs be met. But then we start to discover that the people around us will not allow us to continue in this way. We discover that they expect us to conform to their wishes. We discover that when we do not conform to their wishes we are punished. The punishment may be simply that our mother does not respond to our demands and we go on being hungry or lonely, or it may be an angry voice or a sharp slap.

Along with the angry voice and the sharp slap come certain words which are applied to us and what we have done – 'bad', 'naughty', 'wicked'. We discover that *if we are bad we are punished*.

We soon work out the obverse of this truth, namely, that *if we are good we are rewarded*. We work this out for ourselves, and we are told that this is true. We want to avoid the pain of punishment, we want to please our parents and retain their love, we want to live comfortably with ourselves, and so we become very good at being good. Of course, many times we make mistakes and fail. Many times the adults around us expect us to achieve something that it is beyond our powers to achieve. But before long we become *experts in being good*.

It is not until we become experts in being good that we begin to feel that we have some control over the system of rewards and punishments. Until then we have been the victim of a system which often seemed erratic and unfair, but by the time we become experts in being good we see the system of rewards and punishments not just as a pattern which is followed by our parents and teachers, and which we have learned to predict, but as a universal system, evidence that we live in a Just World. Few children have the experience and wisdom to know that 'Expecting the world to be fair because you're kind is like expecting a bull not to charge because you're a vegetarian'.[2] For at the same time as we were learning how to be an expert in being good, we were being taught the religion of our family.

All religions teach that we live in a Just World where goodness is rewarded and badness punished. Exactly how this system of rewards and punishments operates and who controls the system is different in different religions, but the basic idea remains the same.

Hindus are taught that if they accept the station in life to which they have been born and meet the duties of that station, then in their next life they will be born into a higher station. Buddhists are taught that

83

evil thoughts are followed by pain and pure thoughts by happiness. Jews are taught that evil comes from within them and that it is punished in this life, while virtue is also rewarded in this life, perhaps in material things, but certainly in a close and supportive discourse with God. Muslims are taught that only if they are faithful to Islam will they be saved to enjoy Paradise, and that unbelievers will burn in hell.

Christians are taught that death is not to be feared, provided that they believe in God and carry out His wishes, for then they will be judged by God to be fit to enter the Kingdom of Heaven. Failure to believe in God and/or to carry out His wishes will be punished by an eternity in Hell. The harshness of this doctrine has disturbed many Christians, and down the centuries many people have sought to mitigate the Church's teaching, but such people have been called heretics and often punished most cruelly.

Today many Christians unknowingly hold beliefs which are considered to be heresies by the orthodox Catholic, Protestant and Greek Orthodox Churches. Robert van de Weyer wrote:

> Most Christians support the views of that robust North African, Donatus, who fought against the growing authority of priests and bishops. Orthodoxy teaches that priests have some special sacramental power, and that they alone can preside at Communion. Donatus regarded this as nonsense, teaching that every Christian has a vital ministry – or 'charism' – and that sacramental grace is shared by the whole Christian community. Donatus was accused of subverting the Church, and driving it into exile.
>
> In a similar vein, the ideas of the great mystic Origen are more popular than ever – yet as recently as 1928 the Church of England saw fit to reiterate its condemnation of him. Origen taught that every Christian, through prayer and meditation, can communicate directly with God, without need of priest and theologians. In Origen's view, true faith is a spiritual exploration, in which each person seeks to penetrate the mystery. Small wonder that the guardians of orthodoxy saw fit to ban his writings – as they have banned numerous mystics since his time.
>
> Most striking of all, the arch-heretic Arius refuses to die. He urged people to regard Jesus as a friend and brother, who shared their temptations and struggles; hence he loathed the attempt to spiritualize Jesus, turning him into a divine figure remote from human experience. The bishops outlawed such ideas as undermining the authority of Christ, asserting that he was 'the Second Person of the Trinity'; but now, as then, most ordinary disciples prefer a human Jesus, with whom they can identify.

Robert van de Weyer explained why the Church regarded these views as heresy:

Orthodox Christian doctrine did not emerge directly from the New Testament. Rather it was largely hammered out in the fourth and fifth centuries; and the formulae which carried the day remain the teachings of the churches, Catholic, Protestant, and Orthodox alike. Most accounts of this process, while recognizing the political intrigues and personal rivalries which plagued the various councils, ascribe the eventual outcome to the Holy Spirit; that the bishops, guided by the Spirit, chiselled out a doctrinal edifice that will stand unmoved to the end of time.

But there is a quite different interpretation of the same events. Christianity had just become, under Emperor Constantine, the State religion; and even after the fall of the Empire, the bishops were anxious to retain their status under the new barbarian rulers. It was essential, therefore, that Christian doctrine should assert the Church's spiritual monopoly, its claim to be the sole true religion. The ideas which were condemned as heretical were, without exception, those which undermined this claim.

Thus if Jesus was simply a human being – a great religious leader, but not divine – Christianity cannot claim to offer the only path to truth. If people have free will, and are not predestined by God to be saved or damned, then the Church cannot claim to be the exclusive company of the saved; contrary to the traditional formula, there can be salvation outside the Church. If everyone possesses spiritual gifts, and if all can directly encounter God, then the hierarchy has no special, indispensable role. The heresies of Arius Pelagius, Donatus and Origen are incompatible with an established State religion.[3]

Many people who have rejected the teaching of religion still believe in some overall Grand Design of the universe where goodness is rewarded and badness punished. Not to have such a belief, they say, would render their lives meaningless. Somehow, they feel, there must be some compensation for the disappointments, losses, sacrifices and pain that occur in the most ordinary of lives. Somehow their efforts at being good must be rewarded.

For some people the working out of the Grand Design of rewards and punishments takes place on a *great cosmic stage* where tragedies abound and rewards for patient suffering come only in Heaven. Indeed, the essence of tragedy is that one fatal flaw can outweigh a lifetime of virtue, and that there is no escaping retribution. George Steiner wrote:

In authentic tragedy, the gates of hell stand open and damnation is real. The tragic personage cannot avoid responsibility. To argue that Oedipus should have been excused on the grounds of ignorance, or that Phedre was merely a prey to hereditary chaos of the blood, is to diminish to absurdity the weight and meaning of the tragic action. The redeeming insight comes too late to mend the ruins or is purchased at the price of irremediable suffering . . . Where the tragic conception of life is in force, moreover, there can be no recourse to secular or material remedies. The destiny of Lear cannot be resolved by the establishment of adequate homes for the aged . . . In tragedy, the twist of the net which brings down the hero may be an accident or hazard of circumstance, but the mesh is woven into the heart of life. Tragedy would have us know that there is in the very fact of human existence a provocation or paradox; it tells us that the purposes of men sometimes run against the grain of inexplicable and destructive forces which lie 'outside' yet very close. To ask the gods why Oedipus should have been chosen in his agony or why Macbeth should have met the witches is to ask for reason and justification from the voiceless night. There is no answer . . . And beyond the tragic there is no 'happy ending' in some other dimension of time and place. The wounds are not healed and the broken spirit mended. In the norm of tragedy there is no compensation.[4]

Many people see their lives in terms of tragedy. To be a tragic hero or heroine alone against an angry sky gives their lives a significance which ordinary happiness would never give. Scorning all comforts and consolations, they clutch the piercing arrows of outrageous fortune to their wounded self and go on believing that they are fulfilling a significant role in the cosmic drama. Such significance is their reward for being good. (Accepting the punishment you deserve is a sign that you are good.)

However, many more people want to see the system of rewards and punishments operating in their favour in their own lives in the here and now, not in some distant time and place. Ordinary happiness, they believe, is their just reward for their expertise in being good.

The State is always willing and able to provide the means whereby the tragedians can discover their tragedy and act it out. The State, through war and a failure to provide adequate care for its poor, sick and handicapped, offers many opportunities for self-sacrifice, while its laws and its law enforcement institutions provide opportunities for tragic self-destruction through law-breaking activities.

At the same time the State is always willing to define the terms of ordinary happiness and to provide, or appear to provide, the opportunities to achieve this happiness.

Thus basic happiness might be defined as having family and friends, a home and possessions, a job, and time and opportunity for relaxation and entertainment. For some people the home and possessions and the time and opportunity for relaxation and entertainment are exceedingly modest rewards, while for others they are exceedingly luxurious, but whether people are happy depends not on what they own and do but on what they believe about what they own and do. If their definition of happiness coincides with what they own and do, then they are happy. If their definition of happiness does not coincide with what they own and do, then they are not happy.

Much of the definition of happiness which people use comes from what they have been told constitutes happiness by their family and their State. The family and the State commonly define as happiness-making those things which they can provide, because then they can use such things as rewards for good behaviour.

Thus, only a mother who can afford to buy her children ice cream will teach her children that ice cream is happiness-making and a reward for good behaviour. A State which can afford to encourage the production of objects like cars, televisions, fancy clothes and holiday hotels will teach its subjects that such objects are happiness-making and a reward for good behaviour. A State which cannot afford to encourage the production of such objects will teach its subjects to scorn them and to regard as happiness-making and reward-giving service to one's country and the respect of one's fellows for such service.

The existence within one society both of people who prefer a significant life filled with excitement and disaster, and of people who prefer peace and contentment, means that people are always at odds with one another. Within the family the tragedian is always aware of sources of danger and responds to them, while the seeker after happiness counsels contentment. Around my ears always as a child were the voices of my parents: my mother, the tragedian, seeing in every person and every situation wickedness, dangers and disasters, while my father would be saying, 'Can't you see good in people? Everything is not as bad as you think. Can't you be happy?' Within the State the tragedians see enemies abroad and advise preparation for war, while the happiness-seekers advise negotiation and compromise. In the last fifty years, despite the efforts of the peacemakers, the tragedians' voices have been the most powerful.

Most of human history has been dominated by the tragedians, and so most of history concerns what happiness-seekers regard as unnecessary tragedies. A State devoted solely to creating the happiness of its subjects has never existed outside the world of fiction.

Aldous Huxley explored such a State in his novel *Brave New World*, which was published in 1932 when test-tube babies had just become a possibility. In the State which Huxley described, all the suffering and uncertainty attendant upon conception, pregnancy, birth and families were done away with. Families were abolished, and all conception took place in a test tube. Most of the troubles engendered by individual differences between persons were avoided by dividing an embryo cell to produce thousands of identical babies. All the aggravation produced by people who do not accept the station to which they were born was avoided by treatment to embryos to produce different classes of subjects, ranging from the Alphas, who were intelligent and did the work requiring intelligence, to the Epsilons, who had little intelligence and who did the most menial tasks. Each class was taught from birth a set of attitudes and opinions which defined precisely who they were, what their place in society was, and how they should respond to other people. Families and all the misery of family life were abolished, unlimited sex was encouraged, was even mandatory, happiness-producing entertainment of all kinds abounded, with movies becoming 'feelies', where the sensual delights shown on the screen were directly experienced by the person watching. The reward for being good was complete happiness, and if such happiness palled there was *soma*, a prediction by Huxley of today's Valium.

The Controller of this brave new world was the only person who had access to what was once the world's great literature, and who could contrast the happiness-seeking world with the tragic world of old. He knew that only the tragic world could produce great art. He said:

> You can't make tragedies without social instability. The world's stable now. People are happy; they get what they want, and they never want what they can't get. They're well off; they're safe; they're never ill; they're not afraid of death; they're blissfully ignorant of passion and old age; they're plagued with no mothers or fathers; they've got no wives, or children, or lovers to feel strongly about; they're so conditioned that they practically can't help behaving as they ought to behave. And if anything should go wrong, there's *soma*. . . that's the price we have to pay for stability. You've got to choose between happiness and what people used to call high art. We've sacrificed the high art. We have the feelies and the scent organ instead . . . Actual happiness always looks pretty squalid in comparison with the overcompensations for misery. And, of course, stability isn't nearly so spectacular as instability. And being contented has none of the glamour of a good fight against misfortune, or a fatal overthrow by passion and doubt. Happiness is never grand.[5]

The belief in the Grand Design of rewards and punishments traps us into a way of living which offers only two alternatives – the tragic, where we see ourselves as possessing some fatal flaw which will ensure that, no matter how good and self-sacrificing we are, we shall suffer, or the happiness-seeking, trying to find happiness in whatever is available to us, and sometimes feeling contented but often feeling the ache of 'Is this all that there is?' The belief in the Grand Design requires us to view every disaster that befalls us as proof of our badness and every good fortune as having a price which we must pay. The belief in the Grand Design stands between us and the real world, preventing us from seeing its events, which come to us in the guise of disaster or good fortune, and from dealing with these events realistically.

But it is not just our belief in the Grand Design which prevents us from dealing realistically with the real world. We are also handicapped because in learning to be obedient we are not given access to the information we need.

To create obedient children who will grow up to be obedient citizens it is essential *to limit the information they are given.*

Parents and State officials censor information to great effect. But people who are hungry for information will always find ways around such censoring, be it, as children, in the parents' absence searching their possessions, or, as adults, circulating banned literature. So parents and State officials find ways of not allowing that hunger to arise.

I frequently travel by train, and I use the time to write and read. My most frequent journey is between Sheffield and London, a two-and-a-half-hour journey in a train which is steady and provides comfortable, spacious seats and tables. On every journey, whether travelling first or second class, I note that there are in my carriage only one or two people, like myself, reading or working. The majority of the passengers simply sit for the length of their journey. A few glance through a newspaper or magazine for a few minutes, then close it and stare into space. None of these people takes an active interest in the passing scenery, nor do they strike up conversations with their fellow passengers. They simply sit, lost, I suppose, in fantasy. It does not appear to be a problem-solving fantasy, for I rarely see a person take out a notebook or piece of paper to record some solution, even amongst the businessmen in first class who might conceivably use this travelling time to think through a problem. The passengers seem to put themselves into some kind of mode of thinking which allows them just to sit while they are transported like a parcel from point A to point B. Two and a half hours of their life have gone by in which they could have been enthralled and entertained by a novelist, or astounded and enlightened by a journalist, let alone transformed by a poet, but they are not perturbed by this loss. As little children the power of the printed word to reveal a story might have intrigued and delighted them, but their education has soured that delight and obliterated their curiosity. They ask no questions about what lies outside the small world which they inhabit.

In *Brave New World* Huxley described just how this change comes about:

The Director opened a door . . . Half a dozen nurses were engaged in setting out bowls of roses in a long row across the floor . . . Between the rose bowls the books were duly set out – a row of nursery books opened invitingly each at some gaily coloured image of beast or fish or bird.

'Now bring in the children.'

They hurried out of the room and returned in a minute or two, each pushing a kind of a tall dumb-waiter laden, on all its four wire netted shelves, with eight-month-old babies, all exactly alike and all (since their caste was Delta) dressed in khaki.

'Put them down on the floor.'

The infants were unloaded.

'Now turn them so they can see the flowers and books.'

Turned, the babies at once fell silent, then began to crawl towards those clusters of sleek colours, those shapes so gay and brilliant on the white pages. As they approached, the sun came out of momentary eclipse behind a cloud. The roses flamed up as though with sudden passion from within; a new and profound significance seemed to suffuse the shining pages of the books. From the ranks of the crawling babies came little squeals of excitement, gurgles and twitterings of pleasure.

The Director rubbed his hands. 'Excellent!' he said. 'It might almost have been done on purpose.'

The swiftest crawlers were already at their goal. Small hands reached out uncertainly, touched, grasped, unpetaling the transformed roses, crumpling the illuminated pages of the books. The Director waited until all were happily busy. Then, 'Watch carefully,' he said. And, lifting his hand, he gave the signal.

The Head Nurse, who was standing by a switchboard at the other end of the room, pressed down a little lever.

There was a violent explosion. Shriller and shriller, a siren shrieked. Alarm bells maddingly sounded.

The children started, screamed: their faces were distorted with terror.

'And now,' the Director shouted (for the noise was deafening), 'now we proceed to rub in the lesson with a mild electric shock.'

He waved his hand again, and the Head Nurse pressed a second lever. The screaming of the babies changed its tone. There was something desperate, almost insane, about the sharp, spasmodic yelps to which they now gave utterance. Their little bodies twitched and stiffened; their limbs moved jerkily as if to the tug of unseen wires.

'We can electrify that whole strip of floor,' bawled the Director in explanation. 'But that's enough,' he signalled to the nurse.

The explosions ceased, the bells stopped ringing, the shriek of the siren died down from tone to tone into silence. The stiffly twitching bodies relaxed, and what had become the sob and yelp of infant maniacs broadened out once more into a normal howl of ordinary terror.

'Offer them the flowers and books again.'

The nurses obeyed; but at the approach of the roses, the mere sight of those gaily coloured images of pussy and cock-a-doodle-doo and baa-baa black sheep, the infants shrank away in horror; the volume of their howling suddenly increased.

'Observe,' said the Director triumphantly, 'observe.'

Books and loud noises, flowers and electric shocks – already in the infant mind these couples were compromisingly linked; and after two hundred repetitions of the same or similar lesson would be wedded indissolubly. What man has joined together, nature is powerless to put asunder.

'They'll grow up with what psychologists used to call an instinctive hatred of books and flowers. Reflexes unalterably conditioned. They'll be safe from books and botany all their lives.' The Director turned to his nurses. 'Take them away.'[6]

Teaching children to associate fear and pain with reading is not carried out so systematically in our homes and schools, but such teaching does occur and it is very effective. Many parents, having themselves been taught to fear and despise reading, do not encourage it in their children. There are a great many homes where there are no books, although the parents could afford to buy them, or there are just a few books, kept in a special place and rarely referred to, playing no part in everyday life. Many parents fear that a child absorbed in a book is not merely acquiring ideas which the parent fears, but also that the child is out of reach of the parents and has rejected the parent. My mother would try to prevent me from reading by implying that I was a fool to always have my head 'buried in a book', and she would warn me that I would 'ruin my eyes with all that reading'. Fortunately for me, my father treasured books and all the knowledge from which his family's poverty had excluded him. (He left school when he was only eleven to work to support his family.) By reading I could share my father's joy, defy my mother and escape into a world much larger than my family home.

My love of reading survived my schooling, but many children's love of reading does not. In many schools, reading is not defined as a pleasure but as an activity requiring obedience and conformity and incurring few rewards and many punishments. The school's insistence on correct spelling makes writing difficult, and, while teachers may say that they encourage free expression, children know that their teachers have views about what may be freely expressed. Of course there are teachers who want children to find learning exciting and important, but their efforts are continually hampered by the education system and those people who demand that children should be taught to be obedient and conforming.

Moreover, the general ethos of the school mirrors the ethos of a society which despises intellectuals and artists and strives to reduce any outstanding person to the same dimensions as all other people. Every country has a phrase for this. In England it is 'too clever by half'.[7] The Japanese speak of nails which stick up and have to be hammered down. Australians speak of 'tall poppies' which, in the American phrase, have to be 'cut down to size'. So children the world over learn to deny their intelligence and originality behind a mask of modesty and conformity, but most find it safest to deny completely that they are intelligent, original, inquiring and creative. Instead they define themselves as stupid in all areas except in matters to do with earning their living and carrying out their domestic duties, and even then they have to be careful about being appropriately modest, not challenging their elders and betters, and behaving in ways similar to their peers.

So the natural curiosity of children dies, and as adults they do not question the limited and biased information which the media provides.

Robert Ornstein and Paul Erlich in their book *New World, New Mind*[8] see the failures in education as playing a major part in the disasters which have befallen and will befall the resources of the planet which we need for our survival. In an interview in *USA Today* Ornstein said:

> The world we live in is entirely different from the world we evolved to cope with, with the result that our minds are out of whack with our world. This has given us major problems like pollution, overpopulation, the destruction of the atmosphere, the extinction of plant and animal species and the threat of nuclear annihilation.
>
> Our old minds are designed to look at things as they affect individuals and to respond to immediate dangers – like tigers approaching us, or a sudden thunderstorm, or an earthquake. Large-scale, continuous threats are not instantaneously obvious to us, so they get ignored. For instance, one terrorist attack will cause millions of people to change their travel plans, but all the US citizens ever killed by terrorists would not add up to the number who get killed every day in this country by handguns or automobile accidents.
>
> Part of the problem is that our education is almost irrelevant to

many of the changes that are taking place in the world. People are taught algebra with great precision in schools, but I've never met anyone who's ever used algebra after the age of 13. On the other hand, they're not taught probability, which is something they need every night when they watch the news. People need to understand the nature of the world they actually live in as opposed to the world we're taught to believe in – the kind of bucolic world which only exists now in cereal ads. And we're changing the world so fast that we believe the curriculum needs to be changed every decade. Our past is no longer a good guide to our future, and understanding what could happen in our future is what education needs to be about.[9]

'The bucolic world of the cereal ads' is the world of the Grand Design whose rewards are portrayed in advertising. The world of the Grand Design has no use for probability, so why teach it?[10] Rewards and punishments will follow as the night the day. Though they might be a long time in coming, and though we see the virtuous suffering and the wicked flourishing, we, believing in the Grand Design, have no need to calculate the odds that God will not reward our expertise in being good. To understand what Ornstein is saying and to act upon it would require us to give up our belief in the Grand Design, and then to contemplate the complexity of the network of causes which lead to an event.

Also, to understand what Ornstein is saying and to act upon it, we would have to confront *the censorship which the State imposes on us*.

State censorship operates by stopping its citizens from having access to information, by limiting the information it gives to its citizens, and by lying.

Many governments prevent their citizens from discovering new information by simply preventing these citizens from moving from place to place. All countries require their citizens to obtain passports to travel abroad, and some countries, like Russia, have passports for internal travel. Citizens do not obtain their passports as a right. A passport is a gift by the government to citizens who meet the government's standards of goodness. Naughty citizens, like naughty children, have to stay at home.

In issuing a passport a government also determines where travelling citizens can go. When I got my first passport in 1968, issued by the Federal Government of Australia, it contained a stamp forbidding me to visit North Vietnam, since Australia was then at war with Vietnam. The Australian Government now allows its citizens to visit Vietnam, but no such unlimited freedom is given to US citizens, even though to make such a journey is very necessary for some US citizens.

After the First and Second World Wars, many ex-service men and women visited the scenes of conflict, partly to pay their respects to their colleagues who died, and partly to help themselves lay the ghosts of their wartime experiences. Out of such journeys could come great healing.

No such journeys were possible for the American veterans of the Vietnam war, for their country remained at war with Vietnam, even though the fighting had ceased. These veterans found it extremely hard to come to terms with their experience, and many remained deeply troubled, unable to settle into ordinary life. Many killed themselves. The Akron chapter of Vietnam Veterans decided that a small relaxation in the rules preventing visits to Vietnam would allow groups of them to make the journey in the hope of healing old wounds. A BBC television team followed one such group and made a film, *Back to the Edge*,[11] which told the story of three of these veterans. One of them, Joe La Fatch,[12] had never spoken of the events in his war experiences which troubled him the most. Now, on this journey, he not only spoke of these terrible experiences but he found that he could let go of his hatred and much of his pain. In June 1989, the US Government took members of the Akron chapter to court, threatening them with a $50,000 fine and a ten-year jail term unless they stopped their healing visits.[13]

Much of the healing which Joe La Fatch and the other veteran experienced was in ceasing to see the Vietnamese people simply as wicked and treacherous enemies, with all the hatred that that entailed, and instead seeing them as ordinary people like themselves. Governments and other institutions which want to maintain their power and prestige actively prevent their subjects from making the discovery that the enemies of the State and the institution are just ordinary people.

In my childhood in Australia in the thirties and forties, the population was divided into two antagonistic groups, the Protestants and the Catholics, thus continuing the battles begun long ago in Ireland. The Protestant children went to state schools and the Catholic children went to Catholic schools, and the only times they spoke to one another was when they hurled insults at one another. Protestant parents would warn their children against the dangers of mixing with Catholics, and the priests forbade Catholic parents to send their children to state schools. The ultimate horror for families was a 'mixed marriage', not just because of the social stigma, but for the impossibility of one of the couple's families setting foot in the other family's church.

At the end of the Second World War the Australian Government embarked on a programme of enticing migrants to settle in Australia, and many of those who came were from Italy, Malta and Catholic Eastern Europe. By the early sixties the Catholic church in Australia could no longer cope with the numbers of Catholic children it was required to educate, and so the Archbishop gave Catholic parents permission to send their children to state schools. Within ten years the antagonism between Protestants and Catholics had vanished. Now they, or at least the younger generations, know one another, and if they fight it is over the ordinary things which friends and neighbours fight over.

Meanwhile, in Northern Ireland the Catholic bishops refuse to allow any relaxation of their rule that Catholic children must not attend state schools. The killings of Catholics by Protestants and Protestants by Catholics continue. The only gleam of hope is the package of reforms which came into force on 19 February 1990. In this the Department of Education at Stormont officially recognizes a new form of school, the integrated school, and will provide 100 percent of the teaching costs of these schools. In addition, changes to the curriculum include a course called Education for Mutual Understanding and Cultural Heritage. The Catholic Church refuses to recognize the integrated schools, while the fundamentalist Protestant churches see the schools as an attempt to corrupt their children with dangerous ecumenical doctrines.[14]

Just as citizens do not have an automatic right to a passport, so they do not have an automatic right to information – or so governments believe. Britain's secrecy laws are based on the premise that information on matters of national concern (and what matter cannot be defined as being of national concern?) belongs to the government and not to British people.

Seeing themselves as owning the information, the government decide whether or not to give some information away. Why should they not keep such knowledge to themselves, since knowledge is power?

In California a research project called Project Censored identifies important issues, information about which has been kept from the public by the government and organizations which benefit from such secrecy. Each year Project Censored lists the ten most censored stories for that year. In 1989 this list included the following issues:

Global Media Lords Threaten Freedom of Information

Five major media corporations already dominate the fight for hundreds of millions of minds throughout the world and they concede that before the turn of the century they may control most of the world's important newspapers, magazines, books, broadcast stations, movies, recordings and video cassettes. Source: *The Nation*, 6/12/89, 'Lords of the Global Village' by Ben Bagdikian.

Turning Africa into the World's Garbage Can

Africa, already suffering from poverty, drought, famine, locusts, 'contra' wars and the AIDS epidemic, appears destined to become the world's toxic waste dump as international sludge dealers try to dump US and European waste onto at least 15 African countries. Source: *In These Times*, 11/8/89, 'Western Developmental Overdose Makes Africa Chemically Dependent', by Diana Johnston.

Guatemalan Blood on US Hands

The Bush administration strengthened ties with the oppressive Guatemalan military last year at the same time that human rights violations by the military rose sharply. One unpublicized violation occurred last year when a US citizen, Sister Diana Ortiz, working as a teacher in Guatemala, was kidnapped, beaten, tortured, and sexually molested by three men, one of whom was a uniformed Guatemalan police officer. Sources: *Guatemalan Update*, 2/90, 'US Aid Said to Encourage Rights Violation'; *Guatemalan Human Rights Commission/USA*, 12/24/90, 'US Citizen Kidnapped and Tortured in Guatemala'.

The Chicken Industry and the National Salmonella Epidemic

The chicken industry's drive for profits, aided by relaxed inspection practices by the US Department of Agriculture, has led to a national epidemic of 2.5 million cases of salmonella poisonings in a year, 500,000 hospitalizations, and 9,000 deaths. Source: *Southern Exposure*, Summer 1989, 'Chicken Empires', by Bob Hall, and 'The Fox Guarding the Hen House', by Tom Devine.[15]

If anything shows how, in the process of bamboozlement, the bamboozlers are as bamboozled as those they wish to bamboozle, it is in the area of censorship of environmental information. The bamboozlers act as if the dangers which are being created on our planet cannot possibly threaten them.

There was a time when the rich and powerful could keep themselves safe, ignoring the plight of the poor. For instance, the steel barons of Sheffield built their homes on the west side of Sheffield where the prevailing winds kept the smoke and the filth of the steel mills away, blowing such smoke and filth over the homes of the poor. The rich and powerful of today seem not to have noticed that times have changed. They cannot protect themselves from acid rain, radiation, and food and water which appear to be wholesome but are in fact poisonous. They have been successfully bamboozled, for they cannot see what is happening to them, which is the aim of such bamboozlement.

The most straightforward form of censorship, and the most popular, is lying. Parents and teachers lie to children; governments and their agencies lie to their citizens. Parents, teachers, governments and their agencies all claim that their lying is virtuous. They lie to protect their children/citizens. However, if children or citizens lie, that is wicked.

The reason that parents, teachers and governments want children and citizens to be truthful is because truthful subjects are easier to control. Everything they do or think is on display. They reveal their disobedience and they are punished.

Because children are taught by their parents and teachers that it is wrong to lie, children, who sooner or later discover that their parents and teachers lie, become very confused about lying and truth telling. They find that they have to lie to protect themselves, but because they are convinced of the wickedness of lying, they cannot lie without feeling guilty and being frightened of being found out. (Children who fail to be convinced of the wickedness of lying and so will willingly lie to protect themselves are labelled by the representatives of the government (teachers, social workers, psychiatrists, psychologists) as 'delinquent' or 'psychopathic', and punished.)

This confusion prevents most children from working out a policy about lying which would then help them decide when it is necessary to lie in order to survive, and when, in the long term, it is better to tell the truth. In working out such a policy a person would examine different modes of lying and discover that, while it is possible to lie to other people and not merely survive but even benefit from such lies, to lie to oneself is a certain recipe for disaster. Unfortunately, education by moulding and bamboozlement promotes lying to oneself. The lie which children so educated learn to tell themselves is, 'I am a sinful person who has no right to exist, but I am fortunate in having a good parent/teacher/government/God looking after me. I can repay them for their unselfish care of me only by being and doing what they want.'

Once children have learned how to lie to themselves, they can then lie to themselves about lying to other people by telling themselves that it is virtuous to lie to others in order to protect them. Thus children can grow up to be parents/teachers/government's and God's representatives.

This 'I am bad but am watched over by a good parent/teacher/government/God' aspect of the belief in the Grand Design prevents people from seeing that parents, teachers, governments and God's representatives do lie, and just *how* people with power present their lies.

The reason that so much propaganda is effective is because so many of the people to whom the propaganda is directed do not recognize the principle once enunciated by Goebbels that a lie told once is still a lie, but a lie told a thousand times becomes the truth.

It does not matter if we have seen the truth before our eyes. Television pictures of the Chinese army massacring civilians and burning their bodies in Tiananmen Square flashed around the world, and many thousands of Chinese were witness to the scene. Nevertheless, the

Chinese Government then embarked on telling a lie, a most outrageous lie, a thousand times over.

In the first official account of the events in Tiananmen Square on June 3 and 4, China claims that 100 troops and 100 civilians were killed, but none in the square itself. The report, drawn up by the propaganda department of the Beijing Party Committee and carried by the New China News Agency, describes the events as 'a shocking counter-revolutionary rebellion'.

'The facts are these: at 1.30 p.m. on June 4 the Beijing municipal Government and the martial law headquarters issued an emergency notice after troops entered Tiananmen Square (to warn the people to leave the square) . . . The notice was broadcast repeatedly for three hours and most people in the central square left after hearing it . . . At around 3 a.m. the sit-in demonstrators sent representatives to the troops to express their desire to withdraw and this was welcomed by the troops. At 4.30 a.m. the martial law headquarters broadcast the following notice: It is time to clear the square and the martial law headquarters accepts the request of the students to withdraw. After hearing this, the students joined hands and left the square in an orderly manner at about 5 a.m. Troops vacated a wide corridor in the south-eastern corner of the square to allow the students to withdraw unhindered. A few students who refused to leave were forced to leave by policemen. By 5.30 a.m. the clearing operation of the square, which had lasted half an hour, was complete. During the whole process of this clearing operation no one died.'[16]

It is very easy from our standpoint outside China to see this outrageous lie. The lies told by the people who should be concerned for our welfare are harder to see.

When Marie Curie discovered radium she was well aware of its radioactive properties. Such radioactivity, she declared, was harmless to humans, and she often carried pieces of radium in her cardigan pockets. She died of cancer.

Marie Curie's attitude was adopted by the nuclear industry. People who benefit from the nuclear industry by gaining wealth and power always insist that nuclear power is safe. Any evidence that might reveal this statement to be a lie they try to suppress, often most effectively. When an accident occurs they insist that no great damage has been done, that the industry's safety procedures are infallible, and that the industry's operations were not responsible for any damage people might suffer.

Thus, every time research is published showing that there are significantly high clusters of childhood leukaemia in the areas around Britain's nuclear plants, the nuclear industry responds by saying that such research is inaccurate and invalid, and that leukaemia is caused by things that have nothing to do with the nuclear industry. The nuclear industry denied the seriousness of the accidents at Windscale (the Central Electricity Generating Board dealt with this by changing the name to Sellafield), Chernobyl[17] and Three Mile Island[18] by not revealing what actually happened during and after these accidents.

A nuclear plant, opened in 1944 at Hanford, Washington, has been the subject of an inquiry by a panel of scientists and doctors, set up by the Federal Government.

The panel found that between 1944, when it opened, and 1947, the Hanford weapons plant poured so much radioactive iodine into the air that 1,200 children living nearby were exposed to cumulative doses ranging from 15 to 650 rads (one rad is roughly equivalent to the radiation from a dozen chest X-rays). About 13,500 people, or 5% of the area's total population, may have taken in doses of 33 rads or more – about twice the three-year dosage the Nuclear Regulatory Commission considers safe for workers exposed to radiation as an occupational hazard.[19]

Just what this meant in personal terms was shown by Tom Bailie, one of the Hanford 'downwinders'.

The worst is finally over for us. Or has it just begun? As 'Downwinders', born and raised downwind of the Hanford Nuclear Reservation in Washington, we learned several years ago that the Government decided – with cold deliberation – to use us as guinea pigs by releasing radioactivity into our food, water, milk, and air without our consent. Now we have learned that we can expect continuing cancer cases from our exposure to their 'experiment'.

Is this what it feels like to be raped?

The exposure began the same day as our lives began. Several years ago, when the Government admitted that the release had been made, we were assured there would be no observable health effect. Did the Government really look?

Unknowingly, we had been seeing the effects for a long time. For us, the unusual was the usual!

During my childhood I remember seeing men dressed in space suits walking in front of uniformed soldiers carrying shovels and sacks. They waved to us as they moved past. Usually, they brought us candy and, one time, cowboy boots. What we did not know at the time was that these were nuclear cleanup crews.

What we did not know was that other kids didn't get 'neck massages' from the school nurse (looking for thyroid swelling) or have Geiger counters passed over them; that men in beards and thick glasses did not sample everyone's water and milk weekly;

that farm animal mutations do not happen everywhere. We thought everyone had deformed calves, sheep and kittens; that miscarriages, human and animal, were the norm. Common news was of neighbours and loved ones getting cancer. These were the usual things in our isolated world.

I was born a year after my stillborn brother. I struggled to breathe through underdeveloped lungs and suffered numerous birth defects. I underwent multiple surgeries, endured paralysis, endured thyroid medication, a stint in an iron lung, loss of hair, sores all over my body, fevers, dizziness, poor hearing, asthma, teeth rotting out and, at age 18, a diagnosis of sterility.

The usual was watching the other kids die in St Mary's paediatric ward. I finally learned to walk, but could never play sports. I stood on the sidelines with the rest of my classmates, watching the healthy kids who moved into our area play sport. We never could. We grew angry and defensive from the teasing and abuse.

[Because of our] questioning of the Government our patriotism has been impugned, our credibility questioned. We have been redlined by the banking community since 1985; the Farmers Home Administration foreclosure notice is sitting on my desk. We have been put off by politicians – except for a brave few – until we victims have become a popular issue. We have been slandered as the 'glow in the dark' by friends and strangers alike. We have been told to shut up, and have received death threats. I survived one attempt on my life. It's enough to make paranoia override common sense and to make me carry a gun.

Who the hell do these people in the nuclear gang think they are? In my family we were taught not to lie. How can we citizens defend liars? The world now knows about Hanford's releases. We were the children on the front lines of the Cold War. We deserve fair and equitable treatment. Are we just so much nuclear waste? Will there be compensatory damages? Moscow was condemned for its three days of silence about the Chernobyl nuclear accident. What about Washington's 40 years of silence?

There is a fine line of morality that none of us can cross and still claim membership of the human race. The Government's nuclear gang deliberately crossed it. The price we had to pay, you say? We think we were worth more.[20]

The nuclear industry can no longer deny that high levels of radiation are dangerous, so they have to lie by omitting and minimizing the evidence. The industry's claim that nuclear power is cheap has been shown to be false, since in the accounting certain high costs were not taken into consideration in order to produce figures which appeared to show that nuclear power was cheaper than coal power.[21] Now the

'Greetings. We are from the government. We are here to help you.' [22]

only claim that nuclear power is superior to power produced from fossil fuels is that nuclear power does not contribute to the production of acid rain which so damages the environment.

In 1983 a German plant sociologist, Gunther Reichelt, noticed that tree damage significantly increased downwind of nuclear plants in Germany, France and Switzerland. A nuclear physicist, Roland Kollert, developed a hypothesis to explain this finding, and the two of them published a paper in 1985 entitled 'Tree Damage through Radioactivity?' The reaction of the scientific community was not what we might expect of scientists devoted to the pursuit of the truth.

[Reichelt and Kollert] voiced a carefully substantiated suspicion and asked their scientific peers to refute or accept it. Neither of the two happened . . .

The nuclear industry in the Federal Republic (as elsewhere) has always been, and still is, heavily subsidized and protected by the government. Over the years, a strange alliance has been formed between the government and science. Big think-tanks employing thousands of scientists were created which – just like the nuclear industry – depended on government support for their continued existence. In turn, the government depended on these think-tanks for support and justification of its nuclear policies . . .

Reichelt and Kollert had violated a hitherto well-guarded taboo. They had precipitated doubts about the environmental effects of nuclear power. Should their findings hold true, new questions

101

about environmental impact would be added to the old debate on human health effects and social compatibility. The consequences of such a discussion were threatening and, besides, uncontrollable: the future use of nuclear power might be exposed as being entirely without justification. The fear was that the beleaguered nuclear industry could not withstand this new assault.

At the time of the Inquisition a government confronted with this situation would have had a simple solution: Reichelt and Kollert would have been banned, their book burned, the issue indexed. Nowadays more subtle methods are used for the same purpose.

In a modern democracy a government would not want – does not need – to run the risk of being accused of openly suppressing the search for scientific truth. There are other ways of suppressing uncomfortable scientific findings. With scientists employed by a government-funded institute, as most are in the nuclear field – certainly those who are well-established – the case hardly ever arises. Possible sanctions are so numerous, invisible and effective that self-censorship can usually be relied upon. On the other hand, outsiders to the system are less easily controlled and therefore more dangerous. They are also more vulnerable.

A government's primary rule in dealing with dangerous outsiders is to exploit their vulnerability. The first method is that of countervailance: unruly outsiders are discredited as scientists by 'ruly' insiders. Failing that there is starvation: scientists are cut off from information, participation and funds. Finally, corruption can be used: the scientists are brought into the system in order to be silenced. In the case of two hard-headed rebels such as Reichelt and Kollert, who were unlikely to sell out, only the first two methods were employed.

To begin with, the Government asked its commission of radiation protection, Strahlenschutzkommission (SSK), for a counter-review. The SSK is a high-powered group of pro-nuclear scientists and technicians advising the Government on emission standards. A special *ad hoc* working group submitted its report in March 1986, concluding predictably that no causal connection could be established between tree damage and radioactivity. This conclusion was accepted by the Government as its official opinion in Parliament in April when it confirmed that 'utterances about the interrelationship between radioactive emissions from nuclear facilities and tree damage lack any scientific foundation' and that 'no need for further research can be ascertained' . . .

The state forestry research agencies . . . claimed that for methodological and empirical reasons Reichelt's findings could not be confirmed . . .

Reichelt was portrayed as a crank who had misled the public through phantom chartings. Kollert was seen as an ignoramus who had propagated crackpot theories for political reasons . . . [They] have replied to their critics . . . [but] have not been given the opportunity to meet their adversaries for a frank exchange of views . . . Vital information which could have helped to buttress their [case] was regularly refused . . . [They] have temporarily moved on to do other research.[23]

These are terrible matters which should cause us much anxiety, but most of us cannot pay attention to such matters because the things which we feel we must protect ourselves against are much more personal and in our lives almost every day. We have learned not to be interested in matters which seem not to touch us directly, and we have learned *to be afraid of humiliation*.

The humiliation which Reichelt and Kollert suffered is not unusual. All of us in our childhood have been humiliated by other children and by adults, all with the intention of punishing us for not conforming, for being ourselves, and for stating the truth as we see it. We can be made to feel humiliated in many different ways, but there is a ritual theme for humiliation of each of the sexes.

Boys and men are humiliated by other males by being told that they are not proper males and that their masculinity centres both actually and metaphorically on their testicles. Most of what most men do and think is built on their assumption that they must protect their testicles. So most men spend their entire lives in competitive activities with the aim of proving that they are proper males. They have no time for or interest in matters other than sex, sport and work, which they interpret as being competitive rather than cooperative activities. Hence the popularity of the *Sun* and the other tabloid newspapers whose aim is not to enlighten but to bamboozle.

Although most women spend most of their lives trying to help men maintain their basic assumption that they must defend their masculinity against humiliation, women privately find this assumption very funny. However, women do not see as funny the ritual humiliation that they inflict on one another.

Girls and women are humiliated by other females by being told that they are not 'attractive'. 'Attractive' is defined differently in different times and places, but women's magazines are devoted to promoting the current definition of 'attractive' and to urging women to conform to it, something which requires much time and effort. 'Women's interests' as defined by the media are not concerned with enlightenment but with the necessity that women should conform.

Most women spend much of their lives trying to be 'attractive' to men and 'attractive' to women. Often these two 'attractives' do not coincide, for what men may define as 'attractive', women may define as 'cheap', and then a woman has to work hard at trying to find some kind of compromise. If she opts to fulfil 'attractive' solely in terms of the women's definition of it, she may fail to attract a man, and if she opts to fulfil 'attractive' solely in term of the men's definition of it, other women will scorn, criticize and condemn her. If a woman decides that she cannot ever fulfil even modestly the demand to be 'attractive', she then sees herself as fatally flawed, irredeemably inadequate, and when a woman feels she can no longer go on striving to be 'attractive' she crumbles into old age. Competence and intelligence in all other areas of living cannot compensate her for failing to be 'attractive'. As all women television presenters know, what their viewers comment on most sharply is rot the clarity of their presentation or the incisiveness of their interviewing, but their failure to maintain the viewers' standard of attractiveness.

Thus men spend so much of their lives defending their 'masculinity' and women maintaining their 'attractiveness', all in an effort to avoid humiliation, that they have neither the time nor energy to question what lies behind this threat of humiliation. They do not see what the bamboozlers are about. They simply work hard at being good, and working hard at being good is an essential part of the world that they have been taught to see.

Teaching People How They Should See Their World

Everything we see, we see in terms of a story. The story form is the fundamental form by which we perceive.

We may, for instance, go into our room and see a new table standing there. Until we can fit a story around that table it remains mysterious and disturbing. We ask ourselves, 'Where did it come from?', 'What is going to happen to it?' The table, being there in the present, is in the middle of a story, but a story without a beginning and an end is an incomplete story, and we hate incomplete stories. They make us feel uncomfortable. So we create a beginning and an end.

We might do this by seeking out the facts. We might question certain people and establish, say, that the table is a present to us from our aunt, and since our aunt whom we love expects her presents to be cherished, we shall keep and cherish the table. We have created the story of the table.

But suppose such facts are not forthcoming. Suppose no amount of questioning reveals any information. Do we just leave the matter there, accepting the presence of a table with no history? No, we do not. If reality will not reveal the story, we will create the story out of fantasy. We will create a *myth*.

So we tell ourselves that the table is a gift from an unknown admirer who spirited it into our room, and in the fullness of time other gifts will appear. Or we might tell ourselves that, when two universes, parallel in time, accidentally intersected, the table was left behind. We can choose to create a multitude of myths. We might hold such myths lightly, seeing them as nothing more than charming ideas to explore, but one myth might catch the imagination of other people and be told and retold until it loses the quality of being a fantasy and myth and becomes, for the listeners and tellers, the absolute, literal truth.

We need the story form because it is what enables us to stitch together the string of present moments, which is all we can ever experience, into a line which ties us to our past and which we can follow into the future.

In creating a past and future for the events we experience only in the present, we find that our actual, experienced reality gives us very little information. Technology and science may have burgeoned in the last century, but still the majority of events which we experience cannot be supplied with a completely factual beginning and end to their story. So we create myths.[24]

For instance, a man might develop cancer. His doctors can supply the part of the story which is factual – that certain cells in his body have proliferated, and if left unchecked will cause him to die. But the rest of the story – answers to questions like, 'Why did this happen to me?', 'What will happen to me when I die?' – can be told only in terms of a myth, perhaps, 'I am a wicked person, but if I bear my suffering bravely I shall be rewarded in heaven'.

We create myths, and we learn myths from those around us. Every group of people possesses and uses a body of myths, and the language of these myths becomes the rhetoric, the language of persuasion, of the group by which the group defines itself, creates cohesion among its members and advertises itself to the world.

Thus the myths of the Australian aborigines use the rhetoric of the Dreamtime and the Songlines. The myths of Americans use the rhetoric of the American Dream, God and freedom. The myths of psychiatrists use the rhetoric of illness and the body. The myths of the English use the rhetoric of British justice and continuity. The myths of the USSR use the rhetoric of the State and the people.

So long as we recognize myth as myth and rhetoric as rhetoric we can use and enjoy them, but once we take myth for reality and rhetoric for truth we are in trouble. We lose touch with reality, and, having lost touch, we cannot deal with it effectively.

Yet, teaching people to see myth as reality and rhetoric as truth is what the bamboozlers do in order to make people obedient and conforming. They do not present the great religious myths of the world as attempts to answer the question, 'How should I live my life?', and the national myths as attempts to wield into an harmonious whole diverse and aggressive people. Instead, they say that other people's myths are nothing but lies and fantasies, whereas our own myths are the Truth, and we should revere and follow them.

The myths which we are taught to see as the Truth take many forms, and as we grow up in the midst of the rhetoric of these myths we find it difficult to see these myths and rhetoric clearly and perceive their functioning.

Thus, when I use my rhetoric about the Grand Design of the Just World where goodness is rewarded and badness punished, my listeners do not always readily grasp that I am talking about the myth which they have been taught since early childhood. Yet, if I ask them whether as small children they had been taught to believe in Santa Claus, most of them will say that they did.

Although the Saint Nicholas myth had existed in northern Europe for centuries, telling the story of the saint who rewarded good children with gifts, the myth of Santa Claus or Father Christmas did not become popular until early this century. There were two main reasons for this. First, there was a general rise in the standard of living of the middle classes which provided the wealth necessary to buy their children presents, and the manufacturers responded eagerly to this new, expandable market. Second, working within the 'goodness is rewarded and badness punished' model for raising children, many parents and teachers were coming to feel that an emphasis on rewards rather than on punishments would have a stronger effect. In the nineteenth century the emphasis had been on punishment. Children's literature like *Eric, or Little by Little*[25] and *Struwwelpeter*[26] told in horrific detail what happened to naughty children, while child care 'experts' advised the parents about the necessity of the most cruel punishments for children.[27]

Children brought up by the Just World myth in which the punishment element is emphasized learn to see their life in terms of punishment. They are always anxious. Children brought up by the Just World myth in which the reward element is emphasized learn to see their life in terms of reward. If they are good they expect to be rewarded, and if they suffer they expect to be compensated. When the rewards and the compensation are not forthcoming they are baffled and confused, and become angry, bitter and resentful.

One of the difficult tasks we must accomplish as children is to learn to distinguish what goes on in our internal reality of thoughts, feelings and images from what goes on around us in our external reality, and to locate events accurately in each reality. Small children always have difficulty in distinguishing dreams from waking, and often feel that their mother knows what they think when actually their mother has simply made an accurate interpretation of the child's actions and facial expression. In adult life we can still have difficulty in locating events accurately. Certain dreams can leave us confused as to whether they were real events, while our powerful feelings can impose on our surroundings colours and significances which do not exist in reality.

It is essential that, quite early in childhood, we learn to distinguish events in our internal reality from events in our external reality, for this is, in essence, what sanity is. Once we cease to be able to distinguish internal and external reality we become unable to create structures of meaning which have any reliable relationship to external reality. Once we cease to check our structures of meaning against external reality, which includes other people's structures of meaning, our structures become increasingly idiosyncratic, comprehensible only to ourselves. To other people we are mad.

Because we are prevented from understanding that we each create our individual structure of meaning, we often do not realize just how much of our structure of meaning is fantasy, that is, stories which we tell ourselves but which we have not checked against our own lived experience. We read a travel book and create a picture of a distant land. If we visit that land we find that it is different from our fantasy and change our internal picture accordingly. We study science and learn about scientists' fantasies which are called theories or educated guesses. We interpret what other people tell us about themselves and their experience, and our interpretations of what we are told are fantasies, for rarely can we check the information we are given against experience which is identical to the experience of our informers. People tell us about God, and we interpret what we are told to create our own fantasy or picture of God. There are as many pictures of God as there are people to hold them.

Some people understand this and thus know that whatever supreme power may or may not exist in our external reality, all we can know of this power are our fantasies about it. However, some people insist that their fantasies about God are not fantasies but the Absolute Truth, and their insistence on this can be so strong that some of their listeners come to believe that God, as they define God, exists in their external reality.

The more such fantasies seem to exist as real events in our external reality, the less able we are to maintain the distinction between internal and external reality which is essential if we are to cope with living. For many people God remains a very important player in their external reality. This can be a comfort if they picture God as being benevolently disposed towards them, but when they have learned to picture their God as unceasingly engaged in punishing them for their wickedness, they suffer much pain and confusion. Their every misfortune they interpret as evidence of God's attention to them, and this, while painful, is a source of pride which they are reluctant to relinquish. They

107

prefer to see themselves as being singled out for God's wrath than as being simply an ordinary person leading an ordinary life.

Because we grow up in the milieu of the myth of the Just World and the rhetoric which accompanies it, and because no one will tell us that it is just a myth, *we do not see when the myth is used to manipulate us.*

A myth which endures is one which can adapt to different times and places, assuming current fashion and being told in the current idiom, but retaining its essential message. Thus the myth of the Just World was told in the stories of ancient heroes, and in fairy stories, and, with the coming of the cinema, in every film where, no matter what the ostensible story was, virtue triumphed and wickedness was vanquished. The great American cinema heroes, John Wayne and Gary Cooper, embodied and enacted the myth of the Just World. To invoke these actors' presence in any way was to invoke the myth of the Just World as an Eternal Truth.

The most popular President of this century, Ronald Reagan, not only invoked the myth of the Just World constantly, as politicians are wont to do, but invoked it always in terms of a Hollywood movie. To many Americans he was, like John Wayne and Gary Cooper, the embodiment and enaction of the myth of the Just World.

In the complex world of American politics, no one man can project the image of the mythic hero without the aid of many people, just as a movie actor cannot project the image of the mythic hero without the aid of the producer, the director, the camera crew, and the financial backers. The success of the projection of Ronald Reagan as the mythic hero posed problems for the two men who wished to succeed him as president, George Bush and Michael Dukakis, and their supporters.

The journalist Maureen Dowd told how George Bush's team dealt with this problem by using another version of the myth of the Just World to manipulate the voters:

> Bush's clever aides knew that he was never going to match Ronald Reagan's John Wayne act. So they had worked to come up with a different persona to peddle. Someone macho, but macho in a more oblique way.
>
> As Peggy Noonan, the Vice-President's speech-writer, had told me, 'George Bush is like the bumbling but appealing American heroes played by Gary Cooper in the 1940s. He has a quality of being a nice fellow trying to get along and do OK, and people unconsciously identify with a lack of spectacularness. They say: It's all right, George, we're not articulate, either.'
>
> Roger Ailes, Bush's media wizard, continued the comparison: 'Like Cooper, Bush doesn't want to fight. He would like to talk everything out, but this guy's got a steel core when it's necessary.'
>
> Despite my doubting friends, who did not believe that even

'Coop' could ride to the rescue, it came to pass. Ailes and Noonan took Bush apart like a stuffed doll, dismantling the image of a wimpy, desiccated aristocrat and putting it back together in the lovable shape of Gary Cooper. 'I may sometimes be a little awkward but there's nothing self-conscious in my love of my country,' said George playing Gary at the GOP convention, with a new, deeper voice. 'I am a quiet man – but I hear the quiet people others don't.'

Suddenly, after Bush delivered Noonan's boffo acceptance speech, there was a political whiplash. Now, all heads turned to the Republican side of the court. Disgruntled Democrats began complaining that Dukakis came across as an 'eat your peas' sort of person. Bush grew taller in political cartoons.

'The real story is how empty-headed people are that they could change this much, this quickly,' complained Carter Eskew, a Democratic consultant. 'It proves that Americans don't take their politics very seriously.'

It also proves once again that the handlers of candidates are more important than the candidates themselves, and that perception presides over reality.[28]

To maintain 'the lovable shape of Gary Cooper', Bush went to war.

Just as we find it hard to see the operation of the myth in the stories we are told to entertain and manipulate us, so we can find it hard to see the operation of the myth in the history we are taught.

Indeed, at school we are told that we are being given historical facts as solid and unchallengeable as the ground beneath our feet. We are not told that history is written by the victors, and were history to be written by the vanquished how very different the story would be! Lest any child with an undesirable amount of curiosity suggest that the vanquished and oppressed might tell the story differently, we are taught that the reason that the victors were victorious was because they were good. Victory was their just reward.

As a child I was taught that the British had, with great self-sacrifice, taken over the rule of the countries that comprised the British Empire in order to bring enlightenment and British justice to people who were incapable of looking after themselves. Fortunately for me, I had a father who was well-read in socialist interpretations of history, and who showed me that what historians call 'facts' are simply different ways of interpreting events, and that inconvenient 'facts' are excluded from the history which is recorded and taught.

'Thus,' wrote the historian Christopher Hill:

Patriotic history tends to be sentimentally anecdotal – Alfred and the cakes, Drake and his bowls, Nelson's 'Kiss me Hardy'. More serious patriotic history of the traditional sort was described by a former Regius Professor of Modern History at Cambridge, Sir G.N. Clark, as 'lies about crimes'.

Hill went on to describe some of the crimes which are conveniently omitted from the history books used in British schools, and how not knowing about these crimes prevents the present-day inhabitants of Britain from understanding why there are black people living in Britain and why they should not be the object of racial hatred.

The wealth of the first British Empire was very largely founded on slavery, of which we won a virtual world monopoly from the beginning of the 18th century. The labour of a slave in the West Indies, said the economist Charles Davenant in the late 17th century, 'is worth six times as much as the labour of an Englishman at home'. Six times: it is quite a large figure if you think about it. ('Worth', of course, means 'worth to his employer or owner)'. No wonder the Society for the Propagation of the Gospel, which owned slaves in the West Indies, did not wish *them* to be instructed in the principles of Christianity lest they get ideas above their station. The churches, and English liberal opinion generally, played a great part in the 19th century in getting slavery and the slave trade abolished; and all credit to them. But by that time there were economic as well as humanitarian arguments against it. And by that time the cancer of slavery had spread all over the world. We were not *exclusively* responsible for this, but we must bear the primary responsibility. It was the cornerstone of our 18th century predominance.

The profits of the slave trade, and of slavery, contributed greatly to the accumulation of capital which made Britain the country of the first Industrial Revolution, and so consolidated her position as the greatest world power. Nor is it only a matter of economics: it affected culture, too. That great historian Richard Pares, as he sat in the magnificent Codrington Library in Oxford, surrounded by a superb collection of books, used to reflect sorrowfully that it had all been paid for by slavery. The profits, and the human suffering, were enormous. We shudder when we read that 20% of the slaves shipped from Africa did not survive the middle passage: perhaps they were not the least fortunate. But there was a similar rate of mortality among seamen in the ships which transported the slaves. Comfortable profits were made even after these assets had been written off.

The presence of descendants of slaves in our country today, in large numbers, poses social problems. They come here because the economies of the West Indies have not recovered from the concentration of slave-grown crops to the detriment of other forms of economic activity. For this we are mainly responsible. Is this not something that a new curriculum might encourage children in British schools to think about?[29]

But encouraging children to think about the consequences of the admirable and less than admirable actions of their elders would encourage them to think about politics, and that is undesirable. So well brought-up British children are taught that talking about politics is 'not done'.

When I was travelling in Israel in 1988, I went on a number of guided tours where our guides were men in their late fifties or early sixties who spoke English with a middle-European accent. They had survived the concentration camps and had taken part in the building of Israel. They were proud of Israel's achievements, and, like all Israelis, they were passionately concerned with politics.

One such guide collected me and other tourists from several hotels on the outskirts of Jerusalem and took us on a tour of that part of old Jerusalem where tourists were relatively safe. As we approached the Jewish quarter he joked, 'Everybody who lives in this city is crazy. In half of this city a woman can't go out without her husband's permission, and in the other half a man can't go out without his wife's permission!' But as we drew closer to the exquisite buildings in the Jewish quarter, he explained how the quarter had been largely destroyed in the fighting between the Jews and Arabs in 1948, and how the quarter had been rebuilt. He explained the circumstances of this fighting and why it was not safe for us to explore all of the Old City, and as he did I heard an English woman behind me saying in prim, shocked tones, 'He's talking politics!'

Only someone whose education had been aimed at preventing critical thought could believe that politics can be separated from life and never talked about in public.

Nevertheless, to be able to separate the political from the personal aspects of our lives, while at the same time being aware of the complex interaction between the political and the personal, is very difficult and requires us to see the continuity of everything that exists and to use the network concept of cause. This is difficult, and it is not the way we are taught to see the world. *Our bamboozlers want us to see the world in ways which are simple.*

To get a large, diverse group of people to see their world in the same way requires the teaching of a few very simple ideas. In England the ideas of 'our island race', the monarchy, and the myths of British history give the illusion of a shared unity and purpose to a people with very different backgrounds and interests. It is an *illusion* of unity and shared purpose, not a real unity and purpose, because throughout British history British subjects without power and wealth – the poor, the working and lower-middle classes, the Scots, Irish and Welsh, the

111

colonials, the colonized – have been used by the wealthy, powerful and privileged to establish, maintain and increase their wealth, power and privilege.

The huge spaces of America and the immensely diverse groups of immigrants required even simpler ideas to hold Americans together as a group with a common picture of the world. These simple ideas are God, family and the flag. The idea of God is used in the way that the Russians use the concept of the State – something which over-arches everything, which explains in general everything but in particular nothing (to say that God causes everything does not explain how, say, lightning is caused), and which cannot be questioned. Surveys of religious belief in the USA show that around 96 percent of people profess a belief in God, a much higher percentage than that in Britain.[30] The concept of the family is honoured in the breach. The number of single-parent families is significant and increasing.[31] Just as British television promotes the myth of unity in a society divided by class by telling many sentimental stories about the aristocracy, so does American television tell many sentimental stories about families. We watch many stories about the lives of amiable dukes and lovable parents and children, but very few stories, sentimental or otherwise, about single black women struggling to bring up their children in poverty, or about teenagers abandoned by their families and struggling to survive.

The British can understand and share the American simple notions of God and the family, but they find it hard to understand how the American flag, the Stars and Stripes, is treated by Americans as an icon. Simon Hoggart, writing in the *Observer*, tried to explain this to the English when the burning of the Stars and Stripes became such an issue:

Unlike 'LA Law', hamburgers and pop music, American patriotism doesn't really export. Which is why the current flap over the flag is so puzzling to us foreigners. If you've not been keeping up, the trouble began in 1984 when a young man called Gregory Johnson was arrested for burning an American flag outside the Republican convention in Dallas, the while shouting, 'America, I spit on you.' (Even his defenders describe Mr Johnson as a contemptible worm, presumably to demonstrate their own patriotism . . .)

Anyhow, he took the case up to the Supreme Court, which ruled last month that flag-burning was a form of free expression and so protected by the First Amendment.

You'd have thought the Court had just declared matricide legal. Other decisions, which diluted equality laws and allowed juveniles and mental incompetents to be executed, were forgotten as the horror sank in. George Bush, with his famous tin ear, said he

112

accepted the Court's ruling, then after lunch with his vicious little campaign manager, Lee Atwater, changed his mind, declaring that his love of the American flag was 'visceral' (though, to extend the metaphor, presumably in need of an artificial laxative).

He has proposed an amendment – the first ever – to the Bill of Rights, making 'desecration' of the flag an offence. The Bill of Rights may be the noblest document ever used to govern a country, and one wonders why this political time-server, with his wretched consultants and sheaves of opinion-poll print-outs, thinks he has any right to change it.

A few brave folk argued that a First Amendment which gives the untrammelled right of free speech – unless it upsets someone – isn't worth the parchment it's written on. Others pointed out that flag-burning laws are most popular with the kind of regimes which always need fresh reasons to lock people up.

But they've been pretty well howled down, led by Congressmen who spoke through the night, desperate to get their ersatz outrage on the record. Few will dare to vote against the amendment.

This extraordinary, emotional attachment to the flag is hard for us to understand. We're used to seeing the Union Jack on shopping bags, underwear, smirched on football hooligans' faces, even on Reebok shoes which are made in Korea by a US firm.

Americans address the flag when they recite the pledge of allegiance. (I once saw a six-foot-high Californian raisin clad in brown polyester pledging, while trying to put his hand over where his heart ought to be.) Their national anthem is all about the flag. On a beach last year I watched a family pitch camp with deckchairs and a cooler – then solemnly take out a flag on a telescopic pole and stick it in the sand, perhaps as a guide to confused submariners.

Commerce and the flag are unfailingly united. No shopping mall is complete without one. And the bigger the flag, the more likely it's to be found flying bravely over a used-car lot. Every schoolchild is taught elaborate rules for handling the flag, which mustn't touch the ground or fly at night. Even the old Confederate flag, the 'Stars and Bars', is revered in the South, where it flutters over two state houses, to the anger of black people who see it as an emblem of slavery.

The flag isn't just a symbol of America but its embodiment which of course is what made it worth Gregory Johnson's while to burn it. Thanks to all the fuss, flag immolation has now become quite fashionable in some circles.

This year, our last Fourth of July, it rained most of the day. But the kids went to the parade, and waved little flags kindly provided, in the interests of trade, by the local estate agents. In the evening, we had friends around for the traditional barbecued spare ribs, and saw the wonderful fireworks at the Washington Monument from the roof of our house. That seems to me to be a celebration of America's virtues, pleasanter and healthier than frothing over a flag.[32]

The furore about the burning of the flag epitomizes how the State bamboozles us by denying us the expression of our own truth, and, indeed, denying that we have a truth. Yet for all of us our own truth is that we have a dilemma from which we cannot escape. This is that we need some sort of government, some sort of organization, which will deal with the affairs of the group to which we belong and provide the services which we, both as a group and as an individual, need, yet, whatever form of government we have, that government will, at times, fail us and, through its laws and inadequacy, frustrate and inhibit us and consequently anger us.

Good governments, like good parents, accept the truth and legitimacy of our anger. They let us express our anger (freedom of speech) and they take what we say seriously. Bad governments, like bad parents, refuse to accept that we have any right to be angry and they show us that they regard our anger as proof that we are mad and bad. We are punished and silenced.

Unfortunately, most governments are bad governments, but what else could they be, for the people who comprise such governments have little of the second kind of intelligence, the wisdom of understanding themselves and other people. They were brought up by parents and teachers who, in showing them that they could not have everything, educated them according to the principles of containment and moulding, that is, bamboozled them.

4

'You Can't Have Everything' – Parents

One would be in less danger
From the wiles of a stranger
If one's own kin and kith
Were more fun to be with.
OGDEN NASH

So there we are as infants, knowing, however wordlessly, that we want everything, and knowing what we know about ourselves (our inner truth) though what goes on around us is confusing and unfathomable. Then along come society, the State and our family, each saying, 'No you can't have everything, but if you are good you will be rewarded with what we tell you is something you will like.' We try as best we can to make sense of this, but we are hampered in our efforts because right from the beginning our family is engaged in bamboozling us, usually with the best of intentions, because they love us, and usually unintentionally and unknowingly, because they themselves have been bamboozled.

In the first few months of our life we discover – abruptly, if we are unlucky in who happens to be our mother, or slowly, if we are lucky – that our own subjective truth is disregarded and that we cannot have everything that we want. We are told, 'I don't care if you are hungry. You'll just have to wait,' and 'You're not lonely. You're overtired. Now go to sleep.' As a baby we cannot argue with such pronouncements, but as soon as we have enough language and mobility to argue, we do, only to find that we have run up against an implacable wall of authority. Sometimes we might be able to cajole this authority into indulging us, but nevertheless, this authority, in the form of our parents, grandparents, older siblings, aunts and uncles, neighbours, priests, teachers, policemen, gives us one clear message, that as much as we are loved as we are, we are not satisfactory. To become satisfactory we must be obedient and good.

To question this authority is bad.

We might venture to ask, 'Why should I do as I am told?', but we find that there is no discussion of this issue which is vitally important to us. We are simply told,

'Because I am your mother.'

'Don't answer back.'

'Because I know best.'

'Because if you don't, something bad will happen to you.'

'Children should be seen and not heard.'

'Honour thy father and mother.'

These seem to be diverse messages, but we realize they each carry the same message, namely that there is an Authority which is Absolute and Real, Implacable and Unchanging. This Authority might be presented to us as God or Allah, or the State, or it might not be specified other than as the fixed and structured world in which we live.

Whichever meaning we are given for the Absolute Authority, we accept it and make it ours, for even though this Authority inspires our fear, it gives a stable structure to the everyday uncertainty and flux of our lives.

So we welcome this Authority and do not realize that we have suffered the first bamboozlement. An important Category One idea has been defined to us as a Category Two certainty. Authority has been presented to us as being part of the nature of life, not as a meaning which a person, or group of people, has created.

The Dogma of Authority

Authority, to be Authority, has to insist that the law which creates that Authority is Absolute and True. *Authority does not allow alternative construings.* If Allah's word is law, then all other gods are without truth or virtue. If father's word is law, then anyone who contradicts him is wrong.

Nowadays child-care experts talk disparagingly of 'Victorian fathers' who, like Elizabeth Barrett Browning's father, held a tyrannical rule over their children. Instead, such experts advise parents to be 'consistent' in their discipline. Mother and father should present a united front to the children. Parents who do this actually achieve the same result as the 'Victorian father', that is, they teach the child that there is only one Absolute Truth. Children growing up in such families do not even know of other ways of seeing the world, and by the time they do discover that people outside the family see things differently, they have so absorbed the dogma of the family that all other constructions of meaning seem strange and reprehensible.

Lucky children grow up in families where the parents do not present a united, single view. Father holds one point of view and mother another, and, while this can make for confusing and uncertain situations, the children learn that there is no one Absolute Truth, but that each of us creates our own construction of reality. Children who hold fast to this understanding and do not seek an Absolute Truth to believe in hold fast to their freedom. Thus they grow up to be threats to Authority.

Authority, whether the State or the Church or the parents, does not like threats to Authority. The dogma of the Authority must be maintained, for if it is not, Authority will no longer be Authority. So the President-for-life of Malawi, Dr Hastings Kamuzu Banda, kept a great poet, Jack Mapanje, in jail,[2] and parents become angry or withdraw into an offended silence when their children contradict them.

There are many parents who cheerfully endure a great many contradictions from their children, but even they become frightened and angry when their children produce ideas which contradict the beliefs the parents hold about basic moral rules. Perhaps the child believes that other people's property is not sacrosanct, or that falling in love with someone of the same sex, or a different colour, is natural and good. Then the most tolerant of parents can find in themselves a surprising degree of intolerance, and a desire to force the child into conforming with the parents' beliefs. Jo Brans, writing about the research done by Margaret Taylor Smith into the question, 'What happens to mothers when an adored son or daughter makes a decision about their lifestyle which is distasteful or shocking to the mother?', said:

> Within the privacy of the middle-class nuclear-family home, the mother has taught her child certain basic liberal American values: The future is of your making. You can be whatever you want. All of us are innately of equal worth. Racial and social discrimination is wrong. Money and position are less important than personal happiness and personal honesty. Discerning right and wrong is an individual matter. Let your conscience be your guide; your own heart will tell you what to do.
>
> The mother means what she says. She is not insincere. But she assumes her child will also comprehend what she doesn't probably say: that such values are, in her mind, to be interpreted within certain implicit social norms, as, in fact, she has interpreted them in her own behaviour.
>
> Suppose her child takes literally what she means to be taken theoretically. Racial discrimination wrong? The child marries a black. Personal honesty matters? The child comes out of the closet. Let your conscience be your guide? The child drinks what he pleases, smokes dope, shoots up if he likes; his conscience says it is perfectly okay.
>
> The mother feels double-crossed, when in fact she may have been obeyed too well. One mother after another has said, in effect, 'I told my child to think independently and to do what was right, but I didn't mean to do *that*.' And she will almost certainly feel aggrieved when the consequences of the child's actions deprive her of satisfactions she would normally expect to have as a mother.[3]

If Authority represents the Absolute Truth, then what that Authority says must be True. *So every Authority develops a dogma in which obedient citizens, children and the faithful must believe.* Part of this dogma concerns the hierarchy that maintains the Authority. English children are taught to be loyal to the Queen. Catholic children are taught to revere the Pope. Sri Lankan children show their reverence for their parents by kneeling and kissing the parents' feet when greeting them. In other cultures the reverence for their parents which children are required to show may not be displayed so dramatically, but all of us can recall the rules we were expected to follow in being with and talking to our parents and teachers. These rules went beyond being just sensible rules to follow in order to converse clearly and pleasantly, such as not talking when your mouth is full of food. They were rules to keep children in their place. For instance, in the schools where I was a pupil and later a teacher, teachers would be forever saying to individual pupils, 'Don't speak to me with your hands in your pockets,' though having hands in pockets in no way prevented clear speech. To Authority in those schools, hands in pockets represented a disregard of the teacher's authority. Hands clearly in view and hanging at the child's sides represented being naked and helpless before Authority.

Sometimes the dogma about the hierarchy of Authority is presented to children more subtly. In many families, daughters, when they are little, are allowed to treat their father in ways which might be regarded as disrespectful. The little girl can claim the father's attention, climb over him, demand favours. Yet all the time, in unspoken but powerful ways, she is being shown that, in the dogma of the Authority represented by her father, men are better than women. She is not being treated by her father as a person in her own right. She is merely being indulged.

Once we have learned the dogma of Authority, and follow it, we are relieved of the great burden of having to think for ourselves. Just as saying 'I'm a Pisces' saves us from the labour of trying to understand why we do what we do, so saying 'I'm a Catholic', or 'I respect the values my parents taught me', saves us from having to work out for ourselves, day by day, how we ought to behave.

Having arrived at a set of beliefs which saves us from the labour of thinking, we want things and people to remain the same, just as Authority wants us to remain the same.

So it is often said that 'People do not change'. 'Do not' here means both that changing *does not* occur naturally and that changing *should not* occur naturally. Thus other people always impress on us that we *cannot* change. Our parents define us as having certain characteristics and these, it is implied, are as unchangeable as our sex and the colour of our eyes. If we attempt to change, or simply experiment with behaving in different ways, we are punished and prevented, perhaps by the direct infliction of pain, or by ridicule, or by being frustrated when trying to carry out what we intend to do, or by being made to feel guilty for attempting to break the moral rule of not attempting to change. A simple remark from a loved one will make most of us relinquish our desire to be, even momentarily, different from what we always are. 'That's not like you,' our loved ones might remark, and we hastily abandon what we are doing and return to our old ways.

This is the greatest difficulty people encounter when they go into therapy, yet many therapists concentrate on the individual and ignore their client's social situation, which does not help their client to recognize and deal with this issue. Hence much of individual therapy fails. In the same way, many attempts to diet or to give up smoking fail. If your family does not want to undertake the mental effort of thinking of you as a thin person instead of a fat person, or a non-smoker instead of a smoker, they will do so many small but subtly powerful things to keep you overeating or smoking.

'People do not change' confuses naturally occurring phenomena and moral rules. A naturally occurring phenomena simply *is*; moral rules imply choices. If changing as a person was a natural phenomenon which could not occur, like rivers flowing up mountains, then attempting to change would be wasted effort. But if change as a person is a moral rule, then we have a choice about changing or not changing. An 'is' is not an 'ought', and an 'ought' is not an 'is'. However, *Authority does not want us to change, for if one change is possible, then all change is possible.*

Families will use all kinds of direct and indirect ways of preventing their members from changing, but the most popular method is humiliation. Edward Blishen described how this ritual humiliation operated in his family, at the same time preventing individuals from changing while giving them the pleasurable feeling of belonging to the group.

There were five of them . . . The eldest, Uncle Charlie, made his presence felt by his absence. Largely, as I understood it, through being an insurance agent, he'd propelled himself out of Paddington, where they'd all begun, and New Barnet, where they now lived, and resided (a word he insisted on) in Hampshire where he was known as Charles. 'Any news of *Charles*?' Uncle Jim would ask, after they had spoken rudely about the cakes provided by my grandmother. 'You could make a bloody garden path with these, mum!'

It was not a genial joke. They were not genial. Each, in some cruelly simple way, was comic to the rest. As the joke about Charlie was his wanting to be Charles, so my father was mocked for being a clerk. They pretended to believe that at the Board of Education (itself risible) he sat on a tall Dickensian stool. The absurdity of Uncle Jim lay in his being maritally mysterious. Uncle Harry's weakness was being married at all, and to Aunt Gwen, who had not much of a gift for being anyone's wife . . . Uncle Tom caused unkind laughter by breeding pigs, but especially by referring to them in affectionate terms. 'He'll be sleeping with those bloody pigs next!' And Uncle Len was comic for simply being very small. He'd had a stunting disease in childhood, wore a cloth cap in all circumstances, was deeply simple and had a crooked smile . . . Christmas brought out, I suppose, the worst in them, but I thought of it as the best. Their edgy hostilities took on a festive quality. It was as if they flung Christmas puddings at each other. They were awful about each other's wives, and worse about each other's children. I was a laughing stock for being widely regarded as certain to win a scholarship to the grammar school. Across the years I see that the wives were not offended, because there was a frightful charm about the rudeness of these brothers: and you felt, the target of it, momentarily famous, favoured, the warm centre of their jocular unkindness. I remember being strangely happy one Christmas because Uncle Jim said I was a skinny little thing, and Uncle Tom told a cousin of mine not to push me about because it might do damage to my amazing brains. The idea of anyone having brains was always a great joke. My father had to fight hard to keep at bay the allegation that he had them, too.[4]

Not Understanding Category Two

Because we have, so early in our life, been deliberately confused about Category One, the meaning we create, and Two, the nature of life, we do not come to understand the properties of Category Two.

It is in the interests of Authority that we continue to be confused about the properties of Category Two, because if we come to understand these properties we shall realize that we have been bamboozled about Category One and Two. So, whatever education we receive, it does not include an understanding of the properties of Category Two as I have defined them (see p. 35).

To understand Category Two we need to understand that whatever reality is, it is continuous and in continual flux, and that what we perceive is not a divided and packaged reality but simply the structures which our bodies and our education allow us to make. In my experience, the people who have the greatest difficulty in understanding this are psychologists and psychiatrists, who see nothing illogical and contrary to experience in their belief that biochemical change causes thought. People who have not had a scientific education do not have so much difficulty.

Diana, worried about her daughter who was depressed, told me how she had noticed that her daughter seemed more distressed in the week before her menstruation. 'Could there be some hormone causing her depression?' she asked.

Very briefly I explained that if we used a model of thought which said that a biochemical change caused thought, we would have to apply that model to *all* thought – not just thoughts like 'I feel hopeless', but to all thoughts – and that would not do.

Diana, who is an artist, immediately said, 'Yes, of course.' She knew that to explain art in terms of biochemical change is not appropriate. She recognized too that the onset of menstruation meant for her daughter the conflict between wanting a child and fearing that she could not cope with a child.

If only psychologists and psychiatrists could find this as easy to understand as Diana did, but they do not. Whenever this point arises when I am talking to psychiatrists and psychologists, I explain how a model of thought has to be applied to all thought, and that, using this model, we have no way of evaluating thoughts and deciding that one is better than another, since the process of evaluation itself would be nothing more than the outcome of biochemical change. In such audiences there are some who understand this, but there are many people who do not. It seems that the process of training that psychologists and psychiatrists undergo includes the instruction, 'Do Not Think About Thought!'

Authority, claiming to be part of the nature of life, presents the world as divided up into discrete boxes, all labelled and unchangeable and operating according to their intrinsic nature.

In Elizabethan times, Authority as the Church taught that the world was constructed of boxes arranged in the Great Chain of Being, which ranged 'from the foot of God's throne to the meanest of inanimate objects',[5] the centre point of the chain being man, a little lower than the angels but above the beast. A place for everything and everyone, and everything and everyone in its or his place. (Women were 'its'.) As the State asserted its power over the Church, kings took over the notion of the Great Chain of Being, but now they were at its head and the boxes became the hierarchy developed in feudal times – duke, earl, knight, squire, villein and so on. This hierarchy transmuted into the hierarchy of class which we have today, and which our families present to us as being part of the nature of life.

Perhaps because Authority in Britain, as represented by the English royalty and aristocracy, lived on an island, and so was not so threatened by the continual religious and political wars in Europe from the sixteenth century onwards, or perhaps for other reasons, British people have enjoyed considerable freedom of speech and thought. This freedom has always been patchy – many British people down the centuries have been persecuted for criticizing the Authority of the Church and State – but the English State has never developed an authoritarian, rigid system of education and a wholesale censorship of speech and writing, as is so common in most countries. This freedom of speech is recognized with joy by those who grew up in less fortunate countries. George Weidenfeld, later the highly successful publisher Lord Weidenfeld, wrote:

I had arrived in this country in August, 1938, and spent a few weeks in various boarding houses, sustained by the Refugee Committee at Bloomsbury House and by doing odd jobs, translating and giving lessons . . . Above all, 1939 was the year I learned British ways; the nuances of what it means to be free and critical. Of course, even before Hitler, Austria wasn't a free country. We had what you might call a clerico-fascist regime; partial censorship; partial discrimination; creeping, rubber-soled anti-Semitism. So I had not been in a free milieu; I had an authoritarian conditioning, a respect for authority, an emblematic perception of the state, a kind of naive belief in the superior being, the philosopher king who must be just.

The idea that in Britain you could put a yardstick on Shakespeare was amazing. In Germany to have said, 'You know, Goethe wasn't all that good, there are some very weak passages in Faust, let's discuss it,' was like calling God a felon.

If one has, as an Englishman, been brought up in a permissive, free society, one can have no idea of what it is like to be exposed for the first time to the fresh breeze of free speech. It is not simply what you can or cannot say. It means that strongly entrenched views – like those of feudalism – can suddenly be thrown overboard. It means iconoclasm and scepticism. These are habits of mind I could never have learned in Austria.

I am even more convinced today of the unique qualities of British life. They are unique – and I say this with greater conviction than I would have 50 years ago – when it comes to sheer values, tolerance, and the capacity for friendship.

Nowadays, for instance, the Germans are very consciously decent and tolerant; they have a very nice society; the Federal Republic is a fantastic success story. The British, however, have an inner certainty which stems from Britain having been an island, from having overcome the problems of feudalism and chosen democratic, libertarian ideas long ago.

I sometimes wonder why the British do not know how well off they are. Britain hasn't changed since I first came here; it is still the most tolerant and humane society.[6]

Unfortunately, many English people do not recognize and cherish the freedom they have to make and to hold their own individual constructions of meaning. Like Lord Weidenfeld, I am aware of how lucky I am to be able to write what I want to write. This book could be published in very few countries. It is highly unlikely that it will ever be published in the USA, a country where the State and the Churches allow the freedom to get rich or to starve, but not the freedom to question such freedom. To ask such questions is to hold 'liberal' ideas, almost as reprehensible as being a 'Communist'. (In the Bush-Dukakis contest for the presidency, the Republicans sought to discredit Dukakis by calling him a 'liberal'.) It is unlikely that this book would be published in the USSR, for, even if more democratic forms of government are introduced, the centuries-long belief in the Absolute Authority of the ruler, be it the Czar, the Party, or the President, and of the family, will exist so long as their education system remains one of moulding the child into the obedient citizen. In a great many countries, my fate, should I try to present these ideas, would be imprisonment, torture and death.

The freedom to see and to say that the world is not ordered in the way that the Authority of the Church and State say it is is a precious freedom, but the English who do not recognize this could so easily let this freedom slip from their fingers. The British Government keeps a great deal of information secret and says it has the right to do so. The British Government, whether led by the Conservative or the Labour Party, will interfere in the freedom of the media whenever they feel under threat. When many British Muslims joined the Ayatollah Khomeini's jihad against Salman Rushdie, did the English unite to defend their freedom of speech? No. Politicians looked to their constituencies and counted the number of Muslim votes, and many writers, jealous of Rushdie's success, uttered weasel words of abject compromise and surrender. The Rushdie affair certainly sorted the cowards from the brave.[z]

Issues about freedom of speech are fought out in the public arena, but such issues are first discovered and attitudes adopted in the family. Children who see that their parents never criticize authority because they are frightened to do so grow up following their parents' way of behaving. They want to please their parents and earn their parents' love, and so they behave as their parents do. This is why in repressive regimes most people do not fight for their freedom and, indeed, turn against any of their fellows who try to do so. A few children from homes where parents never criticize Authority do rebel, but their rebellion is usually somewhat confused and always painful. They know what they are *against*, but so much time and effort is taken up in the act of rebellion, and in defending themselves, that they have little left over for elaborating their own constructions of meaning, and

123

finding constructions different from and more happiness-producing than those of their parents and their parents' Authority. This is why successful revolutions go on to produce regimes as authoritarian and damaging as the one the revolutionaries rebelled against. *Plus ça change, plus c'est la même chose.*

Children who see their parents criticizing Authority take this to be the ordinary way to live, and so they grow up believing that having your own opinion and presenting it is part of the natural order of things. In politics they favour democracy, and they acquire no religious beliefs nor favour a God who stresses that we should choose between good and evil rather than a God who demands obedience. While they might believe in the existence of some Authority, they believe that a good Authority takes account of the individual's point of view.

A belief in the freedom of thought and speech does not mean that such thought and speech is necessarily sensible and logical, or full of the intelligence of the second kind. Free speech can simply show how bamboozled we are.

Thus many people, speaking freely, show how thoroughly confused they are about the properties of Category Two. They see events occurring according to linear cause – A leads to B, and B to C – because this is the way causation has been taught to them by their parents. For them, as for those who dare not criticize Authority, the prime example of linear cause is the rule, 'If you are good you will be rewarded, and if you are bad you will be punished'. Not realizing that they live in a non-linear universe, they construe their actions in a linear way, and are then surprised and dismayed by the range of events which follow from their actions.

Most of us, believing that goodness is rewarded, believe that when we give something we have a right to expect something in return. We might have acquired this belief from our parents who were forever telling and showing us that we had to repay them for their goodness in looking after us. So, just as we repay our parents, we are waiting for other people to reward us for our goodness.

Charles had married Mary, a widow with three small children, and had coped very well with the children and with Mary's slow recovery from injuries received in a car accident. Then one day a chance remark by a neighbour forced him to tell Mary that he had been having an affair. Mary said to me, 'He told me that over the past year he had been having an affair with one of my closest friends. He said, It was available and I thought I deserved it.'

Charles is a diligent worker, a well brought-up child who had been taught that goodness is rewarded and wickedness punished. What he had not been taught is that all acts have consequences. He believed that his goodness as a worker and as a husband deserved a reward, but what he did not realize was that such an act of unfaithfulness would have far-reaching, devastating consequences. Within a short space of time he had lost his wife and his lover.

Like Charles, many people grow up believing that they have a right, granted by Authority, to be rewarded for their goodness. They argue that, since they gave up being themselves in order to be good, now they should get their just reward. They have a *right to be happy*.

Writing about this, Neil Ascherson observed:

> It was unprecedented, in the late eighteenth century, to say that an individual's rights were sacred in a way that his duties were not – and Communist jurisprudence in our own day still insists that every right implies a corresponding duty.
>
> The specially French contribution was to give to 'rights' an earthy emphasis on individual property. As everyone knows, the Revolution generated a France of peasant proprietors, hotly patriotic and yet almost beyond the reach of government, possessive and jealous, obsessed with water rights and distilling licences. That France is now passing away. But that special attitude which Marxists accurately called 'petty-bourgeois', survives. Take French women's magazines. It's at once striking how often the word 'bonheur' is used, and how the term carries an extra load which the word 'happiness' does not.
>
> 'I shared my bonheur with Jean-Paul, but he didn't return it', 'I lost my bonheur but I found it again', 'Because of my new life, my bonheur is much richer and deeper than it was before', 'Claudine stole my bonheur', and so forth. Here, happiness is regarded as a piece of property which a human being is born possessing by inalienable right. It can be developed, like a plot of land: it can be shared or realized and invested: but if it is ruined or expropriated or stolen, then a universal law of justice has been violated. That law, as endlessly discussed in showbiz journalism and magazine romances, is the right of man and woman to possess happiness. The American in 1776 sanctified 'the pursuit' of happiness. The French prefer it shot, stuffed and in the larder.[8]

Because we have been taught that the Absolute Structure of the world has the form A leads to B and B only, *we do not develop our ability to create alternative hypotheses to explain why certain things have happened and what multitude of things could happen.* Ask a young child to think of as many reasons as possible that tadpoles turn into frogs, or as many things as could happen if a rocket is shot into space, and the child can think of an endless number of possibilities. But by the time children are leaving childhood they have been so ridiculed by adults for having such fantastic notions that few of them will dare, even in the privacy of their own thoughts, to create and explore alternative hypotheses.

Moreover, having learned the beliefs and prejudices of their family and their family's community, they know what kind of hypotheses they would be expect to produce. Asked, 'Why are there so many wars?', 'Because Allah wills it', replies the adolescent from the Muslim community, 'Because people are wicked', says the adolescent from the fundamentalist Christian community.

Being able to produce only one hypothesis and being unaware of alternative possibilities is very satisfying, for it gives a sense of stability and security, and a belief in the accuracy of the predictions made. We believe that the dogma of Authority provides a solution to all problems, and that all we have to do is force other people to accept our point of view. Not realizing that everything that happens has both good and bad implications, we fail to see that for most problems there is no perfect solution.

This failure to create alternative hypotheses and to recognize the inevitability of imperfect solutions leads groups of people, usually most caring and well-intentioned people, to argue that their solution to a problem is the one and only correct solution.

When a social services department took a seventeen-month-old child of a black father and a white mother from a white foster mother, who had cared for the child since birth, to place him for adoption with a black family, a battle raged between those people who were absolutely certain that the child would be damaged by the breaking of the bond with his foster mother, and those people who knew that a child of mixed parentage needed the support of a black family in order to survive in a society which is very unkind to blacks. For over a week the letters pages of the newspapers were filled with letters from people supporting one side or the other. On radio and television, people representing one side or the other were interviewed. The battle was between mother-love and racism. No one said, 'This is a situation in which whatever is done, it will in some way be wrong. What we need to find are possible solutions where we can try to mitigate the unavoidable harms.' No one said, 'It is not true that breaking a child's first bond will *inevitably* lead to disaster, or that growing up in a black family will *inevitably* benefit the child. We do not know what is likely to happen to this child and to the people responsible for his care. Neither the love from his foster mother nor the understanding from a black family can protect him from all the disasters which could possibly befall him. We can talk about probabilities, but we cannot *know*.'

However, in order to live with any degree of equanimity with such an understanding of our inability to predict the future, we have to have developed a considerable ability to tolerate uncertainty. Few of us manage to develop this ability, for *we have been taught that there is only one correct interpretation of everything that happens, and that anyone who does not agree with this interpretation is either mad or bad.* So we grow up being expert at arguing and fighting, but not at creating compromises. Indeed, the vast majority of people (men more than women) believe that to compromise is to be, at best, weak, and, at worst, bad.

We are not taught that everything in the universe is connected to everything else. Instead, we are taught that God, or Allah, made the world and all in it, and that we should be grateful for the things which He made and which we can use.

There is a children's hymn called 'Think of a World without Flowers', where the children are asked in successive verses to imagine a world without flowers and trees, without animals, and without people, and to thank God for providing the flowers, trees, animals, and the people on whom the children depend. Such an interpretation of the world does not show the children that if there were no flowers, trees and animals there would be no people. Our survival depends on the present pattern of the interconnection of all that exists. If we destroy this pattern, we destroy ourselves.

However, the Church teaches that God made the plants and animals and the earth's riches for us to use, provided we are good. Being good means being grateful. So, thanking God for His gifts to His children, Christians have, down the centuries, taken and used what they see as their right to take and use. The men who destroy the rainforests to grow food, who destroy the fields to mine for coal and other minerals, who eradicate species of animals to provide the necessities of life, who use the earth's resources to provide power, do not see themselves as being wicked. They see themselves as acting according to the structure and organization of the world which they have been taught to see. They are good, God rewards them, and they are grateful. A few Christians, fearful of such destruction, say 'We should not waste God's gifts', but others reply 'There's plenty more where these came from'. Just as children cannot understand that their parents' wealth is limited and think that parents have a bottomless pit of wealth from which they can draw money for sweets and toys, so most Christians believe that their all-powerful God has limitless ways to reward and protect them. If they are good, God will save them. Muslims have the same belief about Allah, and many of us, Communists or capitalists, about the State.

When we believe that the world we live in is *actually* divided into the categories which we have been taught to use, we find it easy to decide that certain categories are unimportant and can be ignored. Thus *we become blind to important interactions.*

Hence parents use the category 'children forget', and ignore what happens to children and what children make of what happens to them. Such parents believe that children will remember being taught how pleasant it is to be clean, but not how unpleasant it is to be sexually abused or beaten. Scientists use the category 'purely scientific', and believe that they can ignore the social and political setting of their work. Psychiatrists use the category 'patients' attitudes are subjective', and believe that how patients view their treatment has no influence on the outcome of that treatment.

Just as we are taught that the world is divided into categories, some of which we can wisely and safely ignore, so we are taught that what we think and feel (our internal reality) is divided into actual categories, some of which we can safely and wisely ignore. Thus *we fail to see that what we do follows from the whole pattern of constructions we have made.*

We believe that we can act 'objectively', not taking account of our 'subjective' wishes, needs and fears. We do not see, for instance, that our desire to bring order into a disorderly situation arises from our experience of our sense of existence as the gaining of order and control, and our fear of our annihilation in chaos. We believe that we can act 'altruistically', not taking account of our own selfish desires. We do not see, for instance, that by acting altruistically we gain the love and admiration from other people which is necessary for our survival. Many people, when they discover that the rewards for their altruism are not forthcoming, when the people to whom they have devoted themselves desert or betray them, are horrified to discover that they did expect a reward for their goodness. Until then they had believed that they did good only for goodness's sake. Discovering within themselves the very selfishness they had been taught to despise, they hate themselves and fall into despair.

Having been taught that our internal reality is divided into categories which do not necessarily have any connection with one another, we fail to develop those habits of thought which allow us to sort out our thoughts and feelings, see our conflicts clearly, and work out our priorities. These habits of thought, the techniques of introspection, are not habits which we can develop on our own. We need other people's help.

As small children we need the adults around us to help us learn to distinguish what goes on inside us from what goes on around us. How do we distinguish a dream from real life? When a child wakes up in fear, loving parents give comfort with 'That was only a dream'. As small children we need to discover that our thoughts are private. Parents who wish to control their children often try to prevent their children from discovering this. They pretend to the child that they know what the child is thinking. Ursula told me how her mother would say to her, 'If you tell a lie I shall find out,' and to this day she cannot rid herself of her fear that her mother knows her thoughts, particularly the thoughts which Ursula regards as base and despicable. Consequently Ursula cannot free herself from her need to be, at all times, good, a most exhausting way to live one's life.

As we grow up we need people to tell us that there is nothing wrong with having certain thoughts and feelings. We need to know that all people, faced with frustration, feel angry, and that if this frustration goes on and on, we can feel a rage which mounts to impulses to murder. The trick in living is to know how to dispel, or keep under control, such murderous rage and hate by elaborating fantasies, thus removing the pressure to act upon this rage and hate, and how to acquire skills in expressing anger in socially acceptable ways. We need to know that loss feels like pain and fear, and that in such loss we all feel weak and helpless. Instead, as children we are told that anger is wicked, and that to think of doing something is as wicked as doing it. We are told that if we show our distress we shall be despised. So *we are actively prevented from understanding and creating effective ways of dealing with our emotions.*

So we grow up not understanding our processes of thought, feeling and action, and, lacking the techniques necessary to understand ourselves, we lack the skills necessary to understand other people. We believe that other people ought to think and feel like we do, and when they fail to show that they do, we believe that they are wicked and we must oppose them, or that they are stupid and of no importance and we must ignore them.

So we treat other people very badly. The majority of families are rent with arguments and bad feeling, so that family gatherings are more stressful than happy, and childhood feelings of envy and hate are not resolved but solidified and enlarged. Instead of taking seriously the point of view of those we regard as immature, stupid or mad, we dismiss them. Children are ignored or laughed at or told that they are wrong, people with learning difficulties are treated as if they are not really human, and those people who are distressed, anxious and depressed are dismissed with 'That's your illness speaking', while those people who try to help the people they see being badly treated are themselves badly treated, being criticized as 'do-gooders' and kept short of the money they need to carry out their work.

The State uses our lack of understanding of our fellows to its advantage. The State creates an enemy, and we turn our fear and anger on this supposed enemy. The State defines a group of people as being unimportant, and we accept that these people can be treated as objects of no importance. So we go to war, and cheer as ships are sunk and cities bombed. We go to war with some relief, because then we can turn our anger, fear and suspicion away from our relatives and neighbours and towards the State's enemy. Older people in England remember with nostalgia the closeness and warmth they shared with their fellows during the Second World War, a closeness and warmth not known in peacetime.

The fear and anger that arises from our not understanding one another is always a threat to the stability of the State, for groups of people fighting amongst themselves can make the State ungovernable, and, even worse, the fear and anger may be directed at the government in power. (This fear and anger is fostered and used by those people who wish to overthrow the government.) So the State always needs to have an enemy. When Mr Gorbachev showed himself to be so friendly to the USA, thus refusing to play the role of the enemy which his predecessors had played so effectively, President Bush had to find another enemy, while at the same time appearing to have peaceful intentions. So in September 1989, President Bush declared 'war on drugs'. No matter that drug-taking in the USA was intimately related to racism and unemployment, and that the most deadly drugs used in the USA were not the illegal drugs, the object of Bush's 'war', but the legal drugs of alcohol and nicotine and the mind-altering drugs prescribed by doctors. Bush wanted to unify his people and direct their anger outwards, and so he declared war. When the war on drugs proved unsatisfactory, Bush, having previously ignored Saddam Hussein's cruel treatment of the Kurds, made Saddam Hussein the enemy for having invaded Kuwait.

The State also benefits from our lack of understanding of ourselves and our fellows because, without such understanding, we cannot combine with our fellows to change the way in which the State operates. Moreover, we fail to see how the State and other powerful groups manipulate us.

Politicians get themselves elected by being able to identify some of their voters' wishes and fears and then promising to fulfil these wishes and soothe these fears. Political parties spend vast sums of money employing people to identify these wishes and fears and determining how they could be turned to the party's advantage. Industries spend vast sums of money trying to identify which groups of people might want to buy their products, and then advertising the products in ways which appeal to these groups.

When political parties and industries get their analyses and predictions of our behaviour wrong, we can then be aware of their intentions to manipulate us, but when they are right, or close to right, we, not understanding ourselves, can be quite unaware that we are being manipulated. We are often unaware that the politician's or advertiser's message speaks straight to our wishes and fears, and we respond immediately, not pausing to analyse the message and our response. In the same way, we have learned to respond to our parents' instructions immediately, not pausing even to think of the reason for our immediate response, which is 'If I don't do as my parents tell me they will cease to love me'.

Adults who have tried to understand themselves have become aware of how they still give themselves this powerful injunction, 'Obey your parents or suffer', even though their parents are no longer powerful, being old or dead. Once we become aware of this we can see how we have generalized this rule to institutions which present themselves as being good parents – the State, the Church, and the industries which sell to the public. Indeed, the less good our parents were to us, the more readily we impose on institutions the characteristics of a good parent and respond to the institution as we would respond to a good parent – with love, loyalty and obedience. We try to be good. We obey, lest we suffer.

Good children do not criticize their parents. So, just as we did not question our parents' instructions and information (we might have criticized them for insisting that we come home *before dark*, but we did not question that we should *come home*), we do not criticize the instructions and information given to us by the Church and State. (To some extent we have learned to be wary of advertisers, but then they are after our money, not our obedience.)

Thus we do not see that *when the Church and State tell us that they give us both security and freedom, they are bamboozling us.* They are pretending to us that we can have large amounts of both freedom and security, when in fact the more we have of one the less we have of the other. Parents do this when they say to children, 'I don't care what you do with your life, darling, so long as you are happy', that is, 'Be free and be secure', and 'Be free and make me secure'. Giving the instruction 'Be free and be secure/happy' is like giving the instruction 'Go swimming but don't get wet'.

The State, be it Communist or capitalist, is always assuring its people that they are free (the government of the USSR insists that its people are 'free from fear and want'), and that they are secure in the care of the State.

Some religions, the more mystical kind, preach a faith built on trust of the unknowable, and so require their believers to tolerate a great deal of uncertainty and insecurity. This is why the mystical forms of the world's religions are the least popular. The most popular form of the world's religions is the fundamentalist whose basic tenet, be it fundamentalist Christianity or fundamentalist Islam, is that if believers follow the rules they will have complete security. Believers are also told that within the framework of the rules they have complete freedom, which is the same as saying 'Within the confines of your prison cell, you are completely free'. These religions do not show their believers that in gaining complete security they have given up their freedom, and with that their hope and unexpected joy.

A young man of my acquaintance was born into a strict Mormon family and, unlike his older brother, accepted the beliefs and practices of Mormonism without question. He went to a Mormon school where, in his final years, he met the girl he intended to marry, once he had graduated from Brigham Young University. Before going to university he showed his special devotion to his religion by going on a Mission to bring the message to the heathen. His Mission took him to Sydney, a city of particular beauty, self-indulgence and sin, but he was not seduced by any of that city's charms, any more than he was envious of the life of his errant brother who, rather than sinking into degradation after abandoning his faith, had done rather well and, after a series of affairs with beautiful women, had married the most lovely and accomplished of them. If he looked at the possibilities outside his religion, what he saw was not freedom but fear, for he had been taught that all risk is dangerous. His life was totally secure, the plan fully mapped out – school, mission, university, marriage and the duties of husband, father, businessman, Mormon, and, after death, reunion with his Mormon family in a Mormon heaven. Provided he kept to the plan, there was no risk, no insecurity. There was also no hope that life might be more exciting and adventurous. He could not dream the wild, improbably delightful, creative dreams that young men dream. He was sad, but did not know it, and thought of himself as serious. He was often ill, with draining, enervating illnesses which doctors could not diagnose except vaguely, 'a virus', 'there's a lot of it about now'. He did not know that the cure for such illnesses is the heart-leap of surprise and joy.

Because we are taught that our goodness will be rewarded as the day follows night, we do not learn to perceive and to accept that there are many situations in life where we cannot have our cake and eat it too. Somehow, we believe, the functioning of the Just World will reward our goodness.

No matter that what we want is excluded by the nature of life: we can want as one of our rewards the love of other people, and we can want as another of our rewards power over other people. Many people find it impossible to accept that when we are in a position of authority, those we have power over are quite likely to dislike and criticize us. Power and love are not compatible, because the fear and sense of helplessness which power provokes in its subjects are incompatible with love.

One of my clients, John, had been recently promoted to a very senior position, but felt anxious and worked excessively hard. He wanted to think of himself as being caring and sensitive, but his new job required him to make and put into effect many decisions which were unpopular with his staff. He agonized over such decisions, but saw his senior colleagues act without such qualms. He called them 'authoritarian bastards' and dissociated himself from them. In a discussion with him about this, I said, 'You get yourself into this anxious state because you are not prepared to admit that you actually like power. You want to be an absolute dictator who is universally loved.' He thought that this was very funny, but agreed. He is still working on this problem, but has not yet discovered a way in which he can please everybody all the time and tell them what to do.

Of course some parents and teachers do try in their education of children to show them the difference between Category One and Category Two, and to help them see and appreciate the attributes of Category Two. This is education by enlightenment. However, *the State does not want education by enlightenment, for that means creating individuals who are questioning, who can imagine different possibilities and identify priorities.* Such people are not obedient.

Richard von Weizsäcker, the President of Germany, was a nineteen-year-old private with the Ninth Infantry Regiment in Potsdam in 1939. Fifty years later he said:

> We were no better and no worse than our fathers, who 25 years earlier had been drawn into the First World War. And we were no better than our children, who today pass judgement on us. We, like the soldiers of other countries, were trained to obedience. We had not been brought up free to demonstrate our opposition under the protection of a liberal constitution. We had the same sensitivities that all humans have, but during a time of difficult decisions, we lacked political vision.[9]

Education by moulding and bamboozling fails to meet the child's needs, creates envy and greed, and leaves the child expecting something in return for what he gives up; and, since it does not address our wanting everything, it leaves an ache and causes confusion.

Children brought up in this way do not see what has been done to them, and so, when they become parents and teachers, they do the same to their children.

Why Parents Bamboozle Their Children

Parents feel the need to bamboozle their children because, not understanding their children, and believing that there is something in children which is dangerous, they are frightened of them and so need to control them. Not understanding their children enables parents to see them as objects which they can own and use. They fear the child's anger and hate, which they see as unacceptable and wicked, and they often feel overwhelmed by their child. Moreover, they have a great need to show that they are good parents, and in this way the child is expected to meet the parents' own needs.

It is parents who do not understand themselves who cannot understand their children and so become frightened of them. They worry about their children, and much of their worry relates to their fear that they may not be able to keep their child under control.

I write a column for a women's magazine, *Chat*. My column is called

'Family Chat', and I answer readers' letters about any of the problems that can arise in families. The most common problem which parents write to me about is that of children who are sometimes angry and disobedient. The contents of these letters show how the parent focuses on the child and does not see how the child is responding to the whole situation, that is, the parent does not perceive the continuity and interconnection of everything that is. Moreover, the parent does not attempt to see the situation from the child's point of view. The parent's point of view presented to me is simply, 'My child is bad. How can I make my child be good?'

In the space of the six hundred words I am allowed, I try to present the child's view of the situation, and to suggest that when we see another person's point of view we can work out effective ways of helping that person change, and that if no change is possible, our understanding helps us to be tolerant.

My answers advocating understanding and tolerance often enrage readers, especially when I advise understanding and tolerance of a child's anger, as the following letters show. One mother wrote:

> I am worried about my 7-year-old son. When he does not get what he wants he kicks things around and throws whatever he is carrying. Once he even scratched his face. He says things like, 'I wish I was dead', and 'I hate you'. He is an only child and gets all the attention. My husband takes him swimming and football and he gets plenty of love, so he is not deprived of anything.

I answered:

> Would I be right in thinking that even though you have a good family and a nice home, sometimes you feel very frustrated and angry and, if you weren't so well behaved, you would kick things and throw them, and even though you love your husband and son there are times when they are so aggravating you could, momentarily, hate them? The people who frustrate us the most are our nearest and dearest, and our natural response to frustration is anger and hate. If, at the time you feel frustrated and angry, someone points out to you that you should be grateful for all the things that you've got, that doesn't make you feel any better. In fact, it makes you feel a great deal worse.
>
> Being a wife and mother is often very frustrating, just as it is to be a husband and father. It is even more frustrating to be a child, because adults are always frustrating you – for your own good, of course. For a family to live together happily each member needs to understand and accept that anger is our natural response to frustration and that we can hate the ones we love. Thus when one member of the family gets angry the others don't punish him,

or criticize him, or get angry back, but just let him express his anger and afterwards, if he wants to, let him talk about what made him angry. Sometimes an explosion of anger is enough for us to get rid of it, and sometimes we need to talk it through with someone who is sympathetic and uncritical.

It is very important in a family that when one person says 'I hate you', the other people in the family don't take it personally. When we are very angry we hate everybody and everything, but that is just the way we feel at the time. Anger and hate expressed like that vanishes. However, if we are not allowed to express our anger and hate, it does not disappear but stays and grows. If you punish your son or make him feel guilty for saying 'I hate you, mummy', he may *really* come to hate you.

My answer so incensed one reader that he wrote, not to me, but to the editor to complain about me:

Dear Sir,

The advice from your consultant Psychologist is typical of modern thinking and leads directly to the problems that beset society today.

Children should be taught from the time they leave the womb that the spiritual rule is to always consider the needs and feelings of all other beings and cater for that in their everyday behaviour.

It is irresponsible to advise parents to allow a child to rampage around the house working out an uncontrolled temper venting hate and spite on those around. The end result of this is the grown youth imposing on that local community by way of graffiti, muggings, vile language, bullying and crimes various, just because there may be some rules of society that are an inconvenience.

There cannot be two sets of rules. The rules of the home and of society should be viewed the same. Every child should be taught to adhere to those rules first in the home, the other will follow automatically + a small percentage. Any change should be by mutual dialogue.

Hate is NOT love, it is an opposing factor. A child needs to be taught this. To say 'I hate you' is completely self-indulgent. It is quite wrong to allow a child to think otherwise and impose this wilful self-indulgence on to the rest of society.

My advice to all parents is to ignore modern, 'trendy' child psychology and concentrate your own and your child's mind along more spiritual guide lines. The rules are simple and uncomplicated but teaching them to your child is a 24 hour a day task for the whole of the formative years.

The writer of this letter demonstrates the belief that the education of children must be by moulding and controlling, and his views, though perhaps not expressed so forcibly, are held by a great many parents and teachers. Such people do not see (though they must know, since they were once children) that obedient children are frightened children. Anna Mitgutsch in her novel *Punishment* described one such obedient child and her mother:

'Girls are toilet-trained by age one and a half; boys may take a little longer,' she, the experienced mother of the best brought up child, said to young, inexperienced mothers. She had many bits of advice for such women, who wanted to raise a child as obedient and well trained as me. 'You have to strike children or they won't amount to anything; if you love your child, don't spare the rod. Children demand it; they're always testing how far they can go. Even newborns tyrannize over their mothers, and all the more so when they reach the defiant stage; you've got to nip that in the bud. We never had any tantrums at our house; at the first sign of rebelliousness you start in, you whack them until you break them of it.' When someone gave me a piece of candy, I said please and thank you with averted eyes, my face unhappy with the strain of obligation. People were polite: How nicely she says please and thank you; they praised Mama and overlooked my scared, joyless face. But not everyone was polite enough to feign blindness, and once in a while a woman who understood children would say, 'Like a trained monkey,' and incur my mother's lifelong enmity. 'Don't look so glum,' people on the bus would say, and I would start to cry. 'What black eyes you have; you must have forgotten to wash them,' people would say to tease me, and at home Mama would say, 'Eat more so that your cheeks will get plump and you won't have such starved-looking eyes.' I was afraid of people because I sensed my mother's fear.[10]

Most parents would say that they want their children to be obedient children because that way their children will enjoy happier, more fruitful lives. Some parents say to their children, 'It's a good idea to do what your teachers tell you because that way you'll avoid getting into trouble, and you'll learn lots of useful and interesting things.' Showing the child that being obedient is something the child can *choose* to do gives the child a sense of being in control, not being helpless. But teaching children that they have a choice about being obedient means that on occasion the child will choose not to be obedient. This could be inconvenient for the parent. It could also be dangerous.

Such disobedience could be dangerous for the child who chooses to embark on activities which could lead to injury or death. Such disobedience could be dangerous for parents who see in the child, but are perhaps unaware of seeing, their own rebellious, independent self whom they have been taught to see as wicked and to fear. All too often the child whom the parents and teachers punish is not the actual child who receives the pain but the child within themselves, the child that they once were. Seeing another child being disobedient arouses in them the fear of impending punishment which they felt as children, and to bring the fear under control, they have to make this child obedient. Seeing another child being disobedient can also arouse envy in parents and teachers. How dare this child get away with what they were punished for! This child must be punished just as they were punished. Thus do the older generations, all older generations, deplore the behaviour of younger generations. Every older generation says, 'I don't know what the youth of today are coming to!'

When we do not understand other people and see no reason why we should try to understand them, we find it easy to see these people as objects. Thus, down the centuries, parents have seen their children not as persons but as objects for the parents' use.

So children are sold into slavery,[11] and abused as sexual objects.[12] Parents who would recoil in horror at the thought of selling their children or using the children to relieve their own sexual urges still see their children as workers whom they control and from whose work they expect to benefit, as this story from the *New York Times* shows:

Already overworked, farmers say they cannot survive unless the family helps in the field. Farm families do about 60 percent of all farm work in the country, experts say. Children are expected to work 'from the time they're big enough to climb up on anything,' said Mr Fields of the American Farm Bureau Federation, who, from the time he was 8, worked with horses at his family's West Virginian cattle farm. 'People have to decide whether they want food in this country or do they want to be do-gooders,' Mr Fields said. 'Accidents can happen to anybody.' In Iowa, barely a week passes without a report of a child being killed in a farm accident.

Darren Fehr was 13 when he lost his left leg four years ago. He had just come from football practice, and his father needed help cleaning out the silo where a screw-like augur was sucking the grain into a hole. His father left to answer the telephone, and the shovel Darren was using got caught in the augur. He tried to free the shovel. 'I knew if the shovel broke my dad would have my hide,' he said. The spinning blades caught his sleeve, grabbed and broke his arm. As he tried to free himself, the blades grasped his pants leg. 'It started chewing my leg apart and moved me towards the hole,' Darren said. 'It chopped my leg all the way off. I was afraid I was going to end up in the wagon in pieces.'

No one could hear his screams in the silo. His brother happened to walk by and shut the augur's motor off. It took eight people half an hour to free Darren from the device.

He now has an artificial leg, and still does chores around the farm. But if asked if he wants to be a farmer, Darren says, 'I'm not planning on it.'[13]

Parents who, as children, were punished for expressing the anger and hate they felt towards their parents find it extremely difficult to accept their own children becoming angry with and hating them. They feel safe only when the child is showing love to the parent, or at least being quietly obedient. This fear of the child's anger and hate, plus the child's demands and dependency which parents doubt they have the ability always to meet, often create in the parent a feeling of being overwhelmed by the child.[14]

Parents who have learned to be good children want to be good parents. Being a good child meant pleasing their parents, and being a good parent also means pleasing their parents. For many mothers, showing your mother that you are a good mother is more important than showing your child that you are a good mother. Such mothers do not see that in doing this they are trying to meet their own needs – getting their mother's love – rather than trying to meet their child's needs.

Of course such mothers, and the mothers who try to understand their child's needs and to meet them, are under tremendous pressure not to meet their child's needs. Mothers are not honoured in our society, as shown by the amount of sentimentality the topic of mothers always attracts. But mothers are certainly criticized. If their children show an independent spirit and speak up for themselves, the mothers are told that their children are 'spoilt'. If the child behaves badly, the mothers are encouraged not to inquire why, but to punish the child immediately. Often a mother finds herself torn between the public pressure to control her child and her love for the child, and often, under such pressure, mothers find themselves acting with more cruelty towards their children than they wish. The guilt they feel is terrible, as is their fear that they have harmed their child irreparably. This is one of the reasons that people who are parents do not wish to see any connection between childhood and adult life, neither the childhood of their children nor their own childhood.

Protecting themselves, they bamboozle their children.

How Parents Bamboozle Their Children.

Parents are powerful. Their baby looks at them, in Alice Miller's words, like a sunflower looks at the sun. The parents do not merely provide their children with sustenance and shelter, they provide them with definitions of who they are, what they should think, and what they should do. They can give the child definitions which encourage self-confidence and clarity of thought. Or they can bamboozle.[15]

The worst bamboozlement of all that parents can impose on their children is teaching them that they are intrinsically bad.

Parents may go on to teach their children that such badness can be controlled and, perhaps, even overcome by striving to be good, but no matter what hope of salvation is given, the children have been provided with a lie on which to build their world of meaning. Inevitably they grow up confused and afraid.

Children are not born bad. Neither are they born good. They simply *are*. Goodness and badness are meanings which we create and impose on ourselves and one another. The belief that within a newborn baby lurks some intrinsic *badness*, like Original Sin or dangerous instincts, is no more than a fantasy. To impose this fantasy on a child and say it is the Truth is to bamboozle and to injure. The belief that within a newborn baby lurks some intrinsic *goodness*, like the soul of a saint or a source of benevolent power, is likewise a fantasy, and equally bamboozling and damaging. Children simply *are*, and we can rejoice in their existence, their newness, and their individuality.

Being defined by no more than 'We love you because you exist' is a wonderful start to constructing a world of meaning. The basis of such a structure is simply 'I am and I am accepted'. Then the world can be looked at directly and there is no need to lie and dissemble. No confusion need arise.

But to tell and to show children that they are bad is to confuse them, for children cannot find this badness within themselves. They have to rely on the information given to them by other people, and this information is inconsistent and not explained. Just how confusing this is is shown in a poem written by Elizabeth, a woman who has had a most troubled and confused life.

Poem to Mama

I had a fierce Mama
That hammered me down,
With a fierce face.
Did I know, somewhere even then,
  That it was terror,
   Behind the fierce face?
   Maybe I did,
And was afraid of the fear.
If the person who's your Mother
  Has such terror within her,
  Then the world
Is a terrifying and insecure place.
  Fear is so contagious.
  And what was it
That had to be crushed?
  My vulnerability?
  Sometimes I thought
That sex was only a convenient hanger.
  If I could have recognized
What it was
That was so unacceptable in me
I would have tried to separate it
  From the whole.
Was it my femininity? My vulnerability?
  Or that I was weak?
  I don't know.
When you're a baby, you don't know.
You only know you're not acceptable
The way you are.[16]

Parents do not merely teach children that they are intrinsically bad. They show them how to behave in ways people commonly construe as bad. This is how Sean learned his 'bad behaviour'.

I first became aware of Sean when his father hit him. I was in the foyer of a hotel, choosing postcards from a stand, when there was a scuffle behind the stand and I heard the sound of a hand landing hard on flesh and then a child crying. A man emerged from behind the stand, dragging a skinny boy of about six behind him.

I saw a lot of Sean over the next three days for he and his parents were in the same tour party as me. Sean did not endear himself to the other members of the party, for he ignored all friendly overtures from strangers and was frequently querulous and crying.

One of our sightseeing tours was to Massada and the Dead Sea. Massada is the remains of a palace built by Herod on a high cliff overlooking the Dead Sea. Later it had been taken over by the Zealots, a Jewish sect who had preferred to commit mass suicide rather than surrender to the Romans. (At least, it was the male leaders who decided on the mass suicide. The women and children were not asked if they would prefer to live. The Old Testament enshrines the tradition that children should be sacrificed for their parents.)

I enjoyed the ride in the cable car to the top, but soon found that our enthusiastic guide was telling us far more than I wanted to know about that pile of old stones. Sean must have been even more bored than me, but he walked about quietly in the hot sun holding his mother's hand.

Sean's mother did all the things the rest of the tour party were doing, but she seemed always to be lost in her own thoughts. As I stood at the edge of a group whom the guide was instructing, Sean and his mother walked by. Sean was saying in a quiet, reasonable and polite voice, 'I want to go to the bathroom.' His mother gave no sign that she heard him. Again he politely repeated his request, and again she ignored him. When his third polite request was ignored, Sean, no doubt desperate, began what in Australia we call a grizzle, a whining, complaining, irritating sound which children use when they feel miserable and hard done by and cannot put their feelings into words. Many parents respond to a grizzle with, 'If you don't stop crying I'll give you something to cry for,' and either terrify the child into submission or force the child into greater rebellion.

On this occasion Sean's grizzle was effective, for through it he got his mother to recognize his need. She led him to a private corner of the ruins and he relieved his bursting bladder.

Grizzling and crying might be the only way Sean can communicate effectively with his mother, but such methods were totally ineffective with his father, as our visit to the Dead Sea showed.

On the way to the resort beside the Dead Sea where we would lunch and swim, our guide warned us that we should not attempt to dive into the water there. As I discovered to my cost, she should also have warned us to keep our knees together. That strong salt water on tender parts stings most painfully. Sean found this as well, and he clambered out of the water, clutching his bottom and crying miserably.

Sean's mother was floating quietly a few yards out in the murky water and Sean's father was standing on the bank. Instead of understanding Sean's plight he began berating Sean for being selfish and spoiling his mother's holiday. 'Don't you think your mother ought to have a chance to enjoy herself?' he demanded. Sean looked guiltily towards his mother, but he still cried with the pain.

Sean's mother heard the commotion, stood up and waded towards her son and husband. As she went past me I was saying to my companion, perhaps a shade too loudly, that our guide should have warned us to keep our knees together. Whether she heard me I do not know, but she did understand Sean's predicament and led him away to the showers nearby. Her husband complained to her about Sean's behaviour but ignored what she was doing for Sean.

Sean was still crouching naked under the shower when I went there to wash off the salt. I tried to engage him in conversation but he just stared at me silently and then turned away.

A lonely life lies ahead for Sean, for he had learned that the only way to attract his mother's attention was to be querulous and cry, but that this behaviour brought criticism and hostility from his father and other people.

Parents who see their children as being intrinsically bad, and who fear that they may not be able to keep this badness under control, are more likely to punish their children for bad behaviour than to reward them for good behaviour. Often the punishment they deal out is nothing more than an expression of their own pain and hurt, frustration and anger, all aroused by events quite unconnected with the child, for one of the most important functions children have for their parents is to be the scapegoat for their parents' rage. Some parents admit this. Others justify their punitive actions by claiming that that is the only way to teach children to behave correctly.

Children learn from whatever their parents and teachers do to them, but they rarely learn what the parents and teachers intend.

When the punishment is physical violence (beating, punching, whipping, slapping) the child's first reaction is hatred for the parent. Edmund Gosse, in his memoir *Father and Son*, wrote:

It was about the date of my sixth birthday that I did something very naughty, some act of direct disobedience, for which my Father, after a solemn sermon, chastized me, sacrificially, by giving me several cuts with a cane. This action was justified, as everything he did was justified, by reference to Scripture – 'Spare the rod and spoil the child.' I suppose that there are some children, of a sullen and lymphatic temperament, who are smartened up and made more wide-awake by a whipping. It is largely a matter of convention, the exercise being endured (I am told) with pride by the infants of our aristocracy, but not tolerated by the lower classes. I am afraid I proved my inherent vulgarity by being made, not contrite or humble, but furiously angry by this caning. My dear, excellent Father had beaten me, not very severely, without ill-temper, and with the most genuine desire to improve me . . . I have to confess with shame that I went about the house for some days with a murderous hatred of my Father locked in my bosom.[17]

When the physical punishment continues, hatred is joined by fear of the parent. Fear drives out love.

One of the bamboozlements which emanates from the Bible is the injunction that we should love and fear God. Love is an emotion which impels us towards the object of our love. Fear is an emotion which drives us away from the object of our fear. When we both love and fear the same object, we find the conflict of emotions extremely painful, and unless the object of our fear can change, no longer to inspire our terror, we weary of the conflict and cease to love. It is easier just to fear.

Parents who use physical punishments against their children often, in later life, wonder why their children, on whom they have lavished so much time and care, are so distant from them. The children may be physically distant, living far away and rarely or never visiting, or, though physically close, living nearby and visiting frequently, may be emotionally distant. They do their duty by their parents, and they celebrate Christmases and anniversaries appropriately, but they are impervious to the parents' advice and concern, and their traditional statements of filial affection lack all warmth and conviction. Some such children, believing that they ought to love their parents, mistake worry and guilt for love. For many such parents the nature of their relationship with their children is no different from that which they had with their parents, for they were beaten by their parents as they beat their children, but now they realize, sometimes only dimly, that no matter what we might achieve, what warms and sustains us in later life is the closeness and warmth of the people we have known for a very long time. (Nevertheless, many psychiatrists explain the high incidence of depression in the elderly as resulting from a gene.)

Some parents, rather than beating their children, try to control them by threatening loss of love. 'Mummy won't love you if you do that!' This is a bamboozlement because, if the parent loves the child, then she loves the child all the time, and if she does not love the child, she has no love to threaten to withdraw. A truthful, clear statement would be, 'If you do that I will not behave towards you in a loving way even though I do love you.' But this is not a threat which will inspire fear and obedience. Children, convinced that their parents love them, can tolerate a great deal of unloving behaviour from their parents.

For some children, being threatened with the loss of love is the greatest cruelty a parent can show towards them. Coping with a beating is not impossible for them, because in beating them the parent is taking notice of them. But those children who experience their sense of self as being in relation to other people (extraverts) fear that if they are left completely alone they will disappear. The terror of losing their parents' love, of being totally and utterly rejected, forces them not merely to obey their parents but to relinquish their own way of seeing things, accept their parents', and so remain tied to their parents for the rest of their life. They remain for ever children to their parents and never become adult friends to their parents.

Other children are not so threatened by the withdrawal of love, for they live within the security of their own thoughts and feelings (introverts). They dislike being alone, but loneliness does not threaten their sense of self. They can cope with being alone. Thus, when their parent threatens them with the withdrawal of love, they can use the same tactic on the parent: 'If you won't love me I won't love you.' In this battle the parent wins the first few skirmishes, for the child finds it uncomfortable to share a home with an adult who refuses to speak to him, but in the long run the child wins. Withholding his love from his parent, he becomes indifferent to his parent, and, when the opportunity offers, he leaves home. If, in later life, the parents say to the now adult child, 'I didn't mean it when I said I didn't love you. I loved you all the time,' the child will respond, in deeds if not in words, 'You lied to me in order to manipulate me. When I needed your love you withheld it. I learned to live without your love, and now I do not need it.'

Perhaps the most popular method for keeping children under control is making them feel guilty. The parents present themselves as being completely altruistic and self-sacrificing. Any child who resists them is ungrateful, and to be ungrateful is to be bad. Unfortunately for parents, this is a game which children learn to play very early on, and in families where the parents would never dream of raising a hand to a child, and the children are models of decorum, the battle over who will make whom feel guilty rages fiercely throughout the entire lives of the participants. (More about guilt later, for guilt is a great bamboozlement.)

When I was a teacher in Australia in the fifties, I was expected to enforce the school's rule that the children should not speak as they walked along the corridors and in the classroom unless they were spoken to by the teacher. I was not surprised by this, for the same rule had been enforced when I had been a pupil. I was surprised when I came to England and found that this unnatural silence was not imposed on all school children, and that in the more enlightened schools children were encouraged to work in groups and discuss their work with one another. In such schools the lack of a national curriculum allowed the teachers to develop programmes suited to their particular school and to individual children.

But such education by enlightenment was not supported by politicians who wanted an obedient, uncritical populace, or by parents who believed that children need to be controlled. The development of the National Curriculum in 1989 was a battle between those who wanted to impose complete control on teachers and pupils and those who saw the National Curriculum as simply sensible guidelines, helpful in providing an enlightened education aimed at giving children the knowledge they needed to function effectively in adult life, and to think critically and independently. I hope that the bamboozlers never win this battle and that the National Curriculum never solidifies into the dogma of the national curriculum in the USSR. Martin Walker, a journalist and father of small children, wrote:

> My first sight of a Russian kindergarten – it was 9 a.m., and it was potty drill by numbers. On the first stroke, all the children stood by their lockers and removed potties. On the second stroke, came the teacher's command to drop trousers and sit. On the third stroke, perform.
>
> Thus at school, in a drawing class, there will be 32 children all copying from the same blackboard precisely the same flower, with the same number of petals, the same length of stalk, and the same colours in the same places. This is an approach which makes sense when it comes to mathematics, but it is a curious technique for the drawing of flowers.
>
> Ritual is all. When they recite poetry, which they do very well, and know reams of Pushkin by heart, the children all make the same gestures in the same places. It is uncanny, seeing it done the same way in Alma-Ata near the Chinese frontier as in Murmansk, up in the Arctic Circle . . .
>
> I wonder how Gorbachev's hopes of a Soviet democracy are going to develop with kids who grew up drawing the same kind of flower, and reciting the same Pushkin in exactly the same way.'[18]

An education which insists that all children of a particular age should learn the same thing at the same time teaches children that individual, personal feelings, knowledge, desires, interests and needs are of no importance. They then become confused when they see adults behave in ways which they know are forbidden to them.

"Don't you ever think of anything but money?"[19]

Children who point out the discrepancy between what adults say and what they do are punished for being disrespectful. This confuses children, but it also leaves them determined to do as adults what they were forbidden to do as children. Their unmet needs will be met when they grow up. This hope carries children through the pain, confusion and disappointment of childhood, but it means that as adults we behave very childishly, trying to fulfil the needs and wishes we have brought from childhood. When in adult life we cannot satisfy these needs in the ways we intended, we feel cheated. We believed that the bargain we had made with our parents and teachers was that if we were obedient children we would, as adults, get what we wanted.

Just what we wanted and expected to get in adult life can be much and various, but most children who see their future as including becoming a parent expect that as parents they will get from their children the gratitude which their parents demanded from them.

Many parents who wish to control and punish their children try to make their children feel guilty by saying, 'After all I've done for you, how could you do this?' When my mother used to say this to me when I was a teenager, I would retort, 'I didn't ask to be born!' It seemed to me ridiculous that there was some place filled with unborn babies, all anxious to be born and ready to be very grateful to their parents for going through the set of motions necessary to transport one of these unborn babies through conception and birth. Since my mother would never discuss any subject that had the remotest connection with sex, my answer usually ended the discussion, but she must have been disappointed that she did not get from me the gratitude which she had given all her life to her mother. All her life she had been tied to her mother, and she had been devastated by her mother's death.

Many people, perhaps most, remain tied to their parents by the demand that children should be grateful to their parents. They are unable to see that if we indulge ourselves in those activities which lead to the birth of children, we have a duty to care for those children, and that those children have a duty to care for the children they produce. They cannot see this because they have been bamboozled by their parents' demand for gratitude, and have comforted themselves by believing that they will be rewarded for their goodness by the gratitude they will receive from their children.

It is not just our parents who tell us that we should be grateful for being born. The Church tells us this, and in very powerful ways.

Many people have experiences which they would call 'religious' or 'spiritual'. These are experiences of wonder and a sense of belonging, being part of everything that is. These experiences can be the readily available, direct wonder and reassurance of being close to some sight of great natural beauty, or they can be something strange, wonderful and unique, the kind of experiences which Alister Hardy describes in *The Spiritual Nature of Man*.[20] In giving a meaning to these experiences, some people talk about 'Nature' or 'all that there is', while others talk about God. Of those who talk about God, some use this word to refer to a power which is above and beyond our comprehension and yet exists in all things, while others give to this power a more personal connotation, seeing God as a power with whom they can have a personal relationship. Whatever these experiences may be, and however the person interprets them, such experiences recapture and remind us of the sense of belonging and the rightness of our existence with which we were born. The freedom, uncertainty, incomprehensibility and yet rightness of everything that is come to us as reassurance and exhilaration. We feel whole, unfragmented, and real. We no longer feel that we have to be good in order to have the right to exist. We are pleased that we exist.

Such experiences have never interested those who make up the authority of the Church, and in fact they have always discouraged such experiences because these are private and personal, and create a sense of worth. The Church demands that religious experiences be group activities under the supervision of Church authorities, be it taking the sacrament or speaking in tongues.

These experiences in which we reaffirm our intimate relationship with all there is require no priest or bishop, brethren or elder, to mediate between us and God. The Quakers recognized this, and that such mediation was unnecessary, and so they were persecuted by the Church and State. These experiences affirm in us our own rightness and worth, something which the Christian Church denies.

Instead, the Church teaches that we are born in sin. As the psalmist said, 'Behold, I was shapen in iniquity, and in sin did my mother conceive me.'[21] We have to be grateful to God for allowing us to be born, yet the only way we can be born renders us sinful and unacceptable in God's eyes. If we believe this, and most of us growing up in Christian homes believed it to some greater or lesser extent (after all, were we not being told this by our elders and betters?), we see ourselves as being intrinsically bad and unacceptable. Such a belief made us helpless. We could not go back to the unborn state, and we could not rid ourselves of the taint of original sin. We had to depend on those in power over us to tell us what we should do. To save ourselves we had to be obedient.

The teaching some of us received in Church and Sunday school emphasized the kindliness of Jesus and how He was hurt if we misbehaved. Our sins hurt Him, and we should feel guilty. This teaching impressed me because my father had found that if he looked hurt at my misdemeanours I was rapidly contrite and well behaved. Though I long ago gave up worrying about whether I had hurt Jesus, I still worry if I think I have hurt someone, and I try to make amends.

The teaching that others of us received in church and Sunday school emphasized God's punishments for wickedness. This was very much the style of the nuns and priests of the Catholic church in the Australia I knew in the forties and fifties. I remember a friend laughing as she told me how her five-year-old daughter had been told by the nuns that if she misbehaved in church God's hand would come down out of heaven and slap her. Little Pi believed what she had been told and she was afraid. She was a very good little girl. Many adult Catholics who no longer practise their religion have told me how, when disaster strikes or they feel that they have erred, they feel frightened in the same way as they were frightened by the nuns and priests of their childhood. One friend, Frank Flanagan, told me how, when he was in his twenties, he decided to leave the Catholic church. On the following Sunday he committed the mortal sin of not attending mass. 'I didn't go to mass,' he said, 'and I didn't go out of the house either – just in case.' I cannot ask Pi whether she still feels frightened, because she died of cancer when she was twenty-one. Frank soon found the courage to leave his house, and remained courageous to his death nearly fifty years later.

The idea that we are guilty and will be punished for something over which we have no control is very confusing. So is the idea that our actions and thoughts are being scrutinized by God, and perhaps by our relatives in heaven. When a friend's mother, Lady Betty, was dying in hospital at the end of a long life, she could not rest for fear of what lay ahead of her. 'My mother will never forgive me,' she said. 'She will have heard me say that I hate her.'

Many children are taught to fear hell, and many are taught to fear the devil. Believing in the devil can be useful, for blaming the devil can save us from the difficult task of deciding who is responsible for what happens and how we should react once we have apportioned this responsibility.

After the bombing of the Pan Am jet over Lockerbie, *Today* newspaper reported:

> The minister father of Pan Am victim Helga Mosey said he had forgiven the terrorist bombers. Helga, 19, had been staying with her family in Oldbury, West Midlands before going back to her job in the States. Her Pentecostal father, the Revd John Mosey, said: 'Despite our loss, finding forgiveness in our heart is not a problem. Our anger is directed at the Devil who brings evil into the world.'[22]

By positing the evil in the devil and not in the terrorists or the airline staff responsible for security, the Revd Mosey can feel virtuous while avoiding the problem of how we should deal with the people who are cruel and/or incompetent.

Explaining evil and suffering as the actions of the devil creates the problem of why, if God is all-powerful, does he let the devil exist. One way around this is to say that there is no devil and that whatever happens is what God wills and therefore is good. This is the attitude which many parents try to get their children to adopt towards them. Whatever the parent says, does and orders is good. Why? 'Because I am your parent.'

This is perhaps the most bamboozling of all a parent's attempts at bamboozlement, for it places a sanction on the child's trying to sort out his own lived experience. He sees his parents behaving in ways which are not always kind, loving and just, but he is expected to deny the evidence of his eyes and believe in his parents' incorruptible goodness. He still may not behave in the ways which his parent desires, but he is certainly bamboozled.

How Children Respond

Parents who raise their children using control and bamboozlement create in their children a fear which remains with them in their adult life. Such children continue to feel overwhelmed by their parents, and their adult life is filled with a battle against this sense of powerlessness and the fear of annihilation.

When John first came to see me, he talked only of his difficulties in social situations when, as he burned with embarrassment, he felt entirely weak and useless. Yet he was a fine, big man with a commanding presence, a teacher much admired and loved by his students, and an excellent artist. For the first months of our meetings John talked only of his shortcomings. He spoke of his childhood only to show that he had always been weak and inadequate. Gradually these references to childhood broadened into explaining to me the circumstances of some events.

His mother was quiet, always downtrodden by her husband, a big, masculine man who rode motorbikes and insisted that his little son should have his hair cut so that he did not look like a girl. His father left the family home when John was ten, and John went to live with his grandmother. He met his father only once in his adult life, and then only to discover that his father had no interest in him.

Sometimes, as the months went by, John would talk about his painting. He showed me some of his work – scenes of rugged coastlines and portraits – and it was easy to see that when he was not frozen by self-consciousness he was a very talented artist.

Initially John was surprised when I suggested to him that there was a connection between the difficulties he had had with his father, and the difficulties he had in adult life with men in authority over him. He thought this over, and conceded the possibility. One evening, when we were talking about this, I asked, 'Have you ever drawn a picture of your father?'

He said no, but the next time he came to see me he brought a large package. He said, 'I've done my homework. I've drawn a picture of my father. I didn't think about it. I just did it. I was surprised how it came out.'

The picture was large, at least three feet by two, and much more impressive, more overwhelming than the reproduction shown here.

The picture is drawn from the viewpoint of a small boy looking up at an overwhelmingly powerful figure. John was struck by the fact that he had not, as he could have done, drawn the features of his father's face. But a small boy would not have seen the individual features, just the potential menace of the face. What he saw most clearly was the solid trunk of his father's body and the great hands

'You Can't Have Everything' – Parents

which came towards him, sometimes bearing joy but often pain. When John drew this picture he was forty-nine years old.

What ties us to parents who control and bamboozle us is that they both reward and punish us. The vast body of psychological research on the function of rewards and punishment in learning shows that when animals – white rats, pigeons and people – are *always* rewarded for carrying out some action, they soon come to take the source of that reward for granted, be it a lever which on pressing produces a pellet of food, or an adult who always smiles and welcomes. When animals are *always* punished for carrying out some action, they soon come to avoid the source of that punishment completely, be it a lever which on pressing produces an electric shock or an adult who always slaps. When animals are sometimes rewarded and sometimes punished according to a pattern which the animal can neither predict nor control, the animal remains fascinated by the source of the rewards and punishments, and keeps going back, braving the electric shocks in the hope of a reward, losing money in the fruit machine in the hope of getting more, suffering in the pain inflicted by the parent whose unconditional love is so devoutly longed for.

Many parents and adult children stay together as a family, not because they care about one another, but because the children are still trying to get the parents to reveal themselves as the people their children want them to be. Keith had no practical reason why he should live near and work with his father who had always treated him badly. His father was a rogue, and yet Keith would keep lending him large sums of money for his business. His father would promise to repay the money in regular instalments, but would cease to do this after the first instalment was paid. Keith knew that the only way he could get his father to repay the money was for Keith to have a fight with him and then not go to see him. Keith hated to do this. He wanted a quiet life, and he did not want to hurt his father. (Keith was an extravert and wanted to be liked.)

When I asked Keith why he had not learned from experience and ceased to lend his father money, he said that he kept hoping that his father would 'do the right thing'. Keith knew quite well that there was as much chance of this as Ian Paisley coming to love the Pope, but he could not stop trying. One day, he hoped, his father would show himself to be honest and true.

When the punishments the child has received have been large and brutal, and when the punishing parent has been the sole source of the rewards, the child not only remains tied to the parent but becomes compelled in adult life to seek out other people who will treat the child as the parent did. The heroine of Anna Mitgutsch's novel *Punishment* said:

I have removed the cotton stocking from the blue bruises and am displaying my bloody welts, waiting breathlessly all my life for the next whipping. It's never long in coming, because the wounds are like blossoms, red bait for birds of prey; they sink their claws into the wounds greedily and tear them open until they are sated and peaceful . . . I really don't enjoy being tortured, but I know that I have to be punished because I am a bad person and unworthy of love. When you beat me I know there is order in the world: no one can be trusted and I can stop suffering the pains of love; I can kick you in the teeth because your evident pleasure in torturing me incriminates you. Therefore I change mothers and lovers like shirts, and in the end they all have the same face in my disappointment, from which I arise laughing with pain because I never expected anything else.[23]

Children give their parents enormous power. They want their parents to be the purveyors of the Absolute Truth because that gives them a sense of security. Reality then is not confused and mysterious. It is organized and clear, just as the parents describe it. Many parents accept this power, even parents who see their children's education as the process of enlightenment. They want their children to be enlightened in the same way as they are. Children who invest and are encouraged to invest such power in their parents are shocked and disillusioned when they discover that their parents can be mistaken. Edmund Gosse's parents loved him dearly, but they both presented to the little boy a picture of a father who knew and was right about everything. Gosse recorded his shock at discovering that this was not so:

In the course of this, my sixth year, there happened a series of minute and soundless incidents which, elementary as they may seem when told, were second in real importance to none in my mental history . . . What came to me was the consciousness of self, as a force and a companion, and it came as the result of one or two shocks, which I will relate.

In consequence of hearing so much about an Omniscient God, a being of supernatural wisdom and penetration who was always with us, who made, in fact, a fourth in our company, I had come to think of Him, not without awe, but with absolute confidence. My Father and Mother, in their serene discipline of me, never argued with one another, never even differed; their wills seemed absolutely one. My Mother always deferred to my Father, and in his absence always spoke of him to me as if he were all-wise. I confused him in some sense with God; at all events I believed that my Father knew everything and saw everything. One morning in my sixth year, my Mother and I were alone in the morning room, when my Father came in and announced some fact to us. I was standing on the rug, gazing at him, and when he made this statement, I remember turning quickly, in embarrassment, and looking into the fire. The shock to me was as that of a thunderbolt, for what my Father said 'was not true'. My Mother and I, who had been present at the trifling incident, were aware that it had not happened exactly as it had been reported to him. My Mother gently told him so, and he accepted the correction. Nothing could have been more trifling to my parents, but to me it meant an epoch. Here was the appalling discovery, never suspected before, that my Father was not as God, and did not know everything. The shock was not caused by any suspicion that he was not telling the truth, as it appeared to him, but by the awful proof that he was not, as I had supposed, omniscient.[24]

Out of this discovery Gosse made another discovery, that of his self. Because his parents valued him, he had retained much of his sense of his own worth, and so he could value his self, but, like all children when they discover that their parents are fallible, he had to keep this discovery of self secret. Gosse, describing how he, as a child, had discovered that he could deceive his parents about a small misdemeanour, wrote:

In the first place, the theory that my Father was omniscient was now dead and buried. He probably knew very little; in this case he had not known a fact of such importance that if you did not know that, it could hardly matter what you knew. My Father, as a deity, as a natural force of immense prestige, fell in my eyes to a human level. In future, his statements about things in general need not be accepted implicitly. But of all the thoughts which rushed upon my savage and undeveloped brain at this crisis, the most curious was that I had found a companion and a confidant in myself. There was a secret in this world and it belonged to me and to a somebody who lived in the same body with me. There were two of us, and we could talk to one another. It is difficult to define impressions so rudimentary, but it is certain that it was in this dual form that the sense of my individuality now suddenly descended upon me, and it is equally certain that it was a great solace to me to find a sympathizer in my own breast . . .

Through thick and thin I clung to a hard nut of individuality, deep down in my childish nature. To the pressure from without I resigned everything else, my thoughts, my words, my anticipations, my assurances, but there was something which I never resigned, my innate and persistent self. Meek as I seemed, and gently respondent, I was always conscious of that innermost quality which I had learned to recognize in my earlier days in Islington, that existence of two in the depths who could speak to one another in inviolable secrecy.[25]

Edmund Gosse's book *Father and Son*, first published in 1907, shocked its readers because, for the first time in the history of biography, a son was being critical of his father. Until then sons writing about their fathers could only praise and never criticize, certainly never, as Gosse did, show the intimate web of love and hurt that is the relationship between children and parents. Philip Gosse loved his son, but he also wanted to control him by instilling in him the same passionate, all-encompassing religious beliefs which he himself held. Edmund, having discovered his self, resisted, using the defence which all children under pressure from adults use.

> In earlier years certain sides of my character had offered a sort of passive resistance to his ideas. I had let what I did not care to welcome pass over my mind in the curious density that children adopt in order to avoid receiving impressions – blankly, dumbly, achieving by stupidity what they cannot achieve by argument.[26]

Stupidity used as a defence can become a habit, the resistance to thinking which many adults have. Hence the popularity of the *Sun* over the *Guardian*.

Philip Gosse, having decided that his son was specially chosen by God, pressured Edmund to let this goodness shine forth in holy ways. This made Edmund keenly aware that he could not achieve what his father wanted because he was an ordinary person and wanted to be an ordinary person who enjoyed the pleasures of life. Other parents, having decided that their children are intrinsically bad, pressure them to become good. Such children cannot maintain a sense of goodness in the face of what their parents tell them and what they know of their own childish inadequacies. Many such children comfort themselves with the belief that they are capable, not just of being good, but of being perfect. Perfection becomes their only acceptable standard for themselves and the world.

Believing that you are capable of perfection breeds personal pride, and so does the belief that the world ought to be perfect in the way that you define perfection. Pride will allow us to believe all kinds of nonsensical things, and the belief in perfection is one of these. It overlooks the fact that the only way we can perceive anything is when there is some kind of contrast or differential. We know light only because there is dark, heat only because there is cold, life only because there is death, and perfection only because there is imperfection. If we lived in a perfect world we would not know it was perfect.

The belief in the perfectibility of oneself and the world causes much grief – guilt, shame, anger, resentment, bitterness and disappointment. The holders of this belief prevent themselves from accepting and so enjoying themselves and their world. They would rather be disappointed than happy.

Whenever we know something we also know its opposite, and all this knowledge links together in the continuous network of meaning which we each create. Parents who control and bamboozle their children overlook this fact when they try to ensure that the children learn only what they want them to learn. Because children are a different generation from their parents, their experience of the world around them is different, and so they put together a network of personal meaning which is different from what their parents expect. An example of this was given in the march on Westminster on 28 May 1989, by British Muslims protesting about Salman Rushdie's book, *The Satanic Verses*. Ed Vulliamy wrote:

> When the fighting had subsided at the end of the Muslim march through London on Saturday, Abdul Razvi from Slough, wearing an orthodox lace cap, long robes and a long beard, cupped his hands to his mouth to cry: 'Nave Takbir' – a resounding call to those sitting in the road on Westminster Bridge. 'Allah Huakbar' – God is Great – came the thunderous response; but Razvi's audience did not look like him. They wore denim and leather jackets, Levi 501 jeans and training shoes. They were mainly teenagers; one wore an Aston Villa strip, another sported a T-shirt with 'Dewsbury-Batley Anti-Rushdie Squad' printed on the back . . . One T-shirt read 'Enjoy Cocaine' in a Coca-cola logo . . . Some of the demonstrators' banners would rival for innovation those at a scouse FA Cup final, albeit a little more ghoulish, such as, 'RSPCA Cannot Help a Rush-Puppy' or 'Don't P-p-p-pick up a Penguin' . . . One of the last banners to leave the scene read 'Ayatollah, You'll Never Walk Alone'.[27]

So children, each creating a network of meaning, which incorporates some of their parents' ideas modified by their own experience, grow to adulthood. Their education has taught them nothing of how to be a parent. Their only experience of being a parent is being a child, and so they grow up and do to their children what was done to them.

When Children Become Adults

As children we take the rules of our family to be the rules of the universe, and so we confuse what we could have with what we can't.

We go on to do to children what was done to us.

Because we are taught that we live in a Just World we lose our capacity to enjoy ourselves. We can no longer take each day as it comes, enjoying moments of pleasantness in the present – sunlight on water, a talk with a friend, the satisfaction of a job well done – because everything that happens has to be assessed in terms of the past and the future. Is this a reward for something I have done right? Will I have to pay a price for this pleasure?

Losing the multitude of pleasures that are freely available to us, we then have to construct pseudo-pleasures and try to persuade ourselves that we enjoy them. Sex ceases to be fun and becomes a compulsory activity with rules and standards, virtues and taboos, which supports the industries of pornography and the media. Sport ceases to be fun and becomes a vast competition where the prizes are wealth and notoriety and the punishments for failure ignominy and humiliation. Games of chance cease to be fun and become a multibillion industry[28] where the players believe that they are challenging the operation of the Just World. Travel ceases to be fun and becomes a reward for being good which supports a multibillion industry and which often leads to disappointment and misery, and not just for the travellers.

The feet of tourists are turning the paths of the great gardens of the world into ditches. The exhalations of tourist breath are corroding the columns of the great castles and mansions. The camera flashes of tourists are bleaching the painted masterpieces in galleries and on cave walls. The suntan of tourists is poisoning fish. Then tourists sign their names with pride on the revered sites.[29]

Because we are taught that our own truth is not truth but 'subjective' misapprehensions which, not being 'objective', can never be certain and true[30] and can often be wicked, we lose the ability to understand the sentences which we utter. We no longer see that when we speak what we believe is the 'objective' truth, we are describing how we have constructed our own world of meaning.

Thus a psychiatrist might say, 'I think that the evidence shows that depression is a result of biochemical change.'

A priest might say, 'I believe that in the world we see the working of God's will.'

The psychiatrist and priest would probably have studied grammar at school, but they do not apply their knowledge to their own sentences. If they did they would see how their own construction of meaning is the centre of their sentence on which the rest of the sentence depends.

Complex sentences consist of a principal clause and subordinate clauses. Here, in the first sentence, the principal clause is 'I think', and in the second sentence the principal clause is 'I believe'.

Clauses and simple sentences consist of a subject and predicate. In 'I think' the subject is 'I', and in 'I believe' the subject is 'I'.

Because we have been taught to hide the fact that the sentences we utter arise out of the constructions of meaning we have made, we have evolved many ways of hiding 'I think' and 'I believe' principal clauses in our sentences.

We keep the principal clause silent and say, 'The evidence shows that depression is a result of biochemical change.' Or we use the passive voice form of the verb to hide who is doing the thinking or believing by saying, 'The workings of God can be seen in the world.' Or we make the person doing the thinking and believing impersonal with 'Research shows,' 'One believes.' In scientific journals the prose style required so hides the person of the researcher that we could be led to believe that the experiment did itself and the report wrote itself. This prose style enables scientists to lie about what actually did happen in the experiment, and they all do, for no experiment ever goes exactly as planned with the scientist always in control of events. In religious circles the spoken and written discourses hide the person by assuming that all of the faithful believe in the One Truth, and that this Truth is not a composite of many different truths but stands on its own, an entity separate from the minds of its believers.

This pretence that there is a Scientific Truth or a Religious Truth which exists outside the minds of people prevents us from discovering and improving how we operate as a group. We do not see that we have been born into a family which might, over the years, have constructed a composite meaning which might be 'This family sticks together', and that this construction is interpreted by each member in a different way.

Because we have been taught to disregard our own individual truth, we fail to understand our wanting everything which lies at the centre of our truth. Because we cannot confront this wanting everything, we cannot understand it and then use this understanding to construct a way of living which allows us to match our wanting everything to what the world will allow, so that, while we might not get everything, we get enough to feel satisfied and, at the same time, not cause suffering to ourselves and others. Instead, we develop devious ways of expressing our wanting everything. We become greedy and envious, and we seek power.

5

'Yes I Can' – *Power*

**'Politics is not another subject. It is
everything. It is your life.'[1]**

A vast sea of faces. One man above them, haranguing them. He raises
his hands, and they all roar their assent.

A crowd surging forward. In front of them massed ranks of helmeted men with batons and shields. They break ranks and charge the
crowd, smashing and beating as they go.

A child facing an angry parent. The parent orders, 'Go to your
room!' The child obeys.

The bomb-bay doors of a vast plane open and a stream of huge black
bombs fall to earth far below. Small mushrooms of dust appear on the
terrain.

A penitent kneeling in front of a priest. The priest raises his hand
in blessing. 'Go in peace and sin no more.'

The skyscraper canyons of a big city. People scurrying about. A
newspaper headline, 'Share Prices Shock'.

These are familiar scenes of power in action. They come into being
when we try to impose our constructions of meaning on to other
people. We do this in the attempt to gain everything through the
medium of political, economic, religious or personal power.

Because these scenes of power are so familiar to us, we often fail to
recognize the operation of power in our own lives. We often fail to
recognize that we are always engaged in trying to impose our own
power on others and to resist the imposition of other people's power
on us. We have to do this in order to survive as a person, but most
frequently we engage in the imposition of our own construction of
meanings and resistance to other people's constructions, not just to
maintain and defend ourselves, but in the vain attempt to get everything. We suffer much in this attempt, and we get very little of what
we want.

Imposing and Accepting Constructions

Power is the right to define how others should define.

We all want this right, but we do not want the hard work of working
out the definitions of everything. So we accept other people's defi-

nitions for some areas of our experience, but mark out other areas as our own.

Thus a child will willingly accept his parents' definitions of who he is and where he lives, but try to insist on his own right to define what he eats and what he wears. A political leader will willingly accept the definitions by others which put him in his powerful position, but will want to rule the country in the way he thinks best. Henry VIII was pleased to accept other people's construction about the Divine Right of Kings, but wanted to impose his own constructions about divorce.

There are many ways in which we can impose and accept constructions.

We can find that other people impose their constructions on us forcibly, with such violence and threats that we cower, feeling helpless, and, so doing, we accept the other's constructions and abandon our own. A small child being beaten by his parent abandons his construction that he is loved for himself and accepts his parents' definition of him as being bad. For a few brief weeks in 1989 many Chinese constructed the belief that their lives would be freer and happier, but their army, at the behest of the old men in Beijing, destroyed this construction and reimposed the construction of duty and obedience.

We can find that other people impose their constructions on us benevolently. They engage our interest, and, feeling grateful and supported, we accept their constructions and abandon our own. This is a much more effective way of imposing constructions than using violence. A child being taught by a kindly parent or teacher will willingly accept that person's constructions. 'Television,' wrote David Smail, 'is a much more powerful means of ensuring uniformity of belief than was the Inquisition.'[2]

The benevolent attempts at imposition are not always made for our own benefit. Often we are being persuaded to accept the other's constructions so that certain people can maintain or extend their power.

A vicar who is an official exorcist has sounded a strong warning to stay away from seances or risk receiving dangerous threats. The Revd Tom Willis, the Vicar of Holy Trinity Church, Bridlington, makes the warning in his church magazine. The vicar, the official exorcist for the York diocese, writes 'We are strictly forbidden to contact the dead through mediums, fortune-tellers or seances. To try to do so is a serious sin. People who have tried to contact the dead through their own efforts report, at first, they receive pleasant and accurate information.' But he claims, 'After a while, when they had begun to trust the source of this information, disturbing and bogus messages were passed, threatening death or serious injury.' Mr Willis, who has conducted several exorcisms, said yesterday, '. . . I believe these messages come from disturbed or evil influences or spirits. [People] should steer clear of trying to make any contact with the dead directly.'[3]

Or, 'My magic is good magic and yours is bad.'

When we are aware that others are trying to persuade us to abandon our constructions and accept theirs, we can shield ourselves from their efforts and maintain our own constructions. Children soon learn how to think their own thoughts while being instructed by parents and teachers, and we all learn how to be sceptical of the propaganda put out by politicians and advertisers.

When we want to impose our constructions we can simply display them, hoping that other people will be interested and modify their constructions accordingly rather than being sceptical and resistant. Whether we are small children keen to tell an adult something we have discovered, whether we are writing a book, painting a picture, or preparing a political speech, if we are going to display our constructions we have to feel reasonably certain that our audience will accept what we have to say. In case our audience rejects our constructions, we can hedge our constructions with statements which claim to show that our statements are not merely our constructions but come from some higher authority ('The Bible says . . .'), or are statements of obvious truth ('As all right thinking people will agree . . .'), or are a disinterested search for truth ('To put the record straight . . .').

When simply displaying our constructions fails, and what we want to impose on others is very important to us, we can use violence and become a child bullying another child, a parent punishing a child, a teacher disciplining a class, a dictator, a soldier, a terrorist.

All of these processes go on simultaneously all the time, an intense interaction of the political and the personal. Often the imposition of one person's constructions on to another is done with the best of intentions, but the end result is that we are all caught, unwittingly and uncomprehendingly, in a vast churning web of power.

> It is not that parents harbour any evil intent towards their children, and it is the cruellest of errors to suppose that they do by, for example, dragging the concept of blame into a consideration of who causes whom psychological injury or distress. It is rather that, in a culture in which we have no articulate concept of the loving use of power (and if we had one in the past we have lost it), we are thrown together in contexts – as for example families – in which our relations are going inevitably to be shaped by the social forms of the wider environment.
>
> I do not think it is any exaggeration to say that we are approaching a state of affairs in which we simply do not know how to relate to one another except coercively and exploitingly, and the

effects of this are going to be particularly severe in cases where – as between children and adults – there are gross disparities in power. My reasons for feeling this are based on no mere abstract consideration of social speculations or political theory, but on the endlessly and dishearteningly repeated experience of witnessing the deformation and ineradicable emotional scarring of people who were once children of parents whose only conscious wish was to love them.[4]

This passage written by David Smail, psychologist and psychotherapist, introduces a description of how, within the hierarchy of class, we are caught in the vast churning web of power that is society.[5]

In the turmoil of trying to impose our constructions and resisting other people's impositions, accepting some constructions from other people, and trying to mark out the areas where we have the right to impose our own constructions, we can be helped or hindered by the constructions established by the society in which we live. In a patriarchal society it is much easier for a man to mark out an area as his own than for a woman to do so. In a repressive regime people are prevented by the State from claiming any area of any significance as their own. The food shortages in Communist countries were not simply the result of inefficiency in the food production and distribution industries. The State has no desire to make the purchasing and preparation of food quick and easy, for that would leave the citizens with time to be involved in other matters. The queuing system in shops where the desired purchase is selected at one counter, paid for at another, and collected at another is as much a way of preventing people from resisting the State's imposition of its constructions as is the system of military repression and the secret police.

In the struggle to impose and to resist constructions we battle over what demarcations we can claim as our own. Parents and children battle over who has the right to decide what time the children go to bed. A judge fining a journalist for refusing to reveal a source of his information represents a clash between the State and the individual.[6] The legal case following a Christian Scientist couple's reliance on prayer instead of medical help for their dying child is a battle both between the rights of parents and the rights of the child, and between the rights of religion and the rights of the State.[7]

Often we accept other people's rights to impose constructions in certain areas, and then object to the constructions which they make. Parents of teenagers may grant their children the right to choose their own clothes, and then be horrified at their children's choice of clothes. While the Reverend Ian Paisley accepts that Roman Catholics are correct in their definition of themselves as children in the eyes of God just as Protestants are, he says that they are wrong to believe that a mere man calling himself the Pope or the priest can act in the place of God.

So to be powerful we have to get other people to accept our right *and* our definitions in the exercise of that right.

This is not easy to do for, as Abraham Lincoln said, 'You can fool all of the people some of the time, and some of the people all the time, but you cannot fool all of the people all of the time.' (This quotation, very popular in my youth, is rarely heard nowadays, no doubt because it strikes at the very heart of the advertising and public relations industry.) *Power is an illusion because it is no more than a meaning which the powerful have created and which the powerless accept as reality.*

Hedrick Smith in *The Power Game*, a study of how power operates in the USA, wrote:

> Power depends heavily on the illusion of power. Presidents – past, present and future – have less power than the country imagines, but the successful ones convey the impression of power and get reputations as strong presidents by playing down their problems and trumpeting their few clear victories.[8]

He explained the immense popularity of Ronald Reagan as President by the fact that Reagan likes people and that

> [he] has been helped by a couple of other important intangibles; one is grasping power lightly. Bryce Harlow remarked to me that one vital secret for presidents and other top officials is to avoid appearing too hungry to wield power. Both press and public, he said, mistrust politicians who lust too obviously for power, as, he pointed out, was the case with Johnson and Nixon. Jimmy Carter, too, created problems by being so eager to exercise power that he became enmeshed in too many fights on too many fronts. Certainly Secretary of State Alexander Haig and White House Chief of Staff Donald Regan suffered from power hunger as well.
>
> 'Reagan is not a power hungry guy,' suggested Lee Atwater, who helped run Reagan's 1984 campaign and later became campaign manager for Vice-President Bush. 'Nixon was power hungry. Johnson was power hungry. Carter was power hungry. Look at the guys who were run out of town by the media – the guys who were obsessed with power. Reagan stays detached. He's got a Zen approach to power. He doesn't care about power for power's sake alone. Eisenhower is the only other person who had the same detached way of holding power.'[9]

Hedrick Smith called his book *The Power Game* because, he argues, in the USA power is treated as a game, and

> [w]e Americans are a nation of game players. From Friday night poker and Sunday bingo to corporate rivalry and the nuclear arms

race, Americans are preoccupied with winning and losing. Competition is our creed; it is knit into the fabric of our national life. Sports and game shows are national pastimes. Either we play games ourselves or we take part vicariously. We swim, cycle, jog or play tennis – making it a game by matching ourselves against a rival, against par in golf, or against the stopwatch when we hike or run. Five out of six Americans spend several hours a week viewing football, baseball, boxing, bowling or some other sport on television. One hundred million people tune into television game shows weekly – forty-three million to *Wheel of Fortune*. All over the world, people are playing at commerce on one hundred million sets of Monopoly. Some people see life as a game, to be won or lost, instead of seeing it in terms of a religious ethic or of some overarching set of values.[10]

Seeing power as a game means knowing that power is a construction, a fiction, for the rules which make up any game are fictions; but there are many people who take game playing as seriously as those people who regard their political creed or their religious beliefs as the Ultimate and Absolute Truth. So the Power Game is played fiercely and uncompromisingly.

The rules of all games simplify reality. Games are played in certain places, by certain people, in certain ways. This is one of the reasons why games are so popular. Reality itself is so complex. Hedrick Smith commented:

> There is a strong urge for simplicity in the American psyche, a compulsion to focus on the single dramatic figure at the summit, to reduce the intricacy of a hundred power-plays to the simple equation of whether the president is up or down, winning or losing on any given day of the week. Television and the viewing millions seek to make a simple narrative out of complex events. Television news feeds the public appetite to treat events as binary – good or bad – up or down – progress or setback – winners or losers – and to push aside more complex layers of reality.[11]

Just how true this is was shown in Andrew Stephen's report in the *Observer* in March, 1990.

> There was something both poignant and infuriating about the scene on the lawn across the road from the White House last Friday lunchtime, especially for a reporter from this newspaper. Scores of television crews jostled for good positions, not least because two of the country's leading personalities had turned out: Tom Brokaw and Dan Rather, presenters of the NBC and CBS television news programmes.
> A former hostage, a priest, read the 23rd Psalm. Little girls

wearing yellow sashes paraded solemnly. A man played a waver-ing lament on a horn. Prayers were said under the hot sun. Later, a young mother rushed forward to ask Brokaw to pose with her baby.

It was a peculiarly American occasion: a mixture of very real, deeply-felt emotion and orchestrated mawkishness. Hatred, impotence, self-interest, somehow merged with compassion, suf-fering, human kindness and love. 'We are the American people,' said Peggy Say, sister of Terry Anderson, the American journalist whose fifth year in captivity in the Lebanon was being marked. She was talking directly to his captors: 'You have humiliated us and degraded us. You have shamed us, you have beaten and killed us, and you have angered us.'

The message was painfully clear. America, the great can-do nation could do nothing to free these Western hostages – and it was enraging . . .

It was poignant because the suffering of the hostages and their families was so real, and everyone there so palpably well-meaning. It was infuriating because Farzad Bazoft had *already* been forgotten. Hanged last Thursday, relegated here to an inside foreign news page in the *Washington Post* and a story with a hope-lessly inaccurate headline in the *New York Times* on Friday, and not a simple mention of it at the White House hostages demon-stration. A faraway man with a faraway name had been hanged. Story over. It had been much the same before. The White House refused point-blank to comment on the fact that a journalist from a British newspaper had been sentenced to death by Iraq: the State Department did not even bother to return our calls.

In America, a *cause célèbre* either attracts the Rathers and Brokaws, proliferates, and then starts to impinge hugely on the national consciousness (as in the case of Anderson and the other hostages) or it simply never takes off (as with Bazoft).

The implications, with a President as ruled by public opinion polls and swings of national mood as is George Bush, are alarm-ing. Following brief mentions on the TV news on Thursday, Brokaw, Rather and Co made no further reference to Bazoft's execution. America was not therefore up in arms about it (indeed, only vaguely aware of it), because the story did not fit in easily with the simplicities of TV news.

Had Bazoft been a British journalist working for a British news-paper, it would doubtless be very different. America would be collectively outraged, and therefore so would Bush. But Bazoft was an Iranian. Iran took 53 American hostages and humiliated the United States. Iran was at war with Iraq. That makes the Iraqis the good guys, right? Wrong, of course: but it's too hard to explain in the precious seconds of network TV news . . . It takes the violent killing of a non-Western reporter for the *Observer* to show how such deep, real feelings have now been packaged into easily digestible, all-important airtime, and how arbitrarily, and even cynically, the emotions are thus channelled and policy made by the likes of George Bush.[12]

In March 1991, Andrew Stephen told me that, although he and his staff in the USA searched most carefully, as far as he knows there is no evidence that George Bush or any other senior official ever mentioned Farzad Bazoft during the Gulf War.

The illusion of power is maintained not just by simplification but by unawareness and silence. John Pilger, writing of the changes in Europe in the winter of 1990, said:

In 1977 I interviewed many of the Charter 77 people shortly after their organization was forced underground. I was much moved by their political and intellectual courage in seeking democratic forms of their own. They were adamant in rejecting, as one of them put it, 'the way of Washington, Germany, London'.

They knew that, just as socialism had been subverted in their own country, so democracy had been devalued and often degraded in the West. I attended a secret meeting in Prague in which speaker after speaker warned of the dangers of adopting the 'values' embodied in Nato, an organization which had legitimized the Brezhnev Doctrine and thereby reinforced their own oppression.

They also understood – unlike many of us in the West – that state power in the democracies is enforced not with tanks but with illusions, notably that of free expression: in which the voice of the people is heard but what it says is subjected to legislation and a pliant media. The American sage Walter Lippman, cited by Noam Chomsky, called this 'manufacture of consent' and warned that such 'false consensus' could render a free society passive and obedient.

In 1977 the banned Czech writer Zdener Urbanak told me, 'You in the West have a problem. You are unsure when you are being lied to, when you are being tricked. We do not suffer from this; and, unlike you, we have acquired the skill of reading between the lines.'[13]

The only way we can effectively resist the imposition of other people's constructions on to us is to know that those constructions are no more than constructions. Then we can protect ourselves just as we as children protected ourselves with 'Sticks and stones can break my bones, but names will never hurt me!'

But if we do that we have to see that our own constructions which we seek to impose on other people are themselves nothing but constructions. Whether we as Prime Minister declare 'My government's policies are correct and just and will be implemented', or, as a parent, 'I'm your father. Do what I tell you', we are simply imposing our constructions. If we recognize this, we can never feel secure in the sense of personal significance which power gives us.

"I love the absolute power that goes with my job.
It allows me to be myself." 14

But, no matter if we do achieve great power, enabling us to force other people to accept that we have the right to define a certain part of reality and to accept the definitions which we make, we soon discover that power does not give us everything.

Why Power Does Not Give Us Everything

The trick of being powerful is to get people to believe that Category One definitions (the way in which we each choose to define ourselves and our world) are actually Category Two (the nature of human life).

If we remain aware that we have performed this deception, or have allowed our supporters to do that for us, we know ourselves to be a fraud, and our happiness and sense of satisfaction can never be complete. If we allow ourselves to be persuaded that the Category One definitions which keep us in power are actually Category Two, and that it is a rule of the universe that we are so powerful, we soon lose touch with what is actually happening, and when reality forces itself on us we are dismayed and confounded. King Charles I believed that the Divine Right of Kings was an aspect of God's will which created him as king and gave him the right to make the laws of England. He was greatly surprised to discover that many of his subjects did not share this belief. His inability to see that his Category Two belief was actually a Category One belief led inevitably to his death. His son, Charles II, knew that the power of the king was a Category One definition and that his power could be taken away from him at any time. So he went warily and survived, at least until he fell into the hands of doctors who treated him according to what they thought were the absolute truths of medical practice and inflicted on him a lingering, painful death.

Charles II's doctors would not admit that they did not know how to cure him. Such an admission would have shown them to be much less powerful than they actually were. The medical profession has always had a great reluctance to admit ignorance and a great propensity to claim certainty where the reality is doubt. Doctors do this not just to maintain the power and prestige of their profession. As individuals they need to reassure themselves that the meanings they have given to their experience are reliable and true. They feel uncomfortable when the only meaning they can give to some part of their experience is 'I don't know'.

This is true for all of us. When inexplicable events occur, our feelings range from discomfort to terror, and to cope with these unpleasant feelings we have to give these events a meaning which purports to explain them. Once we have done this, even if the effects of the events still trouble us, we feel more secure. The continued popularity of Unidentified Flying Objects is a testament to this. For many people the fact that the Earth's atmosphere can produce strange sights and our own machinery of vision can play tricks on us is not sufficient explanation for such unusual events. They want an explanation which has the appearance of solidity and reality, no matter what greater uncertainties such explanations bring in their train. The explanation that our planet is visited by people from outer space contains the familiar concepts of 'people somewhat like us', 'distant home', and 'travel'. But then there are questions of what kind of people, how they travelled such vast distances, and why these visits are seen by so few.

The problem for all of us, for as long as we have existed as a species and as individuals, is that so many of the events we encounter are inexplicable. Scientists are increasingly able to explain *how* something happened – the rubber rings on the Challenger's booster rockets failed to act as expected, the earthquake measured 6.5 on the Richter scale, the virus altered the functioning of the auto-immune system. We can be satisfied with the scientists' explanations of disasters when these disasters pose no threat to us. But when they do, knowing *how* something happened is not enough. We need to know *why*. Is this disaster a result of some malign influence directed by our enemies, or a malevolent god? Is this disaster the result of our own ineptitude, stupidity, or wickedness? Are we being punished by those we have injured or by a judgemental god? Or, most frightening of all, did this disaster happen by chance, a random error in the pattern of the universe where we are helpless in the face of the unknown?

The notions that disasters occur by chance came late in the development of our species. 'Primitive' people explained sickness and death solely in terms of revenge by enemies or punishment by gods for wickedness. We, 'non-primitive' people, still find it hard to accept the notion of chance. Many of us, when we discover that we harbour rogue cancer cells, cry, 'Why should this happen to me?' Many of us, when disaster quite unconnected with us strikes our children, feel guilty. 'If only I had been a better person this would not have happened.' We do these things because being resentful or guilty, painful though these feelings are, is easier to bear than feeling helpless in a universe which is indifferent to our fate.

Even if disaster never strikes us, we still have to face the questions, 'Who am I?', 'How did I get here?', 'Where am I going?', 'What is the meaning of life?' Whenever we turn our attention away from the everyday business of living, and experience and question our sense of existing, we encounter something so vast, so mysterious and inexplicable, that we respond with profound sadness and sometimes terror.

Life is strange, and, for me, the strangeness never diminishes. When I have said this to certain people they have recoiled, insisting that life is not strange, that it is ordinary, and the pattern clear. These were the people to whom to admit the strangeness of life was to look into the abyss. Instead, they assured me that if I believed in Jesus Christ I would see all of life as clearly meaningful.

This is what religious belief does. It takes all those inexplicable things – disasters, loss, death, the strangeness of being – and gives them an explanation. Religious belief is our response to our fear of the unknown and inexplicable.

Once we have given something a meaning we feel more secure. But religious belief offers more than this. It offers us a share in some greater power. We need not feel helpless in the face of the unknown.

By prayer, incantation, by living a good life, we are sustained and protected by a great power.

So it is not surprising that religious belief is popular and that every society has evolved at least one religion. However, while all religions claim that their God will make their believers secure and happy in the next world if not in this, such total security and happiness is not possible for one simple reason. Everything which happens has both good and bad implications.

All religions teach that if we are good in the way that the religion defines, nothing bad will happen to us. So when disasters strike, believers find themselves caught in the powerful trap of feeling resentful for having been treated unfairly, or feeling guilty for having been bad. As a way out of this trap, Christians are encouraged to believe that their suffering will be rewarded in Heaven, and this has led many Christians actively to seek suffering and to inflict it on other people for the good of their souls. Many people brought up in the Christian Church believe that they ought not be happy, and, indeed, if we believe that the universe is governed by a Grand Design where goodness is rewarded and badness punished, we can never simply enjoy good fortune but must purchase it with good thoughts and deeds.

Because we create our religious beliefs to explain the inexplicable, the power which we seek to share is the power of magic. Magic has always been popular as a way of attempting to be powerful and to get everything. It is also a way of overcoming our fear that, while we are dependent on this fecund but rather dangerous planet and the vagaries of its weather, we are aware of the planet and the universe, but the planet and the universe are not aware of us. We always like to think of ourselves being at the centre of the universe (my friend Ron Janoff, who is devoted to New York, says that New York is the centre of the universe, but my neighbours in Sheffield would insist that the centre of the universe is Yorkshire), and we like to think that the universe is aware of us. After all, do not the planets in their courses determine our lives? We like to think that Mother Earth cares for us and that, as well as reaping her fruits, we can tap into her magical and bountiful nourishment. The prediction from scientists that the alterations we had made to the Earth's atmosphere would quite soon render the ecosphere incapable of supporting the human species, though other species might adapt and survive, was too harsh a message for many people to receive. Some, particularly politicians who should actually do something about this state of affairs, denied that the message was true, or mouthed political platitudes and did nothing. Many other people turned the message into something both cosy and magical. Dear old Mother Earth needed our help. Out of such wishful thinking came Jim Lovelock's Gaia theory, much admired by those people who want to believe that the human race is the pinnacle of creation, the hub of the wheel around which all else revolves and for which the rest of the world was created. No wonder Copernicus, Darwin and Freud were the object of such hatred!

Lovelock defined Gaia as

a complex entity involving the Earth's biosphere, atmosphere, oceans, and soil; the totality constituting a feedback or cybernetic system which seeks an optimal physical and chemical environment for life on this planet. The maintenance of relatively constant conditions by active control may be conveniently described by the term 'homeostasis' . . . The physical and chemical condition of the surface of the Earth, of the atmosphere, and of the oceans has been and is actively made fit and comfortable by the presence of life itself.[15]

Thus Gaia's optimum conditions are made for life and by life, which he defines as

a common state of matter found at the Earth's surface and throughout its oceans. It is composed of intricate combinations of the common elements hydrogen, carbon, oxygen, nitrogen, sulphur, and phosphorus with many other elements in trace quantities. Most forms of life can be instantly recognized without prior experience and are frequently edible.[16]

Since 'life' has included many millions of species which are now extinct, chiefly through shifts in Gaia's system, we might wonder whether, in adapting to the changes which the human species is making to the biosphere, Gaia might create a form of homeostasis which would be so inimical to our species that we, too, would become extinct. There are many scientists who believe that, unless we change our ways markedly and quickly, this could happen.

But no.

Should there be such major and deleterious shifts in Gaia's system,

[these] we might in the future be able to help her resolve. Still more important is the implication that the evolution of *Homo sapiens*, with his technological inventiveness and his increasingly subtle communications network, has vastly increased Gaia's range of perception. She is now through us thoroughly awake and aware of herself. She has seen the reflection of her fair face through the eyes of astronauts and the television cameras of orbiting spacecraft. Our sensations of wonder and pleasure, our capacity for conscious thought and speculation, our restless curiosity and drive are hers to share. This new interrelationship of Gaia with man is by no means fully established; we are not yet a truly collective species, corralled and tamed as an integral part of the biosphere, as we are as individual creatures. It may be that

the destiny of mankind is to become tamed, so that the fierce, destructive, and greedy forces of tribalism and nationalism are fused into a compulsive urge to belong to the commonwealth of all creatures which constitutes Gaia. It might seem to be a surrender, but I suspect that the rewards, in the form of an increased sense of wellbeing and fulfilment, in knowing ourselves to be a dynamic part of a far greater entity, would be worth the loss of tribal freedom.[12]

Lovelock does not reveal just how mankind is to be tamed. Which is a pity, for the Gulf War and its aftermath demonstrated how ferocious and incorrigible the forces of tribalism and nationalism are.

Many churchmen and people with religious beliefs often talk of God expecting us to look after the Earth, in much the same way that parents expect children to keep their room tidy. To look after our planet so as to please God is still to be a child, and children believe in magic.

Each religion regards the rituals of all other religions as the practice of magic, but their own rituals as communion with and worship of their own God. I have always wondered whether the Christian God did enjoy those dreary hymns and prayers which instructed Him to do His duty. If He does enjoy those traditional hymns He must be a very boring person, and if He is irritated by all those nagging prayers it is no wonder He is so remiss in His care of us. I have always wondered, too, about His desire to be praised. That is not an attractive attribute in human beings, so why should it be in God? On the other hand, a God who does not require constant reassurance of His virtue and power, who does not need to be propitiated through magic rituals, who needs no instructions, but whose peace and wisdom can be experienced through meditative prayer seems to represent the best we can conceive of with our limited experience.

We can conceive of such a God because some of us can conceive of parents who do not demand propitiation and recompense from their children, nor expect their children to meet the parents' needs, nor reward and punish their children so as to force the children to do and be what the parents want, but love their children simply because they exist, and are available to comfort and support their children so as to help them find their own wisdom. Such parents are rare. Most of us have parents who demand testaments of our love, who manipulate us through rewards, punishments, guilt and shame, who expect us to do and be what they want, and who act so as to meet their own needs. No wonder there are so many Gods who are very badly behaved!

We conceive of the power of our Gods in the way that power has been wielded over us, just as we conceive of death and an afterlife in the terms that we have experienced in our life.

It is hard not to do this, even when we think we have educated ourselves and changed our ideas. I was surprised and amused to find that when I visited India I was shocked by the gaudiness of the Hindu temples. As a child I had been taught religion in the austere Presbyterian Church where the 'idolatry' of the Catholic Church, with their statues and pictures of Jesus and Mary, was condemned and cursed. The Hindu temples showed me that I had not eradicated my Presbyterianism. The only time I felt some connection with those temples was when I was taken to one in Varanasi where, around midnight, I saw a crowd of villagers pressing past me. Their faces in the dim light were faces I had seen before in the pictures and sculptures of medieval peasants in European churches, faces and bodies shaped by the harshness of their toil. Such lives need hope, and so often only religion is available to offer lasting hope. Politics of whatever kind always fails to offer hope because politics is about power, not compassion. Most politicians are concerned only with power, competition and greed, whereas the churches do contain a few people who act with compassion.

But only a few. Most churchmen are concerned with power and obedience. This applies to all religions. I remember seeing a Zen Buddhist teacher at the Zen centre in Green Gulch, San Francisco, preaching with all the claims to power, and seeking to gain the personal devotion of his audience in the same way that I had seen Presbyterian ministers, Church of England bishops, Catholic priests, and

173

Muslim ayatollahs do so. Their claim to power comes from their insistence that Category One definitions are actually Category Two. What they preach is, they say, the Absolute Truth.

All religions claim to give to the inexplicable explanations which are part of the nature of life. While such explanations give to many people a sense of security and hope, such security and hope often proves illusory. Every religion has its 'mystical' extreme with a belief in a god like the wise parent I described earlier, but down the centuries those people who espoused such a belief have been persecuted and rejected by their Churches. Gods or parents who love and accept their children without demanding that their children reward them for this create a space where their children can grow up and become independent adults. Churchmen in search of power want their flock to remain children, and as children we cannot get everything we want because those who have power over us, keeping us children, exploit our longing for everything while preventing us from understanding it and, through our understanding, finding a satisfactory way of assuaging our longing.

The fundamentalist section of religions is always popular because, whatever the religion, fundamentalism offers an explanation of the inexplicable which is very simple – goodness is rewarded and badness punished. The Evangelicals insist that their explanation of the inexplicable is all Good News, but this is a refusal to see that everything that happens has both good and bad implications.

While I was in Australia in December, 1989, I was interviewed by the broadcaster Caroline Jones for her radio series *The Search for Meaning*. Later she sent me, at the writer's request, a copy of a letter from an Evangelical minister. He wrote:

> Dorothy Rowe said that Evangelicals teach that if you are bad you are punished. I shuddered at that impression . . . Evangelicals are not the bearers of bad news that if you are bad you are punished, but the bearers of 'Good News' that Christ came that we might have life, and have it to the full. In Dr Rowe's terms, the 'evangel' or 'good news' proclaims God as that reality that lies beyond man, e.g., in identifying himself to Moses God said, 'I am' (Exodus 3:14). That reality took on a human face when Jesus in identifying himself to the Jews said, 'I am' (John 8:58). Dr Rowe was right when she said that we cannot fully understand the reality that lies beyond us, but the good news is that we can come into relationship with it (Him). Jesus said, 'I am the way, the truth and the light. No one comes to the Father except through me' (John 14:6). The search for meaning ends when our constructions of reality begin to merge with the reality of Jesus Christ. To trust in our own constructions of reality as being right is to reject

the true reality of Jesus Christ. Simply put, we place ourselves in the dark and wear the consequences. 'If you do not believe I am the one I claim to be, you will die in your sins' (John 8:24).

I would think that dying in your sins is a somewhat bad implication of the Good News.

The trouble with simple explanations of the inexplicable is that their simplicity is more apparent than real. Take, for example, the many Evangelical preachers who insist that the only way to be saved and enjoy Eternal Life is to know and to believe in Jesus Christ. If you ask them, as I have often done, whether this means that those people born in the thousands of years preceding Jesus's birth and those people living in places where His message never penetrated are excluded from all chance of Heaven, some will fudge, and others say quite explicitly and, to my mind, cruelly, 'Yes'.

Simple explanations of the inexplicable force believers to create barriers between different parts of what they know, and to keep different pieces of knowledge separate, since to bring them together would lead to conclusions which would challenge the simple explanations. Many Muslims will say that the superiority of Islam over all other religions and societies is seen in the care and status which Islam gives to women. They also know that before Islamic law a woman's testimony is worth only half that of a man. As people, they know that to have your truth discounted by others is most painful and destructive. Many Muslim men escape from this dilemma by saying that women do not feel things in the way that men do, that is, they are not fully human. Neither being hurt by being disbelieved nor being reduced to inferiority accord with the claim that Islam cares for and respects women. But, of course, the perceived inferiority of women is nothing to do with the search for communion with God, and all to do with men wanting to have power over women, something which prevents men from ever getting everything they want. A power relationship between men and women is always one of barriers, insecurity and mistrust. Only between equals can there ever be the security, acceptance and intimacy which is reminiscent of the bliss we once knew and lost and long for.

In all systems of power, not just in religions, the people in power create the definitions of rules and obedience, and those without power have to work at interpreting these imposed constructions. The Catholic Church hands down instructions to its flock and expects the flock to interpret these and apply them to the everyday conditions of their lives. I remember, thirty years ago, being in the crowded staff room of a school where all the teachers had to work very hard to keep the children in order and to educate them. One of my colleagues, a young woman, came in hungry and with little time to eat her lunch, a hot meat pie from the school tuck shop. Such succulent pies were sheer bliss to eat when you were hungry. She put the pie on a plate and sat down. As her hand went towards the pie she suddenly said, 'Oh, it's Friday,' and with that she jumped up, threw the pie in the garbage, and rushed out of the room.

Catholics will tell me that the Church has relaxed the rule about not eating meat on Fridays and insist that 'the Church is different now'. But is it?

Not since 1566 has the Roman Catholic hierarchy attempted such a project: the summarizing of the church's central teaching on faith and morals in a single document. Four years in the making, a secret 434-page draft of the new *Catechism for the Universal Church* was sent last December to the world's 4,000 bishops. The prelates were instructed to dispatch their comments on the text to the Vatican by 31 May, after which work will begin on the final version. Since then there has been widespread grumbling both over the document's old-fashioned conservatism and the rush-rush deadline for responding to it. Last week leaders of the US bishops escalated the debate, sending the Vatican a sweeping and surprisingly blunt 51-page critique of the *Catechism*. They also pleaded for more time to consult with theologians and educators over what they called the 'most significant' project of the church's magisterium, or teaching office, since the Second Vatican Council.

The bishops' critique was the work of a six-member committee headed by Alabama's Archbishop Oscar Lipscomb, 58, the chairman of the bishop's doctrinal committee. (Individual US bishops, like those elsewhere, will also be sending separate responses to the Vatican.) The Lipscomb panel's chief objection is that the *Catechism* has not clearly distinguished a 'hierarchy of truths' treating concepts like the meaning of Christ's crucifixion as more important than, say, teaching about angels.

The report chides Rome for ignoring a generation of progressive Bible scholarship. The Roman draft, the Americans say, seems to presume that 'New Testament texts are the product of direct historical reporting' and resorts to 'proof-texting', quoting Scripture out of context to prove a doctrinal point. In addition, the Americans feel that science has been slighted in favour of an almost Fundamentalist approach to creation. Another US complaint is that the English version of the *Catechism* seems to back away from some of the key ecumenical language adopted by the 1962–65 Second Vatican Council. While Vatican II declared that the true church of Christ 'subsists' in the Roman Catholic Church, implying that there is a place for other Christians, the *Catechism* uses an exclusionary phrase, 'has its existence in'. Reflecting the

influence of feminism, the report sharply criticizes Rome's relent-
less use of non-inclusive nouns and pronouns (for instance, in
referring to believers as 'men' or 'sons'), which the American
bishops have been trying to banish from their own documents . . .
Father William Spohn of California's Jesuit School of Theology
characterized the Vatican drafters as religious Rip Van Winkles
who have slept through a generation of progress in moral theology. Underlying such attacks from liberals is a not-so-hidden fear:
that a hard-line *Catechism* will one day be used as a criterion for
disciplining theologians and educators.[19]

Religion, while offering us a share in a greater power through which,
we can hope, we shall get everything – eternal bliss – keeps us as
children and prevents us from thinking clearly. Such childish bamboozlement, while offering us comfort which, in extreme conditions,
we could not survive without, prevents us from discovering, given
our own limitations and the limitations of what is available to us, what
of our wanting everything we might reasonably be able to obtain and
enjoy.

Political systems, like religions, also aim at keeping the populace in
the position of dependent children. Russia, it has been said, is a school
from which no one ever graduates. In capitalist societies politicians
pay lip-service to the idea that people should be educated so as to
become independent adults, but the actual education of children and
the continuing education of adults through the media prevents most
people from reaching this independent adult status.

Independent adult status means, among other things, knowing that
power hierarchies are not an order of the universe, a Category Two
nature of the universe, but something which people have created. As
dependent adults we may be able to see that the power hierarchies to
which we do not belong are constructions by other people, but we
deem such people to be both mad and bad. However, we believe that
the power structure to which we belong is an Absolute Truth, part of
the order of nature.

Believing this makes it hard for us to see just how power is wielded
over us and how we ourselves wield power. Believing this, we fail to
see the interaction of political and personal power, and how both
kinds of power fail to achieve the results their users desire.

We can wield power over others or have power wielded over us
through violence and coercion, rhetoric, display, and discussion and
persuasion. All methods can be wielded both politically and personally. All methods can be effective in getting people to change their
constructions, but none of the methods nor all of them combined
enable those who wield power to get everything they want.

Perhaps the most telling example of how little we understand of ourselves is our refusal to see that we do not get what we want through *violence and coercion*. Violence and coercion destroy. While a great many people who resort to these methods do want to destroy that which they envy and hate, they invariably destroy much else that they wanted. Moreover, violence and coercion initiate such strong and far-reaching effects throughout the network of causes that the effects of violence and coercion are never what the perpetrators set out to achieve. History is littered with examples of this, and many of them are ironic. In the Second World War the violence and coercion of the German and Japanese leaders led eventually to West Germany and Japan becoming wealthy and powerful but peaceful nations, simply because their victors prevented them from being violent and coercive, while their victors destabilized their own economies to build weapons of war to 'preserve the peace'.

Over the thousands of years that we have existed, we have not learned that not only can we not achieve our ends through violence and coercion, but that when we employ these means we ourselves are changed and become less than we might have been.

Rather than confront the damage we do to ourselves when we use violence and coercion, we instead put a magical gloss upon this damage and transform it into the myth of the hero.

Heroes and hero-makers are usually men, but many women, even though they often suffer at the hands of the heroes, have always supported this myth by preferring the hero to the unaggressive man and by encouraging their sons to be heroes. The hero myth is one of the ways we try to hide from ourselves the destructiveness and failure of violence and coercion.

> Without the propaganda of the hero myth, murder is a sordid business. *With* the hero myth, any act of violence is made not only possible but inevitable: the rapist is transformed into the seducer, the tyrant rules by divine right, the terrorist reconstitutes the hero.[20]

The violence and coercion world-wide in the so-called peaceful years since the Second World War has spawned a great many heroes.

> There he stands: young, lean, garbed in black, his face in shadow or masked by a balaclava, his gestures swift and economical as a predatory cat's, his muscled body not only bearing the magic tools of death but a magic tool of death itself, his commitment total. He is a fanatic of dedication, a mixture of impetuosity and discipline; he is desperate and therefore vulnerable; he is totally at risk and therefore brave; he is an idealist yet a hardened realist. Most of all, he is someone wholly given over to a passion. But his passion is death.[21]

The hero (freedom fighter or terrorist, depending on whether he is for you or against you) appears to be fearless in the face of death.

> The terrorists' willingness to accept high risks may also be related to the belief that one's death will be avenged. The prospect of retribution gives the act of terrorism and the death of the terrorist meaning and continuity, even fame and immortality. Vengeance may be not only a function of anger but of a desire for trans-cendence.[22]

Even more, the hero has given up being himself in order to be indifferent to death. Robin Morgan, quoting Joseph Campbell in his *The Hero with a Thousand Faces*, wrote:

> The hero's strength, then, resides in his dying first to 'the logic and the emotional commitments' of a simple joy in existing; his power is rooted in his emphasis on 'the very kiss of our annihila-tion'; his charisma is dependent on his 'love of the fate that is inevitably death'. Valorous, abnegating his own selfhood and severed from that of others, disconnected from a living logic and the pathos of emotional commitments, recognizing only the redeeming ecstasy of a tragic death, *the hero already lives as a dead man*. As a dead man he is fearless, because as a dead man he is unconquerable by any life force.[23]

Heroes are created by violence and coercion. Often the violence and coercion are of the kind employed by middle- and upper-class families in bringing up their children. Such families set high standards, punish failure with rejection and humiliation, and, with physical punish-ments, teach an indifference to physical suffering. Children brought up this way can often feel powerless. To give themselves a sense of power and to maintain themselves as individuals they can turn against their parents/teachers/State and use what the parent/teachers/State taught them to become revolutionaries.

> Charles A. Russell and Bowman H. Miller drew a sociological profile of a terrorist, based on a compilation and analysis of pub-lished data involving over 350 individual terrorist cadres and leaders from Argentinian, Brazilian, German, Iranian, Irish, Italian, Japanese, Palestinian, Spanish, Turkish, and Uruguayan groups active between 1966 and 1976. They focused in particular on eighteen groups, examining the 'modern urban terrorist', as opposed to the rural guerrilla fighter.[24] The groups included those engaged in transnational actions (such as the Japanese Red Army) as well as those involved locally and committed solely to ethnic struggles . . .
>
> 'Over two thirds came from the middle or upper classes in their respective nations or areas. In most instances their parents were

professional people (doctors, lawyers, engineers . . .), government employees, diplomats, clergymen, military officers, or sometimes even police officials. Although these parents were part of the existing social and economic systems, many of them had been frustrated in their efforts to use them as vehicles for upward . . . mobility.'[25] Clearly, terrorism reflects the old maxim that revolutions are made more by those with raised expectations than by the most severely repressed . . .

'Two thirds . . . are persons with some university training, university graduates, or postgraduate students.'[26] The ratio rises to 75 percent among the Latin American groups . . . Most were educated abroad and spoke a second language. Most of the Turkish People's Liberation Army members were Middle Eastern Technical University students or graduates. George Habash, head of the PFLP (the Popular Front for the Liberation of Palestine), is a medical doctor. Yasser Arafat, who formally renounced terrorism in the 1985 Cairo Declaration of the PLO (the Palestine Liberation Organization), is a graduate engineer. Giangiacomo Feltrinelli, a millionaire book publisher, was a major figure in Leftist Italian terrorism . . . Che Guevara was a physician, Andreas Baader an attorney. The Weather Underground, also called the Weathermen – all white, middle- or upper-class, and educated – followed this pattern . . .

Moroccan sociologist and feminist theorist Fatima Mernissi[27]. . . warns that the fundamentalist is neither uneducated nor uncultured. She cites Saad Eddin Ibrahim's in-depth study of thirty-four Egyptian Islamic militants, and his findings that the fundamentalist militant belongs to the middle class, favours scientific branches of knowledge, and performs exceptionally well, especially in medicine, engineering, technical military science, and pharmacy.[28]

One terrorist organization which does not fit this picture is the Provisional IRA (Irish Republican Army), who are predominantly working class. They have more in common with those people who see their home taken over by a foreign power and find themselves homeless and rootless.

Dr Rona Fields is a clinical psychologist based in the United States who has spent two decades working with children in Northern Ireland and in the Palestinian refugee camps of the Middle East. Over time, she re-encountered many of the children she had worked with, after they had become adults and, in some cases, had joined terrorist groups. Many of these children had survived the humiliation and powerlessness of childhoods in life-threatening daily situations. For them, a denial of death combined with chronic rage was characteristic, along with an inability to see any real way of advancing out of powerlessness for the rest of their lives. That this in turn created a flatly Manichean vision of the universe, as black or white, good or evil, should not shock us. Dr Fields found that the only positive models, the only adults who appeared to control their own destiny and to act as if their actions made a difference, were those who belonged to terrorist groups: it was they who filled the children's hunger for strong, protective parents. Most of the children had already endured at least one close brush with death by the time they reached their early teens, either from illness or from direct attack. Some had already been imprisoned. This culturally affected the boys differently from the girls. 'The experience is a terrible blow to their identity as men, one which they redeem by joining these groups.'[29] Culturally *powerlessness is not a blow to the girls' identity as females*; in a way it's convenient training. Guilt at being a survivor, and revenge for wrongs done to one's family, are additional components that influenced the boys. Dr Fields examined Palestinian children who survived the 1982 massacres at the Sabra and Shatila refugee camps in the Lebanon. Before the slaughter, the boys had spoken with resentment against the military training they were encouraged to take from age eight onward, and were particularly angry at the Palestinian paramilitary forces that offered the training. But: 'After the massacre, the boys felt both grief and intense guilt about their earlier feelings of resentment . . . they somehow felt responsible . . . and felt the only way they could make amends was by taking the place of those who had been killed. They were left with a monomaniacal obsession with revenge.'[30]

Either as middle-class revolutionaries or as alienated refugees from a foreign power, the men and the few women who become terrorists are trying to give to their lives a meaning which allows them to feel that they have some personal power and significance. Their childhood experiences have not allowed them to discover that power and significance can come from compromise and forgiveness. They have been taught to define compromise and forgiveness as weak and wicked, and so they remain trapped in unwinnable and wasteful conflicts.

Into these conflicts are dragged many other people – reluctant soldiers and civilians wanting to get on with their lives – and the power expressed as violence and coercion makes them less than the people they might have been.

The poet Wilfred Owen witnessed how ordinary men in the trenches in the First World War lost the capacity to be sensitive to their own sufferings and the suffering of others.

Happy the men who yet before they are killed
Can let their veins run cold.
Whom no compassion fleers
Or makes their feet
Sore on the alleys cobbled by their brothers.
The front line withers,
But they are troops who fade, not flowers
For poets' tearful fooling:
Men, gaps for filling:
Losses, who might have fought
Longer: but no one bothers.

And some cease feeling
Even themselves or for themselves.
Dullness best solves
The tease and doubt of shelling,
And Chance's strange arithmetic
Comes simpler than the reckoning of their shilling.
They keep no check on armies' decimation.

Happy are those who lose imagination:
They have enough to carry with ammunition.
Their spirit drags no pack,
Their old wounds, save with cold, can not more ache.
Having seen all things red,
Their eyes are rid
Of the hurt colour of blood forever.
And terror's first constriction over,
Their hearts remain small-drawn.
Their senses in some scorching cautery of battle
Now long since ironed,
Can laugh among the dead, unconcerned . . .

But cursed are dullards whom no cannon stuns,
That they should be as stones;
Wretched are they, and mean
With paucity that never was simplicity.
By choice they made themselves immune
To pity and whatever mourns in man
Before the last sea and the hapless stars;
Whatever mourns when many leave these shores;
Whatever shares
The eternal reciprocity of tears.[31]

It is 'the eternal reciprocity of tears' which joins us to other people. In sadness we can empathize with others and draw close to them.

Sensitivity to our own suffering and the suffering of others is not an all-or-none state. Rather, we can be sensitive to certain aspects of our own suffering and to the suffering of certain other people, but in other ways we can be quite unaware. We can be unaware that we are unaware, and so we can be thinking of ourselves as being tremendously sensitive and aware when in fact we have become in certain aspects of our lives quite hard and cruel.

When I was travelling in Israel I stayed with a most hospitable and friendly family where their much-loved daughter, a very gentle and loving girl, had had to interrupt her military training because she found the handling of guns and other military activities very distressing. This, I thought, was hardly surprising because, as a child, she had been subjected to enormous pain and fear by armed terrorists. Military training not only reminded her of this pain and fear but also of the helpless rage she felt as a tortured child. She had not, as many people do, turned the helpless rage into a vengeful bitterness. Instead she had remained gentle, and when the military put guns in her hands she feared that she might give expression to her suppressed rage. So I expected that her family would do what my friends in Britain, Australia, and the USA would do for their children, that is, extricate their daughter from an impossible situation. But they did not. As their soldier son made quite clear, it was the girl's duty to complete her military service, and that was what she had to do no matter what it cost her. This family was not exceptional. All over Israel and the Occupied Territories, Israeli and Palestinian families saw themselves as being unable to afford the tenderness which is possible in peaceful times.

Part of the tenderness, 'the eternal reciprocity of tears', is a willingness to let other people say and think what they wish. But people who wish to impose their definitions of reality on to other people cannot allow alternative constructions to be created and uttered, and such people who would do so must be silenced.

In late 1988, as Emperor Hirohito lay dying of cancer, Nagasaki Mayor Hitoshi Motoshima broke a widely observed taboo by criticizing the once deified leader. Responding to a question in the city assembly, Motoshima declared, 'I experienced military life and was involved in education in the military, and I believe the Emperor had responsibility for the war.' Last week the 67-year-old mayor very nearly paid for that statement with his life. As Motoshima stepped out of city hall, a gunman shot him from behind. A bullet pierced his lung; at week's end he was in stable condition at a Nagasaki hospital.

Shortly after the shooting, police arrested Kazumi Tajiri, who confessed to the crime. Tariji, 40, is a member of Seikijuku, one of the more right-wing activist organizations with an estimated nationwide membership of 120,000. In the past year such groups have intermittently harassed Motoshima, screaming 'Heaven's punishment!' from vans parked outside his office and sending letters threatening to kill him . . . Though the Japanese constitution guarantees freedom of speech, the taboo against criticizing the imperial family is almost never violated in public, in part out of deference to the Emperor, in part out of fear of right-wing reprisals. The shooting shocked most Japanese and sent a chilling reminder of the subtle restraints they have come to accept.[32]

The power-seekers who try to impose their power through violence and coercion have learned these methods in childhood when they were educated by harsh and punitive adults. In her novel *Punishment* Anna Mitgutsch describes how one woman, treated cruelly as a child by her family, is cruel to her daughter. We are horrified by the descriptions of the punishments she inflicts on her daughter, and then we read of how this little girl played with her dolls.

> My dolls never slept; all of them were Cinderellas, who had to work and be obedient and still could do nothing right; they were rebellious and obstinate and had to be punished until their noses were broken and bundles of their hair were loose in my hands. 'What are you doing?' my mother would call from the kitchen, 'You are breaking the doll.' 'But that's because she was bad,' I said self-righteously. This time the power and the law are mine, because in my world I am the ruler of fortune and misfortune, and there is no good fortune in my world. 'What has she done?' my mother asks, trying to insinuate herself into my world. 'She won't turn the wheel,' I say and continue my punishing duties, slamming the doll's face against the edge of her buggy until it is full of cracks. 'And why should she turn the wheel?' 'Because I say so.'[33]

Often when I speak or write about the violence which occurs in families, my audience feel that I am not talking about them because in their families no one ever raises a hand to anyone else. What they forget is that what is more often raised in families is voices expressing rage, and the things that can be said and done are experienced as violence by the recipients. Often the perpetrator of the rage becomes very powerful, and can impose his or her will simply by threatening to get angry. Families which live under the threat of rage know little closeness, acceptance and support. Rather, they adapt by becoming apathetic and secretive in their dealings with one another. Ruth Rendell captured this in her novel *Make Death Love Me*.

> Jillian didn't come in. Pam explained that she had stayed at school for the dramatic society and had gone back with Sharon for tea.

This, Alan was certain, was not so. She was somewhere with a boy. He was an observant person and Pam was not, and from various things he had heard and noticed he knew that, though only fifteen, Jillian was not a virgin and hadn't been for some time. Of course he also knew that as a responsible parent he ought to discuss this with Pam and try and stop Jillian or just get her on the pill. He was sure she was promiscuous and that the whole thing should not just be ignored, but he couldn't discuss anything with Pam. She and Pop and Jillian had only two moods, apathy and anger. Pam would fly into a rage if he told her, and if he insisted, which he couldn't imagine doing, she would scream at Jillian and take her to a doctor to be examined for an intact hymen or pregnancy or venereal disease, or the lot for all he knew.[34]

The violence and coercion which is put upon children often takes the form of demanding much from them and imposing heavy sanctions if they fail. Because the sanctions are defined as being part of the order of nature (a Category Two definition), and come with the possibility of rewards which are defined to the children as being great, the children accept the sanctions, make them their own, and when they themselves get power over others, they uncaringly impose the same sanctions.

Terry, a young man whom I have known since childhood, grew up in a family where both parents expected high standards in every aspect of his life, and where his father believed that all that was great and good was to be found in football. Terry's achievements at school were modest, but he did have an aptitude for football, so it was here that he tried to please his parents the most. He belonged to the school team, but the system was that, to give all the aspiring footballers a chance, the players would be changed each week, and the coach would not announce the team for each Saturday's game until the Friday afternoon.

So for Terry, each week was a torture. Would he be chosen for the team? Was he good enough to be picked, or had he done something wrong? The week was also a torture for his parents, since all the time he would be asking them, 'Do you think I'm going to be picked for the team?'

Though his parents sympathized with him and tried to encourage him not to worry if he was not chosen, they did not realize that he had invested his whole identity in being the kind of footballer whom important people, as represented by his parents and football coaches, would find acceptable. In effect, he was asking whether he was acceptable enough to be allowed to exist.

Time went by, and though Terry became a competent footballer, he was not picked to become a professional. So, second best, he became a physical education teacher and, thus, a football coach. Like his first coach, he chooses a different team each week. Whenever his mother reminds him that he is now doing to his pupils what was done to him, he brushes her concern aside. 'The kids just have to learn,' he says. 'That's what the game's about.'

Terry would be aghast if I suggested that, to those boys who sought to justify their existence by playing football, he was being violent and coercive. He was, he would say, trying to instil through his talks to the boys the correct thoughts and behaviour. In this he was using rhetoric.

In the classical oratory of ancient Greece and Rome, *rhetoric* was 'the art of influencing the thought of one's hearers'.[35] The word 'rhetoric' is often used nowadays to mean 'the use of exaggeration or display, in an unfavourable sense'.[36] Rhetoric which is effective is not perceived by its listeners as being an exaggeration or play-acting but is taken as the truth, often the literal truth. The aim of such rhetoric is to prevent us from finding alternative ways of construing our reality, and the language it uses is intended to obscure, not to clarify. It relies on metaphors which are presented as accurate descriptions, and gives to its believers an illusion of power which they can express in the rhetorical language which they have learned.

It is much easier to recognize rhetoric as rhetoric when it has not been aimed specifically at us. When the journalist W.L. Webb went to Egypt in 1989 to observe the workings of modern Islam after the Ayatollah Khomeini had issued his death threat against Salman Rushdie, the rhetoric of some of the people he talked to surprised him.

> Another convert to a more implacable fundamentalism is one of Cairo's leading theatre critics, Safiniaze Qazem . . . She wears the veil, is friendly, but won't shake hands (an unusual fundamentalist requirement), has a voice like a trumpet and a laugh that drowns even the madness of Abassiya Street below her windows . . . but when we get into the argument apropos Rushdie, about the reasons of art and the reasons of morality, the critic suddenly lays down her hand. 'When Nietzsche says God is dead, I don't see him as a great philosopher but as a wretched person. When it comes to Islam I do not give a damn for art or literature or any of these things. Even if we have to do without art or literature for Islam, it's all right. We do not consider art as a sacred thing in itself. This is Greek ideology.'[37]

Rhetoric can be the enemy of truth and freedom. At the same time as Webb's visit to Cairo, the *Observer* published a letter from Karachi signed only, 'Name and address supplied':

Salman Rushdie speaks for me in 'The Satanic Verses', and mine is a voice that has not yet found expression in newspaper columns. It is the voice of those who are born Muslim but wish to recant in adulthood, yet are not permitted to do so on the pain of death.

Someone who does not live in an Islamic society cannot imagine the sanctions, both self-imposed and external, that militate against expressing religious disbelief. 'I don't believe in God' is an impossible public utterance even among family and friends. Muslims hate Rushdie not so much for his irreverence as his doubt; for his questioning 'divine inspiration', for his humanization of the Prophet, who had of late begun to acquire divine characteristics.

In the *Dar-ul Islam* (Realm of Islam) we may not debate such issues even in the privacy of our own homes. We may talk of 'progressive', 'enlightened', interpretations of Islam and curse the mullahs for their orthodox fundamentalism, but we may *never* question the veracity, rationality, justice or moral rightness of basic beliefs. And if we dare recant, then it is the religious obligation of the faithful to execute us.

So we hold our tongues, those of us who doubt. Call it cowardice or hypocrisy, tact or appeasement, we bury our heads in the sand and wish it all away. But it comes home to us in our children, whose intellectual and spiritual straightjacketing begins early in the Realm of Islam . . .

The agony of dissent which finds no support is unbearable. Rushdie in his wretched predicament is comforted by the support of the international community of writers and intellectuals, peers and politicians – and his readers. But for secularists like myself, imprisoned in the theocratic dungeon that is a Muslim nation today, the isolation is total. I weep for my daughter, just four years old, already being taught to recite the affirmation of faith and learning religious dogma by rote at school. I want to tell her what *I* believe but don't want her to be the victim of ridicule by her peers – or worse, should she repeat such heresy publicly.[38]

Haider Reeve, an English convert to Islam, informed *Guardian* readers that

[f]or Muslims, Rushdie has committed *fitna* (sedition) against the religion of his birth, a crime The Koran states to be more serious than murder, and for which the prescribed penalty is death; differences in Islamic viewpoint expressed over the passing of sentence do not extend to the sentence itself . . . Khomeini's religious responsibilities leave him no choice but to act.[39]

The metaphors used by the State and the Church in their rhetoric may have been used initially as no more than vivid pictures, understandable by and appealing to their audience, but when these metaphors harden into dogma they become the means by which reality is perceived and responded to, and they become part of the network of causes and effects. In recent years the metaphors of Eastern philosophies have been seen in the West as fine and liberating. Ya Ding, a Chinese novelist now living in France, writing about Tiananmen Square, showed how the metaphors of Confucianism and Taoism, once hardened into dogma, imprisoned their believers:

> Formerly the Middle Kingdom was divided into seven realms, each with its own identity, which fought for the right to occupy the unique position of 'Master of Heaven'. Out of these permanent upheavals and never-ending wars, all sorts of currents of thought emerged which might be enrolled by one king to aid his conquest of Heaven, or by another facing peril in his realm. Then, hoping for peace and tranquillity, the heart of the Chinese people rallied under the banner of Confucianism, which, based on the principle of compromise, preached respect for order and ritual, for intelligence, tolerance, wisdom and obedience, the virtue of labour and the knowing of one's place. The great moralist also condemned too close relations between human beings, including commercial ones.
>
> In surrounding China with the highest mountains and the largest ocean of the planet, Providence had, while closing down the possibilities for outside conquests, left her with an immense land mass within which to live. So the limits within which the ancient kingdom developed were both geographical and spiritual; all energy was directed inwards and all learning was only an internalization. Lao Tzu created Taoism, which, based on the ideal of the sage, taught people to minimize their daily physical and mental activity in order that the course of things might not be disturbed. In time Buddhism arrived from India and shaped a philosophy of non-say and non-do. The spirit of detachment permeated China, and in particular the middle classes.
>
> The West believes in God but the East in Heaven. But, while God has a name, an image, and leaves concrete messages (like the Testaments), Heaven in China has neither an image nor a concrete message. Remaining vague always, this powerful divinity can reveal itself through the agency of man: the Son of Heaven. Judeo-Christian civilization has only two sides – God and man. Once God was out of the equation the spirit of equality and democracy among men emerged. Whereas in China, despite formal changes in the social system, man always retained absolute

obedience for the emperor – a habit of mind forged over the course of 5,000 years. So, under the title of the popular republic, Mao and Deng became two Sons of Heaven, both demanding complete submission from the population.

Civilization is like a person: with the passing of years it ages and all its merits are transformed into faults. Confucianism, after so many years shaping the Chinese soul, had turned into resignation in the face of destiny, Taoism into smug self-satisfaction, and the 'listening post' of Heaven gave dumb submission to all that came from the authorities. With its vital forces drained, reality ignored, and science stunted, the Chinese nation was, towards the end of last century, at the end of its tether.[40]

The 'dumb submission' of the Chinese people was easily transferred to the Communist leaders. So often, what appears to be a political revolution or an individual conversion is, in effect, no change at all. The titles given to the authority and the followers may have changed, but the relationships and the metaphors to describe these relationships have not changed.

Just as changing from submission to Heaven to submission to the State is virtually no change, so is changing from the absolutes of Presbyterianism to the absolutes of Islam, or from seeking forgiveness from one's parents to seeking forgiveness from the Evangelical God, no change at all. Often, political and religious rhetoricians believe that they have wielded power and changed the beliefs of their audience, and indeed their audience may believe that they have changed, but all that the audience has done is transfer part of their underlying structure of meaning from one situation to another. If the political and religious rhetoricians do not take the time and care to discover just how their 'converted' audience have constructed their world of meaning, such rhetoricians and their masters can believe that they have asserted their power when in fact they have not.

The rhetoric of the Thatcher Government was aimed at changing the Labour-voting, upper working class, the skilled workers, into home-owning, share-owning, loyal Tory voters, but, while this group did vote Conservative for a decade, their underlying structure of meaning was not changed by the Conservative Government's rhetoric. This rhetoric spoke to the skilled workers' underlying structure when it used metaphors to do with economic security, but the rhetoric failed to address that part of their underlying structure of meaning which had to do with equality of opportunity, justice and the worth of individuals irrespective of class. So this group of people did not become loyal Tories. They were merely being expedient in the their care of themselves, and the Tory rhetoricians, believing their own rhetoric, failed to notice this until the whole fiasco of the poll tax became clear to those Tories who subsequently engineered a change of prime minister.

This is the problem with rhetoric. We can get so enveloped in our own rhetoric that we cease to see it as one of the alternative constructions of reality and come to believe that it is reality.

The problem for all the practitioners in the media is how much in their rhetoric they will present the structure of meaning which the State, the Church, and the international financial institutions want to be presented as absolute reality, and how much they will present alternative structures of meaning. All forms of the media are so seductive because they constantly suggest that it is possible for us to have everything we desire. The media tell us stories about people who do, apparently, have everything, and they purport to show us how we too can have everything, provided that we define 'everything' in the way that the media define it. The media offer us personal significance in a way that was unavailable in earlier centuries. Once the king was known to most of his subjects only as a face on a coin. Now we know the minute details of our Royal Family's life. Once the only more or less permanent memorial a person might hope for was a name on a tombstone. Now we can hope for our picture and name in a newspaper, a story about us on television, our life recorded in a book or magazine. Thus we are much more aware of and sensitive to the rhetoric of the media than of our State and Church, and so the State and Church have learned to direct their rhetoric to us through the media.

Much of this rhetoric has to do with knowing what is best for us as individuals. Newsreels of politicians up to the advent of television show how such politicians addressed their audience as being a public meeting in which they, very graciously, were prepared to tell their grateful subjects a little about the affairs of State which they were handling so competently. Their audience dutifully clapped and cheered. Franklin D. Roosevelt was one of the first politicians to recognize that people much preferred to be addressed as intelligent and concerned individuals, and so he instituted his fireside chats.

Soon all politicians were following his lead, and now they each address us as if they were actually in the easy chair beside us or across the kitchen table. Not that what they say is anything more than rhetoric. They are not concerned with discussion, so as to discover our own point of view. They have simply exchanged the rhetoric of the platform for the rhetoric of the individual. So too has the Church changed. No longer must we be the passive recipients of a sermon handed down from on high. Religious preaching is a friendly chat about everyday matters with an everyday and ordinary God and Jesus in attendance. We recognize the rhetoric of the individual because we use it ourselves all the time. After all, do we not know what is best for our nearest and dearest, and do we not always seek to convert their structure of meaning to ours?

Personal rhetoric is concerned with getting the people around us to do what we want them to do. Sometimes we want to enjoy the power of having people follow our instructions, and sometimes we want simply to organize other people in such a way that we can get on with what we want to do and not be disturbed by others. Much of the anger which many men feel towards women who will not behave in the traditional womanly fashion stems not so much from the desire to control women as from the desire that women should be predictably untroublesome.

We are each subjected to personal rhetoric from the moment of birth (some of us were talked to by our mother while we were still in the womb), and we soon learn how to ignore much of the rhetoric directed at us. As I often say, the reason that a baby learns in the womb to identify his mother's voice from all other sounds is so that he can ignore it for the rest of his life.

Some of our parents' and teachers' rhetoric gets through to us and changes our own structure of meaning, but much we exclude, calling it 'nagging' or treating it as no more than noise about our ears. The rhetoric which reaches us contains something which speaks straight to our own structure of meaning, while the rhetoric we ignore either has no connection with our structure of meaning or would affect us so profoundly that we must defend ourselves against it.

Because most of the rhetoric by parents and teachers falls on stony ground, its inefficiency leads parents and teachers to resort to violence and coercion. These methods, too, are inefficient, but they allow parents and teachers to vent their frustration and anger at the failure of their rhetoric.

Usually, along with rhetoric, especially political and religious rhetoric, *display* is used as another way of trying to impose constructions on other people.

Such display is concerned with being the outward signs of power. It says, 'We can impose our will on you', and 'We are different from and better than you'. Each display may emphasize one of these aspects rather than the other. The pomp and ceremony of the British Royal Family no longer includes many signs that power can be wielded over the sovereign's subjects, but everything from the Royal coach to the rules that the Royals must not be touched or addressed in familiar terms emphasizes that the Royals are different from and better than their subjects. By contrast, the displays by Middle Eastern and African military dictatorships do not emphasize the distinction and superiority of the dictators (most of them claim to be a man of the people), but illustrate their ruthless military might. The display by religious leaders combines both aspects in a rather subtle way. The clothes and the ceremony emphasize the singular superiority of the religious leaders, and, while they claim that they are merely the conduit by which their believers can contact the highest Power, they display themselves as being powerful because they are in contact with the highest Power.

The purveyors of such displays have to act as if there is no possible doubt that such display accurately reflects their power and importance. Any hesitancy on their part destroys the illusion, just as any hesitancy on the part of actors in a play destroys the suspension of disbelief which an audience needs to have in order to become enthralled. We all love plays, and so we are always willing to give ourselves over to the enjoyment of one, but to do that there has to be some consonance between the meaning of the play and our own structure of meaning. When that consonance is present, we can see the king arrayed in all his power and glory, but when there is no consonance we see the king without his clothes. Thus many Anglicans and Catholics are uplifted by their church's rituals, but many people like me simply wonder why God likes men to dress up in frocks.

Personal display has the same aims as political and religious display, that is, to impose our constructions on others and to mark out our distinction from and superiority over others. Often the imposition of our will is no more than our desire that other people should accept us at our own evaluation.

Patrick Seale, writing an obituary about Kim Philby, someone he knew well, said:

> He always wanted to be considered a serious person. Behind the well-bred irony was a lot of self-esteem and he was evidently keen that other people should share his high estimate of himself. He believed that his furtive activities had political significance, that he had made a political contribution to our age.
>
> In his various pronouncements from Moscow, his tendency to be a bit smug and self-righteous grew more pronounced. It was as if he was saying that the shabby and callous things he had done, the betrayals of wives and friends, the colleagues sacrificed, were of no importance in the context of the ideological crusade.[41]

When other people refuse to accept us and our display as we wish, we can be mightily affronted. Quentin Crisp described how he experienced this:

> [Mrs Czech] implied, in all the glittering capitals in Europe, homosexuals, so far from being objects of ridicule, were hardly noticed at all. She could not see why I did not live flagrantly abroad or discreetly at home. She was sure the English would never abandon their condemnatory attitude towards me in particular and sex in general.
>
> With all the other unfortunate people whom I had embroiled

in endless screaming matches on this subject, there had been one point of agreement – that homosexuality was of the greatest importance. Mrs Czech merely thought of it as a minor, slightly curious fact of life. This disturbed my essential puritanism.[42]

Those of us who had the great good fortune not only to achieve skills and expertise but to find an environment where we could use such skills and expertise, can display our power and importance with some success. We can think of ourselves as being skilled and expert, and we can persuade at least some other people to accept us at our own evaluation. But, as David Smail wrote:

If the possibility is denied you of doing anything of value in the world, you have to use your ingenuity in order to feel alive while passing the time. If your activity counts for nothing your *person* is likely to become salient – it will become important what you look like (you could decorate yourself, dye your hair) and what you feel like (you may become absorbed in the state of excitation or satiation of your nervous system, stimulation and satisfaction). In his savagely constricted and inexpressibly sad little environment at the zoo, Guy the gorilla passed much of his time in a rather distractedly off-hand indulgence in masturbation.[43]

Kirsty Milne, writing about 'Youth Lifestyles', observed:

The obsession with style, the brand-awareness does mean something. It is the defence mechanism of young people who feel powerless. You may have no say over whether you can get a job. But you have incredible choices in how you look, what you can buy – choices which the advertisers and the product manufacturers can offer you. Consumer choice means something real to this generation. It offers a way of escape and a means of self-expression.[44]

Such personal display, whether of skills and expertise or simply our person, is no more effective in imposing our constructions of meaning on to others than is political or religious display. If people share our construction of meaning they will accept and even applaud our display, but if they don't, they won't.

So, if violence and coercion, rhetoric, and display are not utterly reliable and effective in getting other people to accept our constructions of reality, all we are left with is *discussion and persuasion*. And there is no more ineffective way of trying to get everything through the application of power than by using discussion and persuasion. Whether we are trying to establish political power or personal power, once we enter into discussions with other people, not only are we forced to see how different their constructions of meaning are from ours, but we find that our own constructions of meaning are changing as we take account of theirs. We are forced to see that our construction of meaning is not a statement about Absolute Reality, but rather something specific to ourselves, growing out of our own individual experience and, while perhaps true for us, not true for everyone else.

Once we enter into discussions with the people over whom we wish to have power, we discover that people actually envisage power in different ways. *Introverts* have a vision of how, once they impose their construction of meaning – always a theory about how society, or the family, ought to be organized – everything will run smoothly in rational, logical ways to result in splendid achievements. *Extraverts* have a vision of how, once they impose their constructions of meaning – always a theory about how members of society or the family ought to relate to one another – everyone will come together in love and acceptance and all will live happily ever after. Dreams of Utopia always reveal whether the dreamer was an extravert in search of close relationships or an introvert in search of organization and achievement. When a group of power-seekers fall out, it is often over these different perceptions of the aims of power.

In seeking power, introverts are not hampered, as extraverts are, by the need to be liked. Just to be convinced that they are right, or that they are superior by birth, or intelligence, or wealth, or strength is sufficient justification for their claim to power.

"A table for four incredibly obese, offensive,
yet extremely rich bastards!" [45]

Whereas extraverts always have the fear that, by using their power they will alienate the very people on whom their sense of existence depends. They have to use their charm to keep the interest and affection of those whom they need, and in their efforts to please they may stumble across the truth of that old saying, 'Try to please all and you shall please none.'

Extravert or introvert, in making our claim for power, the structure of meaning we want to impose on others takes on a degree of rigidity which, when confronted by the structure created by others, can reveal itself as dangerously brittle. To prevent ourselves from being annihilated, we have to withdraw from others, set up barriers between ourselves and other people, and harden our structure so that ordinary intercourse between us and others becomes impossible, and we become less and less able to make accurate judgements about what is actually happening. Edmund Gosse, writing about his father who wished to impose upon everyone, especially his son, his vision of God and salvation, said:

> He saw everything through a lens, nothing in the immensity of nature. Certain senses were absent in him; I think that, with all his justice, he had no conception of the importance of liberty; with all his intelligence, the boundaries of the atmosphere in which his mind could think at all were close about him; with all his faith in the Word of God, he had no confidence in the Divine Benevolence; and with all his passionate piety, he habitually mistook fear for love.[46]

Locked into our own construction of meaning, we are often unaware that other people are getting on with their own lives and are quite unconcerned with our claims for power. It comes as a great shock when we discover this. Quentin Crisp, locked into his power struggle to get people to accept him at his own evaluation, later described how shocked and affronted he was to discover that other people were not simply existing to mirror, or deny, or confirm him:

> One evening, while Mrs Czech was giving voice to her broad-minded views and I was shaking my thin-lipped head, I had interrupted her for a moment while I went to the kitchen for a cup. As I passed through the other room of the flat, I came upon Mr Czech and the art student clasped in a passionate embrace. Here were forces of permissiveness that not even Mrs Czech would have condoned . . .
>
> I did not utter a word on seeing them nor did my feet falter but I was shaken by the revelation of two people whom until now I had regarded only as reflections of my own existence, in violent relation to each other. For the first time I had to admit that other people existed. It was not a discovery I welcomed.[47]

Of course, learning to see ourselves as bad and needing to work hard to be good focuses all our attention on ourselves. We cannot live unselfconsciously, giving our attention to the world and the people around us. Instead we become the central figure in our life's drama, with other people no more than bit players. We want other people's attention and approval, for that confirms our importance as the central character. We find it very hard to see that other people have their own drama, much less that we are no more than bit players in those dramas.

Often, in the course of therapy, a client will describe some incident and interpret it as being a scene in his life drama where he is the central character. For instance, one man, Simon, described how, as he was driving slowly down a narrow street, he saw a group of teenage lads coming towards him and behaving boisterously. One of them jumped in front of the car, forcing Simon to bring the car to a halt. The lad stared through the windscreen, and then, apparently satisfied with his prank, leapt back on to the footpath. Simon interpreted these actions as a deliberate challenge to his manhood, and, having parked his car, went in search of the lad. When he did find him and spoke to him sharply, the lad was surprised and denied he had done anything wrong.

This incident was important to Simon for he had always worried about his manliness and whether he was strong or weak. On this occasion he felt that he needed to reassert his power to assure himself that he was not weak and powerless.

I offered Simon an alternative explanation of the incident. When describing the circumstance of the incident he had mentioned that his two very pretty daughters were also in the car. 'The lad,' I said, 'was trying to impress them. He wasn't even looking at you.'

'I never thought of that,' said Simon. 'Now I come to think of it, when I spoke to him he didn't seem to recognize me.'

Whenever we mark out an area where we intend to be powerful, just as we can think that other people are playing their part in our drama, so we can think that the area we have delineated is the most important in our lives and in the world we live in, and in this we can be very mistaken.

As individuals we may not be able to mark out a large area involving other people for the imposition of our power, so we choose some area of our own lives where we can be powerful, and fail to recognize that this area is continuous with everything else that exists. Some people, feeling powerless, decide to exert personal power over their own health, and devote themselves to controlling what they eat and how they exercise. Somehow these conscientious vegetarians and earnest joggers have persuaded themselves that they have power over the area of their life they call their health, and lose sight of the fact that we are continuous with everything else that is and that everything that is is in continuous change. No matter how much we study nutrition and try to avoid contaminated foods, we have little control over what our bodies actually ingest, and the continuous changes in the composition of our bodies, while they might be modified by healthy living, go on remorselessly to old age and death.

There are many men who regard soccer as the whole point and purpose of living, and some of them compete most fiercely for power within the soccer world. This might provide them with a living and save them from indulging in more destructive power-seeking, but their overestimation of the importance of soccer in the scheme of things prevents them from seeing just how the soccer industry affects and is affected by economic and social factors which lie outside the control of the powerful men in soccer. This is evident in their confusion about just who is responsible for the young men who use soccer as a vehicle for their own power struggles with their contemporaries. In other times and places these young men have not been known as 'football hooligans' but as 'our brave boys', ready to die for their country.[48]

The relationship between the concept of 'football hooligans' and 'our brave boys' is shown in a statement given by one such football hooligan to researchers studying the behaviour of football supporters.

> Whilst away representing my country, England, I had one of the biggest buzzes of my life. I thought I was at war for them. The adrenalin that was pumping through my body, aching with pride from the moment we landed was something I have never experienced in my life before. It was better than sex or winning the pools.
>
> Within an hour of leaving the station at Dusseldorf, about 8 of us encountered 15 Holland fans, all older and bigger than us. They were singing about what they were going to do to England. In England you wouldn't have fancied having a go but because we were representing our king and country we ran straight at them and they were gone.[49]

What this excerpt also illustrates is how often the desire for power stems, not just from the desire to be oneself getting everything, but from hate. Often the person in pursuit of power believes that he can never win other people's love and admiration, and so decides, 'If I can't get people to love me, I'll make them fear me.' By all accounts, Hitler and Stalin were not regarded as lovable until they were powerful enough to terrorize people into describing them as charming. George V once remarked to his friend Lord Derby that he intended to make his sons as terrified of him as he had been of his father, and in this he succeeded. Many people do not realize that using power to create fear for ever precludes love. To love someone means being open

197

and vulnerable to that person, and we cannot afford to be vulnerable to those we fear.

Sometimes, hate in the search for power becomes an essential part of a powerful institution. Gore Vidal once remarked that women do not realize just how much men hate them.[50] To find the truth of this remark women need not look further than the Catholic Church.

Uta Ranke-Heinemann, having had her licence to teach withdrawn by the Catholic Church because she questioned Christ's conception by a virgin (Mary's hymen, according to the Church, was intact after she gave birth to Jesus), now holds the chair of religious studies at the University of Essen, from where she wrote *Eunuchs for Heaven: the Catholic Church and Sexuality*.[51] Anthony Burgess, reviewing her book, commented:

> Christ's enemies called him a glutton and a wine-imbiber (Matt. 11:19) but they never accused him of fornication. Sex is the only pleasure deemed sinful, and not only Christ's career but also his genesis have been carefully cleansed of the imputation of physical congress. The Church, which for two millennia has sustained a posture of what may be called celibate machismo, hates women. Clearly Christ did not. It is highly probably that he started his mission as a widower. His tenderness to adulteresses and prostitutes has always been a source of embarrassment to the Church. He was not so tender towards his mother, the only woman of whom the Church unequivocally approves . . .
>
> St Thomas Aquinas . . . Professor Ranke-Heinemann calls 'the Church's misguided Guiding Light' . . . What he called 'Nature's primary aim' was directed towards perfection, monopolized by man. Women accorded with 'the secondary aim of nature, like decay, deformity and decrepitude'; she was necessary for pro-creation, true, but for nothing else, 'a freak product', as the professor puts it, 'of environmental pollution' . . . Aquinas followed St Jerome in calibrating heavenly rewards thus: celibates get 100 percent of ultimate joy, widows and widowers 60, and the married 30. Better to marry than burn, but best of all not to marry . . .

The professor, professing to deal with the Church and sexuality, is rather more concerned about its sexism. She pursues her thesis about its hatred of women through 300 pages, concluding that the Church has 'desexualized homosexuality in its own ranks and then proceeded to nurture it into a male society disdainful of women'. Or, if it's inhuman to despise them, ignore them. The late Pope John XXIII, whose canonization has been wisely delayed, recalls contemplative days at Bergamo: 'As for women, and everything to do with them, never a word, never. It was as if there were no women in the world.' Jesus Christ would have been puzzled by this all-male-club, but who ever said that he had anything to do with Christianity?[52]

Whenever we organize a system for living which cuts us off from contact with a wide range of people, be it a system of priest or nuns, or of old people's ghettos, or of white laagers, we do damage to ourselves because, when we lose touch with the complexity of human life, we are less and less able to construct meanings which closely approximate reality. Power based on exclusivity always damages the holders of that power, or, in Lord Acton's well known epigram, 'Power corrupts, and absolute power corrupts absolutely.'

Nevertheless, we continue to seek power in order to ease the ache of wanting everything. Power, once we gain it, can be delicious, 'better than sex or winning the pools'. The transformation of Margaret Thatcher from a harassed backbencher in sensible Marks & Spencer suits to the regal stateswoman shows just how delightful power can be.

No wonder we continue, in our desire to get everything, to be deluded. Seeking power, we believe that, no matter how other power-seekers failed, we shall do it differently and succeed. No matter that history, over and over, shows us that dictators, who might appear to be able to get everything, fail.

Why Dictators Fail

Whether dictatorships are political or personal, the State or the family, they lead to disaster.

Dictatorships are always based on the deliberate confusion of Category One (our definitions) and Category Two (the nature of life). The dictator needs to assert that his claim to power is part of Absolute Reality. If he tries to point out the limits of his power, his followers, as long as they accept his definition of Absolute Reality, will try to prevent him because they want to share in his power. It was King Canute's followers, not King Canute himself, who claimed that he had the power to command the waves. They did not thank him for disproving this claim.

The collusion between the dictator and his followers to define their own definitions as being Absolute Reality means that they fail to understand their own nature and the nature of their world. They are deficient in the second kind of intelligence. Thus dictatorships inevitably lead to disaster.

The dictator thinks that the world is divided into discrete boxes, when in fact everything that exists is continuous and flowing.
The dictator thinks he is separate from his subjects when in fact he is not.

199

We know that we are in the presence of someone making claims to power when we discover that we cannot touch and communicate with that person in the same way as we can touch and communicate with our friends and equals. The powerful person is surrounded by a barrier.

Sometimes the barrier has a physical presence – soldiers carrying guns, or dark-suited, burly men warily surveying the crowd, or men in smart versions of the uniforms of soldiers from past centuries. Sometimes the barrier is high walls and locked doors guarded by the police.

Sometimes the barrier is invisible – a space which must not be traversed. No one can approach the Queen, or a judge sitting in court, or a bishop at the altar, without first being bidden, just as we have to wait until the doctor, or therapist, or bank manager, or government official, or business director invites us into his office. Once there we may find that the person we wish to consult has placed a barrier – his desk – between him and us. To reach across his desk or to walk around it is to invade his territory and risk punishment.

Always there is a barrier to communication. The Queen initiates all conversations. The judge decides who should speak in court, and the priest in church. The doctor, therapist, bank manager, government official, business director decides what subjects will be discussed, how they will be discussed, and for how long. Persons addressing people in power must use formal modes of address – 'Your Majesty', 'Ma'am', 'Your Honour', 'Father', 'Doctor', 'Mister', 'Sir', while people in power can address their inferiors with inferior terms. Doctor to patient: 'John, I am your consultant, Doctor Hamilton.'

The dictator may think that he has created and imposed the barriers which both protect him and demonstrate his right to impose his definitions on other people, but in fact the barriers work only if those outside agree to recognize and respect them. Once they decide not to recognize and respect them, walls tumble down, bullets fly through the air, space is traversed, words are spoken, and the dictator realizes his inseparability from everything else that exists.

The dictator thinks of causation as being a single line, when in fact it is a multidimensional net spreading far and wide.

The dictator believes that his dictates will be carried out precisely and no further than he intends.

Those in power believe that they know how to solve problems. They give orders, but their subjects may not carry out the orders as the dictator intended, perhaps because they are wilful, or stupid, or simply because they do not understand them. Research into what goes on in doctors' surgeries shows that patients remember little, and then imprecisely, of what instructions the doctor gave them just a few minutes before in his consulting room. Sometimes dictators' orders are carried out as he intended, but the results are not what he expected.

The anti-abortion measures imposed by Nicolae Ceausescu in the mid-1960s are typically viewed as an example of his repressive policies towards women. Yet the ironic fact is that abortion restrictions inadvertently – and literally – sowed the seeds that helped topple Ceausescu's regime 23 years later.

In 1966 Ceausescu surveyed his country's falling birthrate with despair. The cause, he concluded, was a state decree in 1957 that had legalized abortion and made it readily available for a fee of less than $2. By 1965 abortion was the country's primary method of birth control, with four abortions performed for every child born.

But in October 1966 State Decree No. 770 was issued, in effect prohibiting abortion except under extraordinary circumstances. At the same time, the import of oral contraceptives and IUDs was discontinued, and a package of other measures such as birth premiums and reduced taxes for couples with children were introduced. Rumania's mother heroines, as they have been called, responded vigorously. In September 1967 births totalled 63,183, more than triple the number from the previous December. The total number of births in 1967 was nearly twice that of 1966. Newspapers reported instances of three new mothers sharing the same bed.

During the next few years, the birthrate declined as women discovered other means of birth control. But the babies remained. From 1966 to 1976, Rumania produced nearly 40 percent more babies than might otherwise have been expected.

The result was a compressed baby boom . . . In 1989 twice as many 22-year-olds were flooding into the labour force. But Ceausescu was unable to create jobs in the late 1980s as rapidly as mothers had created babies in the late 1960s. Revolutions are carried on the backs of the young, and the sudden increase of the always volatile 18-to-22-year-old age group destabilized Rumania even more dramatically than a similar surge of baby boomers had disrupted American society in the late 1960s.[53]

The dictator thinks of acting so as to bring about a good result, or a bad result, when in fact every action has a multitude of results, some of them good and some of them bad.

Wole Soyinka has long been the critic of dictators. In an interview in London he said:

At a conference in Lagos the year before last, I called on all writers in Africa to lend their craft to seeing the end of dictatorships all over the continent. And I called on all military dictatorships to set a definite date within this century for terminating their obnoxious existence. For me, a dictatorship, especially a military dictatorship, is an insult to the political intelligence of our people. Such dictatorships have never understood that what they're doing is continually to pronounce us – and by implication themselves – as a second-class breed of humanity.[54]

Dictators, be they political or personal, treat their subjects as if they are stupid, and subjects then become so. We all have a strong tendency to behave in the ways the powerful people around us expect us to behave. Teachers who treat their pupils as being intelligent have intelligent pupils, and nurses who treat their patients as children nurse childish patients. But even more than this, when the powerful people around us are menacing us and demanding obedience we know that we shall be safer if we do not think and act for ourselves. Thus obedient subjects become inefficient and ineffectual.

So the dictator, be he a political leader imposing his decrees or a parent declaring 'Do what I tell you because I know best', ensures that, while he intends the best for himself and his subjects, what he does will have outstandingly bad results as well as good.

The great advantage of being obedient is that we do not have to regard ourselves as being responsible for the outcome of the orders given and obeyed. That is our leaders' responsibility. Dictators often demand that their subjects be responsible, but here the word 'responsible' means 'be obedient even when you are unobserved'. Such obedience is an avoidance of personal responsibility, and an avoidance of personal responsibility leads, at best, to inefficiency and, at worst, to disasters. The emergence of *glasnost* in the USSR, and some forms of democracy in other Communist states, was due not so much to an outburst of passionate demands for freedom, but to the sheer inefficiency and unproductiveness of their industry and agriculture, which convinced the leaders that some changes had to be made in the way the states functioned. What has emerged from the examination of the events leading to the explosion and fire at Chernobyl shows that, however brave and hard working many of the staff were at the time of the disaster, the whole enterprise was undermined by long-term inefficiency and neglect of personal responsibility. Unfortunately, understanding how personal responsibility works involves a lifetime of learning and experience, and people trained only in obedience find it hard to adapt to changed circumstances no matter how great the disaster.

> Four years after the Chernobyl disaster near the Ukrainian capital of Kiev, radioactive contamination of Soviet territory is spreading. This is the conclusion of Dr Alexei Yablokov, deputy chairman of the Soviet parliament's Ecological Committee, after a two-day

hearing on Chernobyl last weekend, attended by more than 100 witnesses . . .

Yablokov said that at least 2.5 million people were still living in contaminated areas in the Ukraine, Byelorussia and Russia and about 200,000 in 'very contaminated' areas. The government intended to move out 70,000 of them, but Yablokov said that this proposal was 'too narrow and conservative'.

A spokesman for RUKH, the Ukrainian popular front, said last week that children were dying of leukaemia not only in Chernobyl and the badly contaminated district of Pripyay but also in Kiev. He said that food was still being grown in contaminated fields and radioactive meat was on sale in Ukrainian stores . . .

Yablokov said contamination was spreading in many different ways from the original fall-out areas. Surface and underground rivers, flowing south, were carrying radioactive material into southern Ukraine. 'Radiation struck everything: food, water, forests,' he said. Winds were spreading radioactive dust. So were migrating animals and birds. Forest fires in fall-out areas threw contaminated material into the air which was spread by the winds.[55]

In countries where the education of children does allow for children to have the opportunity to think for themselves and to learn the difficult tasks of personal responsibility, inefficiency and disasters result from a combination of lazy obedience and a resolute, blinkered adherence to simple ideas. The tragic explosion of the Challenger space shuttle was an outcome of the Reagan administration's power-seeking and the refusal by so many politicians and scientists to admit that sunny Florida can get very, very cold.[56]

Training people in obedience leads the trainers to see the people, and the people to experience themselves, as objects. Then the trainers (who are themselves obedient) and the people lose their awareness of the distinction between objects and people. They expect that objects and people can be entirely explicable and predictable, and, often at the behest of those in power over them, they construct machines and systems which they expect to work with total efficiency. So the Titanic met the unpredictable iceberg, and man-made computers act with wilful individuality.

The first sign that something had gone haywire in the AT&T's long-distance telephone network came at 2.25 p.m. last Monday, when the giant map of the US in the company's operations centre in New Jersey began to light up like a football scoreboard. For reasons still being investigated, a computer in New York City had come to believe that it was overloaded with calls, and it started to reject them. Alerted to New York's troubles, dozens of backup computers across the US automatically switched to take up the slack – only to exhibit the same bizarre symptoms. People trying to place calls to the US from all over the world suddenly began to hear busy signals and recorded messages blandly informing them that 'all circuits' were busy.

Thus began the worst computer breakdown in the history of the US telephone system. The incident was also a vivid reminder of how susceptible the world has become to computer failures – natural and man-made. In 20 years of intensive automation, everything from supermarkets to stock exchanges has been computerized. Last week businesses and consumers were forced to face up to the downside of technology that becomes apparent only when the systems fail.[57]

The dictator overlooks that fact that part of the continuous interaction of everything that occurs is the continuous construction of meaning in which every human being is engaged all the time.

In demanding obedience, dictators are insisting that people should not think for themselves but accept the imposition of the dictator's meanings. Since thinking for ourselves is hard work, we are often glad to accept what our leaders and the media tell us, but in our failure to understand how we construct meaning, neither those who seek to impose their own meanings, nor those who receive such meanings, realize that what is given and what is received are two different things.

When we talk about giving and receiving meanings, or imparting and absorbing information and instructions, we use the metaphor of the *conduit*.

This is the term the linguist Michael J. Reddy used to describe the metaphors we use when we talk about communication, that is, in imposing our constructions of meaning on other people. He took the examples

(1) Try to *get* your *thoughts across* better
(2) None of Mary's *feelings came through to me* with any clarity
(3) You still haven't *given me* any *idea* of what you mean

and asked:

After all, we do not literally 'get thoughts across' when we talk, do we? This sounds like mental telepathy or clairvoyance, and suggests that communication transfers thought processes somehow bodily. Actually, no one *receives* anyone else's thoughts directly in their minds when they are using language. Mary's feelings, in example (2), can be perceived directly only by Mary; they do not really 'come through to us' when she talks. Nor can anyone literally 'give you an idea' – since these are locked within the skull and life process of each of us. Surely, then, none of these three expressions is to be taken completely at face value. Language seems rather to help one person to construct out of his own stock of mental stuff something like a replica, or copy, of someone else's thoughts – a replica which can be more or less accurate, depending on many factors. If we could indeed send thoughts to one another, we would have little need for a communications system.[58]

Nevertheless, these metaphors 'seem to involve the figurative assertion that language *transfers* human thoughts and feelings'.[59]

Examining the 'major framework' of the conduit metaphor, Reddy concluded that

[t]he core expressions in these categories imply, respectively, that: (1) language functions like a conduit, transferring thoughts bodily from one person to another; (2) in writing and speaking, people insert their thoughts and feelings in the words; (3) words accomplish the transfer by containing the thoughts and feelings and conveying them to others; and (4) in listening and reading, people extract the thoughts and feelings from the words [see note 60 for examples].

The 'minor framework' of the conduit metaphor

overlooks words as containers and allows ideas and feelings to flow, unfettered and disembodied, into a kind of ambient space between human heads . . . the categories imply, respectively, that: (1) thoughts and feelings are ejected by speaking and writing into external 'idea space'; (2) thoughts and feelings are reified in this external space, so that they exist independently of any need for living human beings to think or feel them; (3) these reified thoughts and feelings may, or may not, find their way back into the heads of living humans [see note 61 for examples].

An alternative metaphor, and one which approximates more closely what we actually do, is Reddy's *toolmakers paradigm*.

I should like to suggest that, in talking to one another, we are like people isolated in slightly different environments. Imagine, if you will, a huge compound, shaped like a wagon wheel. Each pie-shaped sector of the wheel is an environment, with two spokes and part of the circumference forming the walls. The environments have much in common with one another – water, trees, small plants, rocks, and the like – yet no two are exactly alike. They contain different kinds of trees, plants, terrain, and so on. Dwelling in each sector is one person who must survive in his own special environment. At the hub of the wheel is some machinery which can deliver small sheets of paper from one environment to another. Let us suppose that the people in these environments have learned how to use this machinery to exchange crude sets of instructions with one another – instructions for making things helpful in surviving, such as tools, perhaps, or shelters, or foods, and the like. But there is no way absolutely for the people to visit each other's environments, or even to exchange samples of what they construct. This is crucial. The people can only exchange these crude sets of instructions – odd-looking blueprints scratched on special sheets of paper that appear from these slots in the hub and can be deposited in another slot – and nothing more. Indeed, since there is no way to shout across the walls of the sectors, the people know of one another's existence indirectly, by a cumulative series of inferences. This part of the story, the no visiting and no exchange of indigenous materials rule, we shall call the postulate of 'radical subjectivity'.

In the analogy, the contents of each environment, the 'indigenous materials', represent the person's repertoire. They stand for the internal thoughts, feelings, and perceptions which cannot themselves be sent to anyone by any means that we know of. These are the unique material with which each person must work if he is to survive. The blueprints represent the signals of human communication, the marks and sounds that we can actually send to one another. We shall have to ignore the question of how the system of instructions became established, even though this is an interesting part of the story. We shall simply assume that it reached some sort of steady state, and shall watch how it functions.[62]

Reddy then goes on to give an amusing example of how person A, who lives in a woody environment, designs a rake, finds it is useful, and decides to pass his discovery on to B and C. Neither B nor C have much wood in their environments, and so their attempts to understand A's communications lead them each to construct something quite different. Reddy concluded:

In terms of the conduit metaphor, what requires explanation is the failure to communicate. Success appears to be automatic. But if we think in terms of the toolmakers paradigm, our expectation is quite the opposite. Partial miscommunication, or divergence of readings from a single text, are not aberrations. They are tendencies inherent in the system, which can only be counteracted by continuous effort and by large amounts of verbal interaction . . . It seems that the toolmakers paradigm and radical subjectivism simply form a coherent, common-sense view of what happens when we talk . . . I confess that it took me nearly five years to come around to radical subjectivism as 'common sense'. What stood in the way was never a counter-argument, but rather the simple inability to think clearly about the matter. My mind would go to sleep at critical moments, and it was only the mounting weight of more and more evidence that finally forced it to stay awake.[63]

Like Reddy, our education has so bamboozled us that we do not realize that, no matter how willingly we accept what our dictators tell us, we actually create our own constructions of what they tell us, and these in their meaning and implications are always different from what the dictator intended.

Moreover, even when we think we are obediently and correctly accepting the dictator's orders, we all know that if we accept *all* the constructions of meaning which the dictators impose on us and do not preserve some part of our own construction of meaning as our own, some part which reassures us of our individuality and significance, we shall feel empty and valueless and find our lives dreary and point-less. So we practise some form of disobedience, perhaps in the company of others, by telling jokes against the dictator, or by breaking the economic or moral laws of the dictatorship (as shown by the black market in Communist countries and the propensity for tyrannical parents to have delinquent children), or perhaps just in the individual secrecy of our own fantasies.

Despite all the Thought Police, no dictator can know what we think.

The dictator thinks that the meanings we create are discrete categories, when in fact they are linked to one another so that meanings of which we are not conscious can influence our actions.

As meaning-creating creatures forever imposing structures of meaning on a reality which forever eludes us, we have a choice: either we can strive to approximate as closely as possible the truth of the elusive reality, or we can abandon the pursuit and instead live within our own constructions of meaning in, as we say, 'a world of our own'. Most of us deal with this choice by doing a bit of both. In some parts of our lives we strive to construct meanings which approximate reality, and in other parts we relax in the comfort of our own unquestioned and unchallenged meanings. After all, we cannot, as T.S. Eliot said, 'bear too much reality'.

We all know that if we give up making any attempt to know what reality is we soon get into difficulties. Floating on the bliss of drugs or alcohol we make serious errors in our judgement of time and space; living by our own private meanings we cease to be able to communicate with our fellows. Labelled bad or mad, we suffer society's punish-ments. We may strive to avoid such a fate, but then fail to distinguish between when we are trying to construct meanings which approximate reality and when we are living in a world of our own. We do this whenever we are convinced by the utter rightness of our own point of view.

If we are living in a situation where those around us are free to criticize us and point out our follies, painful though this can be, we are constantly reminded of the necessity of seeking the truth of reality. But once we assume a position of power, fewer and fewer people dare to point out when our constructions have little relationship to reality. History abounds with examples of people who, in the pursuit of power, were astute assessors of reality but who, once they had gained power, abandoned such astuteness while assuring themselves of the immensity of their wisdom, and drifted into their own world of meaning, thus ensuring pain and suffering for their subjects and the failure of the enterprise which first set them on the path to power.

The reality which we must seek if we are not to become locked into our own constructions of meaning is both the reality of our external environment and the reality of our internal world of thoughts and feelings.

Whenever I run a workshop on how we construct our world of meaning, the participants are always people who pride themselves on their self-understanding and who have undertaken the workshop because they wish to increase their understanding. I show them how we can ask a series of questions which will reveal how they each experience their sense of existence and see the threat of the annihilation of their self, and how this underlies every decision we make. Then I ask them to get together in small groups and ask these questions of one another. This activity provokes a great deal of intense discussion and outbursts of shock, and merriment to deal with the shock. This shock has two sources. First, there are always people in the workshop who did not know how they experienced their sense of existence and saw the threat of annihilation. Second, there are the people who did know this about themselves but who had always assumed that everyone else experienced their sense of existence and threat in the same way.

If this level of ignorance is present in people who strive to be sensitive and aware, how much greater is the level of ignorance by those who are so convinced of the rightness of their own constructions that they wish to impose them on other people?

If we do not understand ourselves we cannot know what is right for us, and if we do not know what is right for us we cannot begin to approximate what is right for other people. Unfortunately, the more we know ourselves the more aware we are of our own doubts and dilemmas, and the less we can hold the belief that there are once-and-for-all solutions to the major problems in living. So dictators must abhor self-knowledge and feel convinced that other people see things as they do.

The dictator assumes that other people create the same meanings as he does, and that when he acts, other people will interpret what he does as he intends them to.

The constructions which a dictator strives to impose on his subjects are usually aimed at benefiting the subjects. Politicians like to believe that their political system will lead to health and happiness for their constituents. Religious leaders like to believe that their religion will bring salvation to their faithful. Parents like to believe that they can instruct their children in how to lead happy and industrious lives.

The logic of the dictator is circular. He knows what is best for his people and will impose it, so therefore he is wise and good, and because he is wise and good he knows what is best for his people and is right to impose it. From this circular proof it follows that anyone who rejects the dictator's impositions must be mad, bad or stupid, if not all three.

Such dictatorial assumptions overlook the fact that, while we might appear to others to be mad, bad or stupid, to ourselves we are in the business of survival. Unless we see the dictator's notions of what is good for us as coinciding with our own notions, we shall strive to find a way of appearing to be obedient while trying to foster our own self-interest.

Simon Winchester had the opportunity to interview a Chinese Communist cadre in Shanghai:

Communist Party cadres, the supposedly intelligent elite from the party's cells, essentially form the glue that holds the People's Republic together. Though they fall into many ranks, they can be described as performing four principal tasks: they are low-level policy makers, high priests of the Maoist religion, prescribers of doctrinal opiates, and spies. They rarely talk, except to each other. Even more rarely do they talk to outsiders. To do so would be regarded as the worst treachery.

But Mr Li (like many Shanghainese) is a feisty, dogged sort of man. 'I do not like being ordered around. I was brain-washed in those early days when I was young. I have sat back and watched for most of my life. Now I feel like speaking, telling you how disappointed I am.' . . . They told us the party would do wonders for China. I believed it. It was an honest, proud belief. It was my dream too – that after all those years of war and in-fighting, here was an ideal which could change China. My hero was Zhou Enlai – a good, sincere man. Not Mao – I never thought he was equipped to rule. He was too inflexible, too extreme. The Cultural Revolution proved that right . . . It was afterwards that matters got so bad. Corruption was the terrible thing – everyone took money. I did not, I swear that to you. But my brother cadres did.

And it was no good talking to the police here. They took money too. There was a standard price for a bribe – 2,000 yuan. That would buy you anything you wanted. Any problem could be solved.[64]

Corruption develops because an education in obedience does not breed altruism. Dictators, in imposing their supposedly beneficial system, rely for its successful implementation on cooperation among the dictators' subjects. But this does not happen.

To cooperate with other people we have to have acquired not just an understanding that other people see things differently from us, but the capacity to tolerate and respect these other points of view. If we are brought up to believe that there is only one correct way of seeing things, we do not acquire this tolerance and respect.

Moreover, in being trained in obedience we are taught that the people outside our group, be they neither kith nor kin, nor infidels, traitors, or foreigners, are bad and dangerous, and therefore unworthy of our cooperation and largess. Hence, whenever we feel mean, or greedy, or uncertain whether we have enough to sustain ourselves and those we care about, we can readily identify others as an enemy who must not be helped. So the Communist cadres looked after themselves, little of the wealth created in Thatcher's Britain trickled down to the poor, and we choose the people we are prepared to look after with great care. In this way the dictator's plans are thwarted.

The dictator overlooks the fact that there are certain aspects of life which stand in complementary relationship to one another, so that the more there is of one, the less there is of the other.

To force our structures of meaning upon other people we have to create and maintain a distance between them and us. Consequently, the more power we have the lonelier we are.

David Hirst, writing in June 1990, said:

The adulation which Saddam requires simultaneously exasperates and bores him. He recently complained to his ministers that if he were to set himself up as a seller of pebbles, he would find people to buy them for thousands, nay millions, of dinars, people who would tell him that, from such a hand, these were pearls, not pebbles. He clearly suffers all the loneliness of total power, and what, as an undoubtedly intelligent despot, he realizes is its potentially dangerous ignorance.

It was before the fall of Ceausescu, but with what he called the new 'pluralist trends' in the world very much on his mind, that Saddam instructed all Ba'ath party members to submit regular written reports about what the people were saying. For their own reassurance the reports could be anonymous. He got no response, so he instructed party bosses to hold information seminars instead.

At the first of these, Saadi Salih, President of the National Assembly, called on his audience, as 'the eyes and ears of the leadership', to speak out. Again, nobody dared, until, finally, after he had all but begged someone to say something, one bold spirit did pipe up, and confirmed that the people were indeed complaining bitterly, and 'making nasty jokes about the party and the leadership'. But when Saadi, interrupting him, demanded some 'concrete example' of this, the man took fright and refused point-blank. So did everyone else. Saadi stormed out in fury. Perhaps he had forgotten, remarked an exile, that in spite of promised liberalization, the Revolutionary Command Council (RCC) decree of 6 November 1986, which prescribes the death penalty for the deliberate and public insult of the President, the RCC, the Ba'ath party or the National Assembly, remains in force.[65]

All dictators promise freedom and security, but of course this is what they can never give, for all their impositions of their constructions of meaning reduce their subjects' freedom. Such impositions may not increase their subjects' security in terms of food and work, but they do give their subjects the security of knowing what is forbidden.

Not that the lack of impositions produces security. Those supposedly free countries, the USA and Australia, have the highest proportion in the developed world of children living in poverty – seventeen percent of the young population.[66]

We all need the security of enough to eat, a place to live, relationships with others, a sense of belonging, and such structures together form a prison. We need to be able to live healthily and creatively in such a prison, and the only way we can do this is by having the freedom to choose our own prison. This freedom no dictator can give us except by ceasing to be a dictator.

Dictator or Democrat

We can use our power to create meaning to imprison ourselves and others, or to set us free. As David Smail wrote:

> Most of the evils of our society, and certainly by far the greater part of the so-called 'pathological' emotional distress experienced by its members, are more or less directly attributable to the unequal forms of (usually economic) power which are abused and corrupting . . .

If one is to be able to understand the processes whereby people become unable to realize their potentialities in public living, to learn how to make a bodily contribution to the social world, to treat each other with kindness and forbearance as ends rather than means, and to become, as it were, the organic custodians of an unknowable future, the ability ethically to criticize the social structures in which we live is one which is actively to be preserved. Not, of course, that the ability to make moral judgements will of itself change the world, but it is certainly a prerequisite to the kind of moral and political action by which the actual structure and institutions of society may be altered. The ills we suffer are not consequent upon our personal inadequacies or moralistically attributed faults: they are the inevitable result of publicly endorsed and communally practised forms of indifference, greed and exploitation, and require a moral reformation of our public, not our private ways of life. Instead of abusing power, we need to use whatever power we have to increase the power of others, to take care rather than to treat, to enlighten rather than mystify, to love rather than exploit, and, in general, to think seriously about what are the obligations as opposed to the advantages of power. Ideally, the foremost obligation on power is to 'deconstruct' itself.[67]

Such 'deconstruction' can be difficult for people trained in obedience and unwilling to think for themselves, so they do not want the dictators to disappear.

Many people who try to be democratic leaders are appalled when they find that their tentative suggestions about possible courses of action are interpreted by their equals, who wish to be subjects, as absolute rules, as unchangeable and unquestionable as the laws of the Medes and the Persians.

Anyone who sets up as a therapist soon finds that clients impose on the therapist the expectation that the therapist has the power to make them better. Such clients (and there are many) believe that the therapist will be able to utter some magic words, incantations or priceless wisdom, and the client's pain and suffering will vanish. For some therapists the major work in therapy is in getting the client to see that there are no magic incantations and that the wisdom they must find is their own. However, there are many therapists who readily accept their clients' expectations that they have the power to make the clients better, and so behave in the ways of power that apply to the peculiar conditions of the client-therapist relationship. Just how to do this is shown in a story, so often told that it has become apocryphal, about a psychoanalyst who said to a client who believed that he was God, 'All right, I'll let you be God.' One psychotherapist, so I have been told, instructs his clients that they can go on holiday only when he gives them permission. If they insist on taking their holidays in accordance with other conditions in their lives, like school holidays, rules for employment or family need, the clients must pay for the missed appointments. However, the therapist takes his holidays as it pleases him without concern for the client's needs. The client is helpless to do anything about this because, having imposed on the therapist the magical power to cure, the client must keep going back to the therapist in the hope that one day the therapist will exercise this power. This keeps the client paying, and paying, and paying, so, while the therapist is not able to demonstrate his power, he is able to indulge his greed.[68]

When other people impose power on us it is difficult to resist being sucked into the role of dictator, for the taste of power always carries the hint that the longing to have everything will be satisfied. But power cannot do this, for power never fulfils its aims. Finding this, many powerful people turn to greed in the hope that wealth and possessions will satisfy. But they do not.

6

'Yes I Can' – Greed and Envy

'Too much is never enough.'[1]

Experiences of Greed and Envy

Greed can be felt just as an ache, an emptiness, a longing, a hunger, or can be put into words: 'More, yes, more', 'I want that', 'This is mine and you're not having any', 'I know it's greedy, but I'd love a second helping', 'I want to be the richest person in the world'.

Greed seems to be the obvious way of having everything. Most of us translate 'everything' into goods – money, houses, cars, clothes, artistic objects, trinkets, food and drink – and strive to acquire as much of them as we can. Those people who live in poverty have to devote themselves to acquiring food and shelter, but once we are no longer hungry we can look around and see what else we can have.

Every generation has contained people who devote themselves to acquiring wealth and possessions, but certain generations have had more opportunities than others. During and after the Second World War there were many people who strove, often very successfully, to make money on the black market and in selling war surpluses, but they were not overtly encouraged in this by public opinion. All effort, so public opinion went, should be devoted to winning the war and then to reconstruction. The very popular film *The Third Man* was an indictment of those who tried to profit from the shortages of goods necessary for life.

By contrast, the eighties was a time when greed was praised. With a prime minister who preached that the most important purpose in life was to get 'value for money', greed became good. Perhaps the nineties will be different now we have seen the suffering which resulted from Saddam Hussein's greed and envy.

Names were invented for the conspicuously greedy. There were the yuppies, men and women in their twenties and thirties who demonstrated that for greed to impress others the objects acquired must be approved of by their peers. The yuppies were first admired by many, for most of them worked hard to acquire their wealth, and their taste and elegance created opportunities for others to follow, but they soon fell prey to the satirists.[2] Greed, like pride, comes before a fall.

The eighties, too, was the time of the wannabees, the people who want everything but without having to work for it. According to Brenda Polan of the *Guardian*:

The wannabee wants everything the yuppie wants and, in addition, wants to be famous, admired, feted, courted, talked about, recognized and pointed at in fashionable restaurants. The wannabee aches to overhear her/himself gossiped about at an adjacent table by total strangers. Envious strangers.[3]

Of course the wannabee has existed in large numbers in all generations. As children we are all wannabees in our daydreams, but then most of us realize that to become even part of what we want to be we have to work.

When we work hard to acquire a particular possession that means a great deal to us, we can get continuing satisfaction from that possession because it is a testament to our achievement. As I move about my home I feel satisfaction for, having lived in other people's homes, often shabby and uncomfortable places, I now have a house sited and organized to please me, and achieved by my own efforts. In contrast, when our striving to acquire possessions is fuelled purely by greed, trying to satisfy the ache of wanting everything, the possessions acquired, no matter how vast and expensive, fail to satisfy. This is because it is not the actual possessions that are important to us, but the greedy fantasies we have about getting everything.

We have fantasies about acquisition when we promise ourselves that we shall be rewarded for all the sacrifices we have made in learning to be good. A little girl, learning to be docile and feminine, dreams of her wedding dress and her house filled with pretty things. A little boy, learning to be manly and obedient, dreams of the fast cars he will one day own. We elaborate these fantasies as we come to realize that 'Too much is never enough', for, no matter how much we acquire, material possessions can never compensate us for our loss. The ache and the sense of loss remain. The little girl, grown up and married, redecorates and refurnishes her house but is never satisfied. The little boy, now working, rewards himself with a new car every year, and searches the car magazines for the perfect car which has everything.

For some people the fantasies about acquisition are not just a matter of rewards for sacrifices but are a desperate attempt to buy themselves the sense of security they never had as a child.

A great deal has been written and said about the ways in which parents can behave which lead children to feel insecure, yet one of the major reasons for a life-long sense of insecurity is rarely mentioned. This is the experience of growing up in poverty. This experience is ignored because most psychiatrists and psychologists are middle-class and have no first-hand knowledge of what it is like to confront daily the possibilities of homelessness and starvation. Those psychiatrists and psychologists with working-class origins may be well aware of how much their ambition and capacity for hard work were fuelled by a fear of poverty, but, having made it to the middle class, they are loath to draw attention to their humble beginnings. In recent years there has been a running joke which concerns boasting about humble beginnings – 'When I was a child we were so poor we lived in a shoe box.' 'Call that poor! When I was a child we lived in a puddle.' – and many politicians like to boast of their working-class origins so as to claim to be 'a man of the people', but in psychiatry and psychology the experience of poverty is ignored. Social scientists have collected statistics on poverty, and some of them write most perceptively about the effects of poverty on certain societies, but descriptions of the personal experience of poverty come only from writers who, having had such experience, transmute it into fiction (such as Catherine Cookson) or literature as autobiography (such as Laurie Lee).

Thus, when our television screens and newspapers fill with pictures of starving babies nuzzling against their mother's empty breast, we are given the figures of how many children are dying, but not the figures of how many of those children who survive will grow up with an insatiable greed. Those of us who knew the lack of food in childhood never forget it. Haunted by the memory of being hungry, starving children become adults who have a hunger no wealth or power can satisfy.

I never knew the lack of food as a child, but I knew from my earliest days how lucky I was to be able to eat. I was born in the midst of the Great Depression in Australia, and the constant refrain from the adults around me was that I was a most fortunate child, for my father had a job. Not that that made us wealthy. When I was born, so my mother in later years told me, my father was earning five pounds a week. He gave one pound of that to his mother (her husband had died twenty years before in a mining accident, leaving her with six children to support, and the mine owners paid no pension), kept a few shillings for himself, and gave the rest to my mother. How she managed to pay the mortgage and feed and clothe the four of us (I had an older sister) was little short of the miraculous. But she was always anxious about money, and conveyed her anxiety to my sister and me. Christmases, birthdays and wedding presents worried my mother terribly. She hated to appear mean, and she was not, but she had little to spare, and the spectre of hunger and of the shame of homelessness haunted her continually. It came not just from her memories of her childhood as one of six children living in the bush on what little her father earned as a coal miner. The spectre was just over the hill from her marital home, in Happy Valley, where families made destitute by the Depression lived in humpies of old coal-mine props and sacking. If I complained that my growing feet were cramped inside my shoes, I was told how lucky I was to have shoes and not to have to go barefoot like the children of Happy Valley. My mother also warned me that going barefoot would mean that my feet would spread like 'black fellows' feet'. I disobeyed my mother and went barefoot whenever I could, and this saved me from the fate of many children growing up in similar circumstances – crippled, distorted feet.

Such literally crippling poverty has not vanished from rich countries. At present in Britain, the purchase price for adults' shoes includes Value Added Tax, whereas children's shoes are not taxed. Adults' shoes are defined by size, with the result that many rapidly growing older children need adult-sized shoes. When parents cannot afford to pay the extra cost of shoes, such children have to continue wearing shoes which, being too small, damage their feet.

Throughout my childhood my parents constantly told me that the only reliable way to avoid poverty was to have an education. They pointed to the many people who were once prosperous but who were now destitute, not through any fault of their own, but through the machinations of politicians and financiers. My father would tell the story of the man stranded on a desert island who found a ten-shilling note in his pocket (then a goodly sum) and, looking at it sadly, reflected that it was of no value or use in that situation. What I learned from all of this was that I should acquire money in order to avoid the shame and helplessness of poverty, but that I should rely not on money for my security but on my own efforts in skilled work.

This was a powerful conclusion to draw from my economic experiences as a child, for it fitted in with how I had been taught to be good, especially the 'work hard' admonition, and how I knew myself to be, needing to be myself and to develop myself.

Unfortunately for all of us, the conclusions we draw from our childhood experiences and the actual events of our lives do not always mesh together in a neat and happy pattern. While I was constructing my beliefs about economics, I was also constructing my beliefs about love and marriage. Often, when I heard my mother talking about my father, I thought that she was being disloyal to him. She would, for instance, speak most disparagingly of his capacity as a carpenter and plumber, and Dad was certainly much better with words than he was with tools. So I vowed that I would give the man I loved my undivided loyalty.

Thus it was that I allowed myself to hand the responsibility for myself over to someone else. I married, had a child, and when my son was nearly three I returned to teaching. My salary was used to run the household. This arrangement was meant to allow my husband to set up his own legal practice. I had no idea what money he was making and spending. It was inconceivable to me that there were people who did not pay their bills when they had the money to do so, and thus I was slow to realize that my husband had a deep aversion to paying bills. Not to running them up. He did that with great verve and enthusiasm. His aversion to bill paying was eventually brought home to me in many unpleasant ways – importunings from relatives and friends that I should get him to pay them what he owed them, visits and phone calls from menacing strangers, finding my car missing when I needed to get to work and discovering that it had been repossessed. My life was out of my control and I was terrified.

When, finally, we separated, I found that after all my years of hard work all that stood between me and poverty was what I could earn. Everything that I thought I owned – home, car, an insurance which I had always paid – had vanished into the maelstrom of my husband's debts. The spectre of poverty filled me with terror and despair. How could I get control of my life, make my child and myself secure, escape the hopelessness and shame of a hand-to-mouth living, and give my life some meaning which would give me hope and purpose? My friends expected and hoped that I would marry again, but I knew I would not. To marry and to demand of my partner that I operate my financial arrangements totally separately from his would imply a lack of trust inimical to a happy marriage, and I would no more trust my welfare to someone else than a person plucked from a raging ocean would go back into that ocean again.

Secure though I may now be – or as secure as anyone can be in a world which is at the mercy of politicians and financiers – the spectre of poverty has not left me. I may not have acted nor may I act with regard to money in a logical and sensible way, but I now know that no one does. Money – or the lack of it – is integrally bound up in our experience of wanting and not getting everything, of needing to be in control and feeling helpless, of being ourselves and of selling ourselves. It is no wonder that we all act illogically about money, some of us outrageously so.

All of us, battling to make ourselves secure, are haunted, if not by the spectre of poverty, then by the shadow of the tax men. We work hard, and these anonymous people then take from us much of what we earn. We try to reduce what we are expected to pay by a scrupulous attention to what can be regarded as tax deductions, and some

218

of us, by a careful 'forgetting', neglect to disclose this or that taxable income. We are not surprised when large business institutions deprive the tax men of millions by finding loopholes in the law and by 'creative accounting', for honesty is not a prized commodity in the international business scene, but we are surprised when we discover that certain well-known and admired people have not realized that there are in life only two certainties – death and taxes.

When in 1988 Lester Piggott, the very successful and highly respected jockey, was charged and sentenced to prison for failing to declare to the Inland Revenue all of his large income, the British public was shocked. To an outside observer there was no reason for his dishonesty and greed. The following year there was an even greater shock when the greatly loved comedian Ken Dodd was charged with tax evasion. In the USA Leona Helmsley, once dubbed 'Queen of New York', was charged with forty-seven counts of federal tax evasion. Her reported outrageous behaviour and her alleged remark, 'We don't pay taxes: the little people pay taxes,' lost her what popularity she might have had in a city where wealth and the display of wealth are highly valued, but there was still surprise that people as wealthy and knowledgeable as she and her husband should not have recognized the inevitability of taxation.

What these three people have in common is not just their failure to recognize one of life's certainties, but their childhood experiences where the fear of poverty impressed upon them the need for money, and created in them fantasies of acquisition which came to dominate their lives. This can only be inferred from the accounts given of the lives of Lester Piggott and Leona Helmsley, but the trial and acquittal of Ken Dodd revealed much about his childhood.

> Ken Dodd was born 61 years ago to a furiously hard-working family of Liverpool coal-traders. It was an extremely happy childhood, enlivened by his father's wit, but darkened by his gambling, diseased lungs and the bailiffs. Arthur Dodd's fear of them – they called twice – banks and the rest of the financial establishment 'must have rubbed off on all of us,' his son told the court . . .
>
> During the trial the jury heard that Dodd had actually hoarded £336,000 in his attic, an astonishing sum to risk being stolen or lost in a fire. Dodd said he hoarded because money meant to him that he was a star, 'important only because I have nothing else'.[4]

The simplicity of Ken Dodd's way of living revealed at his trial was as astonishing as the sums which he earned and hoarded. Lester Piggott, a very reserved man, lived in a style appropriate to his work and his need for privacy, whereas Leona Helmsley lived with great style and extravagance in the way that many people dominated by fantasies of acquisition do.

For such people it is not enough to feel comforted by sums of money stashed in shoeboxes in the attic and off-shore banks. The fantasies of such people include fantasies of display and rhetoric in which they persuade others of their importance and significance. So Leona Helmsley's face advertising the Helmsley hotels smiled confidently at us from magazines and billboards.

Many people are dominated by fantasies of acquisition which arose not in response to the spectre of poverty, but in response to childhood events, usually because of a domineering parent, which threatened to overwhelm the child. The child protected himself with the 'I'll show you' fantasies that feature in every child's life. The fantasy goes, 'You might humiliate me now, but you wait. I'll show you. I'll be bigger, better, richer, more famous, more powerful than you.' Such fantasies have spurred many a child on to great things. If a child has artistic or intellectual talent, the result in adult life may be great artistic or intellectual work, but if the child has little ability or interest in these fields, or if he knows that the people he wants to impress care only

"Say what you will about greed, but before I became greedy, I was nothing."[5]

for wealth, his 'I'll show you' fantasies become fantasies of acquisition. Thus Donald Trump, the son of a rich man, became much wealthier than his father, and blazoned his name across his possessions for all to see.

So we dream of wealth and possessions, and imagine ourselves receiving our rewards for being good, feeling secure, and reducing to awe and humiliation those who have humiliated and defeated us. Best of all, we see our wealth as investing us with power. We shall be able to impose our definitions of reality on to other people. They will love us, respect and admire us, and do what we want.

Fantasies of acquisition give us much comfort and hope. We might deplore greed, and envy those richer than us, but the existence of the rich assures us that we can have it all.

Thus it is that no country ever evolves a truly egalitarian system. Each Communist country had or has its own wealthy elite. In Israel only four percent of the population live in kibbutzim. Everybody wants something more, some distinction.

When the governments of Britain and the USA, with Margaret Thatcher as Prime Minister and Ronald Reagan as President enjoying a 'special relationship', pursued policies with rewarded the rich and punished the poor, there was a public glorification of greed which was reflected in the arts. In the popular film *Wall Street* the anti-hero Gekko said, 'Greed is good. Greed is right. Greed works. Greed clarifies, cuts through and captures the essence of the evolutionary spirit. Greed, in all of its forms – greed for life, for money, love, knowledge – has marked the upward surge of mankind and greed . . . will save . . . the USA.'[6]

The arts reflect our lives not merely to entertain us but to enlarge our understanding of the moral issues in our lives. However, so dominant is greed in our lives that those artists who attempted to question the morality of greed found that their work was taken instead as a glorification of greed. An editorial in the *Guardian* reflected on this:

Every Friday night over recent weeks the comedian Harry Enfield has been strutting on to the set of the Channel Four programme Friday Night Live, waving great wads of tenners and proclaiming, in his role as a character known as 'Loadsamoney', that the secret of human happiness lies in lots and lots of what he calls 'dosh'. Now he is going to strut off. To his horror (for in private life Mr Enfield is a politics graduate of impeccable left-wing persuasions) a creation intended to be a satire of the money-philistinism of Thatcher's Britain appears to be savoured and loved. Real yobs all over the City, according to eye-witness reports, have begun appearing in pubs, brandishing bundles of genuine banknotes and screaming 'loadsamoney, loadsamoney'. Before long, if present trends continue, the thoroughfares of the nation could be crammed with 'loadsamoney' lookalikes. Mr Enfield alone has the power to discourage such practices. And, no doubt at great cost to his own load of money, he means to use it.

Meanwhile, across the Atlantic, the writer and director Oliver Stone, who made the Vietnam war film *Platoon*, is said to be equally chagrined by some of the audience responses to his new Oscar-winning movie *Wall Street* which opened in London yesterday. This features a villain called Gordon Gekko (played by Michael Douglas), a creature whose creed is greed and who aims if he can to twist and cheat his way to a million dollars a day. You're not supposed to like him. 'I think the pigs and greedies will be offended by the portrait,' Mr Stone opined as the film hit US screens. Not a bit of it. When they got to the scene where Gekko delivers a hymn to grasping avarice not a million miles from the genuine words of the notorious Ivan Boesky ('greed is all right, by the way') some punters, it seems, stood and cheered.

Harry Enfield won't lack for company in the pit he dug for himself. We weren't meant to love Alf Garnet when Johnny Speight unleashed him in a cloud of foul-mouthed racialist rhetoric; but millions did. The great cartoonist Vicky thought he could ridicule Harold Macmillan by drawing an Edwardian caped crusader and calling it Supermac. But people loved Supermac too. The media, and especially the screen, have become a kind of philosopher's stone, transforming base irony into gold – loads of it. Tom Driberg used to warn of the dangers of irony. If you've got to use irony in a newspaper, he used to instruct young reporters, make sure you get it set in ironic type. The world today is littered with tragic, broken figures, weighed down by remorse (though also sometimes by bulging wallets), who are paying the price for not heeding that warning.[8]

Of course irony is not understood by those people who do not understand that we construct our world of meaning. Irony is essentially the juxtaposition of two constructions in order to create a third perspective. Irony is rarely comfortable, even though it does afford those who understand it great amusement.

For some time in the eighties there were many people who took advantage of the opportunity to be greedy without apology. Even the portrayal of greed brought satisfaction.

Michael Douglas, who won an Oscar for his part of Gekko, said to Terry Wogan on his talk-show, 'I like playing a character that has no moral redemption.'[9]

However, as time went on, the purveyors of the 'greed is good' philosophy became more keenly aware that there is something distasteful about a person who is apparently motivated only by greed and self-interest.

Margaret Thatcher, who did not use the term 'greed' but spoke instead of 'value for money', a concept which allows no room for generosity and altruism,[11] found it necessary to justify her actions in a curiously disjointed address to the General Assembly of the Church of Scotland.

> We are told that we must work and use our talents to create wealth. 'If a man will not work he shall not eat,' wrote St Paul to the Thessalonians. Indeed, abundance rather than poverty has a legitimacy which derives from the very nature of Creation.
>
> Nevertheless, the Tenth Commandment – Thou shalt not covet – recognizes that making money and owning things could become selfish activities. But it is not the creation of wealth that is wrong but the love of money for its own sake.

The spiritual dimension comes in deciding what one does with the wealth. How could we respond to the many calls for help, or invest for the future, or support the wonderful artists and craftsmen whose work also glorifies God, unless we had first worked hard and used our talents to create the necessary wealth? And remember the woman with the alabaster jar of ointment.[12]

Her theology was questioned by Mark Corner, lecturer in religious studies at the University of Newcastle-upon-Tyne.

A straightforward embargo on riches is unrealistic. But the Bible is far more realistic in this respect than the Prime Minister. For her position appears to be that the rich will accept their obligation to help the poor, whereas 'human nature' would suggest that they are more likely to stay as rich as they can . . .

Perhaps she should turn for a moment from those pious platitudes about individual giving which she culls from a handful of New Testament texts to the prophetic Old Testament denunciations of nations and cities in which the poor went uncared for and the rich enjoyed their wealth.

The prophets could tell her something about the progressive decline of a nation as the fat cats get fatter, as the manners and attitudes of the people grow uglier and as the poorest minority is swept out of sight. And they could tell her that change can realistically come, not when the rich turn from their wealth to help the poor, but when the nation expresses its commitment to the morality of public provision by taking away some of their wealth.[13]

At the same time the BBC television series *Panorama* examined the Government's attitude to wealth and pointed out:

This Government has created a degree of unfairness that has not been seen since the war. The gap between the rich and the poor is widening at a rate it has not done this century.

In response, Lord Young, then a member of the Government, justified his own position. He said:

I don't actually look to see if someone's better off. What I'm concerned about is that I can look after my family, that I can take responsibility for myself. It's the exact opposite of selfishness. It's taking responsibility for myself.[14]

Lord Young's words epitomize the sense of unfairness we all feel when we are criticized for being greedy when, in our own eyes, we have been trying to get what we feel is rightly ours. Why should we not have what we have earned through trying to be good, and what we are owed through our status and privileges? Why should others be given and we deprived? And how can others know that we have been given unless we display what we have?

So, along with our fantasies of acquisition go our fantasies of envy.

The world of sales and advertising thrives on these fantasies. The *Observer* colour supplement carried a two-page spread showing a BMW car, and under it was written:

ANYONE CAN DREAM. ONLY FORTY CAN BUY.

BMW wish to announce the forthcoming sale of a true masterpiece.

A strictly limited edition of the M635CSi.

This year, only forty will find their way onto the streets of Britain. It's no real surprise.

The 3.5 litre 24 valve engine is built by BMW Motorsport using the most sensitive precision tool known to man. The human hand.

Developing 286 bhp, it propels you to 60mph in 6.1 seconds, only easing up when it hits 158mph.

A powerful computer keeps it running sweetly whether it's simply ticking over in the driveway or tearing along the fast lane of the Autobahn.

Slip into the air conditioned interior and you'll recognize the human touch again.

Finest hand-stitched Nappa leather abounds. It clothes the doors, the fascia and the electrically adjusted seats. 27 metres in all.

Step outside and you will find ellipsoidal headlights that give 30% more light, regenerating bumpers and twin tube gas filled shock absorbers.

But perhaps 1988 is not your lucky year. Perhaps you won't be one of the fortunate few.

Then take a good look at the slightly less rare (but by no means common) BMW 635CSi.

Its 3.5 litre engine is capable of a slightly more sedate 140mph with a 0–60 time of 6.8 seconds.

But the computerized engine management system, the interior and the classic lines all remind one of its more unusual stablemate.

So, the choice is yours. The rare M635CSi or the medium rare 635CSi.

Whichever you choose you'll be ending up with a car most people will only dream of.

THE ULTIMATE DRIVING MACHINE.[15]

Envy can be felt just as an ache, a longing, a sense that everything important is happening elsewhere, that everyone else has what we lack. We can put the feeling into words which reveal our envy: 'That jammy bugger's got just what I want', 'It really screws me up to see that old cow wearing the clothes that'd look so good on me'; or we can hide our envy and say, ' I'm against positive discrimination in education. Those who get it don't appreciate it and won't use it', 'I don't know what the youth of today are coming to. When we were young we had to work for whatever we got'.

Envy is prevalent in our society because we are born wanting everything and grow up feeling deprived and not understanding why. Envy supplies the reason why so many people do what they do. We envy and are envied.

Envy on its own can be a useful spur to achievement. We can fancy a certain job, a certain car, a certain prize, and work hard to achieve it. But all too often envy is mixed with hate, and then we are injured by it.

If we envy others and hate them because they have what we have been deprived of, our hate cuts us off from others, and narrows and sours the way we think about ourselves and our world. Our hate will lead us to destroy what we covet but cannot have, as was seen in the orgy of destruction the retreating Iraquis wrought upon Kuwait. If we are the object of other people's envy and hate, we are in danger and are often hurt.

It is difficult to deal with envy and hate. When we find such feelings within ourselves and recognize the deprivation we have suffered, it is hard to abandon such feelings without abandoning the hope that one day something that ought to belong to us will be ours. It is hard to accept that we shall never be rich, or famous, or carefree as those we envy and hate are. (The Tenth Commandment warns us against coveting our neighbour's possessions, but does not warn us against the even greater envy we can feel for those people who enjoy good fortune or do not have the burdens which we carry.) When we find that we are the object of another person's envy and hate, it is difficult, often impossible, to communicate with that person, much less persuade him that we are not worthy of his envy. Belittling or despising our own possessions will not persuade another person not to envy us.

But what makes dealing with envy and hate impossible is our inability to recognize their presence. When we were children we were taught that to be envious was to be wicked. Striving to be good, we could not afford to be envious. But we could not help being envious because every day we were being shown that we could not have everything. So the only way we could deal with our envy was to deny that we felt it. We told ourselves that we could not possibly envy those people who had what we wanted because good people would not want what they had, and only bad people had what they had. We judged them from the stronghold of our virtue and felt towards them not hate, for hate was wicked, but righteous anger. So we envied and hated, and did not recognize that we did.

We had to tell ourselves these lies so as to give ourselves the hope that we were good enough to be allowed to exist, to avoid punishment, and, one day, get our rewards. This had become necessary because we had become convinced of our badness and inadequacy, so convinced that we could not possibly conceive that anyone would see us as possessing anything which *others* might envy. So we made ourselves defenceless against other people's enmity and spite. To the degree that we retain a sense of our own worth, we can recognize another person's envy and enmity towards us, but when we despise ourselves, we interpret acts of envy and enmity directed at us as evidence that other people are right to hate us because we are hateful people, and because we are bad we deserve bad things happening to us. Whenever a depressed person tells me of some act of hate directed at him because of his intrinsic worthlessness, and I offer an alternative interpretation, 'That person envies you', the depressed person always reacts with surprise. How could anyone envy him!

I have told this anecdote using masculine pronouns because men can interpret their world in this way, but more often it is women who do not recognize envy directed at them. Boys are allowed to acknowledge envy in so far as it fuels their competition with other males, but girls are taught that for a female to be acceptable she must not envy and she must be modest, that is, not the object of envy. So women are especially handicapped in recognizing and dealing with envy in their lives.

Men can acknowledge their envy in those competitions where they can feel powerful. They can compete with and envy other men in contests over wealth, power, possessions, physical prowess and sexual conquests. They do not wish to acknowledge their envy in situations where they feel weak and powerless. Instead they tell themselves that they despise those whom they envy. Thus many men despise women, or people of other races, or men whose power and wealth they can never emulate, or men who feel free to express the feminine side of their nature.

Unacknowledged envy underlies the remorseless criticism which many women direct at other women, thus provoking the constant anxiety which many women feel about their 'attractiveness'. Mothers are very good at provoking this anxiety in their daughters, and do not recognize that their constant criticism of their daughters arises not so much from their concern for their daughters as from their own sense of inadequacy and their unacknowledged envy of the young girl, who has not yet made the mistakes which the mother has made and suffered the same disappointment, deprivation, and disillusion.

One of the main reasons that women, down the centuries, have succumbed to the power tactics of men is because their unacknowledged envy of one another, with its consequent distrust and dislike, has prevented women from coming together in groups to confound and outwit their men. What chance would a sultan have had if all his harem had combined against him? What rabbi, or mullah, or early Christian father could have taught that women were dangerous and inferior if the women as a cohesive group denied that this was so? All that women need have done, down the centuries, was value themselves and one another, and teach their daughters to do the same, and acknowledge their power by withdrawing, or threatening to withdraw, their sexual and domestic services, and, most effectively, refuse to tell those lies which nourish a man's pride. Had they done so, the history of the human race would have been entirely different.

However, men have always held that it was a law of nature that women did not get along with one another, and women made this appear to be a law of nature by venting their unacknowledged envy as spite. One of the great achievements of the Women's Movement was to show there was no such law. Much of the attack which men have made on the Women's Movement was fuelled by men's fear that if women discovered that they could cooperate with one another, men would lose their power and privilege.

Our envy, acknowledged and unacknowledged, prevents us, men and women, from cooperating successfully in whatever venture we undertake. When a group of people do cooperate together, as in one of those rare but splendid experiences of a group in search of personal wisdom or practical achievements, such as the Cooperative movement in England in the nineteenth century, great things are achieved, not least of all the joy of fellowship. But all too often, what starts out as a worthy enterprise in cooperation degenerates into a morass of power seeking, back-stabbing, and destruction. Few of the committees of health and social services professionals operate with open, generous cooperation, while the noble ideals of socialism, once applied, soon generate a maelstrom of envy, spite, greed, stupidity, ignorance, cruelty, destruction and death.

The envy which prevents cooperation is often directed at anyone who appears to have some better than average characteristic or ability. 'Tall poppies' are cut down, and, instead of nourishing these people and their talents which we could appreciate and benefit from, we destroy them.

Not one of us ever develops and uses all the talents with which we are born. Criticized and humiliated by those older than us, as children we learn not to display and practise our talents. One man, a dynamic and creative training officer in the social services, told me, 'I am surprised every time I get up to speak in front of a group that the people accept what I have to say. I was the youngest in my family and everybody talked about things I didn't understand. I always felt that everything I might want to say was silly and childish. So I kept quiet.' Children are natural talkers. They have to be taught to be self-conscious and silent.

At school we are taught the 'correct' way to draw, or sing, or dance, or act, or write, and our natural talents wither and die. If we do retain a talent our contemporaries will make us pay for it. When I was a schoolchild, the one and only joy for me in class was writing the composition or essay which the teacher set. My heart would be beating fast when she returned the marked work, and I was suffused with joy on those occasions when she accompanied the return of my work with high marks and spoken praise. But my joy was short-lived, for in the class all around me were sniggers and cruel comments. At least in my primary school my teachers criticized only my spelling and handwriting, not my ideas. In high school the teachers' cold criticism of my ideas – how dare I treat Noel Coward as a dramatist worthy of serious consideration or write about Shelley's politics – reduced me to a silence which it took me thirty-two years to break, and then in a country far away from those Australians who cut down tall poppies.

The cruel envy which children feel, created by the criticism and humiliation which they suffer, continues into adult life.

The narrator of *Coming Second* tells the story of how her parents had refused to let her have piano lessons, but how her desire to play remained a secret passion. Married, with two teenage sons who were brilliant pianists, she decided to learn, but not to tell anyone, especially her husband who took such pride in their sons' musical achievements. Her teacher, Mr Brookes, pleased with her progress, entered her in the beginners' section of a musical competition where her sons were sure to take the major prizes. No one in her family, she was sure, would notice if she slipped away to play her piece. No one did, but:

Just as I was playing the last two chords, the door opened and in stalked Adrian.

All the way back to the hall, I waited for him to say something. But he didn't. Nor while we were waiting for Nicholas to play his new Bartok piece, nor all through the lunch we ate with the boys in the school canteen. He didn't say anything while we filed back to the Main Hall for the Adjudication and Prizes, First for Nicholas and Edward, of course. And for that wonderful singer.

It would have been easier, perhaps, if the photographer hadn't made such a fuss about taking my photograph with the boys, and of course his telling Adrian to take himself off out of the way didn't help . . .

Then the boys went around saying at last they knew where they got their talent from, and Mr Brookes said hadn't it been worth it, all that pain and practice, and although I'd never be another Myra Hess, I'd proved something, hadn't I?

I suppose I have.

Adrian still hasn't spoken to me – oh, he asks where his shirts are and tells me what he wants for dinner – but that's not the same thing, is it.

So that's what the cup has cost me.

There are days when I think it was too much. But then I wonder if I'd been paying too high a price all my married life, and – shall I tell you this? If the house burned down tomorrow, it'd be this little cup I rescued. And I might not give the rest a backward glance.[17]

The poignancy of this story was, for me, its universality. Many people have a secret desire to use a certain talent which they know they have and, if not to shine, at least to be for once a unique individual. Many people dare not do this, for they know that they would be punished by their nearest and dearest who do want any change in the status quo and who envy those who dare to be different.

We confine one another by our envy, and we envy the young. It is this envy which has enabled old men, down the centuries, to send young men to their deaths.

Much of the envy which the old feel towards the young takes the form of 'I suffered, so why shouldn't you?' Senior army officers resist any relaxation of the brutal initiation ceremonies which recruits have

Western eye: The massacre as seen in Vienna's *Kurier*.

to undergo. Consultants resist any improvement in the dangerously long hours which junior doctors work.

Envy arises out of our own sense of deprivation. In envy we cannot let anyone do well. Men in power in the United States Government could not let Allende and the Socialists do well in Chile. Their successors (or were they still the same envious, destructive men?) could not let the Sandinistas in Nicaragua do well. The US Government could have prevented the USSR from having influence in Chile and Nicaragua simply by supporting the Socialist governments and giving them the kind of financial support which the USSR could not afford. But the American men in power were not capable of such generous cunning. They needed an external enemy in order to maintain themselves in power and as an outlet for their enmity and spite.[18]

The belief 'I have been deprived and so should you' strangles so much of what is best in human endeavour. It is not as though those American men who destroyed Allende and who battered Nicaragua had been deprived of the basics of physical survival – food and shelter – but they had been deprived in their families and in their education of all that enriches love and compassion, and so they had no love or compassion for those who might, just might, have what they had never had and forever longed for – someone to love them as they were and who would give them what they needed. The governments of Allende's Socialists and the Sandinistas appeared to be trying to give to their people what these American men had never had. (Not that socialist governments actually do this. Power and greed soon subvert socialist ideals. Politicians of all political persuasions are much more concerned with power than with nurturing.) These men could not allow such mothering, such caring, to exist and they not be the recipients of it. So, like mindless Daleks, they had to destroy.[19]

Destructive envy often operates with the self-justification 'I'm just doing my job'. I witnessed this frequently when I was working in the National Health Service. The people who become psychiatric patients, irrespective of the 'symptoms' they display, have all suffered the losses and the lack of understanding and affection which lead people to conclude that they are bad and worthless. People deprived of Vitamin C develop scurvy, and the cure for scurvy is the giving of Vitamin C. Giving understanding and affection to people who lack these essentials is not as simple and direct as the cure for scurvy, but understanding and affection is the *only* method which has some chance of restoring psychiatric patients to ordinary life.

Traditionally, most of the people deemed mad have been treated most cruelly, and so driven further into their madness. In recent years, a few people caring for psychiatric patients have realized the importance of giving understanding and affection, but whenever they have attempted to do so they have been frustrated and hounded by those doctors, nurses and administrators who envy the patients for getting, or having the possibility of getting, more understanding and affection than they themselves received. Such doctors excuse the poor conditions of care which negate and humiliate the patients with 'If you make everything nice they won't want to leave or be independent', such nurses describe patients who express their needs as 'attention-seeking', and such administrators congratulate themselves on how they ensure that each member of staff has many patients to care for, thus maintaining the principle of 'value for money'.

In envy we try, and often succeed, to destroy what we envy and the people who possess it, and in doing so we deprive ourselves of opportunities for our own betterment. We are part of the continuity of everything that is, and if we can *all* rejoice in one another's existence and enjoy one another's talents, we all are enriched.

But our greed and envy will not let us enjoy such richness.

Why Greed and Envy Will Not Give Us Everything

Being unsuccessfully greedy causes nothing but anguish and heartache, and being successfully greedy causes nothing but trouble. Envious people turn against us, and greedy people steal from us. We have to devote so much time and effort, and spend much money, on guarding what we own. What is the point of having jewels so expensive that they can rarely be worn, pictures so valuable that they must be kept in a vault, and living with security guards and behind high walls and locked gates, so that we are no more than prisoners in a luxurious prison?

What is the point of risking all that is valuable in our lives in order to gain that which cannot rightly be ours? Financiers risk ruin and shame in order to get money which they do not need,[20] lawyers negate the principles of their profession,[21] football managers bring shame and a burden of disappointment to those who had supported them loyally for many years.[22] Why do they do this? Just utter stupidity, a grievous lack of the second kind of intelligence.

Of course, many greedy and envious people deny that they are so and claim that they have an absolute right to what they covet. Many greedy people claim that their desires are not simply their own constructions of meaning (Category One definitions), but are Category Two, part of the nature of the world.

Thus a wealthy Hindu man can simply congratulate himself that his virtue in previous lives has ensured not only that he was not born a woman but that he is entitled to all the wealth and possessions he can acquire.

The Bible, being regarded as a description of the nature of life rather than as one of the alternative definitions of reality, is a rich source of justification for greed.

Greedy people want to treat other people as objects, and not as fellow human beings with whom they should share their possessions. The wealth of Britain was built on slavery, and the justification was found in the Psalms:

> I shall give thee the heathen for thine inheritance, and the uttermost parts of the earth for thy possession. Thou shalt break them with a rod of iron, thou shalt dash them to pieces like a potter's vessel.[23]

Believing in a Just World, we believe that as our reward for being good we ought to be given what we covet. So the Psalms promised:

> Blessed is the man who walketh not in the counsel of the ungodly, nor standeth in the way of the sinners, nor sitteth in the seat of the scornful . . .
> And he shall be like a tree planted by the rivers of water, that bringeth forth his fruit in his season, his leaf also shall not wither, and whatsoever he does shall prosper.[24]

Even Jesus's admonitions to scorn greed can be read as a promise that goodness will be rewarded not just with salvation but with possessions:

> And he said unto them, Take heed and beware of covetousness, for a man's life consisteth not in the abundance of things which he possesseth . . .
> And he said to his disciples, Therefore I say unto you, Take no thought for your life, what ye shall eat, neither for the body, what ye shall put on . . .
> The life is more than the meat, and the body more than the raiment . . .
> But rather seek ye the kingdom of God, and all these things shall be added unto you.[25]

But even in defining the justifications for our greed as being part of the nature of life, we overlook the limitations which the nature of life places on us.

We think the world is divided up into discrete boxes, when in fact everything that exists is continuous and flowing.

To justify our greed we tell ourselves that our search for acquisitions is a separate part of our life, unrelated to our other activities. Thus the men in charge of the tobacco industry, wishing to maintain their profits while appearing to be public-spirited, advertise 'considerate' smoking and sponsor sporting events, while ensuring that increasing numbers of young women and people in the developing countries smoke and thus maintain the tobacco industry's profits.[26]

Such greedy men fail to see that in persuading young women to smoke they are damaging their wives, daughters, granddaughters, daughters-in-law, and the wide range of women whose services they need or whose existence delights them. They fail to see that we live in an indivisible world, and sickness and death in one section of the population renders the rest of us vulnerable. Even in those centuries when people travelled little, but rats and fleas did, plagues swept the world. Now people travel a great deal, and diseases like AIDS, hepatitis, gastroenteritis and malaria travel too.[27]

Greed and envy are private preoccupations, and people so engaged often do not realize how their activities affect other people. Seeing other people in terms of whether they can be used in the process of acquisition does not promote good relationships. Envy, too, can cause people to withdraw from us.

I have a friend who, whenever I mention that I shall be travelling to one place or another in the course of my work, groans in envy and says, 'Aren't you lucky! I wish I could do that. I've always wanted to go there. I don't get a chance to travel anywhere.' This response always silences me, because I know that my 'luck' is very much a result of hard work, planning, and the giving up of many other delightful possibilities. To say so would appear harsh, and to talk further about what I shall be doing would elicit from her more envious comments, the aim of which would be not to learn more about me but to allow her to talk about why she is prevented from travelling. Though I am not one of the factors which prevent her from travelling, I am made to feel that I, being able to travel, have added to her misery. I also feel that she is not actually interested in me and my activities, but rather she wants me to be a mirror whereby she can see herself. Bored and discomforted, I withdraw.

We think of causation as being a single line, when in fact it is a multidimensional net spreading far and wide.

'I'll get this and then I'll be happy.' A leads to B. End of story.

Or is it?

In the years following Partition, the Indian people made great advances in food production, becoming able to feed themselves and to export food. This did not mean that every Indian was adequately fed. The poor still went hungry, and the rich remained greedy; but their greed will destroy their security:

> Flood, drought, erosion – all man made – now threaten to cancel out the progress brought about by four decades of economic development. 'Development' itself – in the shape of mining, modern irrigation that relies on dam and tubewells, of forests that are cut down, and of advanced agriculture that depends on chemical fertilizers and pesticides – is causing the damage.

A third of India's 266 million hectares of agricultural land has been turned into wasteland by erosion, waterlogging or salinity – the ill effects of deforestation and modern irrigation. Another third is classed as 'partially' degraded. The result is that in spite of huge reclamation works, the average Indian now has only a quarter of the agricultural land that was available at the time of independence 40 years ago . . . Development, far from lifting India into the ranks of the affluent, is now coming to be seen as the latest and most ruthless form of colonial expansion. (Significantly, the forests are managed on principles inherited from the British, who treated the forest as a resource to be exploited.)

The new colonialists are India's thrusting, expanding middle class, rural as well as urban, who profit from industry and advanced agriculture without paying the true cost. Their allies are the politicians and officials, down to the corrupt local police who are sent out to confront the ecology demonstrators. The whole process is kept in motion by the developed world through aid, investment and trade.[29]

The advertising industry bases all its output on the message 'Buy this and you'll be happy'. Advertising tries and often succeeds in drawing our attention to a range of different objects which are supposed to have this happiness-inducing quality.

In recent years such happiness-inducing objects have included the sports shoe, but what has been induced is not entirely happy, as Martin Walker reported from Washington, DC:

Suddenly a new kind of foot fetishism is pattering through US crime statistics. In Atlanta, the police have recorded more than 50 muggings this year in which the victims have been relieved of their footwear. The shoes were probably more valuable than the contents of the average wallet . . . High technology which is supposed to justify a price tag of $170, or more than £100, may do wonders for one's basketball game, but the point about these shoes is that few are bought to be worn on court. They are a status symbol, a fashion statement . . . Sometimes when we turn on TV, it is hard to tell whether it is a sports report or an ad . . . Bo Jackson is an outstanding athlete who makes a fortune out of promoting shoes . . . Sports shoes are big business, with America handing over more than $5 billion for namebrand sports shoes last year, the same as they gave in aid to Israel and Egypt combined.

The industry now spends more than $200 million a year on its TV campaign, and this kind of money gets results . . . Demetrick Walker, 17, [is] now serving a life sentence after shooting dead 16-year-old Johnny Bates for refusing to give up his Air Jordans high-tops. 'It's bad when we create such an image of luxury about athletic gear that it forces people to kill over it,' prosecuting attorney Mark Vinson told the court.

Even if they don't kill, there are other dangerous ways of raising the money. I was admiring a brand-new Mercedes convertible parked casually in the street near our office the other day. Two teenage black kids, clanking with gold jewellery, strolled out of the Footlocker, a chain store which specializes in sports shoes. They dumped at least a dozen shoeboxes into the back seat of the Merc, and took off down M Street with a squeal of tyres.

'Guess where they got that money from,' said my companion, a staid American journalist who could not quite keep the envy out of his voice. 'You Brits are partly to blame. You know that brand of shoes, British Knights? It has the letters BK on the sides. The word on the street is that it really stands for Black Kings. Some gangs say it means Blood Killer. Desirable stuff, huh?'

The magazine *Sports Illustrated* has reported that name-brand footwear and associated sports clothing have become a kind of uniform for drug-dealing street gangs . . . In dismayingly large parts of the black community, the drug dealers are the kings of fashion, trend setters who easily become local role models. It's a grim coincidence that these local heroes of crime are wearing the same fashion icons which the respectable black role models – like Bo Jackson – are promoting on TV.[30]

Certain things which we acquire can give us great pleasure, and having fashionable clothes, a good car, a nice house can increase our self-confidence, but no amount of possessions can restore the sense of unquestioned security which we once had and lost. No matter how rich we become, we know that our possessions can be taken away from us. Thieves can rob us, banks can fail, stock markets crash, royal heads roll, and people rise up against their leaders. When we expect that what we acquire will give us everything we desire, we are always disappointed.

We think of acting so as to bring about a good result, or a bad result, when in fact every action has a multitude of results, some of them good and some of them bad.

When we are greedy we often invent reasons as to why our greed, far from hurting other people, will actually help them. We can argue that our greed 'makes work', and that we ought to be remunerated adequately for the trouble we have gone to in helping others.

I was once asked to be a speaker at a women's lunch organized by a charity which supported a small home for physically disabled children. The event was held in an expensive hotel, and was well attended. I sat on the raised dais with a Duchess, a Lady, a Famous

Politician, and an even more Famous Actress. I calculated what the people in the audience would have paid to attend the event – their tickets, the raffles, the cost of getting there, car parking, cloakroom, some of the cost of the fashionable clothes most of the women were wearing – and worked out that if each had simply given the charity the cost of the ticket and instead spent the day engaged in some useful or enlightening activity, the charity and presumably the disabled children would have profited greatly. As it was, the major financial beneficiary of the event was the hotel, while the rest of us could parade our frocks and our egos.

Advocates of forms of charity which, to make money, sell entertainment, food and drink, gifts, and the opportunity for display and contact with the famous, argue that such activities 'make work'. The job of the cooks and waitresses in that hotel were more secure, the wealth of the charitable 'trickled down' to the workers if not to the objects of the charity. Advocates of our present social system would argue that such charitable activities provide the venue for people of a certain social class to meet and talk and add interest to their lives. Both arguments have their merits, but they overlook the fact that charitable activities, whether springing from the very best intentions or being used as justification for greed, can have results very different from those originally intended. Good intentions are easily subverted by greed.

We might consider whether there are better ways of helping other people than those which lend themselves to greed and self-aggrandizement.

The United Nations World Bank was set up with the aim of helping the less developed countries improve their economies and to raise living standards. In recent years the World Bank has imposed austerity programmes on the countries which are now deeply in debt. The burden of these programmes is borne by the poor, not the rich. The principle being followed seems to be the Biblical one, 'Unto everyone that hath shall be given, and he shall have abundance: but from him that hath not shall be taken away even that which he hath.'[31]

A senior member of the bank, Dr Michael Irwin, on resigning, issued a report in which he stated:

> 'Apart from its failure in really helping the many impoverished people in the world, I am very concerned about the Bank's bloated, overpaid bureaucracy, its generally poor management and its unjustified arrogance.' Dr Irwin, 59, who trained at St Bartholomew's Hospital in London, joined the Bank last year as director, health services department, after a distinguished 32-year career with the UN Development Programme and the UN Children's Fund, Unicef . . . After joining the Bank, he served as vice-president, personnel . . . Dr Irwin criticized the lavish perks

and huge salaries of Bank officials – often 25 percent higher than other UN agencies – and described the use of first-class air travel as excessive. '$85 million (£52.8) is provided in this fiscal year.' . . .

Dr Irwin's accusations mirror those made earlier about the IMF (International Monetary Fund) by Davison Budhoo, a former senior Grenadian member of the Fund staff. The charges were presented in book form under the title of *Enough is Enough*. In it, Budhoo says that a Fund official with a big family and on assignment in the Third World 'would receive more than the basic pay of every head of state in the world'. Perks include 'high-class night-clubbing' and first-class travel 'as we go on our way to bust the native in Africa or Asia or elsewhere'.[32]

Africa has long been the object of many people's greed and charitable intentions. Africa now affords us the spectacle of some of the greatest greed and the greatest failure of charitable intentions:

Africa is the world's hungriest continent and it is getting hungrier every year. One hundred and forty million Africans are hungry now, compared with 92 million 20 years ago – and 200 million will be hungry before the end of the century. Most of these hungry people are children and women, and most of them live in the countryside. Many of them, particularly babies and small children, will die of hunger this year, just as many did last year, and as many will next year.

African hunger has become so routine, so much part of the everyday reality of the rest of the world, that no one cares to remember that the reasons for African hunger are man-made, well known and could be eliminated by the international community if the political will existed to do so. At the root of Africa's hunger lie two things: the flawed world economic order and South Africa's wars, particularly against Angola and Mozambique, which have cost its victims $60 billion in the last decade . . .

Now, for the fourth year running, the IMF is taking out of Africa more than it is putting in – a drain of over $2.5 billion in total. And in today's political climate, where the agenda is more than ever set by the super-powers and the obsession with military power is reaching beyond our world into space, the problems of the periphery and their spokesmen are simply shifted off the agenda.[33]

Greed breeds corruption. The *New Internationalist* summarized the situation in Africa:

Corruption is endemic in Africa.[34] It operates at all levels of society, but with governments playing for bigger stakes with less chance of getting caught. IMF Structural Adjustment Programmes have given corrupt officials a great break. Projects frequently don't need to be completed or accounted for, so the money vanishes overseas – this is known as capital flight.

Overseas aid is regularly siphoned into foreign bank accounts, while food aid liberates governments from the responsibility of feeding their people, enabling them to do other things with their money – like bolstering up their armies. And further down the social and political ladder, the flowering of bureaucracies and administrative regulations have brought innumerable opportunities for civil servants to line their pockets with bribes.

Between 1976 and 1986, an estimated $10 billion left Nigeria in capital flight.[35]

The *New Internationalist* offered a way forward.

The West should give aid to African countries prepared to show how the money will benefit ordinary people. Strict conditions should be attached – like the publication of all business accounts, and ceilings on military spending. The eradication of many African administrative regulations would wipe out opportunities for bribery and corruption. And African governments should be made accountable to their people. Aid might be channelled through grass roots organizations to ensure that it reaches those most in need. Voluntary groups everywhere should lobby for all aid packages to be subject to public scrutiny. And donor governments should prosecute home firms that pay bribes to get business in Africa.[36]

Why don't the politicians and financiers in the West insist that the African leaders be honest and restrain their greed?

When merchants, soldiers and buccaneers ventured into the Americas, Africa and the East they found that it was as easy to conquer people by playing on their greed as it was by subduing them by force. The merchants, soldiers and buccaneers understood this because they were themselves greedy. Nothing has changed. The politicians and financiers in the West use the African leaders' greed to further their own desire for power and acquisition.

We overlook the fact that part of the continuous interaction of everything that occurs is the continuous construction of meaning in which every human being is engaged all the time.

Possessions and the things we desire to possess are never simply useful objects. We impose on them all kinds of additional meanings, and these meanings relate to how we have constructed our own world of meaning.

A car can provide an efficient method of getting from Point A to Point B. But if the meaning we give to a car was simply that it is a means of transport, we would not have the plethora of different kinds of cars, with advertisers assuring us that not only will a certain car get us swiftly from Point A to Point B but it will enhance our image in our own eyes and in the eyes of others.

The meanings which we impose on objects are concerned with our need to think well of ourselves and our need to feel that our world is full of people, both people-people and objects-people. So some of us regard certain of our possessions as people, giving our cars, or computers, or sewing machines human names and never discussing anything likely to upset these objects (such as their replacement) in their hearing. All of us invest our possessions with certain human characteristics – such as being friendly, supportive, easy to get on with, or being difficult, spiteful, deliberately obstructive. Just as we were comforted when we had our dolls and teddy bear with us in our cot, so we feel comforted when we know our car is safely in its garage, our favourite clothes are clean and ready to put on, our television is waiting to entertain us, our computer is ready to do our bidding, and our money in the bank is protecting us from disaster.

Our possessions and those objects we desire to possess are part of our world of meaning, but these objects cannot in reality support the meanings we have placed on them. They cannot, as people can, show us that they love us, and so fill the empty spaces in our being, take the ache from our hearts, and restore our sense of belonging. They cannot, as people can, hold us close, protecting us from danger and restoring our courage.

Objects are just objects. They can never satisfy our hunger for them, for what we want from them they have not got and cannot give. No matter how much we feed on objects, we remain hungry. Our greed can never be satisfied.

We think that the meanings we create are discrete categories, when in fact they are linked to one another so that meanings of which we are not conscious can influence our actions.

Wanting everything, we often fail to realize why we define 'everything' in a particular way. 'Everything' might include everything the world has to offer, but as we look about us certain things appear to us to have a special quality which arouses our longing and our greed. Not understanding ourselves, we can fail to see that what looks particularly desirable is those things which appear to promise to fulfil the longings which arise from how we experience our sense of existence and how we see the threat of the annihilation of our self.

Those of us who experience our sense of existence as being in relationship to other people, and see the threat of annihilation as being completely and utterly alone (extraverts, or People Persons), see as particularly desirable those things which appear to promise to ensure that we shall be the centre of admiring, loving attention. Sometimes the things are those objects which we think will attract the admiration and affection of other people, objects which we believe will make us appear to be attractive, or successful, or interesting. Sometimes the things we want to possess are people. They may be an audience which we hope will never stop applauding us, or a series of sexual conquests. The people we wish to own either as an audience or as sexual partners we do not wish to see as people with their own interests and concerns, that is, as being likely to turn their attention away from us. Instead we see them as objects which can meet our need to reassure ourselves that we do exist.

If we lack the skills of a Frank Sinatra or a Don Juan to keep other people's attention focused on us, we can surround ourselves with objects, and fill our home with cuddly toys which we fantasize love us, and/or pictures and mementoes of people who we fantasize have a close relationship with us, and/or clothes, make-up, music, videos which we can use in enactments of our fantasies in which we are loved, admired, powerful and successful, and/or a phalanx of objects which enclose us and shut out the emptiness of a wide world into which we, if unprotected, would disappear. Since our audiences may tire of us, sexual partners reject us, cuddly toys not return our love, and objects cease to inspire our fantasies and obliterate the void, our greed for a faithful audience, insatiable lovers, and desirable, magical objects can never be satisfied.

Those of us who experience our sense of existence as the development of individual achievement, clarity, authenticity and control, and see the threat of annihilation as falling into chaos (introverts, or What Have I Achieved Today People), see as particularly desirable those objects which appear to promise to advance our achievement, to support the theories which we have elaborated in our search for clarity and truth, and to strengthen our organization and control of our environment. Progress up a hierarchy of positions in work or society, the winning of prizes, the accumulation of disciples, money and power all appear to meet our need to secure our sense of existence and ward off the threat of loss of control and falling into chaos.

In our greed we, as introverts, can be quite ruthless. Convinced of the rightness of our theories, be they political, religious, economic, scientific, or psychological theories, we can excuse our lack of concern for or cruelty to others as being 'for their own good'. Preferring to see ourselves as the protagonist on a cosmic stage rather than as an ordinary human being amongst millions, we excuse our greed by claiming that the end justifies the means. In doing so we ignore the fact that, in the continuous network of all that is, every event is both a means and an end, and that every event produces effects that spread far and wide. Thus the Thatcher Government's economic theories, aimed at making the British economy wealthy and secure, involved stern measures which were, so Mrs Thatcher (an introvert) would tell her people, 'for their own good'. The suffering of those people made unemployed by these policies were excused in terms of the end (economic security) justifying the means. However, these means produced other ends – an unprecedented rise in crime, particularly crimes against property. The Thatcher Government did not set an example of restraining greed, and many people who believed that they had been unfairly deprived took what they thought was rightly theirs.[37]

Objects, be they possessions, wealth, position, prizes, or people treated as objects, can never satisfy our need to secure our sense of existence and ward off our fear of annihilation of our self, for objects are always external to us and therefore prone to loss. The only way that we can be secure in our sense of existence and untroubled by the fear of annihilation is for us, as extraverts, to realize that even though we may be alone we do not disappear, and, as introverts, to realize that, as much as we enjoy a sense of achievement, organization and control, everything that is is in constant movement, and that we should see change, not as chaos, but as the source of our delightful freedom.

We assume that other people create the same meanings as we do, and that when we act, other people will interpret what we do in the same way as we do.

To excuse our greed or to get people to act in a certain way, we assume that other people see things as we do. We are surprised and confounded when other people do not excuse our greed or act as we expected.

I have two friends, of whom one has devoted her life to acquisition and the other has inherited wealth. When I told the first friend that the second friend was depressed she snapped, 'But she's got everything!' Our depressed friend was not going to get much sympathy or understanding from her!

Imelda Marcos was surprised at the interest the press took in the shoes she wore at her trial in New York in 1990. A newspaper reported, 'Her counsel, the flamboyant Gerry Spence, is at pains to eliminate from the jury's mind the profligate image suggested by the shoe mountain discarded at the Malacanang Palace in Manila. She liked shoes, he explained, because she had gone barefoot as a child.'[38] For me, the memory of the lack of shoes in my childhood makes it hard for me to discard old, worn shoes, and I have to force myself to buy new shoes.

Ceausescu, who is believed to have salted away for himself up to $8 billion (£5bn),[39] was surprised to find that his subjects did not recognize that what he did was for their own benefit. His misunderstanding cost him his life.

To be successful in manipulating people through their greed, it is necessary to know precisely the priority which people give to certain things.

For the first few million years that the human species existed, we lived in relatively small groups, tribes of about forty or fifty people. Even when several groups came together, as they did when farmers needed markets and towns began to develop, we still thought of ourselves, and continue to think of ourselves, as belonging to a relatively small group. This, combined with our strong tendency to fight amongst ourselves and form and reform our groups, meant that anyone who wanted to be a leader over hundreds or thousands, now millions, of people had to think of some way to keep these people together.

The solution readily to hand was enemies. Small groups had enemies. All the leader had to do was find some enemy against whom all the people could unite.

So tyrants, monarchs, generals, and democratically elected governments maintain their power and hold their subjects together by identifying an enemy who is external to the total group. However, if the total group should become too cohesive, the people might decide to overthrow their leader. So all tyrants, monarchs, generals and elected governments also identify an internal enemy. To get their people to hate the external and internal enemy, the leaders can play off their greed. 'See – your enemy has taken/is about to take that which is rightly yours!'

Every British government has found it easy to provide an external enemy because the British have a tradition of distrusting and disliking foreigners. The dislike of foreigners and the power of the myths of empire made it easy for Mrs Thatcher's Government to define Argentina as the enemy, while Mr Major's presentation of himself as the ideal British man, modest, reasonable, responsible, tolerant, but with right and proper limits for his tolerance, made it easy for the British to change from seeing Saddam Hussein as a ruler to be supported to seeing him as a wicked enemy.

It is easy to perceive the external enemy as all bad because we need not have any contact with them where we might see them as human like ourselves, but defining the appropriate internal enemy is difficult for a government, for we can easily see that our enemies are people like ourselves. English governments use the Sinn Fein Irish as both an external and internal enemy. They are over the water and in our midst. The Thatcher Government in 1989 forbade the media to report what Sinn Fein leaders said in an attempt to prevent the British from seeing the Sinn Fein Irish as human beings like themselves. The Irish in Britain do not form a strong group, and therefore are a possible internal enemy. While it would be easy for a British government to define anyone who might be called black or Asian as the enemy, for there are many white people who would welcome such a message, the black and Asian community is strong, and a strong internal enemy can overturn a government.

Better than the Irish as the internal enemy is that collection of people which the upper and middle classes and the upwardly aspiring working class join together to hate, that is, the layabouts, the scroungers, the lazy, dirty, improvident, badly behaved, ungrateful unemployed. They are ideal as an internal enemy. We provident, well-behaved people need not actually meet them, but just see them so as to disapprove – and they are weak. We can approve of a government's attempts to eradicate and control them, and not see that the government's measures militate against us as well.

A government's successful manipulation of its designated enemies relies on an accurate knowledge of its subjects' attitudes and prejudices. The Thatcher Government did this very effectively until the introduction of the poll tax in 1990.

The dislike which well-behaved, provident people have for badly-behaved, improvident people stems from the fear which well-behaved, obedient children have for badly-behaved, disobedient children because disobedient children can get them into trouble. They also resent 'bad' people being given the rewards which they, the 'good' people, deserve. Mrs Thatcher and her Government manipulated this fear and greed very effectively, but forgot that fear of badly-behaved people is not our primary fear.

Our primary fear concerns survival both in body and as a person. We are frightened when there are threats to our physical survival, and when we find ourselves negated and ignored by those people whom we feel should take notice of us.

These are the very conditions which the Government's imposition of the poll tax created, and the primary fear which both well-behaved and badly-behaved felt overcame old barriers and brought them out together on the streets. Mrs Thatcher tried to reestablish the old enemy by blaming the militant Left and the Labour Party. As a politician she needed her subjects to be orderly and obedient, but she forgot that all of us are in the business of surviving.

We overlook the fact that there are certain aspects of life which stand in complementary relationship to one another, so that the more there is of one, the less there is of the other.

In June, 1990 Kawasaki launched a new motorbike, the ZZ-R1100, '105cc, 4 stroke in-line Four, DOCH, 16 valves, forced induction, 123bhp at 9,500 revs, 0–60 in 2.9 secs in first gear.'[40] Kawasaki took a two-page spread in the newspaper colour supplements and major magazines with a picture of an empty road winding through a barren wilderness, and in the foreground a helmeted rider speeding along on this fast, new machine. The caption read '36, MARRIED AND FREE'.

Evidence that no matter what our elders have told us and what our experience has shown us, we still believe that we can have our cake and eat it.

How delightful it would be if we could enjoy the companionship and security of marriage with the irresponsibility and freedom of a single life! Many people, men particularly, try to achieve this, and their attempts always come to grief. While the rider depicted in the advertisement is enjoying his freedom, is his wife at home, insecure and lonely as she worries that he might have an accident or wonders when, if ever, he will return to her? Or has she taken the opportunity to explore the possibilities of her own freedom to find a man who loves her, not a motorbike, or an occupation more enthralling than marriage. Will he return home to an empty house and complete freedom?

What has emerged, time and time again, in the conversations I have had with people who are depressed, anxious, resentful, bitter, despairing, angry, envious, vengeful, is their belief that they can have their cake and eat it. It seems that when they were being taught to be obedient children, when they could neither have their cake nor eat it, they formed the notion that the rewards that would eventually come to them because they were good would be in the form of cakes which they could both eat and keep. In marriage they would be both free and secure. They could terrorize their children into obedience and still have their love. They could protect themselves from rejection by never giving total love to anyone, yet they would never be lonely. They could live with total selfishness, yet others would look after them with selfless concern. They could have a secure job and never be bored or unsatisfied. They could ingest whatever food and drugs they wanted and never be ill. They could amass wealth and possessions and never be the object of envy and theft. They could live and never die.

Such people, and there are many, react with anger and resentment when someone like myself points out the limitations which the nature of life places on us. How unfair! How unacceptable! They want to kill the messenger who brings such tidings. They burn with resentment against the world which has treated them so unfairly, or they retreat into their fantasies of a life which bears little relationship to the realities of living.

However, the realities of living do not go away just because we refuse to acknowledge them.

We pay a price for our greed which goes far beyond the money and effort we paid for our acquisitions.

In Old Cairo I saw a young woman crossing a busy market street on her hands and knees. Her right lower leg and foot were curled up, crippled, behind her. At her side trotted a three-year-old child.

I was in a car on our way to visit a mosque. Inside this mosque were men studying the Koran. Had I told them about this woman, they would have said it was the will of Allah. Had I pressed them further as to why this woman had to live like this, they would have said that she would be receiving charity, for the Koran commands that alms should be given to the poor. The Bible says that the poor are always with us, and most Christians have treated that statement as a command and not merely an observation. After all, is it not the duty of the poor to be poor, so that the rich can practise virtue?

If we want to be greedy we either have to suffer such sights or become indifferent to the suffering of others and, in doing so, become less of the person that we might have been, for, in doing so, we destroy our imagination, that faculty which enlivens our experience, draws us close to other people, and marks the difference between human beings and objects.

With imagination we can see the beauty of a coral reef. Without imagination we can let a reef die.

At a depth of 30 feet, where the coral suddenly rose in a ledge from the sandy ocean floor, it seemed that the entire reef had been wrapped in plastic string. It looked like the work of the curious artist who wraps Paris bridges and Greek islands in pink sheets. But this was not art.

This was fishing line, dozens of fishing lines, cast off by impatient anglers when their hooks caught in what they thought was the ocean floor. In fact, the hooks are locked into soft coral. The drifting of the boat and the jerks of the fishermen loop the trailing lines around hard corals and knot them into impossible tangles. The results are devastating. Delicate sea fans tangled in line were pulled from the reef. Finger, branching, and staghorn coral was wrenched off by the tuggings from above.

Then there were the plastic bags looped over the brain coral, and starving them of nutrients. Finally were the great gouges in the reef where anchors had been dropped to moor the boats. It does not take an expert to see that the reef is dying . . .

'Right now, the reefs are dying at a rate of about five percent a year,' says Brian Lapointe, who has just completed a reef pollution survey for the Florida Land Trust. 'We have a water quality problem which is really a people problem. The sharp increase in population and in tourism in Florida, and particularly the Keys, has overloaded our waste disposal systems. The septic tanks are leaking into the sea, producing nutrients which are force-feeding the algae, which overgrow and kill the coral.' . . .

The potentially most lethal [threat to the reef] is oil drilling. About 25 miles off the reef, nine oil companies hold some 73 leases . . .

'Greed kills,' says Dr Lapointe. 'If we want a high-density population in this area, then we have to build better sewerage treatment plants, because otherwise the long-term economy of this region is at risk. This area lives on the sea, on the fish and the tourists and the scuba divers and on the reefs. It is in everybody's self-interest to clean up the reefs, if only they could see it.'[41]

Greed kills because it reduces our awareness of what we actually need to live a fulfilling life. Greed kills because it makes us indifferent to other poeple's wellbeing, and that indifference puts our own wellbeing in jeopardy. Between 11 May 1985 and 15 April 1989, over a thousand people died and many people were injured in Britain in a series of disasters which were a result of greed, incompetence, and indifference to human life.[42] Such disasters show that greed cannot keep us safe.

Wanting everything and trying to get everything by being greedy results only in us getting much less than what we would have had if only we had recognized the truth of the old saying,

We Get to Keep Only That Which We Give Away.

If we clutch a rose tightly, the thorns prick us and the petals bruise. If we hold in an iron grip our relationship with another person, the relationship dies. If we hang on to our possessions, guarding them from thieves, we imprison ourselves. People and possessions, like roses, should be held lightly. If we let the people around us be themselves, they are more likely to stay with us, and if we do not invest ourselves in our possessions, we do not hunger for more nor mourn them when they disappear.

To hold our possessions lightly, we need to know why we choose such possessions and why we long for more. We need to understand ourselves.

Many people, reading this chapter, will say, 'None of this applies to me. I am not greedy. I am concerned about other people. I am unselfish and responsible.'

Many people try to get everything by being responsible for everything, just as some people try to get everything by being totally selfish.

7

'Yes I Can' – Responsibility and Selfishness

'Am I my brother's keeper?'

The answer to this question is not 'Yes' or 'No', but the framing of a better question:

'How much should I be my brother's keeper and how much should I look after my own interests?'

or

'What are the limits to my responsibility to myself and to other people?'

There is no simple, once-and-for-all answer to this second question. Any answer must take into account a multitude of factors reaching far into the past and stretching far into the future, affecting a multitude of events. Any one answer can relate only to a particular place and time, and a new one has to be worked out for every situation. We might, with wisdom and experience, develop some guiding principles to help us arrive at our multitude of answers, but we have to accept that every answer is relative. There is no One True Answer.

Unfortunately, trying to find the best answer for every situation is hard work, and many people do not wish to undertake it. Moreover, most people are not equipped to carry out such complex thought. They have been taught to think in absolutes like 'Always put other people first', or 'Look after Number One'. They have been taught that to be good they must be unselfish, and so, to get their rewards, they try to be unselfish, and, to avoid being rejected, they try to appear to be unselfish when they are not.

All they achieve is getting into a muddle. When they give generously to other people and accept responsibility for other people, they find that other people take advantage of them and load them with burdens. When they look after their own interests, they find that other people criticize and reject them. When they act selfishly while appearing to be unselfish, they fear that they will be found out.

Some people – quite a number of people – try to avoid this muddle by opting for the extremes. Some of these people opt for complete, unashamed selfishness, and others opt for being totally responsible for every other being, the whole universe in fact.

These two extremes, being responsible for everything and denying

249

responsibility for anything, are attempts to satisfy the longing to have everything.

What Do We Mean by 'Responsibility'?

Most dictionary definitions of 'responsibility' speak about 'account-ability' which is owed to someone. We can be accountable to other people and to ourselves, and in this process of accountability we often use the word 'responsible' when in fact the reason for our actions have little to do with a sense of responsibility.

We often use the word 'responsible' when we are simply being obedient. Well-trained and unthinking in obedience, we look after the interests of other people, not because we feel responsible for them, but because we fear the punishments we would receive from those in power over us if we failed to act appropriately. Left to ourselves we would not bestir ourselves in the service of our fellows. Civil servants and people in the service industries often display this kind of 'responsibility'.

We often use the word 'responsible' when we are simply wanting to preserve the image we have of ourselves as a good, kind, caring, responsible person. We work out that the discomfort we would feel in looking after the interests of other people is significantly less than the discomfort we would feel if we suspected that our virtue was not as great as we believed. When the discomfort of looking after the interests of others threatens to be significantly large, we can save ourselves from suffering by assuring ourselves that the people in need would be better off by learning to be self-reliant, or that they brought their misery on themselves and deserve to suffer.

We often use the word 'responsible' when we are working out the line of causation which led to a certain event. This concept of responsibility is accompanied by the concept of blame. In seeking to apportion blame we often confuse 'responsibility' as a direct cause and 'responsibility' as accountability. An electrician fails to wire a signal box correctly and a faulty signal causes a train to crash. As a direct cause the electrician is responsible for the crash, but the inspector who failed to inspect the wiring through lack of time, the manager who required his staff to work excessive hours, British Rail directors who required managers to organize extensive overtime to save money, the Conservative Government which required British Rail directors to save money are all responsible in terms of accountability. If the Government is supposed to be accountable to the people (in practice it rarely is) then presumably the public would prefer to travel on trains which did not crash and would conclude that the Government was not providing them with the service they required.

To understand how responsibility works both as a cause and as an accountability, we must use the model where cause is seen as a network of interlocking events stretching far and wide in time and place. Because we are educated to think of cause only as linear, we have enormous difficulty in understanding responsibility, but at least our difficulty keeps lawyers rich. In one sense we are all responsible for everything because everything is connected to everything else. Thus, so chaos theorists tell us, 'a butterfly stirring the air today in Peking can transform storm systems in New York'.[1] Here we need to distinguish a chance connection from one which was intended. Did the butterfly intend to create a storm?

Presumably not. People, however, do have intentions. But though we may hate someone and intend to harm him, we need to have the skill and the opportunity if we are to achieve this. Our thoughts of hate and bitterness on their own will have certain effects – making us feel ill, spoiling our enjoyment of life and turning us into unpleasant companions – but not the effect of harming our enemy. There are people who believe that they can kill by thought alone, but I shall remain unconvinced until someone can show me that housework can be accomplished by thought alone.

Many things happen to us for which we are not responsible in the sense that we did not cause these things to happen. We are not responsible for the set of genes which we inherit from our parents, nor for the child-rearing practices which our parents and teachers used, nor for the social, political, religious and economic conditions into which we were born. *What we are always responsible for are the meanings which we create about what happens to us.*

We are responsible for the meanings we create because we are not compelled to create any one particular meaning (although other people may try to compel us), but are free to choose from among the multitude of possible meanings. We are responsible for our constructions of meaning in the sense of *cause,* and we are also responsible in the sense of *accountability.* We may have to account for some of the meanings we have created to those in authority over us – the law, our parents and teachers – and to the people with whom we have relationships – family, lovers and friends. But *for all the meanings we create we are accountable to ourselves.* We have to ask ourselves, 'Have I created a meaning which is true, or have I created a lie? Have I created a meaning which will cause me pain and frustration, or have I created a meaning which is in my best, long-term interests? Have I created a meaning which, in the circumstances, is the best way forward?'

In our responsibility to others, we can either be responsible in the sense of cause (for example, 'I drove carelessly and was responsible for the accident'), or be responsible in the sense of accountability (for example, 'I am accountable to the managing director for my work'). Our responsibility to ourselves, however, is in the sense of both cause and accountability. We may be able to arrange our lives so that we are not accountable to anyone else, but as we can never step out of the network of causes which comprises everything that is, our task is to determine whether or not our connection with a particular event was so close that our actions had an immediate connection (for example, a woman says, 'My therapist had a heart attack. I feel it was my fault.' Was it? He is fifty, overweight, never exercises, and smokes heavily). But we can never, not for one moment, cease to be responsible for ourselves.

Even when we decide that we shall let other people and powers be responsible for us, it is we who have created that particular meaning, and so we are responsible for deciding that we shall accept the decisions which other people make. When we say 'I can't (or won't) decide', we have decided not to decide, which is itself a meaning. When we decide that we shall be responsible for other people, we may take over control of what other people do, but we can never take from other people their own responsibility for the meanings which they create.

Understanding our responsibility to ourselves and other people requires careful reflection. When we try to work out the limits of our responsibility, both in cause and in accountability to both ourselves and others, we need to assess what our intentions are and what it is within our capacity to achieve.

We can be responsible only for that which is within our competence to perform. Thus, as a mother I can be responsible for providing a secure home and adequate food and clothing for my school-age children, but I cannot be responsible for what happens to them when they are at school. Similarly, I cannot be responsible for how other people interpret my actions. I can act towards you with warmth and friendliness, but if you choose to interpret my actions as evidence of hostility, then that is your choice and not my responsibility. However, if I wish to cling to my belief that I am a very powerful person, being totally responsible both as the cause of just about everything and as being the only person capable of looking after others (all a way of trying to get everything), I can claim responsibility for everything my family does and everything that people think of me.

Many parents of teenage and adult children look back at what they did when their children were little and blame themselves for the difficulties their children now have. Many people, looking back on their childhoods, blame their parents for their present difficulties. What both groups fail to realize is that they are projecting back on to earlier versions of their own experience, knowledge, skills and understanding which were not in existence then. Most parents do the best they can for their children, given the information and experience they have at the time, and the social, political and economic conditions which exist at the time. Most parents learn to be parents only by being parents, and so by the time they have learned what they need to know, the need for such knowledge is past. Rather than blaming parents for failure to be responsible, we should help one another find the understanding we need when we need it.

Understanding responsibility is more than a matter of understanding it as a concept. Indeed, just an intellectual understanding of responsibility can be quite dangerous. We need to be aware of how being responsible *feels*.

The feeling of responsibility for others is the feeling of sympathy, empathy and the wanting to protect. When an earthquake in Australia caused damage and death in places just north of Sydney, my friend Nan said to me of her grandchildren, 'I just wanted to rush up there and put my arms around them and keep them safe.' Just how she would get her arms around seven healthy young Australians and fend off falling buildings and gaping cracks was not a consideration. She was their grandmother and it was her responsibility to protect them.

Vaclav Havel, in his letters to his wife Olga from prison, examined the question and the experience of a sense of responsibility. He wrote:

Several days ago, during the weather report . . . something went wrong in the studio and the sound cut out, though the picture continued as usual . . . The employee of the Meteorological Institute who was explaining the forecast quickly grasped what had happened, but because she was not a professional announcer she did not know what to do. At this point a strange thing happened: the mantle of routine fell away and before us there suddenly stood a confused, unhappy and terribly embarrassed woman: she stopped talking, looked in desperation at us, then somewhere off to the side, but there was no help from that direction. She could scarcely hold back her tears. Exposed to the view of millions, yet desperately alone, incapable of conveying by mime that she was above it all (by shrugging her shoulders and smiling, for instance), drowning in embarrassment, she stood there in all the primordial nakedness of human helplessness, face-to-face with the big bad world and herself, with the absurdity of her position, and with the desperate question of what to do with herself, how to rescue her dignity, how to acquit herself, how to be. Exaggerated as it may seem, I suddenly saw in that event an image of the primal situation of humanity: a situation of separation, of being cast into an alien world and standing there before the question of self. Moreover, I realized at once that with the woman, I was experiencing – briefly – a most physical dread; with her I was overwhelmed by a terrible sense of embarrassment; I blushed and felt her shame; I too felt like crying. Irrespective of my will, I was flooded with an absurdly powerful compassion for this stranger (a surprising thing here, of all places, where in spite of yourself you share the general tendency of the prisoners to see everything related to television as part of the hostile world that locked them up): I felt miserable because I had no way of helping her, of taking her place, or at least of stroking her hair.[2]

Havel is describing the helplessness and pity which we feel for another and for ourselves. He explained the incident:

In itself the incident with the weatherwoman was insignificant . . . [but] it was such an incisive representation of human vulnerability. And if, in that moment, I felt such a powerful sense of responsibility for this particular woman and felt so entirely on her side (though common sense tells me she is doubtless better off than I am, and probably never gives me a thought, if she knows about me at all), then this was likely because the more transparently vulnerable and helpless humanity is, the more urgently does its misfortune cry out for compassion. This dramatic exposure of another, void of all obfuscating detail and all 'appearances', reveals and presents to man his own primordial and half-forgotten vulnerability, throws him back into it, and abruptly reminds him that he, too, stands alone and isolated, helpless and unprotected, and that it is an image of his own situation, that is, a situation we all share, a common isolation of humanity thrown into the world, and that this isolation injures us all in the same way, regardless of who, concretely, happens to be injured in a given instant.[3]

Helplessness and pity are among the most painful emotions we can ever feel. To overcome the pain, which is a combination of pity for the person suffering and pity for ourselves, we rush to be helpful. This can make us feel better, and might even help the object of our concern, but if we do not ever permit ourselves simply to feel the helplessness and pity that Havel describes, but are forever 'making better', we damage those who have inspired our sense of responsibility, for we have become the most dangerous person in the world: someone who knows what is best for other people. We want to control everybody and everything. We want to take away from other people their right of self-determination, which includes the right to make mistakes. If we cannot make mistakes we cannot learn. In assuming the responsibility for others which is rightly theirs, we are trying to stop them from changing.

The feeling of responsibility for ourself is a feeling of power and freedom – the freedom to make our own decisions and the power to carry them out and make our definitions of reality, at least in relation to ourselves, prevail. When other people try to take away that feeling of power and freedom, no matter how benign their intentions, we feel angry and anxious, and usually very little gratitude for the help that we are being given. It is no wonder that those people who devote themselves to being responsible for others get so little gratitude in return!

Being responsible for ourselves means not lying to ourselves. We are honest with ourselves about our intentions, and we do not pretend that our feelings are different from what they are. When we decide not to be so honest in reporting our intentions and feelings to others, we do not lie to ourselves about why we do this. While we might deplore some of our intentions and feelings, we do not condemn ourselves, but rather resolve to do better next time. We take pride neither in our virtues nor in the humility with which we criticize our vices, but recognize that we are valuable and acceptable, and that taking responsibility for ourselves is part of valuing and accepting ourselves. Taking responsibility for ourselves should be as easy as breathing, but for most of us it is not, because our education has been the process of bamboozlement, which is aimed at preventing us from knowing our own truth and thus taking responsibility for ourselves.

In determining what are the limits of our responsibility to ourselves, there is always the delicious temptation to blame others for what we do. When I was backing my car out of my driveway, something I have done hundreds of times, I brought the side of the front bumper bar up against the gate. The heavy rubber bumper bar bent obligingly, as the Volkswagen designers intended, but some paint was scraped from my beautiful car. I would have dearly loved to blame the driver of the car parked opposite my gate and restricting the turning space in the roadway, but I had to recognize that the fault was mine. Introvert that I am, I sometimes treat external reality as being as plastic as it is in my dreams. Sometimes I get away with it, and sometimes, not paying external reality its proper dues, I do not. But how delightful it would have been to blame that other driver! Just as it is always delightful to indulge ourselves in selfishness and excuse our bad behaviour by blaming the weather, or our genes, or 'Them'.

Havel defined responsibility for oneself as

> a knife we use to carve out our own inimitable features in the panorama of Being; it is the pen with which we write into the history of Being that story of the fresh creation of the world that each new human existence always is.[4]

I often speak of our world of meaning, and can be referring, at times, to our collection of everyday meanings about ourselves, our family, work,and home, and, at other times, to the totality of everything we know and experience. Havel is more precise, using the word 'horizon' to distinguish different layers of our world of meaning, from the most physically close, as was his prison, to the absolute, as far as it can go, horizon. This horizon is

'the absolute horizon of Being', against whose background and out of which anything first becomes itself; the absolute horizon of Being as a 'system of co-ordinates' providing everything that exists with a place, a context, a meaning, a discrete existence, and thus, ultimately, genuine Being. It is, therefore, the 'experience of all experiences', the measure of all measures, the order of all orders. Indeed: if I know what I have done and why, and what I do and why, if I can really stand behind this and (in private perhaps) own up to it, I am thereby constantly relating to something stable, something I 'win' from my 'unstable' surroundings, and thus I myself ultimately become 'relatively stable' – something graspable, something that possesses continuity and integrity. In short, I am 'someone', i.e., identical with himself. By standing today behind what I did yesterday, and standing here behind what I did elsewhere, I not only gain my identity, but through it, I find myself in space and time; if, on the contrary, I lose my identity, time and space must necessarily disintegrate around me as well.

In this sense, therefore, responsibility establishes identity; it is only in the responsibility of human existence for what it has been, is and will be that its identity dwells. In other words, if human identity is the irreplaceable locus of the 'I' in the context of the 'not-I', then human responsibility is what determines that locus: the relationship of the former to the latter.

Patocka said the thing most peculiar to responsibility is that it is 'ours, everywhere'. I think this is so because the world is everywhere, 'surrounded' or 'infused' with its absolute horizon, and that we can never step beyond this horizon, leave it behind us or forget about it, regardless of how hidden it is (and in any case it is always hidden:.it is in everything, and nowhere does it exist in and for itself). It may be only our own imaginary construct – but in that case, so is the whole world. Does it matter, though, whether we use the word 'Being" or the word 'imaginary construct'? In doing so, we cannot escape our responsibility, not by even a fraction of an inch![5]

But some people try. Some deny all responsibility for others and for themselves and what they do by being totally selfish, and some deny responsibility for themselves by being totally responsible for others.

'Nothing Is My Fault'

Selfishness in the form of greed – keeping everything for ourself and not sharing with others – is an obvious way of trying to get everything. Selfishness in the form of refusing to take responsibility for the effect our actions have on other people is also a way of trying to keep everything for ourself.

Most politicians, once they gain power, become remarkably adept at denying responsibility for matters which patently are their responsibility. They follow the rule that when things turn out well they take the credit, and when things turn out badly they blame others.[6]

Denying responsibility can unite politicians of different parties and the judiciary in collective deceit. In 1979 the American lawyer Stewart Udall, on a visit to St George, Utah,

> heard the wrenching tales of death and debilitating illness from cancer afflicted Southwesterners who had lived downwind from the Nevada nuclear-test site from the 1950s to the early '60s. Victims were convinced their illness came from clouds of radiation. Udall was outraged to learn that a 1981 US Public Health Service survey had found cancer rates five times higher than normal among the 15,000 white and Navajo uranium miners in the region but concealed the findings from the victims. He began filing claims against the Government on behalf of both the miners and the 'downwinders'.
>
> Udall sold his house in a Washington suburb and moved to Phoenix, Ariz., when for eleven impecunious years he fought unsuccessfully in the courts to obtain redress. Judges consistently held that the Government could not be liable, even though it knew of the danger from radiation and kept its victims in the dark. More than 1,000 stricken miners 'were sacrificed for cold war nuclear weapons', says Utah Democratic Congressman Wayne Owens.
>
> Last week Owens told his colleagues that the victims are owed 'compensation and an apology'. The House agreed, approving a $100 million fund to aid affected families in five Southwestern states. But even if the Senate goes along, the Justice Department has urged President Bush to veto the measure as 'another entitlement programme'. Udall, now 70 and practising law in Santa Fe, N. Mex., is writing a book on Government callousness in the atomic age. The Bush Administration may provide him with another chapter.[7]

In the years when I worked as a psychologist in the NHS I was sometimes asked to interview men who had been convicted of sexual abuse of children. Their explanations always amazed me. They had been

257

overcome by 'a red mist', or the little girl 'just happened' to be in the men's lavatory. There was nothing in their prison experience which would teach them to see the connection between their acts and the outcome, and to take responsibility for what they did, so it was highly likely that these men would act in the same way again once they were released.

One person who has tried to develop ways of helping such men understand themselves is Ray Wyre, who runs Britain's only full-time private clinic working to control paedophiles' behaviour. He said:

> Offenders constantly try to excuse their actions by claiming it was someone else's fault or that it only happened the once, or it was caused by stress at work. Typically the man will try to shift the blame on to the child by saying she led him on, or on to his wife by saying that she was no longer sexually active.
>
> I have heard any number of excuses. Men will try to bluff their way out of the situation by saying, for example, that it was an accident. One offender told me that the abuse of his daughter happened when he turned round and his penis 'just went in her mouth'.
>
> I can see no reason to accept unquestioningly an offender's assertion that he had sex with a child because – and this is a typical excuse – he was under pressure at work. There is no relationship between the two.
>
> I am often challenged on this in court when I appear as an expert witness. What I say is generally the same: I accept that the man may have problems at work, he may have lost his job or his wife may no longer have sex with him. But there are a range of options for him in response to those problems. He can quit his job, or he can seek another one; he can leave his wife or have an affair or go to a prostitute. He can even, more prosaically, go to the pub and get drunk. But if he chooses to have sex with a child, that is not a logical response to those problems and indicates a predisposition to paedophilia.
>
> It is particularly important for police and psychologists to be careful in this sphere, because when a man is charged and convicted he will always try to blame other people – the child, his wife, his boss – for the situation. But in fact it is vital for him to confront the reality of his desires and his offending so that he can learn to control them.[8]

If we accept responsibility for what we do, we can have something taken away from us. Politicians who admit their errors can lose their power and position. Men who see that the expression of their sexual desires injures others, and that this is wrong, have to deny themselves the expression of these desires if they are to be able to live with themselves. Admitting our errors, failures and inadequacies can take away from us the feeling that we deserve to have everything. Hence many people will go on denying responsibility so that they can think well of themselves.[9]

Some people can deny that they are responsible and not be called to account, and others are censured by society. But censured or not, those people who try to get everything by denying that they are responsible for what they do in the end fail to get everything, for other people turn against them and never trust them. Such selfishness provides short-term gains but long-term woe.

'I'm Responsible for Everything'

We are taught that it is wrong to seek power and be greedy, and so we can try to cultivate a guise of humility while being powerful and greedy. Stravinsky once remarked about Schoenberg, 'Though his humility is fathomless it is also plated all the way down with a hubris of stainless steel.'[10]

Most of us, while our hubris or pride is not as strong and impenetrable as that of Schoenberg, do retain a sense that we are responsible for ourselves as much as we are responsible for other people. However, there are some people who feel most strongly that they must always put other people's needs before their own, and that whatever goes wrong is their fault. They berate themselves for being selfish, while performing acts of unparalleled goodness which those of us, like me, who operate on the principle of enlightened self-interest could never emulate. Such people would be appalled if I told them that their humility, unselfishness and sense of total responsibility stemmed from an attempt not only to be good but also to get everything. What greater pride could there be than believing that you are capable of being responsible for the universe and everything in it? Such people might admit that they did indeed see themselves as being so capable, but they would remind me of Jesus's injunction, 'Unto whomsoever much is given, much is required.'[11]

While people who strive to get everything by being powerful and/or greedy might acknowledge, at least to themselves, that they are not so very interested in being virtuous, the people who want to get everything by being responsible for everybody and everything want also to be good. They can demonstrate their goodness through their unselfishness and concern, they can (they hope), by exercising their responsibility, get everything under control and put to rights, and then, in a secure and ordered universe, they can get what they want.

How does such a sense of responsibility develop?

When disaster strikes us we ask, 'Why did this happen? Was it my fault, or someone else's fault, or did it happen by chance?' It takes courage to decide 'It happened by chance', because that means acknowledging our inability to protect ourselves from all danger. To avoid this, we blame others, and have to deal with our resultant anger and resentment. Or we can blame ourselves.

In a television series from Northern Ireland, Nicky Harris, a young mother, told what happened to her after her baby boy, her second child, suddenly died.

I was so self-destructive afterwards because of the guilt. I felt I was trying to destroy myself in some way. I was trying to punish myself because I felt so guilty. I really wanted for somebody to come and put me up against a wall and say, 'You murdered your baby.' I really wanted that. I kept waiting for them to come. The Garda have to make some sort of investigation when there's been a death like that, but they were so nice when we met them in the hospital and they hardly bothered me at all. I kept waiting and kept on saying inside to myself, 'Why is nobody asking me what way he was lying, what was he wearing, what did you feed him before you went out,' questions that would somehow implicate me, because I felt totally responsible as his mother.

Jessica, her four-year-old daughter, was also trying to deal with the problem of responsibility.

I realized soon after he died that she was feeling the same guilt that I was feeling. We always talked, and about a month after he died she said to me, 'Mummy, I know why Jordan died,' and I said, 'Why?' and she said, 'I bounced the bouncy chair too hard. Do you remember when you told me not to do that?' And I felt the guilt flowing out and I was able to deal with it. I just totally knocked that theory on the head. It had nothing to do with it. I thought I'd got that over with, and then a couple of weeks later she came back to me and she said, 'Mummy, I think I've definitely worked it out now.' This is a four-year-old child talking to me. She said, 'When Grandma was sitting over there and you were sitting over here, and I was hugging Jordan, and Grandma said, Don't hug him too tight, you'll kill him.' She said, 'That was it. I must have hugged him too tightly.' Inside I was crying for her for I felt the same way.

What Jessica showed too was how, as little children, we feel empathy, concern and responsibility for those we love.

She was a great source of comfort to me from the very beginning, because half an hour after he died I was sitting at the kitchen table – I was in a state of shock and must have looked terrible – and she came over to me and she put her hands out holding my face like this and she said, 'Mummy, look into my eyes,' and she said, 'When I smile, you smile too. I'll look after you.'[12]

Jessica could easily have become one of those people who feel totally responsible for everything and everybody, but she fortunately had a mother who took the time to help her sort out the difficult question of what were the limits of her responsibility.

Not all parents realize how important it is to do this, and many parents, in the effort to make their children obedient, deliberately lie to them and confuse them about their responsibility to others. Such parents tell their children that the children are responsible for matters which are actually completely outside the children's control.

Philip Gosse did this to his son Edmund.

> He had formed the idea and cultivated it assiduously that I was an *âme d'élite*, a being with whom the mysteries of salvation had been divinely revealed and by whom they had been accepted . . .
>
> My little faults of conduct, too, assumed shapes of terrible importance, since they proceeded from one so signally enlightened. My Father was never tired of reminding me that, now I was a professing Christian, I must remember in everything I did, that I was an example to others. He used to draw dreadful pictures of superstitious little boys who were secretly watching me from afar, and whose whole career, in time and in eternity, might be disastrously affected if I did not keep my lamp burning.[13]

Fortunately children do not always accept what their parents try to force on them. Edmund did not accept the burden of responsibility which his father wanted to place on him, perhaps because by the time Edmund left home he knew that even though his father was disappointed in him he would not reject him. Not all children are so lucky.

At a workshop where I had set the participants the task of recalling an incident from their childhood which led them to draw the conclusion that they were bad and unacceptable, one woman, Ann, told how she had a twin sister about whom she always felt totally responsible because her sister, unlike her, had been born a small, sickly baby. Though her sister was now a healthy adult, competently leading her own life, Ann still worried about and tried to protect her sister. The incident she recalled from her childhood was the guilt she felt when she passed her 11-plus examination and her sister failed. Such a disproportionate sense of responsibility must have stemmed from her parents' exhortations to her to be good and to look after her sister, and her own attempts to bury her envy of a sister on whom her family lavished much care.

Stephen, one of my clients, would tell me of the immense shame and guilt he still felt for being responsible for the break-up of his parents' marriage. He knew quite well that his father and mother did not get along together and that his father had a mistress, but what still troubled him was how, when he was eleven, after a tempestuous scene between his parents following his mother's discovery of her husband's infidelity, his father, leaving the house, yelled at him, 'It's your fault I'm leaving. If you'd been a good boy none of this would have happened.'

There are parents who, not having been looked after by their parents, want their children to look after them. Children who resist having this adult role thrust on them are told that they are selfish, ungrateful and wicked. Children who see that they are being expected to assume a responsibility which is not rightly theirs become angry and resentful. Children who are taught that it is an Absolute Law of the Universe that children should be grateful to their parents for allowing them to be born dare not admit their anger and resentment, and, having assumed responsibility for their parents, go on and assume responsibility for everyone else. Being responsible becomes their way of justifying their existence.

Not many corrupt and greedy stockbrokers come seeking therapy, but many caring, responsible, unselfish people do, for they are burdened and driven by a great sense of guilt. They claim to be respon-

"Would you like to be left alone to feel guilty about Ethiopia before or after the sweet trolley?"[14]

sible for the welfare of an enormous number of people – their extended family, the entire workforce of their firm, the functions of an entire health care system – and have not put their intelligence to the task of considering what they can rightly be responsible for.

To the outside observer Fleur has everything. She is an attractive woman in her late forties, married to a successful surgeon. Their children, charming and well-behaved, are at school and college and showing academic and artistic brilliance. Fleur herself is a distinguished philosopher and teacher, and is engaged in developing new areas of her discipline. They have a wide circle of friends, enjoy some of the pursuits of the English upper classes, and have a beautiful home.

However, things are never as they seem.

When Fleur first phoned me for an appointment she explained that she had been in therapy, which had helped to sort some things out, but that there were still some matters unresolved, and that she felt tense and unhappy.

And unhappy she was, as anyone must be who assumes such responsibility. She was responsible, so she told me, for the happiness and wellbeing of all the members of her family and of all her colleagues. If any of them became angry or upset, she had to ask herself how she had failed, and if any of them criticized her, she accepted these criticisms as true. When a male colleague told her that she was being strident and demanding, she, a very placating and unaggressive woman, tried to become even more placating and unaggressive, while berating herself for her errors. Whenever her mother-in-law told her that she was selfish and uncaring, she, a very unselfish and caring woman, tried to become even more unselfish and caring, while berating herself for her failure. It never occurred to her to wonder what particular axes her colleague and her mother-in-law might have to grind, and to think about how she might better defend herself from their blows.

So impressed was I with Fleur's assumption of responsibility for the woes of every person she encountered that I felt it necessary to try to prevent her from assuming responsibility for mine. One morning I greeted her with an explanation as to why I looked so wan. I was suffering the effects of a self-inflicted injury, a cholera injection arising from my insistence on visiting cholera-prone countries. Fleur immediately assumed responsibility for my state by saying that she would leave me immediately and distress me no further. I wrested responsibility back from her, and our session proceeded.

I had come across a great many women who believed, like Fleur, that they were totally responsible for the happiness and wellbeing of their family and friends, but these were usually women who had left school early and who never applied their intelligence to anything more complicated than a knitting pattern. They had considered moral questions only in terms of the personal. Fleur must, in the course of her studies, have looked at the general question of what are the limits of our personal responsibility. Had I set her this as an examination question, she would no doubt have answered it brilliantly, but, as she said when we discussed this question, while she knew intellectually that what we can be personally responsible for is quite restricted, this was not what she felt in her heart. Her heart told her that she was responsible for all other people's welfare. She had learned long ago that whatever went wrong was her fault.

She had learned this lesson so thoroughly that she had never called it into question. One day when she was describing to me her great propensity to upset people without even trying, she said that as a child she frequently upset her older brother who would respond by hitting her. She recalled one particular event, when she was about thirteen and travelling in a car, with her parents in the front seat and she seated between her sister and brother in the back. She recalled the particular pain she felt when her brother hit her several times across her young breasts.

'Didn't your mother stop him?' I asked.

My question surprised her. She knew quite well that most mothers would try to stop a bigger boy hitting a smaller girl, but she never applied this knowledge to her mother. 'My mother said it was my fault. I'd upset him.'

So it was that when a man, who was her parents' friend and a preacher at their church, would try, in her parents' absence, to give her wet kisses, she dared not complain. Even though his sexual fumbling revolted her, she was sure that somehow she was responsible for it and would be blamed by her parents.

Taking such responsibility upon herself prevented Fleur from seeing that people had their own reasons for being aggressive to her, reasons for which she could not possibly be responsible. In the course of accepting this burden of guilt she denigrated herself even further, and so she failed to see that some of the criticism which was directed at her was motivated by envy.

In families where parents make one child the scapegoat for all the parents' problems, the other children usually copy the parents and direct their hostility and blame on to their scapegoat sibling. Thus not only did Fleur's brother do this, but her sister did too.

'I've always tried to look after my sister,' Fleur said to me, 'but I think she feels I've let her down. Recently she's been rather, well, sharp with me, more than usually, and I must admit I find visiting her difficult.'

Fleur's sister had enjoyed none of the success and advantages that Fleur did. Yet Fleur was again surprised when I suggested that perhaps she was the object of her sister's envy.

Was Fleur responsible for her sister's envy? If she assumed that she was, then to prevent her sister suffering from what is undoubtedly an uncomfortable emotion, Fleur should immediately give up all her possessions and advantages. While this might cause her sister to cease envying her, and instead to despise her, it would certainly cause Fleur's husband and children some distress.

Fleur thought about these matters carefully. Now she could see that the remarks directed at her by her male colleague were motivated by his envy and spite rather than by her inadequacy, and she could see alternative ways of dealing with her sister. But try as she might, she found that her mother-in-law still had the power to cause her great distress.

Fleur's mother-in-law was an ill, lonely, old woman, now widowed from a man who had given her nothing but pain and disappointment. In her case, as in the case of many people, suffering had not improved her character. She became and remained cruel, envious and vindictive. Such people always need a sacrificial lamb, and this was the role that Fleur could play to perfection.

When Fleur first entered her mother-in-law's life, she was not only a nice, well brought-up young woman who was always respectful and caring, she was also a member of that group which her aristocratic mother-in-law despised the most – the working class. So to her mother-in-law's complaints and accusations that Fleur was duplicitous, stupid, uncaring and incompetent was added the degrading treatment of Fleur as a non-person, an object of no importance.

In the early years of her marriage, Fleur bore all this without complaint. There was no point in complaining to her husband because, while at one level he recognized the necessity of taking jobs as far away from his parents as possible, at another level he refused to acknowledge the reality of the profound effects that people have on one another. He was a 'practical' man who didn't want to waste time going too deeply into 'things like that'.

Fleur found her mother-in-law's abuse to be an aristocratic version of what she had received from her family, and she tried to deal with it in the same way, by being compliant and obedient and trying to do her best in everything. She worked out techniques for dealing with her mother-in-law, how to indulge her mother-in-law, how to spare her children any unpleasantness, and how to attempt to head off any major scenes. Fleur was clever, efficient and sensitive to people, and had her talents been applied, with a greater awareness of human cruelty and cupidity, to the problems of the Third World, she could have abolished hunger. As it was, she protected her husband and her mother-in-law from themselves, and her children from cruel adults. The one person she did not protect was herself.

When Fleur as a small child became convinced that her family were right when they said she was a bad girl, she was faced with two alternatives. She could accept that she was bad, and so be bad, following a life of disobedience and crime, or, since such a way of living invites rejection and punishment, she could do what most of us in Fleur's position would do, that is, choose the other alternative: work hard to be good.

Fleur rapidly became very good at being good. She was obedient, polite, clean, tidy, unassertive, responsible, unselfish and hard-working. She became in turn an exceedingly good pupil, student, teacher, wife and mother. Fortunately she was healthy. Such an effort to be good requires considerable physical strength.

However, no matter what we achieve in the effort to be good, no achievement can make us feel secure in our goodness while we accept the insults and criticisms made by our fellows. The reason we accept them is because we suspect that they must be true. After all, are we not bad and working hard to be good? Perhaps we are not working hard enough?

Whatever insult or criticism came winging its way towards her, Fleur took in, like St Stephen receiving the arrows. Her colleague accused her of being a domineering woman. She reviewed her actions and decided that his perceptions must be more accurate than hers. Her mother-in-law accused her of being selfish. She searched her soul, and found some vestige of selfishness lurking there.

Such constant wounding drained her strength and self-confidence, and she slipped towards the morass of despair. However, there was something in her that would not let her drown. She tried to save herself seeking therapy, and from her actions her husband perceived, however dimly, that something was amiss and that he should do something about it.

This led him some time later to seek therapy for himself, and there he made the most astounding and amazing discovery. He discovered that there was a connection between what happened to him as a child and what was happening to him now. The reason he felt anxious and confused was because his mother had treated him badly when he was a child.

Now he could allow himself to feel in full the rage towards his mother that he had forbidden himself to feel. Now he could blame those myriad mysterious feelings which had oppressed him on his mother. He talked to Fleur about it endlessly. Sometimes he would say he was going to see his mother and tell her about the wicked things she had done, and Fleur would dissuade him, pointing out that his mother was old and frail.

In those years when Fleur was discovering the range and power of her mother-in-law's hate, she had longed for him to talk to her about his mother. Now she longed for him to be silent.

'I've worked through all of that,' she said to me. 'I just want to put it behind me and get on with living.'

She could not say this to him because he was so engrossed and enthralled with his discoveries of himself and his past. He would say to Fleur, 'I'm sorry I didn't see what you went through. But we're together now. We can talk about it,' and when the phone rang, heralding his mother's daily call, he would say to Fleur, 'Would you answer that? I'm too upset.'

Obedient as ever, Fleur would answer it, although what upset her most, almost past bearing, was listening to her mother-in-law. 'I can't put her behind me,' she said to me. 'I want to be calm but I can't.'

'Of course,' I said. 'It's your pride that stops you.'

At the word 'pride' Fleur stiffened. Hadn't her parents taught her that pride was wicked, and hadn't she spent all her life trying to divest herself of every shred of pride?

'Pride,' I said, 'is absolutely necessary for our survival. Human beings are weak and puny. If we didn't have our pride we would never have survived as a species. If we didn't have our pride most of us wouldn't survive as individuals.'

Had she not, when she was a little girl, beset by cruel and powerful adults, kept some small but vital part of herself hidden and safe from their prying eyes and demands for obedience? Wasn't her choice to be obedient and humble her way of protecting her hidden self? Didn't her hidden self declare, 'I am I and I will continue to be I, no matter what others do to me'? And wasn't this hidden self angered by every insult and act of degradation, and didn't it long for triumph and revenge?

Could she, I asked, hear my words, not as yet another condemnation of her wickedness, but as a simple description of how human beings manage to survive as people when their fellows try to turn them into mindless automatons?

Our pride, I said, is indefatigable. We pretend that we haven't any pride, and it simply appears in another guise, often more ludicrous than its simple self. There's pride taking pride in itself being so humble. There's pride taking pride in itself for being better able to be responsible for other people than they can for themselves.

Pride can save our lives. It can also drive us to wild, destructive extremes. We should be aware of what our pride is up to, and we should not take our pride seriously. A well-developed sense of the ridiculous keeps pride in check.

So, let's consider how her hidden self, defended by her pride, felt about her mother-in-law. Well, of course, her hidden self felt insulted, demeaned and angry. She wanted revenge.

Now, revenge is always considered to be bad (except when it is righteous revenge and God is on your side). However, if instead of 'revenge' we said 'response', then we could recognize its importance. It seems natural to us that we should make a response whenever we receive an insult or injury which causes us more pain than we can easily absorb and discount. The act of insult or injury seems, to us receiving it, to be the beginning of an event which needs a response from us in order to complete it and achieve a sense of closure. Until we have a sense of closure, we do not have the conditions in which the feeling of forgiveness can arise. Though we often talk of forgiveness as something we can choose to do, in the way we can choose to have a cup of tea, in fact forgiveness is like love, a feeling which we cannot command into being but which arises spontaneously when the conditions are right. Often, when we say we have forgiven someone, all we really mean is that we do not intend to pursue, or be seen to pursue, our hostile intentions towards that person.

So, when we are injured or insulted, we need to consider our 'revenge'. What kind of revenge would create the sense of closure that Fleur needed in her relations with her mother-in-law? Death, perhaps, but the trouble with murder is that your victim cannot admit the error of his ways. What most of us would settle for is a huge, heartfelt, abject, grovelling apology, accompanied by a confession of guilt and ignorance, and a truthful appreciation of ourselves as the most wonderful, admired, brilliant, wise, compassionate person ever to have blessed this world with his/her presence. Sadly, very few of us ever enjoy such revenge. If we do settle our differences, it has to be for less.

This, alas, is what Fleur discovered.

Fleur's husband continued to feel strongly that he should confront his mother with at least some of her failings, and finally he did just this. Fleur's unease about this was well founded, for the old lady withdrew, as she had often done, into a depression, and later entered one of the more distinguished of our psychiatric hospitals. From there she wrote Fleur a letter in which she acknowledged that she had not always treated Fleur as well as she might, and she asked Fleur to forgive her. Whether she had done this at the behest of one of the psychotherapists at the hospital, or whether she was feeling the imminence of death and wanted to make her peace, Fleur could not tell. While, as usual, she wanted to respond immediately, assuring the old lady of her forgiveness and love, and thus try to wrest from her the pain she was feeling, Fleur was also conscious of a strong feeling of unappeasement and distrust. She did not feel that one short plea for forgiveness and reconciliation could wipe out all those years of massive insult, and she wondered if accepting this plea would make her vulnerable to another even more wounding attack. For once she did not rush into her compliant mode, wanting to smooth everything over and make things appear right, even when they were not. She held back and considered what were the limits of her responsibility.

A sense of being responsible for everybody and everything, combined with the belief that one is competent to discharge this responsibility satisfactorily, leads to a life where there is never any time just to do nothing, or to please oneself. There is always another task, another duty. But when the sense of responsibility for everybody and everything is combined with the belief that you do not have the ability to meet these responsibilities, that your essential badness and unacceptability will lead to failure, or, indeed, has led to failure, then added to the sense of constant pressure is the sense of impending doom and constant, overwhelming guilt.

Caroline would describe to me how she would try not to wake out of sleep, for when she did she would be drenched in terror, the fear of imminent punishment for some evil deed she had committed or would commit, a deed that was in some way represented in the dream out of which she had woken. Her early childhood had convinced her that she was intrinsically wicked. After all, did not her parents always tell her she was mad and bad, a terrible disappointment to them both. Nevertheless, out of the goodness of their hearts, they would not see her go cold, or hungry. When she became too depressed to work they gave her presents, and Caroline felt guilty, not just because she did not deserve such gifts, but because her mother had taught her that to take without a sense of responsibility to the giver is wicked.

Caroline saw her sense of responsibility to other people in terms of never doing anything which might hurt anyone else, and so she was always burdened by the belief that when other people expected her to do something (paint a picture, babysit, be grateful), if she failed to meet their demands she would hurt them. She could not reject her friends' demands nor her mother's gifts, even though she saw the years speeding by with her still tied by her sense of responsibility to the one person who could destroy every vestige of her self-confidence with no more than an impatient sigh.

One of the favourite ways parents have of teaching their children that they are bad and have to work hard to be good is to punish them for being angry. Being punished for being angry makes all of us, children and adults, angrier, and if the punishment goes on for long enough the anger becomes murderous rage.

When children cannot express their anger directly, especially when their anger has become murderous rage, they try to deal with such emotions by denying that they exist. But denied emotions do not disappear. They simply come back in other forms.

For extraverts, denied anger and rage come back as fear, the cause of which extraverts locate in their external environment. Simply going outside, or encountering a spider or a dog, becomes too dangerous an activity to be undertaken.

'Yes I Can' – Responsibility and Selfishness

When Adele's mother died, Adele's fear of spiders, which had been a mild nervousness since she was a teenager, blossomed into terror. She had no awareness of being angry with her mother for keeping her at home, never letting her get a job or her own home, nor of being angry with her mother for dying and leaving her, not just alone, but with no focus for her sense of responsibility. She had been the inadequate little girl all her life so her mother would never have to live on her own, and now her mother had left her. What could she do now that her inadequacies were no longer needed?[15]

Introverts who have denied their anger and murderous rage never, like Adele, run short of people about whom to feel responsible. They can feel responsible for the safety of the entire universe.

The comedian Ben Elton uses his universal responsibility as his comic material. Lynn Barber asked him

about Captain Paranoia, and whether his obsessive preoccupation with checking gas taps and plugs is Ben Elton's own. 'Oh God,' he groans, 'that's all for real. Have you checked the gas taps? Better look again. Are the lights off? Is the fire out? Is that creak a mad axeman coming in through the window? I *am* a bit of an obsessive. It irritates my girlfriend sometimes. On occasion I get silly.'

Oddly, he worries about small things – 'gas taps and dinner parties' – rather than about his work. 'I have my work in perspective – I'm pretty healthy about that.' But the thought that he might have left a light bulb burning can drive him demented. Why? 'Because,' he explained, as if to a dim toddler, 'it's *important* not to leave the lights on all day. I mean, what a silly thing to do. The world's in an energy crisis. I was brought up to turn out lights – weren't you? Do you leave *your* lights on when you leave the house?' I nod Yes, and he looks at me as if I have just confessed to some wild affectation like bathing in champagne or lighting my cigarettes with rolled £10 notes: he seriously doubts my sanity.

But what is the fear if you *don't* turn the lights out? What is supposed to happen? 'Well, I could give you all sorts of energy-saving arguments, but the *real* thing is that any power is a fire risk. That is why I check all the plugs. I don't pull them out any more, because I've learned that that is actually more dangerous because you degrade the plug, but you make sure it's all turned off. All my life I've been laughed at for worrying that a light bulb might spontaneously combust, jump across the room, land on that inflammable cushion and before you know it, a conflagration ensues. And my worry is that I might be responsible for something that might hurt someone else, you know? I don't mind me dying in a fire, but what about the neighbours? I think we've gone a bit far with this . . . let's change the subject.'

Wholehearted 'Yes', but now Captain Paranoia is up and running with the ball he won't easily let it go, and somehow every conversational gambit seems to lead back to light bulbs. The crux of the argument is: can a light bulb really start a fire? He insists that it can: 'I was on tour last year and my stage manager in one of the dressing rooms hung a shirt over the light fitting – this was during the day and the light was off, but later someone came in and switched the light on and there was this shirt on the bulb and the next thing we knew it burst into flames and we had a dressing room fire. One day, a bit of paper might be close to a bulb . . . All I'm saying is: I'm very paranoid. I feel a great responsibility. I pick up litter. I think society is about being responsible.'[16]

Not all obsessive introverts can use their obsessions so entertainingly. They are too busy checking that gas taps are turned off, knives are safely packed, hands are scrubbed, and that they have not run over a pedestrian or sexually molested a child. Of course they have done all the right things and refrained from doing the wrong, but, forever doubting their external reality, they have to keep checking to see that, though they would not admit it to themselves, they have given way to the expression of their murderous rage.[17]

The obsessions are attempts to master the traumatic experiences which give rise to the murderous rage. To 'master' means to give a meaning to or draw a set of conclusions from the experience with which the person can live. Because the murderous rage and the pain from being betrayed and injured have not been acknowledged and resolved, the obsessions continue.

The betrayal and injury have usually been inflicted by someone who should have looked after the child but didn't, and the child has not been able to resolve this contradiction. In adult life, such contradictions can arise in society, and the victims be unable to resolve and master them. Then the result may be the loss of the distinction between internal and external reality and the vivid return of painful memories.

The contradiction which society and the army presents to every soldier is that he is required to be both a responsible person and a robot who kills on order:

Michael King will never forget the death of his friend Tony Dacre 'on 27 March, 1985'. Five years on, and his voice still trembles. He knows he bears no blame and that he could have done nothing. But at 21 that made little difference to the way King felt. 'He shouldn't have died; and you carry around the guilt for the rest of your life. I couldn't stop myself feeling guilty. It's irrational guilt, I know. But it's still guilt.' . . .

When Corporal Michael King bought himself out of the British Army in 1988 he left the barracks in County Armagh with only one intention: to escape from what seemed to him an intolerable life. His two years of infantry service in Northern Ireland – street patrols, mortar attacks, deaths of fellow soldiers – had stretched his nerves to breaking point. He had resolved to abandon an eight-year military career, his friends in the regiment, and start anew on the mainland. Within a few months he had landed a good job in financial consultancy, settled with his wife in a flat in the idyllic Suffolk village of Nayland, and was buying a cottage for renovation in Constable country. All seemed set for transition to English civilian life.

Then, on Sunday, 16 April, 1989, while walking home from lunch in the village, he says he suddenly found himself back in Northern Ireland. To his horror, St James's Church, Nayland, its vicarage, the Rattonshaw Rest Home and the surrounding countryside no longer belonged to rural Suffolk but to a melange of places in south Armagh and Belfast. Worse, these picturesque streets and fields concealed a number of wanted IRA Provos. Soon he glimpsed the men who had eluded the Army for years. He knew he must act, not only to protect himself but also the public. His experience of urban combat had taught him what to do. Following the Yellow Card 'Rules of Engagement' as best he could, he hurried home, found his army fatigues, helmet and visor, took out his weapon – now a shotgun kept for rabbit shooting – and established a defensive 'observation post' in his flat opposite the vicarage.[18]

An intense belief in our own responsibility for other people can cause us great misery. We can also inflict misery on others by our sense of our own rectitude.

Everything we do has good implications and bad implications. Being responsible for everybody has the bad implication of always feeling burdened and guilty, but it has the good implication of being a most effective way of controlling other people by making them feel guilty. When you are being so good to other people, how could they not do what you want?

Moreover, claiming total responsibility gives you access to that most desirable terrain, the Moral High Ground.

From such a lofty position we can criticize others for not being as responsible as we are. Lord Linley, driving again after a six-month ban, was observed by a reporter from the *Daily Mail* to be driving without a seat belt.

*"Moses and the tablets will be a little
late — there's a bit of a queue for the
moral high ground."*[19]

Princess Margaret's 25-year-old son was not breaking the law
because his open-top car, produced before 1965, is too old to be
required to have one. Belts are, in fact, fitted and observers
thought that someone so much in the public eye as Lord Linley
should be setting a better example.[20]

The moral attitudes adopted by the tabloid newspapers can be tire-
some, but at least we know they will change with the needs of the
circulation figures. Whereas the rectitude of the totally responsible
person is unchanging.

Why do people dislike Ben Elton? Having met him, I'm prepared
to swear that he's a thoroughly decent bloke who struggles con-

stantly to be considerate and kind and good and to make the world a better place . . . But the *real* problem, the almost insurmountable nose-getting-up problem is his self-righteousness. Why does he have to say he checks all the lights and everything because he doesn't want the house to burn down *and burn the neighbours*? Why can't he just say he doesn't want the house to burn down? He gives a sort of moan of pain at the question and whimpers a bit before answering: 'Because, I tell you, it's an honest fact that I feel connected to other people. That's not being self-righteous, that's being whingeing and paranoid and overly anxious. *Now* of course I wish I hadn't said it; I think that's about the most horrible thing I've ever been accused of – it makes me shiver to think of it – but it's fair, it's fair, and I thank you for saying it.'

He insists that he is not self-righteous, not a martyr. 'I don't *martyr* myself. I don't give *all* my money away – I give *some* of it away, but if we had a proper welfare state I wouldn't have to. If I say I would prefer to be taxed at a higher level, some people say they find that irritating and Jesuitical; I say it's an extremely logical, selfish stance because I am not bettered by beggars accosting me in Tube stations, I'm not bettered by people who have nothing to lose breaking into my flat and stealing my possessions. That might sound self-righteous, but I'm thinking about me and my girlfriend and being able to walk safe in the streets.'

Notice that even while he is denying he is self-righteous, he has leapt nimbly up to the moral high ground and delivered yet another sermon. He is *always* higher up the moral high ground than you are, he is waving down from the summit of K9 while you are still plodding up the foothills.[21]

It seems that both total selfishness and total responsibility alienate others, and neither method allows us to achieve our aim of getting everything. There are other reasons as well for the failure of these methods.

Why Neither Responsibility Nor Selfishness Will Give Us Everything

All our confusion over how we should act, or assess the actions of others, arises from our confusion of Category One, our own constructions of meaning, with Category Two, the nature of the world.

In our moral education, instead of being taught how to understand that each person has a different construction of himself and his world, and that the causes and effects of our actions spread far and wide, we are taught that there is One Moral Law which applies in one way only on every occasion. Moreover, our religious education is directed not at our relationships with other people but at our relationship with God. What He feels is more important than what people feel.

The Church teaches that we sin 'against God'. David, having sent Uriah, Bathsheba's husband, to certain death, repented not for what he had done to two people but because he had 'sinned against God'. The Bible makes no mention of how Uriah felt about David's treachery and abuse of power, nor of how Bathsheba felt about being used by David. The Bible takes for granted that the appropriate punishment for David and the sacrifice which will expiate his sin is the death of his son, the baby Bathsheba had conceived. None of this pain and loss matters. All that matters is whether God thinks that He has been sinned against.

If we try to discover how God feels when He is sinned against, we are told that He feels hurt or angry. If hurt, He expects us to feel guilty, and if angry He punishes us. Making children feel guilty or punishing them are the tactics used by parents who want to force their children to be obedient.

Christians who want to see God as a kindly, forgiving person say that God understands us. But if He does, why does He get hurt and angry about what we do? Parents who love and understand their children know better than to get angry and hurt when their children misbehave. In dealing with our wicked behaviour, God, according to the Church, does not direct us to understanding ourselves and other people. He wants us to focus all our attention on to Him. Jesus advised us to love one another and to forgive one another so that *God will forgive our sins*. He did not suggest that we might simply find that loving and forgiving one another would enable us to live a more happy and fulfilling life.

Parents who want their children to be unquestioningly obedient find God or Allah very useful. As a parent, if you say to your children, 'Do this because I want you to and because I think it's right,' your children will certainly argue with you, but if you disclaim personal responsibility and claim that you are nothing but the mouthpiece of a Higher Power, there is no one with whom they can argue. This was the technique the Ayatollah Khomeini used with his children:

> 'If I wanted to play at a house, and he knew there was a boy there, he would say, Don't go there, play at home,' Mostafavi (his daughter) recalls. 'You couldn't say, Come on Dad, let me go, because what he said was based on Islam, not on his own opinion.'

The consequences of flouting Islam were made brutally clear. He once told Ahmad (according to Ahmad's wife), 'I love you because you are obedient toward God. If you stand against God,

I will stand against you; and if it is necessary according to the law, I will send for your executioner.'[22]

Some parents do not need to claim that a Higher Power has given them the right of life and death over their children. Through punishment, threat, guilt and humiliation they convey to their children that there are certain moral rules operating in the family which are Absolute, Omnipresent and Unquestionable.

Josie is an artist and knows full well that it is her art which gives her life richness and meaning, and that when she does not paint her life becomes arid and she feels herself drying up. But she gets very little work done because of her ever-present guilt and the efforts she makes to prevent other people from feeling guilty.

'Why,' I asked her, 'is it important to you to stop other people from feeling guilty?'

'Because guilt is so destructive. I can't let other people be destroyed.' She described the endless efforts she makes to see that her widowed mother and other relatives have all their needs met and are never given any inkling that she has needs which need meeting.

All her life Josie has avoided making close relationships. She has good friends, and while she responds to their needs, she never shows them any vulnerability or weakness. I wondered if she was lonely, but she said that this was not so, or, if she was lonely, she had no awareness of that.

Yet in her dreams she is always alone. She told me about one very clear dream which she knew had power and significance, but she did not know what. In the dream were large logs of wood floating on a lake. She recalled that the Japanese guards in prisoner-of-war camps used to call their prisoners 'logs of wood'. This was the guards' way of not taking responsibility for the suffering they were inflicting on the prisoners, because logs of wood are not human and so do not have the right to suffer.

This is how Josie had learned to think of herself. No matter what terrible things happened to her, she did not have the right to suffer. She should not fret, or get upset, or complain, or hold any opinion even slightly different from her parents'. This was the Absolute, Omnipresent and Unquestionable moral rule which her parents had taught her when they forbade her to show any distress, since her suffering would shatter their illusion that they were a happy family.

Not being allowed to grieve means that not only has Josie not learned to accept grief as part of the human condition, but she fears that if she once started to grieve she would never stop.

Her only way out of the prison of depression (which she entered through the refusal to grieve) and her all-absorbing sense of total responsibility is to challenge the Absolute Law which her parents imposed on her, but this will involve much grief, though perhaps not as much as the grief suffered at the end of the war by those Japanese guards who denied their responsibility to others.

To be totally responsible or totally selfish it is necessary to ignore certain aspects of the nature of life.

We think that the world is divided up into discrete boxes, when in fact everything that exists is continuous and flowing.

Being totally responsible requires a great deal of worry. This worry is concerned with working out all the possible situations where things can go wrong and what must be done to protect all those people who, no matter how old and experienced they might be, must be protected by the worrier. However, some expert worriers believe that their worrying alone can prevent disaster.

I have two friends, Nan and Helen, who are amongst the world's most expert worriers. They worry chiefly about family and friends, but there is no disaster, real or imagined, which they cannot see as likely to inflict their nearest and dearest. Their interest in world events, in politics, economics, science and medicine is chiefly in terms of the disasters which could inflict their loved ones and which they must prevent. There is usually very little they can actually do to prevent such disaster (washing clothes or growing organic vegetables does not prevent aeroplanes from falling out of the sky), and so they worry. (Expert worriers always harbour the belief that worrying about something can prevent that thing actually happening. They also believe that worrying about people's welfare is to show that you care about them. Not to worry means to be careless and to care less.) Nan and Helen do most of their preventive worrying at night when most of us are asleep. As they each live on opposite sides of the globe, between them they give twenty-four-hour protection to those on whose behalf they worry. I attribute my good luck, health and safety to the fact that I am (I think) on both their worrying lists.

I can joke about my friends' protective worrying, except when I see them looking tired and worn after a sleepless night, and then I feel angry at the way in which so many of us, as children, are not only made to feel that we are responsible for everything and everybody (which is bad enough), but also have the dangers of the world impressed on us, while at the same time such confidence as we might have to deal with these dangers is drained away.

We cannot be responsible for everybody and everything, because no one can have the power to be the sole cause of everything, nor to be able to protect everyone else from all dangers. We are not even powerful enough to be the cause of all benefits to our loved ones and to protect them from all harm. To have such power we would have to be able to separate ourselves from everything that is, and then intervene in everything that is. Only God is deemed to have that power.

Because we are not 'taught about the interconnections between all events, we find it very difficult to work out what are the limits of our responsibility. Thus when some very grave disaster strikes us, we can feel overwhelmed by a sense of responsibility and guilt.

One of my colleagues, Cynthia, phoned me to tell me that Janice, her eighteen-year-old daughter, had suddenly begun to act very strangely. She had thrown all the electrical equipment she had in her bedroom out of the window, and had barricaded herself in. When her father went to remonstrate with her, she attacked him with a knife, saying that he was the devil. The neighbours called the police, and Janice was now under sedation in a psychiatric hospital. Cynthia was convinced that Janice's breakdown was totally her fault. She was Janice's mother, so she must be to blame.

I knew there was no way I could convince her otherwise over the phone, so I suggested that we meet to talk. I was not surprised that Janice had attacked her father, for I knew that, while he presented to the world the appearance of being a warm, caring person of the utmost goodness, at home he was a petty tyrant and a faithless husband.

I had thought that Cynthia had endured his tyranny and infidelity for the sake of the children, and that once they had left home she too would leave. I knew that at work she was an expert at putting on a cheerful face in difficult circumstances, but it was not until we talked that I realized that under no circumstances would she allow herself to complain. As she talked about her marriage, she kept apologizing to me for complaining, and, when talking of her daughter's plight, she began to cry, she – who would encourage her clients to cry, telling them about the healing powers of tears – writhed in embarrassment. 'You must think I'm terrible,' she said. As she fumbled for a tissue she said, 'My parents would be ashamed of me.'

I asked her about her parents, and she spoke of her adored father and her loving, chronically ill mother, and of the little girl who always had to 'be brave' and 'count her blessings'. In her family no one complained, for complaining was a weakness and a vice. She grew up believing that it was wrong to complain even to herself. Thus, when in the first months of her marriage she became the victim of her husband's total selfishness, she could not protest, but bore it all with the fortitude which, she hoped, would make her parents proud of her.

So what responsibility did she have for her daughter, who now believed that her radio and radiator emitted dangerous rays and messages intended just for her, and that her father was the devil? These kinds of experiences, usually labelled 'psychotic' or 'schizophrenic', come about when the person concerned loses the ability to see external reality as solidly real. All introverts always find that external reality is not quite as real as their internal reality, and they need to have confidence in their own judgement to be sure that they can act as if the external reality they see is actually real, and to distinguish the events around them from their thoughts and feelings. Once this confidence in their judgement is undermined, they feel very frightened, and they begin to act in ways which other people find bizarre and crazy.[23]

Introvert children need the adults around them to behave in reasonably consistent ways so that they can grow up with confidence in their own judgement. Unfortunately, Janice had two parents who did not behave consistently. Janice was well aware that her father in public life was very different from her father in private, and, like the devil, he assumed different guises. Janice knew that her father was cruel and selfish, for she observed what he did to her mother and sisters, and she suffered what he did to her. Yet, instead of acknowledging her own or her daughter's suffering, her mother insisted that everything was fine, that her husband's behaviour was understandable and excusable, and that he was 'a good father' and Janice should be grateful for what he did for her.

The tragedy of this situation was that Cynthia was not acting out of wilful selfishness, but out of her sheer goodness, wanting the best for her children, wanting to please her parents, not wanting to harm her husband in any way, and to be fair. Yet her need to be good, to assume responsibility for everyone and everything, prevented her from seeing just what was her responsibility. Children need to develop the ability to be responsible for themselves. They cannot do this if the adults around them lie to them. Children can deal with uncomfortable truths. What they cannot deal with is fairy-tale lies which they suspect, but dare not say, are lies. By maintaining the fairy-tale lie that all was well in the family, Cynthia failed to acknowledge Janice's suffering at the hands of her father, thus undermining her daughter's self-confidence, and, by denying the reality of what Janice saw happening, undermined her ability to make secure judgements about external reality.

What Cynthia was not responsible for was her husband's behaviour. He was responsible for that. Nor was she responsible for her parents' happiness, though they had forced this responsibility on to her.

Cynthia had been taught to see the world as being composed of discrete boxes. 'Don't complain – protect your parents.' 'Be good – be totally responsible.' She was not shown that everything is connected to everything else, and all is in constant flux. Working out the limits of our responsibility in such a world is very difficult, and Cynthia was given no help in learning how to do this. Instead she was taught the simplistic notion that she was responsible for everything, including her parents' happiness.

Parents who prevent their children from complaining and showing that they are suffering are sacrificing their children to maintain themselves. This is the tradition in our society. The Bible contains many stories of children being sacrificed for their parents, but no stories of parents being sacrificed for their children.[24] Some children, thus sacrificed, die, but the sacrifice which most make is the person they might have been and the life they might have lived.

When parents do not allow their children to complain about their suffering so that the parents will not have to acknowledge their own unhappiness, such children, being made to be responsible for their parents, can grow up with a sense of being totally responsible for everybody and everything. If someone in the child's life shows the child that she is aware of the child's suffering (such a person is often the child's grandmother), such children can acknowledge to themselves that they are suffering, even though they might despise themselves for indulging in self-pity. But if there is no one in the child's life who supports the child by at least showing that she is aware of the child's suffering, the child does not recognize that he is being treated cruelly. Such children are able to grow up to inflict cruelty, which is total selfishness, on others. Alice Miller has pointed out that to combat cruelty, a person must first be able to recognize it as such.[25] This is why cruelty is so common.

We think of causation as being a single line, when in fact it is a multidimensional net spreading far and wide.

One of my responsible friends told me that if, when she is driving, she hears a car horn behind her, she immediately assumes that she has done something wrong. The fact that car horns get sounded for a multitude of reasons means nothing to her in this situation. If something has gone wrong, it is her fault.

Being responsible for everybody and everything is a prime example of the way we are taught to see causation as a single line – A leads to B, and B to C. Such a way of thinking causes enormous confusion in our notions of responsibility, blame and guilt.

We get very confused over the allocation of responsibility and blame to the ills that befall us, be they the ills of the body or of the mind – anxiety, depression, all those wayward feelings and actions which psychiatrists call the mental illnesses. We say that we cannot be blamed for acquiring a physical illness because that is something which just happens to us. We did not bring it on ourselves. Whereas we can be blamed for the ills which affect our mind – our worry and despair – because these are the result of what we do to ourselves. This simplistic notion of cause and blame has a number of unfortunate consequences.

We learn quite early in life to explain our disasters in terms of physical illness. Rather than say, 'Mummy, I'm frightened,' we learn to say, 'Mummy, I feel sick.' One woman told me how, when she was a little girl, she was indecently assaulted by an uncle. 'I didn't tell my mother what had happened to me because I knew she would blame me. She saw that there was something wrong, so I told her I was bilious. She made quite a fuss of me, so every time after that when I was upset I told her I felt I was going to be sick. I spent much of my childhood with my head over a bucket. I always seem to have problems with my tummy. As an adult it took me years to work out what was happening. I still have problems with my bowels.'

While working in the NHS I met many people who were sent to see me by doctors who had carried out extensive investigations and found no physical cause for the physical pain and discomfort each of these people felt. They were all quite insulted to be sent to a psychologist and attended only because they were obedient patients. They were certain that there was something seriously wrong with their body and that the doctors were negligent or mistaken. Whether the doctors were I had no idea, but what I found was that these people had no language in which to discuss feelings. Painful feelings they felt only as bodily pain, and they could see no connections between the sad and frightening events in their lives and their distress.[26]

To define an area where they alone might be experts, psychiatrists claimed that there are such things as mental illnesses which have physical causes. According to the theory that no blame is attached to a physical illness, this should mean that no one could be blamed or stigmatized for having a mental illness, but in practice anyone who has a mental illness is seen as blameworthy and inferior. In the USA, where the psychiatrists' view dominates, a person's standing in the community can be ruined by the suggestion of a mental illness. In the contest between George Bush and Michael Dukakis in 1988, the Republicans tried to destroy Dukakis by putting about the story that he had been treated for depression. Dukakis had to make strenuous efforts to refute the story. There was no suggestion that, if Dukakis had been depressed at some time in his life, this demonstrated his humanity and suggested that from such an experience he had gained wisdom.

The extensive research which shows a strong causal connection between nicotine and alcohol and a wide range of potentially fatal illnesses throws into doubt the distinction between physical illness/ no blame and self-inflicted illness/blame. There is in the medical and nursing professions a strong tradition of treating with little sympathy those people who attempt suicide or, under great tension, harm themselves. Should smokers who develop lung cancer or drinkers who have liver damage be treated in the same way?

Even more confusing is the increasing body of research which shows a connection between how we deal with stress and the cause and outcome of cancer and heart disease. When Professor Hans Eysenck said at a conference on cancer that only good people, that is, quiet, self-effacing, unselfish people, got cancer, and the *Guardian* carried an article on the connection between not expressing anger and developing cancer,[27] many people were outraged. One woman wrote to the *Guardian*:

> Please do not use your responsible paper to promulgate half-truths which may encourage patients, relatives and friends to employ a 'Pull your socks up' approach, with an 'It's all my/your fault' response when it fails.

Another woman wrote:

> Carcinogens cause cancer, and suppression is not one of them. Professor Eysenck should consider the effect of his words before he opens his mouth. To jumble together a lot of misleading data and conclude that a calm, suppressed character will assist in the onset of cancer is unmitigated nonsense. I urge all woman unfortunate enough to have cancer to take with a large dose of salt all you read about a 'negative' attitude being a contributory factor. If you are a nice, calm person who would rather suffer in silence than make waves, carry on like that, but let your loved ones know how brave you are and perhaps they will help you over come any helplessness you feel.[28]

Using the notion of linear cause, these women, like many other people, cannot grasp the idea of a complex net of causes which leads to the development of cancer and affects the outcome of the disease.

When we believe that we do not have the right to defend ourselves from the demands and aggression of other people, that is, when we are quiet, self-effacing and unselfish people, we often find ourselves in situations which we believe we cannot master, and so we feel in danger of being overwhelmed, or, in popular parlance, we feel under stress. Ordinarily our body wards off disease with a complex mechanism called the autoimmune system. There is much research which shows that stress reduces the efficient functioning of the autoimmune system. Why one person develops a particular disease once this happens depends on what noxious material is available in the environment, on other potentialities in the person's body (like a genetic mutation from a father who had been exposed to radiation), and on the person's way of living. Research also shows that something as simple as learning to relax improves the efficiency of the functioning of the autoimmune system. In short, if you don't want to get ill, value yourself and stand up for yourself, and if you're ill and want to get better, believe that you deserve to get well.

More confusion about responsibility, blame and guilt arises when people believe that we are at the mercy of a force of evil.

Brendan O'Friel was the governor of Strangeways prison when, in April 1990, a group of prisoners rioted and took over part of the prison in a 25-day siege. After the siege ended, Mr O'Friel, a Jesuit-educated Catholic, called a press conference for the journalists reporting on religious matters:

> Surrounded by his chaplaincy team in the prison officers mess at Strangeways itself, Mr O'Friel had one word on his mind: evil.
>
> For these men – and Mr O'Friel in particular – evil is much more than overused hyperbole for bad: it is a real and tangible force for disruption in the world; and diabolic challenge to their Christian mission among the prisoners.
>
> Long pauses and parenthetic asides punctuated his speech as he tentatively explained this vision, growing in confidence as he continued. 'Now, I don't know, there is something in this incident that makes me feel it was in part – and of course there are many other explanations – but that it was in part something of a battle between good and evil.'
>
> His argument, as it developed, was full of symbolic gestures, moments of redemption and sadness that ultimately affirm his world view. It was also full of the reality of evil. 'When I use the words explosion of evil,' he said, 'those words were very carefully chosen – they had been thought about for several days.'
>
> He paused and enunciated the key symbolism of the struggle, phrase by phrase. 'Notice,' he said, 'that the incident started in our main chapel. It was followed very rapidly by the destruction of the only building that was totally destroyed in the whole incident: the other chapel, the Roman Catholic chapel.
>
> 'One of the first things the prisoners did when they broke on to the roof of F wing was that they pushed the cross off,' he explained patiently. 'Then, during the course of the incident, we had a number of incidents of desecration, including the wearing of vestments from the chapel on the roof. The point was that the incident ended on the chapel roof.'
>
> The history of the riot and its immediate and not-so-immediate causes take on a new significance through Mr O'Friel and his chaplains. They place the riot and occupation as the final battle in a hard-fought campaign of mission within the prison, which last year saw at least 200 inmates make a 'commitment to Christ'. It is an idea which fascinates him: that improvements in the prison, and the success of the mission, may have awakened the dark forces against him.
>
> 'I have got this very clear feeling that one aspect of this happening was a straight good – evil conflict, and I come back to my expression of an explosion of evil. It could be that part of the total explanation of what happened in Strangeways was a real manifestation of evil.' . . .

There are difficulties, even contradictions, in his argument. Questions that remain unresolved. How, he was asked, could the men be held responsible for their actions if they were guided by an evil force? 'The burden of freedom,'he replied. 'Are these the sort of thoughts you will be putting before the inquiry?' asked a journalist at the back. Brendan O'Friel smiled. 'I haven't got my head round that.'[29]

This is indeed a hard idea for any of us to get our heads around. If it is evil (A) which causes us to do wicked things (B), then we can be no more blamed than we can be when a flu virus invades our body and makes us sick.

Unless, of course, we are free to choose between the promptings of an external force and our own moral verities. But if we do have free will, does that mean that God does not know what the future will be? Does that mean that we are not pawns of an already determined fate, puppets in a play created by God or Allah? Does that mean that we are free to make our own choices, and that we are responsible for ourselves?

For Muslim pilgrims, a high point of the hajj to Mecca is the trek to Jamarat Al 'Akaba in Mina, one of the three stoning points of Satan. Each passing pilgrim must cast pebbles at this rock pillar in a ritual that symbolizes the faithful's struggle against evil. At 10 a.m. last Monday the believers suddenly faced a more earthly trial.

As throngs of the faithful, clad in traditional terry-cloth robes, crossed a pedestrian bridge in Mina, a railing gave way under the pressure. Seven worshippers plunged 8 metres, smashing into even greater waves of people at the mouth of a 550-metre-long tunnel dug through a mountain to ease the pietists' journey. The rain of bodies brought traffic to a halt, but at the tunnel's opposite end other hajjis, unaware of the human blockade, continued to shove forward. Soon the passageway was jammed with some 50,000 people, many times more than its capacity. Next, according to survivors, for reasons unexplained, the lights in the tunnel went out and the ventilation system failed – on a day when the temperature outside was a searing 44 degrees.

Then came the mad panic. In the scramble to escape, hundreds were crushed under the frantic feet of their co-religionists; others collapsed in the airless heat. 'It was terrible,' an Arab survivor told Saudi television. 'When one stumbled, scores trampled him and hundreds fell on top of them.' According to Islamic teachings, to die while on the hajj ensures immediate ascension into heaven. On that day, 1,426 Muslims earned the privilege.[30]

King Fahd of Saudi Arabia explained, 'It was fate. Had they not died there, they would have died elsewhere and at the predestined moment.'[31]

This is a useful way of explaining the tragedy. It was the Saudi Government who had built the bridge and tunnel.

Nirad Chaudhuri pointed out that the king was simply stating Islamic doctrine:

> Islam is a religion of unquestioning submission to the will of God, as it is embodied in the *surah fatihah* of the Koran, the daily prayer of the Muslims: a nobler and purer prayer does not exist in any other scripture. In this aspect the Muslim is not very different from the Christian who says: 'Thy will be done.'
>
> But in addition, the Muslim is also a believer in fate as an independent power on the life of a man. He calls it *kismet* or *nasib*. Nobody can resist it. John Stuart Mill recognized its true character and wrote: 'Pure or Asiatic Fatalism, the Fatalism of Oedipus, holds that our actions do not depend on our desires. Whatever our wishes may be, a superior power, or an abstract Destiny, will overrule them, and compel us to act, not as we desire, but in the manner predestined.' . . .
>
> The Muslims, however, also believe in a third irresistible power, which is evil. Evil cherishes ineradicable rancour against human greatness and happiness, and brings misfortune on kingdoms, peoples, and individuals indiscriminately and out of sheer malice. They call it the Evil Eye. Its dread presence hovers over all men and only the mercy of Allah can save men from its hatred.
>
> What was common in all forms of fatalism – Greek, Hindu and Muslim – was that in practice they gave men strength and fortitude to go through and bear suffering without losing the will to live. Thus there is nothing morally wrong with fatalism of any kind, nor is there in Muslim fatalism in its normal operation. But the Muslims in certain cases extended the idea of fatalism one step further so that they might not feel uncomfortable from a sense of guilt after they inflicted sufferings on others from motives of ambition or greed.
>
> Of this, I should give an authentic historical example. Alivardi Khan was the ruler of Bengal from 1740 to 1756 . . . Alivardi was the general of the legitimate ruler, Nawab Sarazaran Khan, and seized his throne after killing him. But after his accession he went to the mother of the assassinated prince and begged her forgiveness on his knees saying: 'My Lady, do not harbour ill feeling against me, for what has happened was ordained by inexorable fate.'[32]

Alivardi's excuse is the one commonly used by those who try to get everything by being totally selfish. It was, they claim, fate, or an evil force, or their hormones, or their uncontrollable passions, or market forces, or the needs of the Party, which led them to do what they did. They are not responsible for what they did, and so they cannot be blamed.

Those people who want to be totally selfish benefit from the confusion over responsibility and blame because it often enables them to avoid responsibility and blame. Those who want to be totally responsible also benefit from the confusion, for, in claiming total responsibility, they are also claiming great power. They could, they say, have acted differently if they had chosen to do so. No matter that at the time they had inadequate knowledge and experience, and were subject to many restraints (as, say, when we are parents of young children). They prefer to claim this because it gives them a sense of being in control of events. To say otherwise, to say that they did the best they could at the time, but that their knowledge and experience were limited, that there were conditions present which they could not control, would be to recognize their helplessness in a vast and changing universe. Better to feel guilty, for guilt is a claim to power.

We think of acting so as to bring about a good result, or a bad result, when in fact every action has a multitude of results, some of them good and some of them bad.

People who assume total responsibility believe that the outcome of what they do will be good. They worry that it might not be good enough, that they might have overlooked some aspects of their responsibility or not done as much as they could, but, they are sure, the results of their efforts will be good.

By 'good' they mean 'good for us', the objects of their responsibility. Parents who feel totally responsible for their children are not going to let their children go wilfully on their own way, making mistakes and living lives the parents do not approve of. Adult children who feel totally responsible for their parents are not going to say of their parents, 'They've made their bed. Now they can lie on it.' Instead, by bullying, cajoling, using the same guilt-arousing tactics which their parents once used on them, they try to force their parents to lead the kinds of lives the children approve of. When their parents fail to conform (many parents cannot even comprehend what their children want, much less produce the desired behaviour), they worry.

Many such totally responsible people are too well practised in guilt, self-blame and humility to claim in public that they do know what is best for everyone, but privately they feel that this is so. They base their conviction on their belief that, while they have shortcomings, about which they feel shame and guilt, they do know how to be good.

Other people – or, at least, most of them – do not know how to be good, and so need their guidance. Other people need to be pointed to the light and shown the way.

Once such a totally responsible person gains power, the veil of modesty can be swept aside. Hugo Young, a biographer of Margaret Thatcher, spoke of 'her conviction that she alone could bring the necessary wisdom and understanding to whatever issue was on the agenda at the time', and 'her searing sense of her own rectitude together with the need at all time to prove it'.[33] The journalist Andrew Gimson wrote:

> The unifying theme of her prime ministership is her attempt to remoralize the British character. She does not express it like that, and may not even think of it like that, but there can be little doubt that by the time she finishes with us or we with her, she intends us to be an exceptionally hard-working and thrifty people.[34]

Being forced to resign as prime minister by her party in no way altered Margaret Thatcher's aims. She still, so she believed, knew what was best for her people.

But being assured of one's goodness and the rightness of one's aims does not ensure that *everything* will turn out well. No amount of goodness and wisdom can ensure that *every* result of our actions will be good.

At a shipboard drinks party given by a major Australian bank, a businessman told me that it was only with great reluctance that, in 1980, he had established a branch of his Australian business in London because he was convinced that Britain was finished both economically and industrially. However, now his business in London was flourishing, thanks to Mrs Thatcher's economic miracle. He went on to praise her policies fulsomely. I murmured a few words to the effect that, in my experience, such policies applied to the NHS led to patients getting worse treatment, not better. He agreed, explaining that his wife was a sister specializing in nursing geriatric patients, the ones who have lost most by the changes. Before I could ask how he and his wife had reconciled their opposing experiences of the Thatcher policies, he explained, 'My wife had to leave the NHS. She does private nursing now.'

Organizations in the rich, developed world have poured billions into the Third World in order to do nothing but good. The men who ran these organizations believed that they knew what was best for the Third World. Thus, in the Groundnut Scheme:

> Around 50 million dollars were spent in the late-colonial 1950s on a grandiose scheme – conceived in London, executed in Tanzania – to grow groundnuts. The expert expatriate agriculturalists destroyed vast areas of grazing land before they realized that intensively mechanized groundnuts would not grow. Still, the experts' hearts were in the right place, weren't they?[35]

By the mid 1970s, the men who would do good had realized that they needed to find out what their would-be beneficiaries actually needed, and then supply them with that. Thus all would be well. The Village Fishponds programme around Lake Victoria was one such scheme:

This really seemed to have done everything right. It obeyed all the rules – or all the catch-phrases, depending on your degree of optimism or pessimism about Western approaches to development. Sustainable, low-tech, community orientated: this had the works. Lake region dwellers have a fishing culture already. Add small ponds to their back-yards and you get protein for all.

The fish they put in were Nile Perch which are carnivorous and change from small fry into monsters six feet long in a couple of years. Some escaped into Lake Victoria, where the biggest native species are less than twelve inches. The Nile Perch had no competitors and it has exploded. The lake people can now catch bigger fish more easily. Hooray.

There is a slight snag. There used to be 300 different species of fish in Lake Victoria. The Nile Perch have eaten 180 of them. It is the biggest mass extinction of vertebrates in modern times. Well, with a growth rate like that, you'd expect the Nile Perch to have a big appetite.

That's not all. Victoria fisherpeople dry their catch in the sun. Nile Perch are too oily, and had to be smoked. So the fisherpeople cut down their trees for charcoal. Soil erosion and desertification are following. Perhaps some eucalyptus plantations might help.[36]

There has also been the slight problem that, having rendered extinct 180 species in the lake, the Nile Perch have nothing left to feed on and have started eating each other. A little thought will show that this is not a viable long-term strategy: you can't get by for long eating yourself.

Already the ecological balance of the lake has been destroyed: the fish that used to eat the algae in it are extinct. It is quite possible that an algae bloom will cover the lake, absorbing all the oxygen, making the lake stone-dead sterile and killing any remaining fish species with the temerity to survive this small-scale, ecologically-sensitive and culturally-appropriate development project. What will the fisherpeople catch then?

Also, Lake Victoria is the size of Switzerland and covering it with algae will have an appreciable, though unpredictable, effect on the climate. So, a desert, eroded soil and deforestation in the most fertile area on earth; 180 species rendered extinct and the number rising; 10,000 square miles, the largest fresh water lake in the world stone-dead; and the world's climate doing who knows what. That's some development project.[37]

Parents who believe they know what is best for their children, and adult children who believe they know what is best for their parents, are horrified when they discover that not everything has turned out well. They blame themselves, rather than see that everything that happens *always* has good results and bad results. Children either follow their parents' directions and then blame their parents for the parts of their lives that do not suit them, or they react against the parents' directions, only to make most of the mistakes the parents had predicted and a few more besides, or, worse, their lives turn out well and they prove their parents wrong. Parents of adult children who believe they know what is best for their parents either become recalcitrant and difficult, thus causing their children endless worry, or they sink gratefully into childish dependency, thus causing their children endless work.

Burdened by worry and work, the people who feel totally responsible create in themselves a kind of loneliness. Their superior goodness and wisdom sets them apart from others who regard them with awe and, feeling unworthy, dare not approach them too closely. Moreover, because they are busy pointing out the way to others, such responsible people do not spend time with themselves, getting to know themselves and looking after themselves. They become alienated from themselves.

So do the totally selfish people whose guiding principle is 'Grab what I can and think only of myself'. This attitude alienates them from others, because no one likes being treated as an object which may or may not have value for the selfish person, and we withdraw from someone who treats us in this way. Since we only get to know ourselves through our interaction with other people, totally selfish people do not get to know themselves. Totally selfish people might acquire wealth and possessions, and they might avoid a great deal of work and the burden of responsibilities, but the price they pay for this is loneliness.

We overlook the fact that part of the continuous interaction of everything that occurs is the continuous construction of meaning in which every human being is engaged all the time.

Just as every action has good results and bad results, so every meaning that we create has good implications and bad implications. People who want to be totally responsible are seeking perfection – perfection of action and perfection of motive. The imperfection of the world offends them, but they hate to recognize that if the world were perfect they would be superfluous. Moreover, if the world were perfect we would not know it was perfect. We have a concept of perfection only because there is imperfection.

Nor do they wish to confront the fact that their drive for perfection and their need for total responsibility arises from their need to compensate themselves for their childhood suffering. No doubt they would protest that their aim of perfection and safety for other people arises from love. Not understanding themselves, they are unaware that we need to distinguish between that feeling which we call love which arises when another person meets, or promises to meet, our needs and that feeling which we also call love and which is inspired *simply because that other person exists.*

With this second feeling, which I, at the risk of sounding romantic, call true love, we have no urge to interfere in the lives of the people we love. If we see them in danger, we do what we can to protect them because they have the right to exist, and not because their existence is necessary to our existence. Thus we do not spend our lives in constant anxiety that the people we need will die. If there is something we can do to enhance those people's lives we do it, but only after we have ascertained that this is what they want. We never assume that we know the people we love better than they know themselves, or that, even when we believe that our wisdom is superior to theirs, we have the right to force or manipulate them to do what we want them to do. This means that we have to keep to ourselves our anxiety when we see the mistakes they make, and we refrain from making them feel guilty just so we can keep them near us and enjoy their company. We love them because they are, and we always wish them well, even when that 'well' does not include us.

If our love is not this kind of love, then what we feel arises from our own needs to assure ourselves that we are good, that other people need us and will not abandon us, that we shall not be overwhelmed by the chaos of the world, or that we can justify the privileges we enjoy. (The tradition of the British aristocracy that they should care for their servants and other inferiors may have inspired many good works, but it is essentially a justification for their privileges.)

True love, as I have described it, is the kind of love that we all want. In some way we experienced such love when we were in the womb, for then we were accepted as we were and our needs were met. Once we were born and encountered people, we discovered, if we were lucky, the joy of being accepted simply because we existed and because the adults around us sought to understand and meet our needs. Such bliss lasted for a few brief weeks, but the memory of such love remained. We might have tried to restore such bliss by becoming the responsible person our parents demanded, or by deciding to give ourselves the total acceptance and concern we wanted, but our continuous construction of meaning which followed on these decisions never succeeded in gaining for us the love for which we longed.

The continuous construction of meaning of the totally responsible people and the totally selfish people are complementary. Totally selfish people need totally responsible people, and totally responsible people need totally selfish people. They often manage to marry one another, to their mutual unhappiness. They battle for power, but avoid direct confrontation and honest statements of what they want. The responsible one allows the selfish one to behave outrageously because then the responsible one can feel guilty, in control and good, and the selfish one allows the responsible one to be saint-like and long-suffering because then the selfish one can manipulate the responsible one through guilt. Their children suffer.

We think that the meanings we create are discrete categories, when in fact they are linked to one another so that meanings of which we are not conscious can influence our actions.

Both extraverts and introverts can choose to be totally responsible or totally selfish, but, as ever, they make their choice for different reasons, and they have different ways of trying to carry out their aims.

The overriding need of introverts who wish to be totally responsible is to impose order. This is one of the reasons why guilt is so important to them, so they do not have to feel helpless in the face of chaos. They are highly skilled in creating theories as to why they should be so responsible and why the world needs their expertise and goodness. These theories may be about personal morality or public morality, or about politics, economics, or science, and they may have only the slightest relation to reality, but, whatever the theory is, the totally responsible introvert is convinced that its execution is for our own good. Believing that they know what is best for other people, totally responsible introverts can be the most dangerous people in the world, for they can be convinced of their own rectitude while inflicting great cruelty on others.

The overriding need of extraverts who wish to be totally responsible is to keep other people around them. They do this by making other people dependent on them. This is usually done with the greatest kindness and concern, but the recipients, unless committed to being totally selfish, feel guilty if they reject any of this kindness and concern so as to do and be what they want. 'If you reject what I offer, you reject me,' the totally responsible extravert cries, and the loved ones surrender themselves. How could they hurt someone so kind? They are cossetted and cared for, undermined, weakened and trapped.

If, at the same time as wanting to be totally responsible, the introvert and extravert feel a profound self-hatred, their need to be totally responsible damages them as much as, or more than, it damages others.

Ben Elton's obsessions are a small example of how totally responsible introverts who doubt their own worth and goodness become dominated by the thought that through their negligence they may injure others. There are many people whose lives are dominated by other much worse obsessions. There are people who keep sharp knives locked away, lest these knives in their hands stab their family, people who check and recheck that gas taps are turned off, lest a gas explosion destroy their home and the people in it, people who check and recheck that doors are locked, lest burglars break in and murder the family, who fear to drive lest they inadvertently kill someone, who fear to be near a child, lest they inadvertently molest the child. These fears and the repeated checking to prevent the feared disaster are accompanied by the most violent and often bizarre fantasies, which come to mind unbidden and cause the obsessional person enormous distress.

These fantasies are particularly appalling to totally responsible obsessional people because they pride themselves on their lack of aggression and anger. They are calm, organized, rational, compassionate people. These fantasies seem to be completely alien.

The reason that the fantasies appear to be alien is because, as children, these people were taught most forcibly that to be angry was to be wicked. Yet, in learning to be responsible, they often felt angry at being taught forcibly, and once they began to demonstrate their expertise in being responsible they often felt angry with the people who so readily loaded them with burdens and punishments. This anger had to be denied, but denied anger does not disappear, and often turns to hate and murderous rage. So the anger, hate and murderous rage return in fantasies, and everywhere the obsessional, totally responsible people look, they can see possible dangers to others against which they, the responsible ones, must guard. Life becomes a nightmare.[38]

Totally responsible extraverts who believe that they are essentially bad and valueless dare not allow themselves any respite from meeting other people's needs and encouraging others to be dependent on them. Every waking moment they spend in work and worry. They dare not risk losing the affection of a single person or having a single person dislike them. They dare not say, 'No. I need some time for myself to do what I want to do.' So their life slips by, their pleasures are few, their achievements are minimal, and they find themselves taken for granted by those on whom they have lavished concern.

Totally selfish introverts need to establish control and organization and to achieve. All this is worked out in terms of a theory which the introvert has developed and which is put into operation with a single-minded determination and without regard to the needs and wishes of others. The theory may be in terms of their great uniqueness, as shown by the way they can beat all contenders and push back the limits of achievement, usually in terms of sport or entertainment. The theory may be in terms of a religion, and these totally selfish introverts, in the guise of superhuman wisdom and goodness, plan to convert millions, destroy the infidel, and lead the faithful to salvation and glory. The history of Christianity and Islam abounds with such people. The theory may be in terms of power, and such people, in the guise of knowing what is best for those whom they wish to have power over, become dictators. There has never been a shortage of such people, just as there has never been a shortage of those totally selfish introverts who create and implement their theory in terms of acquiring wealth. All such totally selfish introverts can be the object of much admiration from afar, but those who know them either lie to themselves, trying to convince themselves of the selfish introvert's worth, or they despise the selfish introvert. Whatever, they suffer at the selfish introvert's hands.

Totally selfish extraverts are in the business of keeping people around them, and this they do with charm. There is something particularly attractive about such lively, observant, amusing extraverts, and when their apparent lack of aggression and their immediate interest in and concern for other people deludes us into thinking that they are really unaggressive, except in the defence of those who need defending, and that their concern for others is profound and not merely an immediate brief response, we cannot see the utterly ruthless selfishness and self-involvement which motivates their every action. Many otherwise sensible introvert women are dazzled and seduced by such men, and then devastated to find that a buccaneer does not make a good husband. Totally selfish extraverts can be very successful at keeping their followers around them by sudden bursts of generosity, but, since much of the charm depends on youth, beauty and sexual prowess, fewer and fewer people approach them to be dazzled, and many of those who have been dazzled desert in disillusionment. The totally selfish extravert has to resort more and more to artifice and self-delusion, unattractive attributes in middle and old age.

When the totally selfish introvert and extravert lose confidence in themselves and turn against themselves, their efforts to achieve their aims have to be greatly increased. They are plagued by anxiety and depression, and to maintain themselves resort to acts of selfishness which observers find quite breathtaking. I often see this in couples, for the totally selfish person, whether introvert or extravert, usually has the foresight to find a partner who has a strong sense of responsibility and guilt. If the partner attempts to break free, the totally selfish person threatens to commit suicide or become depressed, or, if necessary, makes a suicidal gesture or retreats into depression. Outwitted, the responsible partner conforms to the totally selfish person's wishes. Such selfish partners see their predicament as a matter of survival, and, since they do not regard other people as being human like themselves, they use other people in the same way as they would use any object to save their lives. Such couples live in mutual misery, and defeat all efforts by doctors, therapists, family and friends to resolve their difficulties. A few totally selfish people eventually realize that some degree of unselfishness is needed in order to repair and maintain the relationships on which they depend, but by then so much damage has been done that those they have injured cannot always bring themselves to forgive them.

We assume that other people create the same meanings as we do, and that when we act other people will interpret what we do in the same way as we do.

Totally responsible people, being convinced of the rightness of their views, assume that if other people do not hold the same meanings as they do, then they *ought* to do so. (Mrs Thatcher called her critics 'irresponsible'.)

Totally responsible people try to force their morality on to other people, and other people resist. Mick Jagger was interviewed by a panel of establishment worthies in 1968, after he had just escaped prison for a drug offence. They told him he should set an example to young people. He denied this. He said that his private life was his own affair.[32] Humphrey Bogart used to say the same. He said that his responsibility to the public as an actor was to give a good performance, not to set moral standards.

Totally responsible people are appalled at the wickedness and irresponsibility of other people, and this greatly adds to their constant anxiety. They battle against despair which, at every piece of evidence that others do not see the world as they do, threatens to overwhelm them in complete hopelessness. They find that others do not appreciate their worth and the rightness of their views, and that others misinterpret what they do. This they can neither understand nor accept. Some totally responsible people, in their relationships with others, live in constant miserable confusion, while other totally responsible people impose on their confusion a simple paranoid structure: 'Those who are not for me are against me!'

Totally selfish people have never wasted any time trying to understand how other people think and feel. They simply believe that anyone who does not think like them is a fool.

Yet anyone who does think like them is a competitor, and that creates anxiety. Totally selfish people believe that the only reason that other people do not behave as they do is because they, as well as being fools, are cowards, yet when other people's criticism of their behaviour has serious implications (like jail, bankruptcy, divorce), or a competitor is winning, the totally selfish people become extremely confused and frightened. Since they do not understand other people, and because they have no close relationships which might sustain them, their fear and confusion can be resolved only by the imposition of a simple paranoid structure: 'Those bastards are out to get me!'

Paranoia is an extremely popular defence.

We overlook the fact that there are certain aspects of life which stand in complementary relationship to one another, so that the more there is of one, the less there is of the other.

The rhetoric of totally responsible people is all about being responsible. They constantly urge others – children, family, friends, neighbours, voters, subjects, the faithful – to be responsible. On many occasions their meaning for 'responsible' is 'do what I want without my having to remind or supervise you', but sometimes they are actually urging others to accept their individual responsibility for themselves, to take other people's needs into account, to think before acting, and to act with sense and foresight. But once totally responsible people do this they are in difficulties.

We cannot make another person be responsible by ordering that person to be so, for even if he proceeds to make his own decisions without asking for permission, he is still simply carrying out an order. He is not exercising personal freedom. When we want someone to assume personal responsibility, all we can do is create a space where he can do so. Then we must not interfere or direct, and we must accept what he does even if we do not approve. Thus, in teaching a child to handle money responsibly, we can discuss with the child how he might spend his pocket money, but once we hand the money over to him he is free to do what he wishes with it, and to live with the consequences. If he spends it all on comics and has none left to buy his school lunch, we neither punish him for his stupidity nor give him extra money, but rely on hunger to teach him wisdom.

To teach someone to accept individual responsibility, we have to give up control, and this is what totally responsible people cannot do. Other people's freedom of individual responsibility is incompatible with their need for the security of total control. Unable to accept the complementary relationship of freedom and security, they bewail the irresponsibility of those whom they would control.

Totally selfish people encounter another kind of complementariness, namely the way in which we resist when other people press us to give them something, yet when we are not pressured to give, give generously. An old proverb, often used by parents to stop a child from expecting his desires to be met, is 'Those who want can't get.'

Our resistance to importunings is an important aspect of our need to resist others imposing their structures of meaning on to us. This basic need gets reinforced by our desire to prevent other people from getting everything just as we were prevented, and to punish others for getting more than we do. Sometimes we resist simply because what we are being asked for we have not got.

So totally selfish people ask, and meet resistance. When responsible people have what the selfish people want, they can develop ploys which play upon the responsible person's guilt and their need to be helpful, but these ploys work only in personal relationships. With other people, totally selfish people discover that to ask is to be resisted. They feel frustrated and angry, and when in their reckoning they have been good and deserve their rewards, they feel bitter and resentful. Life is so unfair!

Being Responsible for Ourselves

Both being totally responsible and being totally selfish are denials of responsibility for ourselves. Totally responsible people are so busy with other people's affairs, so busy being unselfish, that they give themselves an excuse for not considering the complex questions of the limitations of their responsibility for others and the requirements of responsibility for themselves. Totally selfish people are so busy denying responsibility for themselves while trying to guard their own interests that they never learn from their mistakes. Denying responsibility for oneself has serious consequences, as Havel has shown:

> To relinquish this full responsibility to oneself, to compromise one's integrity and sovereignty, not to widen and strengthen, but on the contrary, to narrow and weaken the control of one's 'I' over one's actions (including those ascribed to the 'instincts' – another alibi that shifts the blame from the 'I' to the 'not-I'), ultimately means only one thing: to turn away from Being, to give up on one's own mysterious connection – in one's origins and aims – to its fullness and integrity, to cancel out one's complex way of relating to it – and to disintegrate into fragmentary, isolated, self-enclosed events, interests and aims that lack any transcendence beyond one's 'existence-in-the-world', to dissolve in that existence and thus in the 'non-I' and so, ultimately, to deprive oneself of genuinely human being, that is, being as the inner coherence, direction, transcendence, meaning, purpose of human existence, anchored in the fullness of Being and oriented toward it. In other words: it means dissolving oneself in the world, in the world of phenomena, particular aims, random occurrences, isolated things, 'merenesses' and disjointed worries. It means apparently simplifying one's life – but at the cost of losing oneself, the miracle of one's separated being which, precisely because of its separation, aspires towards the integrity of Being. It means losing the identity of what is anchored in Being and reliably related to it, that is, the only thing that holds our 'I' together and makes us truly human. To know all this and to express it, obviously, is in no way difficult; but it is not easy to experience it existentially, as I have learned through hard personal experience. For there is nothing like experiencing personal failure to give you a more intense understanding of responsibility – that is,

if you manage to open yourself to it wholly and without prevarication – as responsibility for one's self.[40]

Some people are so prepared to deny their responsibility to themselves while trying to get everything that they are prepared to suffer, even to die, to achieve this.

8

'Yes I Can' – Martyrdom and Revenge

'Too long a sacrifice
Can make a stone of the heart.'
W.B. YEATS[1]

Martyrdom and revenge are methods we can adopt in the attempt to force the world to be what we want it to be, and thus give us everything.

Sometimes we find it necessary to endure some suffering so that we can be the person we want to be. This is not martyrdom but our wanting to live and die on our own terms.

Our tour party in Jerusalem included a married couple, Harold and Yetta, who appeared to be a typical middle-class couple in late middle age. They could not be called old, though that adjective is often applied to people of retirement age, because they were so fit and active. Yetta was slim and pretty, and Harold had the straight back and brisk, no-nonsense movements of a military man. They were polite and reserved in the English way which keeps intruders at bay, and it was not until we had found ourselves in a situation of possible danger – our small party were the only tourists venturing into the Arab town of Hebron on the West Bank – that we relaxed with one another, as groups do in danger, and I could ask Harold a personal question. What was the tattoo on his arm?

Since I thought of him as being a middle-class Englishman, the tattoo looked most out of place. An English gentleman does not have tattoos. This one was in deep blue in an obvious place on his lower arm. It was a six-pointed star, the shape which in Israel is called the Star of David.

I asked Harold this question privately, as we were walking away from the Tomb of the Patriarchs. He told me the story so easily that I asked him to repeat it later to the others as we lunched in a garden in Jerusalem. Yetta said, 'Oh, not that old story again,' but, undeterred, Harold told it.

He had been a soldier in the British army in France in 1940. He had managed to get back to England, but he and his fellow soldiers knew that their army was very disorganized and lacked the most basic equipment. There was no way they could repel a German invasion which they were sure would come in the next two weeks.

299

Harold and his friends also knew what the Germans were doing to the Jews. His friends said to him, 'Don't worry. You don't look Jewish. No one will tell them. You'll be all right.'

As soon as he got leave, Harold and his brother went to a tattooist and had the Star of David and each other's name tattooed on their arms. Rather than lose that which distinguished them from Englishmen and so merge into comparative safety, they preferred to remain as distinct individuals, even if this meant imprisonment and death.

Had Harold's action led to his death at the hands of the Germans, he might have been claimed as a martyr for the Jewish cause. But he was not a martyr and did not intend to be. He took responsibility for himself. He knew that to maintain one's sense of integrity it is often necessary to give something up.

Vaclav Havel, writing from prison, made the same decision.

My grand plans (to study, write, 'work on myself', etc. in prison) have proved immensely naive, of course; I had no idea what it would be like here (despite having heard so much about it – but the experience may indeed be impossible to communicate to anyone else). And so of all of that only one thing has remained: the chance to prove – to myself, to those around me and to God – that I am not a lightweight as many may have seen me, that I stand behind what I do, that I mean it seriously and that I can take the consequences . . . In any case, it was a deliberate choice on my part and I can't be accused of making a virtue of necessity after the fact. At the same time, I have no desire to become a professional martyr; my position followed quite naturally and logically from the logic of the situation as it evolved, and from the inner logic of my attitudes and my work, in other words, from my own identity. To put it simply: I had to act as I did; there was no other way.[2]

The Meaning of Martyrdom and Revenge

People who resort to martyrdom and revenge are struggling with the problem, 'I am bad. How can I show myself to be good?' However, it is not enough just to demonstrate personal goodness. To the martyr and the avenger the world is not satisfactory, so the martyr and the avenger are determined to make the world over into what it should be, that is, to impose their structure of meaning on to reality. Going on hunger strike or planting a bomb are extreme methods for imposing structures of meaning, but martyrs and avengers prefer to hold extreme ideas. They despise middling uncertainties and shades of grey. They want a world of sharply delineated black and white certainties. They want everything, and they want it to be just as they think it ought to be.

The martyr claims to be humble, self-effacing and unselfish. However, martyrdom requires an audience. This may be the populace at large, or our social, political or religious group, or our own observant self who assures us that our suffering is of the greatest magnitude and that our self-sacrifice is of supreme virtue. And so, in the eyes of the audience, we become a person of immense singularity, the centre of attention, admired, praised and rewarded. Our reward may lie in Paradise or Heaven, or in the remorse and guilt that our loved ones suffer. The trouble is, there are so many martyrs. How can we show the world that our capacity for suffering is greater than anyone else's?

To be a suitable aspirant for martyrdom and revenge, you need to believe that suffering is good for you. Indeed, an enjoyment of suffering shows a real talent for martyrdom and revenge. Those who do not enjoy suffering are the ones who scamper out of the way when the crosses are being handed out. Of course, there are many people who play the martyr role while avoiding actual suffering so that they can keep their family in order, but the success of this strategy requires a lack of shame on the part of the ersatz martyr and considerable gullibility and guilt on the part of the family.

Martyrdom, real or assumed, also requires a lack of the sense of the ridiculous. An avenger who has retained a sense of the ridiculous seeks to embarrass rather than to destroy those who have injured him, and has great fun in the process. But *Schadenfreude*, the delight in another person's discomfiture, is not sufficiently satisfying for those to whom revenge is the most serious matter in their lives.

An acceptance, or even enjoyment, of suffering and an extreme and totally serious way of constructing meaning are the essential requirements of the successful martyr and avenger. This means that the martyr and avenger are never more alive than when they are suffering. They may dream of the day when all their enemies are vanquished and they are gathered to glory, but they have few concepts of how they might live in peace and happiness. So, no matter what happens, they will not let anyone take their suffering away from them.

Martyrdom and revenge arise from a state of helplessness and weakness, the kind of helplessness and weakness we experience as children in the power of adults. We need to survive not only physically but also as a person, so we do what we can with the meagre materials we have available as a dependent, inexperienced child, and for some of us this means employing self-sacrifice. Most of us manage to save ourselves, but problems arise when, as the years pass, we do not realize that the techniques of survival which were so necessary in childhood are no longer needed once we become independent adults. Unfortunately, by then such techniques have become habitual,

unthinking, automatic responses, and have acquired some secondary advantages (such as reassuring yourself of your goodness as evidenced by your self-sacrifice or your unwavering loyalty to your group's programme of vengeance).

All of us sacrifice ourselves in order to be good and not be abandoned or punished by those adults in whose care we are, but not all of us choose self-sacrifice as the principal way in which we protect ourselves, only some of us. One woman described to me how, as the eldest of a large family, she had no memory of any time when she was her mother's special, adored child. Instead, as soon as she could fetch and carry (which eighteen-month-old babies can do), she placed herself at her mother's beck and call. 'It was only by looking after my brothers and sisters that I could get my mother to show any interest in me.'

Some children, burdened with such work, become resentful, and, as soon as they are able, flee from all such responsibilities, but this woman, being convinced that she had no right to consider her own needs while others had needs to be met, continued to serve others for the rest of her life, and there was never any lack of people who needed her care.

Until her mother's death in old age, this woman hoped that one day her mother would tell her that she loved her, not for what she did, but because she existed. This blessing never came. Many children, discovering that their parents will accept them only if they are unselfish and self-sacrificing, and finding that, no matter what they do, unqualified love is never shown, create fantasies where they perform acts of self-sacrifice unparalleled in the history of the world, the scales fall from their parents' eyes, and they see their child as the one worthy recipient of all their love. The child, in fantasy, may choose to accept the parents' love, or may prefer a touch of revenge, not spurning the parents, for that would be too mean-spirited, but by being singled out by God's gracious hand and swept into heaven. Some children, knowing that their parents could never, under any circumstances, have the wisdom to perceive the child's special worth, drop the parents from the fantasy and replace them with a Great Hero, or God, or Allah, whose love surpasses all other love.

As children we comfort ourselves with many fantasies. Most of them we abandon when they are no longer useful, but some we build into our life story and then seek to fulfil them. The world offers many opportunities to fulfil our martyr fantasies, just as there are many opportunities to fulfil our revenge fantasies.

Revenge fantasies in childhood give us hope. No matter what humiliations are heaped on us, one day we shall triumph over those who have injured us. Actual revenge when we are children is difficult, for that can get us into even more trouble, though the teenage years do offer plenty of scope for upsetting and humiliating parents. However, when our humiliations and defeats have been great, we need to plan in fantasy something which is astounding and earth-shattering. Sometimes all that the vengeful child wants is an apology from the parents, and when this is not forthcoming, the child embarks on the enactment of that fantasy which Eric Berne calls the 'See What You Made Me Do, Ma' game. Psychiatric hospitals, prisons and cemeteries contain many people who played this game to its bitter end. Often the revenge the child wants is the torture and murder of the parents, but he dare not be conscious of this lest his parents read his thoughts or his own conscience punish him as his parents would punish him. In such fantasies, the parents' place is taken by some stranger, some person or people whom the child has been taught by his society to see as the Enemy.

Through the fantasies we construct about martyrdom and revenge, we bring together the political and the personal. We can use fantasy as a way of exploring reality (for instance, in planning a journey or a task, we fantasize carrying it out and see what practical issues the fantasy reveals), or we can use fantasy to release emotion and to give comfort, courage and hope. For the second use of fantasy to succeed, reality should not be allowed to intrude. The outcome is without qualification, being good for us and bad for our adversaries, and the characters and actions can represent other people and desires which, in cold reality, we would find reprehensible. To create this kind of fantasy we need to draw on concepts and myths of our society. Thus Catholic girls model their fantasies of self-sacrifice on the Virgin Mary or Mother Teresa, and Hindu girls on Sita, and some boys see their vengeance and triumph taking place in the streets of Johannesburg and other boys in the streets of Jerusalem.

When in adult life these fantasies are acted out in the social and political arena, the personal and the political, martyrdom and revenge, come together in an inseparable whole. In the way that the dramatis personae present themselves, tell their story and have their story told, certain elements may appear to predominate.

Sometimes it is the personal and the martyrdom.

Lynette Phillips made sure the world would know precisely why she was killing herself. Before the 24-year-old Australian burned herself to death in Geneva, she typed out the political manifesto she intended publicizing by her death, mimeographed it on orange paper, and posted copies off to the media . . .

The letter is headed by the bald, type-written title: 'Self-Immolation'. It is signed 'L. Phillips', in neat schoolish hand. Underneath the signature are the words: 'Lynette Phillips (Shanti), Proutist Universal Citizen, a lover of humanity.' Alongside the signature is a roughly sketched Prout Symbol showing a rising sun, representing progress, and a swastika, representing luck.

Under the 'Self-Immolation' heading, Ms Phillips adds a subtitle to her death: 'Protest against inhumanity, injustice and irrationality prevalent in our society.'

'I belong to an organization, Proutist Universal, that believes in establishing one human society, based on moralism and universalism (citizen of the Universe),' she begins . . .

'Morality is dying. Law is mere verbosity for high fees and argument's sake . . . Anyone who speaks out is imprisoned or otherwise suppressed . . . All the moralists, all positive, forward thinking people must unite and fight to establish a new social order, based on the expression of humanity's fullest potential – spirituality and universal citizenship . . . This act of self-immolation is my own choosing and planned in secrecy. Divulgence would have meant prevention. It grew from a burning desire, an inner need to do something, to help stop the criminality of our exploited lives on earth . . . May the light emanated enlighten all other hearts. May this action pave the way for the establishment of a new social order that is devoid of exploitation, misery and injustice.'[4]

Only a fantasy which is unrelated to reality could go from a burning desire to a burning body, and expect that the light given off by a burning body could enlighten anyone. Lynette must have suffered at someone's hands and learned to see the social order as wicked, so her message and her martyrdom try to highlight the political, but point to a personal message of revenge.

Sometimes the political and the martyrdom appear to predominate.

Palestinian recruits, aching to the bone on what was only the first day of military training, sat in a semi-circle on the baked earth, hidden from Israeli reconnaissance planes by torn bushes of blazing gorse and sang,

'Oh you who hold the key to the sky, open it for me,
I am coming.
My Comrades have gone before me, they are already in heaven.
They kill me on earth and shoot me,
I am coming.'

A slim, soft-spoken officer put the youngsters through their paces: crawling, with weapons, under barbed wire a bare foot from the ground: throwing karate punches: assembling weapons, running, running, running until they fell to the ground. The recruits, all in their mid teens, sweated and groaned under the dehydrating sun. They tripped, dropped their weapons, tore their

clothes and lacerated their bodies. Some stood to attention backwards. But when they sang, they did so with their eyes closed,
and without moving a muscle.

'My mother wears funeral clothes and sits alone for the feast,
she looks at my photograph and shouts to God in the sky.
I have come.'

In most parts of the Lebanon where the Palestinians have
rebuilt their strength after the Israeli invasion of 1982, small,
mobile camps like this one run by the Democratic Front for the
Liberation of Palestine are training fighters to cross the Israeli
borders and attack military targets.

'We are here to support our brothers in the occupied territories,'
the leader of the camp said gravely in an interview a few days
before the DFLP guerrillas crossed the border and killed two
Israelis – one of them a lieutenant-colonel from the crack Givati
brigade – before being killed themselves.[5]

Sometimes all that the onlookers see is the political, without seeing
the personal revenge which underlies it. Trotsky wrote:

The motive of *personal revenge* has always been a considerable
factor in the repressive policies of Stalin. Kamenev told me how
the three of them – Stalin, Kamenev, and Dzerzhinsky – in Zuba-
lovo, in the summer of 1923 (or 1924?) spent the day in heart-to-
heart conversation over wine. They were bound together by their
campaign against me, which had recently been initiated. After the
wine, on the balcony, the talk touched on a sentimental subject –
personal tastes and predilections, something of that sort. Stalin
said, 'The greatest delight is to mark one's enemy, prepare everything, avenge oneself thoroughly, and then go to sleep.'[6]

One very popular pastime is the construction and enactment of fantasies of martyrdom and revenge using religious themes.

One Hindu sect, the Nagos, try to hasten their exit from the weary
round of death and rebirth by abandoning their fantasies and all their
possessions and embarking on a life of denial and penance. Not satisfied with living naked and by begging, some of them determine to
deny themselves even more. One man took a vow not to sit or lie for
twelve years, and now props himself by means of a swing. Another
man holds his right arm above his head and, as the months pass, the
muscles wither and the hand contracts into a claw. Such martyrs
become objects of great veneration.

The two world religions which have the greatest number of followers, Christianity and Islam, have specialized in martyrdom and
revenge as ways of dealing with that most prevalent activity, sin.

The outstanding difference between Christian practice and the eastern tradition lies in the Christian concern with sin. The legend of man's initiation into sin in the Garden of Paradise, and his need for redemption by bloody sacrifice, first of a lamb and in the end of a divine being, hangs like a baleful star over the Christian mystic's head . . . Preoccupation with sin and suffering . . . sectarian feuds and wars, persecutions and heresy hunts . . . distinguish Christianity from the other great religions. Preoccupation with sin is the exact opposite of the Buddhist practice of forgiving oneself before exercising compassion towards one's neighbours.[7]

Jesus's message about forgiveness has been more commended than followed in the Church.

Love your enemies, do good to them that hate you, bless them that curse you, and pray for them which despitefully use you. And unto him that smiteth thee on the one cheek offer also the other; and him that taketh away thy cloke forbid not to take thy coat also.[8]

Whereas Paul's message about revenge,

The Lord Jesus shall be revealed from heaven with His mighty angels, in flaming fire taking vengeance on them that know not God, and that obey not the gospel of our Lord Jesus Christ who shall be punished with everlasting destruction from the presence of the Lord and from the glory of His power.[9]

has been preached and received with great enthusiasm. But revenge needs martyrs, and 'the blood of the martyrs was the seed of the church'.[10]

The story of the early Christian martyrs shows how martyrdom can be used for political ends. 'The religious societies of the Western world,' wrote Donald Riddle, 'have always been noted by their success in controlling the individual by means of the group.'[11]

Any situation of persecution involves as its two primary aspects conflict and control. The persecuting group attempts to enforce its demands on the persecuted; while the persecuted, unless, as sometimes happens, they submit to the demands of the persecutors, are under the necessity of controlling those of their number who are faced with the personal issues of the matters in hand. The persecuted attempt to control the persecuted, while the persecuted must control those who are or may become the victims of untoward activity.[12]

Christian groups early in the second century became the object of persecution because the Roman law explicitly designated any new cult as illegal. Other cults, like the cult of Isis, were prosecuted for the same reason. The Christians encountered public disapproval because they were thought to be atheists, immoral (their habit of kissing one another suggested more serious intimacies) and unpatriotic since they did not attend public games and spectacles. Once charged with being a member of an illegal cult, all a person had to do was to deny that this was so. But such denials weakened the early Church. What the Church needed was people who would publicly confess that they were Christians. If such confessors would then go bravely to their death, other Christians would feel greatly heartened at this demonstration of the worth and importance of Christianity, and pagans would be drawn to this faith.

So it was very much in the Church's interest that those charged should confess, be tortured, and die rather than deny their faith. Accordingly, each Church group developed what in business parlance nowadays is called a package which would produce the desired behaviour and promote the Church.

As in any promotional package, the rewards were set out, and in this case they are without rival. The prospective martyr was promised immortality. At first this was in terms of being raised from the dead on Judgement Day, but when the idea of being transported to heaven or hell at the moment of death became popular, the martyr was assured of a triumphant entry into heaven, with the Lord Jesus welcoming him, and God, forgiving all his sins, would gather him into His Glory. Once ensconced in heaven, the martyr could enjoy triumph over demonic powers, the opportunity to intercede with God for his earthly companions, and the sweetness of the revenge of being able to judge his erstwhile adversaries. Meanwhile, back on earth, the martyr's memory would be venerated. Any possessions or bodily parts left behind took on magical, curative properties, his name was entered on a list of martyrs (many of whom became saints), and the story of his confession put into written form, which in those days was called a martyrology, but which nowadays is called a press release. This indeed was getting everything!

To make sure the prospective martyr remembered the importance of what he was being offered, the punishments for denying the faith were also kept to the forefront of his mind – the everlasting torments in the fires of hell, and, before his eventual death, immediate, devastating and grotesque misfortunes.

All of this was thoroughly discussed in each group in preparation for arrest, and techniques for answering the court's questions were developed and practised. The casting of one's eyes to heaven while confessing 'I am a Christian' was recommended, as was fixing one's mind, not on the horrors of torture and death, but on immortality.

Salespeople are well aware that customers can be most enthused about a product while with the salesperson but, if left on their own, are likely to reconsider. So the rule is, never leave the customer alone. Thus, from the moment the person was charged with being a member of an illegal cult, members of his group devised ways to visit him, providing comfort and support, and assuring him that he was always in the presence of Christ and the heavenly host.

> It is not to be thought that martyrs in any significant number could have undergone their fate if they had been abandoned in it by their fellow Christians. They were able to meet their crisis only because they were members of societies which kept effective the influence of social bonds.[13]

The importance of martyrologies in establishing this successful cohesion cannot be underestimated. They had reached their typical form by the middle of the second century.

> They were written ostensibly as reports of the confessor's examination and the martyr's death . . . The martyr is pictured always as master of the situation in which he is placed. He is not convicted by his judge, but by his wise answers his judge is refuted. He is never carried to an unwelcome fate by untoward circumstance, but is always pictured as laying down his life himself. The confessor is always successful in his defence, even though he must needs be given a sentence of condemnation. The martyr is always the fully delineated hero . . .
>
> [The martyrologies] were written in part to inform, but much more importantly to edify. Their most essential purpose was to suggest, with appropriate sanctions, that the experience of the martyr was one which it was desirable to imitate. To generate this wish, and to multiply this attitude, the martyrologies were written and assiduously circulated. Their content was subtly presented, so that the reader through the heroic history of famed saints was equipped with an answer for every question, and, more effective than this, was taught that the fate of the hero was so richly glorified that the reading of such stories not seldom was found to be sufficiently impelling that their readers themselves joined the noble army of martyrs.[14]

The first martyrology, wrote Donald Biddle, was the Gospel according to Mark, which was used as a source by the writers of the Gospels according to Matthew and Luke. In Mark there is the apocalyptic message that Jesus was the new Messiah, but there is also the story of betrayal and martyrdom of Jesus. New Testament historians have some consensus that Mark was written in Rome about AD 70, in the time of Nero.

> Nero figured largely in Christian tradition as a persecutor . . . [although] there was no attempt by this emperor to eradicate the

Christian movement, of which he was probably unconscious, and
. . . if Christians suffered during his regime they suffered, not as
Christians, but as victims of a trumped-up charge which had
nothing to do with their religion.[15]

But the casual cruelty of Nero and the might of the Empire were major
threats to the early Christian groups. In their weakness, they used the
defence of the weak – martyrdom and the promise of future revenge.
And, like so many individuals, the Church did not relinquish these
defences once it had gained strength and independence. Instead, suffering, martyrdom, the Way of the Cross, became the essence of its
teaching, and, with the gaining of strength, revenge upon the
Church's enemies who, since 'He who is not with me is against me',
were deemed to be many.

So the Church deemed suffering to be good. Suffering was the only
means by which we could overcome our inherent defect – being born
in sin – for if we suffer in penance for our sins and humbly ask for
God's forgiveness, He, in His great mercy, might grant this, and we
would be assured of eternal life. The early Church made it easy for
the faithful to undertake years of painful penance, but difficult for the
penitents to end their penance, so that some penitents chose martyrdom for a swift end.[16]

The gross physical suffering which penitents chose, though still
popular in places like the Philippines where young men choose to be
nailed to a cross for the Good Friday procession, became less popular
in western Europe, but the degree of suffering sought and inflicted in
the name of Christ did not diminish. How could it, since suffering
was both a punishment for sin and the means of atonement for those
sins? The faithful were taught that, when suffering comes upon them,
they should not concern themselves with the practical question of how
this suffering was caused, but rather *Why*. Is this a punishment, or
has God sent this suffering in order to teach me something? Whenever
little Edmund Gosse fell ill, his father did not hasten to find him a
cure.

> He cultivated the belief that all my little ailments, all my aches
> and pains, were sent to correct my faults. He carried this per-
> suasion very far, even putting this exhortation before, instead of
> after, an instant relief of my sufferings.[17]

By teaching people to concentrate on the *Why* of suffering, the Church
taught them to be unquestioningly obedient. When disasters occurred,
they should not waste time asking what physical events might cause
haystacks to burn down or a plague to kill, or what actions by those
in power in the Church and State might lead to increased taxation or
wars, but rather they should focus on their own wicked selves, the

cause of all their misfortunes, and the increased efforts they should make to atone for their wickedness. Lest anyone stumble across ideas which might suggest alternative explanations for life's vicissitudes, the Church severely restricted access to education and, just as the early Church had perfected the promotional package, so the medieval Church perfected censorship.

As the city and national states emerged in Europe, their leaders were pleased to work closely with the Church in creating and maintaining an obedient, ignorant and unquestioning populace. Whenever leaders and churchmen fell out, it was over power, not principles.

The State made full use of the strategy of making suffering and self-sacrifice central in the lives of individuals, and provided the populace with plenty of opportunities to suffer. To the belief that suffering was punishment for wickedness the State added the belief that poverty was the result of stupidity, incompetence and laziness, and with this came no compensation. Suffering might lead to salvation, but poverty carried no remedy. The poor are always with us.

State leaders who had not had the benefit of a Christian upbringing could also make the discovery that suffering and self-sacrifice makes obedient citizens:

Like the Church, Communist China has always believed in teaching by example. There is a saint for every shift of party line, every new political campaign. Until recently, such models were culled from the ranks of managers, entrepreneurs and newly-rich peasants . . .

Today's post-Tiananmen model citizens embody a different set of virtues: self-sacrifice, personal suffering, disregard for economic incentives and, most importantly, total, unquestioning obedience. Most are Communist Party members (fewer than 10 percent of officially designated 'national model workers' are not). Many boast tales of agony: a crematorium worker who suffers constant nausea as a result of 15 years spent collecting the ash of dead bodies; a postman who nearly drowns trying to deliver the post in a storm. What characterizes today's model more than anything else is their singular lack of personal ambition. They know their humble place and are happy with it . . .

The greatest paragon of the proletarian values now in fashion died more than two decades ago. This was Lei Feng, a legendary bore, celebrated army driver and champion hand-grenade thrower. Famous for his desire to be no more than 'a rustless screw in the machine of the revolution', Mr Lei spent his days washing his comrades' socks, putting out fires and helping the elderly across the street – exploits which were all captured for posterity by the providential presence of photographers. After a brief and failed attempt to present Mr Lei as a model of financial cunning and flare (officials suddenly discovered he had invested his money in a high-interest bank account), Mr Lei is now back in his original role.[18]

The State maintains its power by teaching that martyrdom and revenge are virtues when they are practised in the State's interest. Lest its citizens be too virtuous in this regard, society divides up these virtues – men should seek revenge on the State's enemies and women should sacrifice themselves for others.

Women's Martyrdom and Men's Revenge

When establishing their profession at the end of the eighteenth century and the beginning of the nineteenth, doctors were well aware that they could do little to relieve suffering. So they claimed that pain was integral to life. The agony of surgery was thought to be essential to the process of healing. Never mind that many patients died in the agony of blood poisoning contracted during the operation. The invention of anaesthetic was opposed by many physicians since physical pain was part of our atonement for our sins. If Queen Victoria had not lacked a talent for martyrdom (although she had a talent for grieving) and demanded an anaesthetic in childbirth, British women might still be giving birth with the pain and suffering which never befalls a man. However, the doctors, having themselves suffered the pain of a British boy's education aimed at teaching an indifference to pain, especially the pain that others suffer, taught that pain was necessary for the development of masculinity. There is nothing like having your leg sawn off to prove that you are a man, unless it is killing other people!

Such doctors saw little reason to try to reduce the suffering of working-class women because society considered that working-class women were robust, inured to suffering. Society women were deemed to have a special sensitivity to suffering, and their sickness to be a source of female beauty. So the doctor's role was to comfort, not to cure.[19] Women were constricted and controlled by being forced to accept the role of the languishing invalid, and women could express their anguish with their lives through this role. Many women developed illnesses and disabilities which were without physical foundation. Freud called this condition 'conversion hysteria'. After the First World War, illness was no longer seen as the mark of femininity and breeding, and this neurosis disappeared. Its place seems to have been taken by anorexia nervosa.[20] At least one society woman used illness in a more practical way to obtain freedom. When Florence Nightingale returned from the Crimea she knew that her mother and sister would expect her to join them in their empty round of social life, so she developed an illness which necessitated her staying in bed, but which did not prevent her from collating and interpreting statistics and dealing with her correspondence. Nor did it prevent her from rising to sally forth to collect more statistics and harry the generals and politicians.[21] But then Florence was no martyr.

While working-class women were considered to be able to work endlessly, bear many children, and live in unhealthy conditions and feel no physical pain, they were expected, like all women, to see the whole purpose of their lives as self-sacrifice. Though no woman could ever emulate the virtue of Christianity's paragon of virtue, a virgin mother, nevertheless Christian women must be unceasing in their efforts to attain great virtue, and this they could do by self-sacrifice. Not only should they sacrifice themselves for others, but whatever misfortune befell them and their families, women should blame themselves. No wonder so many women never created anything other than children and homes, for artistic creation requires a degree of self-interest. But when they did, their art reflected their pain. In the sixteenth century, the poet Mary Carey, on the death of yet another of her children, wrote:

> I only now desire of my sweet God
> the reason why he tooke in hand his rodd?
> Methinks I heare God's Voyce, this is thy sinne;
> And conscience justifies ye same within;
> Thou often doth present me with dead frute;
> Why should not my returns, thy present sute;
> Dead duties; prayers; praises thou dost bring,
> affections dead; dead hart in every thinge:[22]

The Christian belief in the appropriateness and virtue of a woman's self-sacrifice and martyrdom has so permeated Western society that in the twentieth century many women who would say that they had no allegiance to any Christian church still define their virtue in terms of self-sacrifice. Those women who say 'I am not a feminist', and who speak of feminism in disparaging terms, are usually responding to the well-instilled fear and guilt they feel at the slightest inkling that they might act, or want to act, in their own interests.

Not that the self-sacrificing woman is not held in esteem in other societies. Hindu girls are taught to model themselves on the self-sacrificing Sita who devoted her life to her husband Rama. The Indian psychoanalyst Sudhir Kakar commented:

> The ideal of womanhood incorporated by Sita is one of chastity, purity, gentle tenderness and a singular faithfulness which cannot be destroyed by her husband's rejections, slights or thoughtlessness. We should note in passing that the Sita legend also gives

us a glimpse into the Hindu imagery of manliness. Rama may have all the traits of the godlike hero, yet he is also fragile, mistrustful and jealous, and very much a conformist, both to his parents' wishes and to social opinion. These expectations, too, an Indian girl incorporates gradually into her inner world.[23]

Equally, Muslim and Jewish girls are expected to devote their lives to their family.

The jokes about Jewish mothers epitomize the woman's self-sacrifice (the goy lover of a Jewish young man demands that he prove his love for her by bringing her the heart of his mother. He kills his mother and rushes to his lover's house with the still-warm heart in his hands. On the way he trips, and he hears his mother's voice saying, 'Careful, my son'), and her refusal to ask for anything for herself ('How many Jewish mothers does it take to change a light bulb?' 'None, I'll just sit here in the dark'). But the jokes also show that, no matter how much we tell ourselves that we are self-sacrificing and self-denying, we still want something for ourselves. Martyrdom requires recompense. ('Mrs Cohen, your son has an Oedipus Complex.' 'What does it matter so long as he loves his mother.') They also show that martyrdom requires revenge. ('When I die I want to be cremated and my ashes scattered in Bloomingdales. That way I can be sure that my daughters will visit me twice a week.') The revenge of the mother-martyr is usually to create in her family unassuageable guilt. ('Mother, what can I ever do to repay you?' 'You should live so long!'). But sometimes the mother-martyr will go further.

Women usually want their revenge to be subtle and secret because they want to appear to the world as nice, feminine women, but they often have a sneaking admiration for a woman who, in seeking to revenge herself on a faithless male, abandons niceness. There was considerable joy amongst French women when Pierrette Le Pen, having been told by her ex-husband Jean-Marie Le Pen, the French National Front leader, that she could do housework for a living, posed as a scantily dressed maid for *Playboy*, while Fay Weldon's novel of envy and revenge, *The Lives and Loves of a She-Devil*, is enormously popular with women.

A vengeful woman is very disturbing to a man, even when he is not the object of her vengeance, for she upsets the natural order of things. Revenge is man's work. In fact, if men gave up revenge, how on earth would they fill their time? It is not just the endless wars and internecine terrorism and the industry which supports these that fill their time, but the stories of men seeking and warding off revenge which dominate the entertainment industry, so that if men are not actually engaged in revenge they can be entertained by it.

The so-called New Man who has taken over elements of women's

traditional role may find satisfaction in nurturing, but such men have also encountered the less pleasing aspects of that role. Many men looking after a young family have discovered that there is something about the daily company of people less than three feet high which drains away self-confidence. (Women in a similar situation are told that they have post-natal depression caused by an alteration in hormonal levels.) Such men have also discovered that domestic martyrdom breeds a desire for recompense and revenge.

Martyrdom, where we are lifted to the highest pinnacle of virtue and admiration, and revenge, where our enemies grovel at our feet, have always offered the lure that through them we can get everything. But this promise can never be fulfilled.

Why Martyrdom and Revenge Will Not Give Us Everything

We learn about martyrdom and revenge in terms of absolutes. To the Irish Nationalists, Cromwell was, and still is, utterly bad, while to the Irish Loyalists the Pope is utterly bad. The rules we learn, 'I must sacrifice myself', 'I must have revenge', are absolutes. No moderation or qualification is allowed. So again we confuse Category One, our definitions of reality, with Category Two, the nature of life.

We think that the absolutes of our martyrdom and revenge must be the one and only Truth because we are prepared to suffer so much for them. We refuse to consider Oscar Wilde's observation, 'A thing is not necessarily true because a man dies for it.'[25]

Absolute Truths have absolute demarcations, and so, again,

We think that the world is divided into discrete boxes, when in fact everything that exists is continuous and flowing.

Thinking in absolutes is lazy thinking. It is much easier to do everything for your children than to work out, day by day, where your children need your help and where they are capable, or should learn to be capable, of meeting their own needs. Parents who try to bring up their children on the principle that children should learn to be independent and self-reliant find themselves involved in endless discussions and negotiations with their children, and they are constantly told by their children that they are simultaneously 'treating me like a baby' and 'never here when I need you'. How much easier it is to respond to every demand with 'I'll do it'!

It is much easier to think in terms of injury and revenge than to try to work out the complexities of the rights and needs of all conflicting sides. Can we blame faithless lovers totally for their defection, or should we consider society's pressures and our own actions and expectations? Perhaps only God and Allah working together could arrive at a just resolution of the conflict between the Arabs and the Israelis,

while if Jesus came to Northern Ireland to bring an end to the Troubles He might well find Himself, His efforts at reconciliation defeated, trudging up Black Mountain with a cross on His back.

We think of causation as being a single line, when in fact it is a multidimensional net spreading far and wide.

The thinking behind martyrdom and revenge is always of the simple linear kind. 'I was injured. Now I will take revenge.' 'I shall sacrifice myself. I shall be saved.' This is wishful thinking and bears little relationship to reality. It is the same kind of thinking which we use when we believe that the solution to our problems is to kill ourselves.[27]

When we plan our martyrdom, revenge or suicide we create a fantasy in which we see ourselves carrying out the planned act followed by the consequences which we desire. Such a fantasy is deliciously seductive, and we do not want others to destroy it by pointing out how it differs from reality. Indeed, those people who want us to carry out acts of martyrdom and revenge can manipulate us by playing on this fantasy, elaborating it and assuring us that events will turn out just as we hope they will.

But fantasies of martyrdom and revenge, like those of suicide, are simple stories, and reality is complex and never what we expect. We imagine ourselves to be suffering in great nobility and we forget – perhaps we do not know – that pain *hurts*, and that in the extremes of pain there is no way we can dominate our bodies and control our pain. Many first-time mothers, having faithfully attended antenatal classes, are shocked to discover that, no matter how well they have practised their breathing, giving birth hurts, and that the birth process goes on in its own way, irrespective of how diligent the mothers were as pupils and how much they want to give birth according to their teachers' gospel. The actual pain of dying is very different from the fantasy. In their death agonies, martyrs are supposed to be silent, but, if they are, their silence is more likely to be result of that degree of pain where, as I have experienced, no word or sound is possible. Martyrs are supposed to speak words only of determination and certainty of glory, but even Jesus at the point of death cried out, 'My God, my God, why hast thou forsaken me!'

In our fantasies of revenge we always see things going according to our plan. We might assess the risks and dangers, but our wishful thinking, apart from our general inability to predict all the far-reaching effects of our actions, prevents us from seeing that the results of our actions will be different from what we expect. We might, for instance, plan a revenge which will not result in our death, but our colleagues might think otherwise. Going on hunger strike is quite a popular way of trying to avenge yourself and your group and to force your construction of meaning on to other people. Gandhi did this often.

However, few hunger strikers actually emulate Bobby Sands and die of starvation. Some hunger strikers in Spain were being saved from this fate when

> a doctor who supported the force feeding of hunger-striking terrorists was shot dead in his consulting room in Zaragoza. A member of the Grapo left wing terrorist group was identified by the interior minister as the killer.[28]

We think of acting so as to bring about a good result, or a bad result, when in fact every action has a multitude of results, some of them good and some of them bad.

The fantasies which we create about martyrdom and revenge always have the same simple outcome – the good triumph and the wicked are punished. Martyrs and avengers believe in the Grand Design where goodness is rewarded and badness punished, but they do not always trust God, or Allah, or the workings of karma, or the Just World to act as expected or sufficiently quickly. So martyrs and avengers take upon themselves the duty of putting the Grand Design into operation. They prefer justice to happiness, and in the end get neither, for whatever this world is, just it is not, for every benefit carries a disadvantage, and every ill wind blows some good.

When, in fantasy, we plan our martyrdom and revenge, we dream only of the good results of our actions and ignore the bad. When Lynette Phillips planned her immolation, she may have considered the grief her actions would bring her family, but this would have been in terms of her revenge on them, not in terms of the actual pain they would feel. Avenging children know nothing of the pain their parents feel when they review what they have done as parents and regret the effects their actions have had on their child, or when they simply see their child suffering. Avenging children believe that their parents do not love them and therefore cannot feel the pain of love and loss. All they can feel, so the avenging children believe, is the pain of humiliation, or the pain of being stamped on, hit or stabbed. Avenging children discover that they were wrong only when they themselves become parents.

Similarly, Lynette Phillips would not have taken into account the reaction of people generally to her action. Very few, if any, would take her seriously and choose to mend their ways. Most would regard her as mad. There would be some gossip and stories in the media, but being remembered is not much of a reward, for there are so many of us to be remembered and time rushes on.

The continuing popularity of vengeance despite its futility provides outstanding evidence of the human race's general stupidity. Perhaps for the first few thousand years of our existence, when few of us lived more than three or four decades, and when there was no written

319

history, we did not realize the futility of vengeance for we did not see its long-term effects; but our subsequent failure to learn shows our utter stupidity. We may plan and enact our revenge within the family or in the political arena, but while some people may benefit from our revenge (private revenge keeps mental health professionals and drug companies in business, and political revenge keeps armament manufacturers wealthy), the people who suffer are ourselves and our own, for all that revenge breeds is more revenge.

We overlook the fact that part of the continuous interaction of everything that occurs is the continuous construction of meaning in which every human being is engaged all the time.

We assume that our martyrdom and revenge will solve our problems, and that with that all problems will be solved.

A woman may assume that once she has taken revenge on her husband who has failed to meet her expectations as to what a husband should be, he will see the error of his ways and become the person she wants him to be. Meanwhile, her husband is distressed and angered by her continual complaints and criticism, does not know what to do to please her (like many wives, she wants him to be strong enough to protect her and weak enough for her to boss him around), and while he does not want to be annihilated as a person, he depends on her and admires her. So they remain together and fight. She never gives up the hope that her revenge for her disillusionment will one day be complete, but even if one day he capitulates, begs her forgiveness, and becomes her slave, they will be left with the continuing problems of their children, none of whom, having lived with the spectacle of their parents fighting, can form satisfactory relationships, and so all lead lives of great misery.

If one of the continuing factions in the Lebanon achieved successful and final revenge on all the other factions, who then laid down their arms and forswore all retaliation, the country would remain devastated. Any government, however well-meaning and wise, would find it difficult to establish order on a people who have been forced, in trying to survive, to create meanings very different from those which they held when the fighting broke out. Many farmers, unable to grow the crops which supply food but which require time and stability, have turned to the quick and profitable crop of cannabis, and now a great many people in Lebanon make much money out of the drug trade, while the fighting and destruction have left a burden of grief which will be carried for many years to come. Similarly, in Northern Ireland the meaning of the Troubles has changed. Men who are violently politically opposed cooperate in dividing the spoils in a black-market economy, while what was a struggle between Protestants and Catholics in Northern Ireland has now been linked to international terrorism.

'Yes I Can' – Martyrdom and Revenge

Unless we understand that we are all in the business of constructing meaning, and that this meaning changes over time, then as we plan how to defend ourselves against those who want to injure us, and how to maintain our sense of personal integrity, the meaning we construct will get further and further from reality, and the chances of the success of our ventures will become less and less.

We think that the meanings we create are discrete categories, when in fact they are linked to one another so that meanings of which we are not conscious can influence our actions.

Martyrs and avengers pride themselves on being unselfish. Martyrdom is seen as the ultimate altruism, while political revenge is seen as being for the benefit of others. Even personal revenge is seen as upholding some universal principle, and so failure to uphold this principle, such as not defending one's honour or not punishing disloyalty, can be seen as injury to humanity at large. (Martyrs and avengers have great love for humanity. It is people they cannot stand!)

So martyrs and avengers are not keen on any inspection of their ultimate priority, or the way they experience their sense of existence and see the threat of annihilation of their self. This ultimate priority contains no vestige of altruism. It is all about survival.

Extraverts and introverts, in the business of survival, choose martyrdom and revenge for different reasons and carry it out in different ways.

For extraverts, the attraction of martyrdom and revenge is that, if carried out successfully, the martyrs and avengers become the cynosure of all eyes. They are admired, adulated, loved and remembered – or so they hope. For introverts, the attraction is the achievement of their ultimate goal. They have put the world to rights, gained the satisfaction of getting something important done, and earned the approval of those people of whom they approve – or so they hope.

Martyrdom and revenge are always social acts, even when the martyr and avenger act alone. Extraverts fear rejection and abandonment by their group. How many early Christians, I wonder, went to a martyr's death because they could not withstand the threat that if they denied that they were Christians they would be expelled from their Church? That must have been a hard choice, for there are many extraverts who, no matter how strong their faith in God and heaven, fear death because that means leaving their friends and family behind. Introverts fear the chaos which would ensue for them if the theories which they had created to organize and control their world were shown to be false. Introverts are prone to doubt, for external reality always seems doubtful to them, and they cause themselves much anguish when they allow themselves to doubt their most cherished theories. In such situations introverts act in order to try to prove to themselves that their theories and their judgements are sound, and the greater their doubts the more extreme is their action. How many early Christian martyrs, I wonder, were introverts determined to prove to themselves that their faith was strong and that what they believed was true.

One of the reasons for the popularity of God and Allah is that their presence can give to extraverts and introverts what they need most to make them feel safe. Extraverts can find in God or Allah the self-affirming relationship which they seek, and introverts the standard which they seek to emulate, the certainty and the ultimate approval. But, just as God and Allah can provide all that is needed, so they can withhold the ultimate safety. Belief in God or Allah can give great serenity or great anguish.

We assume that other people create the same meanings as we do, and that when we act other people will interpret what we do in the same way as we do.

Martyrs and avengers are often misunderstood.

To be a successful domestic martyr you need a family well trained in feeling guilty. Once you are sure that they will respond with guilt to the merest suggestion that you are suffering, you can spare yourself the inconvenience of suffering, indeed of ever doing anything which you do not enjoy doing. Just the gentlest of sighs, the slightest darkening of your brow, is all that is needed to remind them

> How sharper than a serpent's tooth it is
> To have a thankless child.[29]

But if you have failed to train your family in guilt, all your unselfishness, all your self-sacrifice and suffering, are in vain. God may appreciate your martyrdom, but your heartless, shameless family will go their own sweet way, noticing you only to complain to themselves and one another what a bore and irritation you are. Of course they will still expect you to do things for them, but they expect this in the same way as they expect the sun to rise each morning. Unless suffering is your only joy, you may as well abandon martyrdom and give yourself over to selfish pleasures. Your family will not change.

To be a success in private revenge your enemy must take you as seriously as you take yourself. It is humiliating to have an enemy who ignores you, or, worse, sees your vengeful activities as funny and joins in the joke by heaping on you all kinds of public ridicule and humiliations. One such man of my acquaintance spirited away the avenger's much prized car, carefully removed the inside panel of the driver's door, inserted a large fish, replaced the panel and returned the car. It was weeks before the owner traced the source of the smell, by which time the car was thoroughly impregnated with an offensive odour. Enemies who do not find your attempts at revenge funny are likely to treat them, not as legitimate and honourable actions, but as criminal activities which demand certain consequences. Try explaining the justice of your vengeful cause to the police and the court!

The acts of public martyrdom and revenge are equally never interpreted by others in the same way as by martyrs and avengers. Even their friends, who call them freedom fighters, may regard them as foolish, or as attention-seekers bringing the movement into disrepute and danger,[30] or as expendable pawns, while their enemies call them terrorists and treat them accordingly.

We overlook the fact that there are certain aspects of life which stand in complementary relationship to one another, so that the more there is of one, the less there is of the other.

Martyrs and avengers insist that the world is as they see it, and that people must behave as the martyrs and avengers deem to be best. Such attitudes make good relationships impossible, for the essence of a good relationship is mutual acceptance, and that means accepting one another's faults as well as one another's virtues.

This acceptance of other people in their entirety is an aspect of freedom. In giving other people the freedom to be themselves, we give ourselves freedom. By imprisoning others in our demands that they do and be what we want so we can have certainty, we imprison ourselves.

Clare came to see me because she wanted to work on some of the issues arising from her recent divorce, not just her confused feelings, but practical issues to do with how she should now earn her living. She had a number of options, including a good job back in her native Australia, but this would mean separating her ten-year-old son from his father. What was most important to her, she told me, was to compose. She had always composed bits and pieces – setting poems to music, making some piano arrangements, even an operetta – but now she wanted to settle to composing a major work, perhaps a concerto or even a symphony. All she needed was to make some decisions and get things sorted out. The problem was that she could not make decisions.

At first I thought that this inability to make decisions was what many women experience after a divorce, simply because when the constraints of marriage are removed, they have a wealth of options. Clare certainly did, for the divorce settlement left her with a house and a small income, and, with her education and work experience, she had the choice of many jobs. But then I came to see that her inability to make decisions was more than the difficult task of sorting out options, each with its own advantages and disadvantages.

We talked about her family, and over the weeks I learned of her unhappy childhood with a father who terrorized her, older brothers and sisters who teased and persecuted her, and a mother who was too busy and, later, too ill to protect her. I learned, too, about her marriage. Her husband had consistently lied to her in order to keep secret his many affairs with other women. Like her family, he had betrayed her many times over, and this betrayal threatened her very being, just as when she was a child she often felt her sense of existence being annihilated by the cruelty of those who had power over her. As a child she had found one way to defend herself against the threat of annihilation, and, as it was a successful defence, she used it against the threat which came from her husband's actions.

The reason that Clare could not make decisions was that she had little time to think about alternatives and their implications. Instead, all her thoughts and imagination were absorbed in a drama of revenge. She brooded, counting over her husband's lies and infidelities, reviewing past events and seeing them, no longer as ordinary events, but as further evidence against her husband, and each of these events she hoarded like jewels which ripped and tore at her as she clutched them to her breast. In pain, she planned revenge. She fantasized murder, but the fantasy did not content her for long, and she had to repeat it over and over, elaborating it, working it out in detail, changing the setting, the means, the outcome. She fantasized his repentance, how he would come to her begging her to take him back and vowing eternal fidelity, and she fantasized the humiliations she would heap on him. She fantasized her brilliant success when she became the cynosure of all eyes, admired, powerful, and he, wandering on the edge of her adoring audience, wistful and longing just to touch the hem of her garment. The stage of her mind carried only one play, that of two lovers, locked forever in combat, unable to let one another go.

The one thing that would destroy her, so she told me, would be if he walked off the stage. So long as she continued to receive reports of his many affairs, her drama of revenge could continue. But if he married and became an ordinary married man, her fantasy would have no focus in external reality. 'If I saw him in the supermarket with his wife and child, that would finish me. I would just fall apart.'

Revenge is one of the means by which we hold on to other people. As a child, Clare had not just been hurt by her family, she had feared that they would desert her. So, by fantasizing her revenge on them, she reassured herself that they would stay with her. Whatever revenge she fantasized, be it their punishment and humiliation, or their admiration and longing for her at the sight of her awe-inspiring success, every drama assured her that their eyes were on her and she was powerful.

Such drama carried Clare through childhood and saved her from falling into total despair or losing contact with the world around her, and so such fantasizing was a successful defence of her sense of existence. But in adulthood she could not relinquish them. At the Conservatorium in Sydney, so she told me, she pursued her studies with only part of her mind. Most of her attention was absorbed in fantasies of revenge, but now not just about her family. With unerring aim, she found just the kind of men who would hurt and betray her. She always had someone to play the other actor in her drama.

Fantasies, when we are using them to reassure ourselves that we are not a no-thing but a significant being, have an absorbing, seductive quality. We have to indulge ourselves in them until we have drained them dry, and then we can discard them. Such fantasies can save us, and they can also destroy us, for it is always much easier to lose ourselves in fantasy than to venture out into the harsh world of reality which makes no allowances for our pretensions. It is much easier to fantasize about being a great composer than actually to become one. It is much easier to fantasize eternal relationships than to try to hold real relationships together.

In marrying and having a child, Clare had made a commitment not just to a real man but to her internal representation of this man, a representation which was to play the other actor in her drama. To lose a real husband was a blow, but to lose her partner in her internal drama was a loss she felt she could not face. She felt that if this happened she would become nothing but a lone wanderer in an empty universe, or else she would explode into shattering fragments.

It was not just that she had little time to think about her practical affairs. It was that when she did, each practical possibility had to be assessed in terms of the multitude of possibilities that her fantasies of revenge could supply, so there was no end to the pros and cons of every option she could consider. So no decisions were possible, and she remained trapped.

To give up all thoughts of martyrdom and revenge is difficult when we have been beset by humiliations, injustices and disasters often arising from the actions of those people who should have cared for us. So we might occasionally allow ourselves to indulge in a little martyrdom and revenge.

There is no reason why we should not indulge in a little martyrdom if it makes us feel better and helps to restore a self-esteem that has taken a battering. But we need to remember that we do good because it makes us feel good. Other people might benefit, but so do we. If you like to think of yourself as being kind and helpful, and an occasion presents itself where you can be kind and helpful even though it involves you in some self-sacrifice, there is no reason why you should not reinforce your construction of meaning about yourself. But if, in doing so, you tell yourself you are a selfless martyr who acts only out of altruism, you are lying to yourself, and there is no more dangerous activity. Everything we do has the ultimate aim of surviving as a body and a person. We lay down our lives for others because we want to think well of ourselves, and we commit suicide because we want to live and die on our own terms.[31]

It is only when we recognize how our need for survival underlies everything we feel and do that we can recognize how important other people are to us, and how we must strive to understand them as people and not as objects which we can use. Only then can we act in our own best long-term interests. Using other people to prove how altruistic and good we are is a very foolish and very selfish activity.

There is no reason why we should not indulge in a little revenge if it restores our battered self-esteem, allows us to master an experience so to close it and let it go. Such revenge should not be deadly or destructive, but should add to our lives some joy and love.

The joy may be that of *Schadenfreude*, delight in another's discomfiture, as epitomized in the legendary James Cagney film *Strawberry Blonde*. Cagney played Bif, an eager, simple young man, always used and outwitted by his friend Hugo, who made off with Bif's first love, the Strawberry Blonde, and then trapped him into taking the blame for Hugo's dishonesty in business. Bif went to jail, and there qualified as a dentist. Once released, he set up in practice, supported by a loving wife.

One day Bif had a phone call. Hugo was in town, had a raging toothache and needed a dentist. Bif agreed to treat him, and, to the horror of his wife, prepared to kill Hugo with an overdose of gas. Hugo arrived with his wife, and, from the way the pair of them argued, it was soon clear that the Strawberry Blonde despised Hugo and made his life a misery.

Bif asked Hugo to sit in the dentist's chair and said that he would examine the tooth. But instead he reached in with a large pair of forceps and, without any anaesthetic, wrenched out the tooth, much to Hugo's agony. Everyone, except Hugo, laughed, and Bif said, 'I haven't got anything against you any more, Hugo, but I wouldn't be human if I didn't take revenge.' The film ends with Bif rejoicing in his fortunate life.[33]

The love that revenge can create is that which we call forgiveness.

In Nicaragua, Tomas Borge wrote *Mi Venganza Personal* after he had been tortured by the dictator Somoza's National Guard and his wife had died at their hands.

> My personal revenge will be the right
> Of our children in the schools and in the gardens.
> My personal revenge will be to give to you
> This song which has flourished without panic.
> My personal revenge will be to show you
> The kindness in the eyes of my people

Who have always fought relentlessly in battle
And been generous and firm in victory.
My personal revenge will be to tell you good morning
On a street without beggars or homeless.
When, instead of jailing you, I suggest
You shake away the sadness there that blinds you,
And when you who have applied your hands in torture
Are unable to look up at what surrounds you,
My personal revenge will be to give you
These hands that once you so mistreated
But have failed to take away their tenderness.[34]

Only in such forgiveness do we have any chance of getting everything,
for

> You can't have anything unless you let go of it.
> You only get to keep what you give away.[35]

The Best Is Good Enough

'If ignorance is bliss, why aren't there more
happy people in the world?'

ADRIAN LOVE[1]

Why indeed?
Why are we sad?
Is it because we dare not understand and dare not think? Is it because we cannot name, much less resolve, the sadness which permeates our every breath, our very being, so that those moments of sublime joy, bursting strength and optimism, or deep, restful contentment seem to be rare, fragile, special, transient, miraculous, unique strokes of luck, or gifts with a price we have to pay?

Why are these moments of ultimate bliss also filled with longing? Longing that the bliss not be transient, that we might rest in it as securely as we once – when was it? We cannot remember. Was it – never? Lest the sadness of never knowing secure bliss be unbearable, we try to comfort ourselves with fantasies of the past, a Golden Age when everyone loved one another and kindness abounded, or with fantasies of the future when we would rest safe in Jesus's arms.

We do not understand our sadness, and when we try we become confused. We are given so many different explanations, and we cannot begin to work out which is right. We suspect that there is something which we need to find, but when we begin to search, like an investigator looking for a well-hidden crime we are warned off, told that it is dangerous to go into such matters. Some things are best left alone. We may heed this warning because we fear that our past contains a secret which, if revealed, will destroy us. Or we may press on, believing that truth, however unpleasant, is better than lies.

Occasionally we stumble across a clue, and cry, 'Why wasn't I told this before?' *This* may be some family secret, or some information which applies to us all, but, whichever, we are angry that we have been kept in the dark for so long. Yet the clue can make us even more confused. We stumble around, feeling that we have not got the tools necessary to solve the problem. We do not even know what tools we need. We know what to use to find out why our car will not start or when the gravy goes lumpy. But what do we use to find out about ourselves?

Perhaps we are stupid, just like our parents and teachers always said. Let's give up, and turn our minds to the things we do understand. Let's turn on the telly or go to the pub.

Yet we all know quite well that when we do need to understand something, we work at it until we do. Even some scientists, those guardians of secret knowledge, admit that this is so.

> When people see a personal or practical use for science and are sufficiently motivated, they often show a remarkable capacity to learn, Dr Brian Wynne of Lancaster University told a meeting on the public understanding of science at London's Science Museum. Researchers found that people with AIDS, environmentalists, bird-watchers, amateur astronomers, and many others were well able to seek out and use scientific information.
>
> One of the studies, by Professor John Durant, disclosed that most adults seem to know little about some of the most elementary science, but have an excellent grasp of the practical logic of drug-testing and the inheritance of genetic defects . . .
>
> Dr Wynne said, 'People do not use, assimilate, or experience science separate from other elements of knowledge, judgement or advice. Practical policy should be less concerned to feed people a controlled, single correct scientific understanding and more concerned to provide flexible social access to diverse sources of scientific information.'[2]

When computers become important to us, we can learn about computers. When diet becomes important to us, we can learn about nutrition. When we become important to ourselves, we can learn about ourselves. Just as we can discover that we do possess a mathematical and scientific intelligence, so we can discover that we do possess the second kind of intelligence. We can understand about ourselves.

All we need to do is to try.

The tools we need are, first, an understanding of how we are engaged all the time in creating meaning, second, how society works using power and responsibility, third, how education can liberate or imprison us, and, fourth, how there is much more to love and understanding than saying 'I love you' and 'I know just how you feel'.

Our Worlds of Meaning

Creating meaning and using meaning is all that we can do. When we act, we might not be thinking about what we are doing, but we are using the meaning we have already created. In using the meaning we have created we modify that meaning. Thus we might drive our car without thinking about it because we constructed our meanings about cars and driving long ago and have used them often, but if something happens – an accident or breakdown – we modify our meanings: 'I'll take that corner more slowly in future', or 'It's time I changed my car'.

Everything we know about lies within our world of meaning. We talk about physical causes or attributes of things and people, and even claim that we are being scientific and separating our personal constructions of meaning from the real, objective world, but all we talk about are the constructions of meaning which we have made. We talk about 'objective' as against 'subjective', 'physical' as against 'mental', as if 'objective' and 'physical' lie outside 'subjective' and 'mental'. We do not see that 'objective' and 'subjective', 'physical' and 'mental' are all constructions of meaning which we have created.

So trained are we to think in terms of 'objective' and 'subjective', 'physical' and 'mental', and not to question what we have been taught (another example of how we are taught to see Category One as Category Two), that many people find it hard to grasp that everything we know lies within the despised 'subjective' and 'mental'. The very suspicion that this may be so frightens and angers many people. A whole school of psychology, behaviourism, which was most influential for some twenty years and which still has many adherents, was created so as to deny, if not the existence, then the importance of thought and feeling. I have a friend who, having often invited me to teach in his organization, is very familiar with my point of view but who insists that social, economic and political matters lie outside our constructions of meaning. He writes papers where, he states, he puts aside personal constructions of meaning and addresses the real world of society, economics and politics. But what is writing a paper other than the putting of our thoughts on paper?

If all we can know is our constructions of meaning, how can we be sure that our constructions relate to anything outside ourselves? Perhaps we just imagine it all.

I pondered this question when I was a child and had not yet encountered the philosophers who had also pondered it. Finally I decided that if I had imagined it all, I would have created something far finer than what I was encountering. I might not have been able to imagine something finer than the Pacific Ocean and the Blue Mountains, but I certainly would have been able to imagine much nicer people. I would never have dreamed up Hitler.

Having decided that there was a real world, I then decided that, even though I could never know exactly what it was like, I should try to get to know it as exactly as possible. In my first lessons in calculus I was fascinated by the concept of one point getting closer and closer to another point but never reaching it no matter how infinitely small the distance between them became. This seemed to me to show how we should deal with the truth of the real world: by seeking to get as close to it as we possibly can. Although our goal is always beyond our grasp, our task in life is to get as close to the truth as we can. The truth that we seek is the truth of the world in which we live and our own inner truth, and each truth depends on the other. Our search for truth is the responsibility which we have for ourselves.

The world is there, but what we see of it depends on how we perceive it.

If ever you have fallen out of love, you will know how what we see changes when our feelings change, irrespective of the fact that we know that the object of our perception has not changed. That person, who to us in love lit up our world and made everyone else insignificant and even odious by comparison, now appears to us as banal, shameful, perhaps even physically smaller. How could I ever, we wonder, have loved such a person!

Similarly, the people we fear seem large and loom over us as adults did when we were children, yet if we ran a tape measure over them, we would find no significant discrepancy between their size and ours.

Even though in the real world everything is continuous with everything else, what we see is a world divided. However, no two people see exactly the same divisions. For instance, I see two people, a woman and a small child. What the woman sees is one person, herself, which contains a bit which keeps running off and getting into danger.

What attributes we give to the divisions we see depends on what we have learnt and what is useful to us. Growing up in an Australia which was divided between Catholics and Protestants, I reckoned that I could pick a Catholic at five hundred yards. This skill vanished with disuse when I came to England. Instead, I believe I can identify the class of every English person I see without my having to hear that person speak.

Recognizing that we live in a world which we can never know exactly, and that what we perceive is structures which have less substance than a set of matchsticks, can be frightening, and so we look around for something which gives us some sense of solidarity and permanence. In our daily lives we see the transitory nature of everything, and we ask, 'What is the purpose of my life?' We try to arrive at an answer which tells us what is the meaning of life. Beyond all the meanings which we can create and destroy there is, we hope, a meaning which does not change, which is absolute and forever. Vaclav Havel calls this his 'absolute horizon':

A search for the meaning of life, then, is in fact a search for the absolute horizon. It is as though we were constantly striving for something beyond and above us, something firm, something we wish to grasp and hang on to and which we in fact – or so it seems to us – do grasp and hang on to. It is, of course, a troublesome and paradoxical process: we know we must hold on in order not to fall, yet not only do we not know, nor will we ever find out, what we are holding on to or what is holding on to us, but we are never certain that we are holding on to anything at all: there is no way to confirm it, and in such matters, we have no choice but to believe in our belief.

We do not know the meaning of life – just as we do not know the mystery of Being – and yet in some way we 'possess' it – as our own, immediate version of that 'anchoredness' or as our way of longing for it. There is no direct answer to the question of what life means, but indirectly, each of us answers and must answer it anew every moment of his life. It is the darkest and most distressing mystery – and yet it is our final hope, the only firm point in life and the only reason for it: were we in some way not to 'possess' it, search for it or at least feel its lack, we couldn't begin to live as what we are, that is, as creators of the 'order of the spirit', as 're-creators' of the world, as dignified beings, capable of stepping beyond ourselves, that is, beyond the shadow of our animal foundations.[3]

Havel asks us to accept absolute uncertainty as our absolute, and hang on to that. He asks that of himself, and his understanding is not the outcome of some whimsical philosophizing but of hard experience. He knew the hardships and terrors that followed when his compatriots and neighbours refused to live with absolute uncertainty but settled for less, the absolutes of Communism and the Church. He knows that we can never live peacefully with one another until we accept the certainty of flux and the flux that is in all certainty.

When we, unable or unwilling to accept absolute uncertainty, turn our absolute horizon into a person and impose on that person our own human attributes, we simply extend to our absolute horizon all the dilemmas, conflicts, misunderstandings and cruelties which bedevil our relationships with real people. When we see, or are taught to see, that this absolute horizon in the guise of a person has issued absolute decrees which we must obey, we relinquish the freedom which uncertainty and flux give us, and we put ourselves in a prison of our own making.

The prison is the way we define the parameters of our lives. We do this in such a way that we leave ourselves with only one outcome. We say 'I have no choice', when what we mean is that the alternatives are unacceptable. We refuse to accept that there are always alternatives, because if we did accept this, we would have to acknowledge that we have not been compelled but that we have made a choice. We would have to acknowledge our responsibility for ourselves.

There is a legend that monkeys can be caught with a container which has an opening small enough for the monkey to get his paw inside and grasp the piece of fruit left in the container, but not large enough for the monkey to withdraw his hand while still clutching the piece of fruit. The monkey, not wanting to give up his prize, is trapped.[4]

We are as stupid as the monkey who gets his hand and thus himself caught in the monkey trap. All he has to do is open his hand, drop the fruit he had reached in to get, and he is free. But he does not do this. He wants this insignificant piece of fruit, he will not lose it, and so he loses his freedom and his life. In our prison of absolutes which we have created, when we refuse to accept responsibility for what we do, and try to hang on to what little of the everything we want we have managed to acquire, we give up our freedom.

Power and Responsibility

Because we are forever creating meaning, we are forever responsible for ourselves. We can choose to deny that we are responsible. We can say that we were compelled to do something, or to believe something, but here we are simply making a choice which we think will be in our own best interests. (Why give up the pleasure of being able to blame someone else when things go wrong?) Sometimes the alternatives offered to us by the physical world can be limited. A soldier with a gun offers us the choice of surrender or die, or a malignant cancer offers us the choice of a painful death with or without medical therapy. But the alternatives offered by our ability to create meaning are infinite. Shall I die heroically, shamefully, pointlessly, resentfully, angrily, happily . . . ? John MacLachlan, suffering from AIDS, wrote:

> Given the likelihood of my death quite soon, I have only two
> choices. To remain fearful, and to die an uncomfortable death

much sooner, or to confront and defeat fear and die reconciled after living longer and better. To be a victim of that fear or, in terms of my life, a hero. But victims and heroes die, of course. But heroes die victorious; victims die only victims.[5]

Or as Brian Keenan said of the men who held him hostage for four years, 'They took away my liberty, not my freedom.'[6]

Our ability to create and choose between alternatives ceases only when our cortex ceases to function. (Or do we take this ability with us into heaven and hell? Will we construe these places in the same way as the angels do?)

As meaning-creating creatures, we form a natural democracy. Each of us creates our own meaning. We are responsible for the meaning we create. We are responsible for ourselves. We cannot do anything other than create meaning. We are equally adept at creating meaning. We are equals.

Yet we do not live democratically. No society does. Even the ancient Greeks who supposedly invented democracy had slaves. All the supposedly democratic nations of the modern age are societies of privilege, poverty and alienation.

Why is this so?

First, because we rarely accord to those who have constructions of meaning different from ours the respect we give to our own constructions and those of the people who think as we do. ('Anyone who does not agree with me is mad or bad.')

Second, because we wish to impose our own constructions of meaning on to other people, that is, be powerful.

Third, because we want to avoid being responsible for ourselves, that is, we do not want to grow up, and we want power without responsibility.

Being responsible for yourself can be difficult and painful. Nureyev found this when he defected to the West.

> The hardest lesson he had to learn in the West was to take responsibility for his own life. 'In Russia, you know, you grew up with an absolutely in-built instinct that somebody older, taller, bigger, dictates your life. He decides what you are going to do – the authority, the father, you know? You are trained in submission. And so to make decisions and learn to act on your own is a very painful process – and very long. You have to tell yourself you cannot wait. But at the beginning I was waiting, waiting, and no big Daddy comes along.'[7]

Sometimes our situation is so extreme that we need to locate the responsibility elsewhere so as to relieve the pain, in the same way as we might take aspirin or alcohol to relieve the pain. Sometimes it is necessary not to accept responsibility for oneself in order to survive. From her prison cell Jane wrote:

> Also I have Pre-menstrual Tension and the sick bay have run out of Efamol. But at least just knowing that it's PMT which seems like feelings of unbearable loneliness makes it easier to cope with.

In another letter she said:

> I'm trying to think of something good to tell you, but it's hard when I've got PMT, although knowing that it's PMT helps, knowing it's endogenous (is that right?) hormone or chemical balance rather than thinking that the world out there is really like it seems. Although I got no letter again today, which is real.[8]

Fundamentalism, the belief in the absolutes of goodness being rewarded and badness punished, flourishes among the poor, dispossessed, powerless and ill-educated. (Many American fundamentalists are neither poor nor dispossessed, but they are ill-educated, having been taught very little about the world outside their state, and they are politically powerless. Their wealthy leaders are powerful, but not them.) In pain and poverty we long for someone to look after us. The essence of fundamentalism is the relinquishing of responsibility for oneself and handing it over, in rhetoric to God or Allah, but in effect to those religious leaders claiming to speak the word of God.

Our willingness to hand over to other people and organizations the responsibility which is ours (just as the colour of our eyes is ours) stems from our inchoate desire to sink into the mindless bliss of being totally cared for, totally supported, our original wanting and getting everything. We do not want to accept that, just as our eyes are organized to see only one part of the spectrum of light and no other, so our sense of time is ordered to perceive time only as progressing, never as standing still or going backwards. No matter how great our longing, we cannot return to the womb or the Garden of Eden.

So our fundamentalist beliefs and practices will always disappoint us, or worse. Edmund Gosse, having at last escaped from the fundamentalism which his father had pressed upon him, wrote:

> Let me speak plainly. After all my long experience, after my patience and forbearance, I have surely the right to protest against the untruth (would that I could apply to it any other word!) that evangelical religion, or any religion in a violent form, is a wholesome or valuable or desirable adjunct to human life. It divides heart from heart. It sets a vain, chimerical ideal, in the barren pursuit of which all the tender, indulgent affections, all the genial play of life, all the exquisite pleasures and soft resignations of the body, all that enlarges and calms the soul are exchanged for what is harsh and void and negative. It encourages a stern and ignorant

spirit of condemnation; it throws altogether out of gear the healthy movement of the conscience; it invents virtues which are sterile and cruel; it invents sins which are no sins at all, but which darken the heaven of innocent joy with futile clouds of remorse. There is something horrible, if we can bring ourselves to face it, in the fanaticism which can do nothing with this pathetic and fugitive existence of ours but treat it as if it were the uncomfortable ante-chamber to a palace which no one has ever explored and of the plan of which we know absolutely nothing.[9]

When we hand responsibility for ourselves over to other people and organizations, we lose whatever ability we had to think clearly. Having been handed the Truth, we cease searching for reality's many truths. We lose the ability to tell truth from falsehood, and we become gullible, prepared to believe anything our leaders tell us. Again and again we are seduced into accepting and generating magical thinking, believing that we can affect events and protect ourselves by means of the stars, or crystals, or incantations and prayers, when we should be taking a very close look at what we and our leaders are actually doing.

There is still no end to the cruelty and suffering which we see and sometimes experience. We ask our Church leaders why, and they explain that the problems of cruelty and suffering are being caused by human wickedness and tell us that the cure is to love God, who will save us. But this in no way explains cruelty and suffering, nor how they can be overcome. Gullible, non-thinking people cannot see this, yet they would see quite clearly that to say that a car will not start because it is inherently wicked is an explanation which explains nothing, and that what is needed is an understanding of the workings of the car. They would also see that a prayer to God might get the car started, but they know that this is not a reliable method. (Some people explain God's unreliability in answering prayers by saying that God answers all prayers, but sometimes the answer is no. Human beings usually have the courtesy to tell you when they cannot or will not answer a request for help, but God seems not to respond in this way.)

So widespread is our desire to avoid being responsible for ourselves that we connive at the way our social, political and religious organizations also avoid genuine responsibility and thus avoid a sense of genuine identity, while at the same time pretending, as we individuals pretend, to be honest, genuine and concerned. Havel wrote:

> Just as man conceals his turning away from the world by pretending it is not a turning away at all, so these social organisms hide their turning away from the world and themselves in an analogical fashion. For this reason we may observe how social, political and state systems, and whole societies are inevitably becoming alienated from themselves. The difficult and complex

task of serving moral ideals is reduced to the less demanding task of serving projects intended to fulfil those ideals in a concrete way; and, when such projects have won the day, there is a further reduction to the even more comfortable task of serving systems allegedly designed to carry these projects out; and finally, it degenerates into a situation, common enough now, in which the power which directs these systems (or more precisely 'possesses' them) simply looks out for its own interests, or else the systems, in a purely utilitarian fashion, adapt themselves to the demands of that power [for instance, a charity becomes fashionable, its one-time revolutionary leaders are petted and praised by members of the Establishment, and its fund-raising becomes a society event] . . .

One consequence of this alienating process is the enormous conflict between words and deeds so prevalent today: everyone talks about freedom, democracy, humanity, justice, human rights, universal equality and happiness, about peace and saving the world from nuclear holocaust, and protecting the environment and life in general – and at the same time, everyone – more or less, consciously or unconsciously, in one way or another – serves those values and ideals only to the extent necessary to serve himself, i.e., his 'worldly' interests – personal interests, group interest, power interests, property interests, state or great-power interests. Thus the world becomes a chessboard for this cynical and utterly self-serving 'interplay of interests', and ultimately there are no practices, whether economic, political, diplomatic, military or espionage, which, as means sanctified by an allegedly universal human end, are not permissible if they serve the particular interests of the group which carries them out. Under the guise of the intellectually respectable notion of 'responsibility for everything' (i.e., for the 'welfare of mankind') – that is, pretending to relate to the absolute horizon – huge and uncontrollable forces and powers are in fact responsible only to the particular horizon from which they derive their power (e.g., to the establishment which put them in power). Pretending to serve the 'general wellbeing of mankind', they serve only their own pragmatic interests, and they are oriented exclusively toward 'doing well in the world' and expanding and proliferating further – wherein that very expansion and proliferation which flows directly from the expansive essence of focusing on existence-in-the-world is interpreted as service to 'higher things' – to universal freedom, justice and wellbeing.[10]

So rare is being responsible for oneself amongst people in public life that Gary Trudeau had to salute one American politician who recognized her part in the Savings and Loan scandal and resigned. Her action was not understood by her colleagues.[11]

Doonesbury

BY GARRY TRUDEAU

Alas, Congresswoman Lacey Davenport is only a character in a cartoon strip.

In prison Havel mediated upon a shameful episode in his life when he failed to think clearly about what he was doing and to see the consequences of his actions. Responsibility to oneself, he decided, means standing behind what one does:

> For it is only by assuming full responsibility for one's own elsewhere, only by assuming full responsibility today for one's own yesterday, only by this unqualified assumption of responsibility by the 'I' for itself and for everything it ever was or did, does the 'I' achieve continuity and thus identity with the self . . .
>
> It is not hard to stand behind one's successes. But to accept responsibility for one's failures, to accept unreservedly as failures that are truly one's own, that cannot be shifted somewhere else or on to something else, and actively to accept – without regard for any worldly interests, no matter how well disguised, or for well-meant advice – the price that has to be paid for it: that is devilishly hard! But only thence does the road lead – as my experience, I hope, has persuaded me – to a renewal of sovereignty over my own affairs, to a radically new insight into the mysterious gravity of my existence as an uncertain enterprise, and to its transcendental meaning. And only this kind of inner understanding can ultimately lead to what might be called true 'peace of mind', to that highest delight, to genuine meaningfulness, to that endless 'joy of Being'. If one manages to achieve that, then all one's worldly privations cease to be privations, and become what Christians call grace.[12]

Education and Freedom

Once we can see how we are always in the business of creating meaning, we can then see that education is not a matter of stuffing children's heads with facts and teaching them vocational skills, but that education is a matter of creating meaning. The question is, 'Whose meaning?'

Should the meaning be the children's? Should education be the process whereby children explore and so enlarge their own world of meaning, using their natural curiosity, enthusiasm and creativity? Or should education be the process whereby the adults in power over the children impose their constructions of meaning on to the children and negate and inhibit the children's own world of meaning?

The first kind of education is education for freedom. By 'freedom' I do not mean the freedom of wilful selfishness. This 'freedom' is no freedom at all, for the person indulging in such 'freedom', be he a soccer hooligan or a dishonest rich industrialist, is not free but is driven by an insatiable hunger for he knows not what. The freedom of which I speak is the freedom to recognize and to use our capacity to choose. In such freedom we experience ourselves as neither driven by outside forces and demands, nor imprisoned and inhibited by outside barriers and our own fear, guilt, and shame. Freely making our own choices, we stand behind what we choose. Freely we choose to accept responsibility for ourselves. Freely we choose to make commitments. Free, we do not fear freedom.

Such freedom does not imply a lack of concern and commitment for other people. Rather, because we are free, we freely choose to enter into caring for and commitment to others. Caring and commitment are neither burdens nor prisons when they are freely chosen. Because we are not trapped, feeling that the people on whom we depend will drift out of our grasp, we do not have to try to maintain an iron grip on others. Our relationships with others are not as prisoners on a chain gang but as dancers in a most delightful dance.

We are born knowing how to do this dance, and we long to dance. A newborn baby's eyes focus on a face, and the dance begins. Children want to dance, to be involved in their family and in society. Children become unsociable and difficult ('spoilt') not because they are free but because the adults around them are inconsistent and untruthful. Such children are not free but frightened. There is nothing so imprisoning as being afraid.

Adults are inconsistent and untruthful with children because they do not see children as their equals, having the same right to existence as they have. (Does not the Church teach that children should be grateful to their parents for having been born?) They patronize children and are sentimental about them, and sentimentality always leads to cruelty, for sentimentality relates only to a fantasy, never to a real person. (Try being sentimental about a dirty nappy or a runny nose!) Adults behave like this because they have been educated in the system whereby other people's meanings have been imposed on them. They have been lied to, and so they lie to others, and to themselves.

On BBC Breakfast TV there was a news report that Customs and Excise had made their biggest haul ever of cannabis and cocaine in a shipment from South America. A woman who had established a voluntary group in Liverpool to help children and teenagers on drugs was interviewed. She said, 'We are absolutely delighted with this success. We opened a bottle of champagne to celebrate.'[13] Many more people die of alcoholism than do of drug addiction.

An education which is concerned with negating and inhibiting the child's own construction of meaning is ultimately crippling and destructive. But the sacrifice of the child for the parent, the family, and society is so traditional that few people see it, much less question it. Even in Bali, that most beautiful island, the Barong Play, concerning the eternal fight between good and evil, begins with a woman, Dewi Kunti, promising Ranga, the evil monster, that she will sacrifice her son Sadewa to him.

Just as we find it hard to see how we create meaning because we live within meaning-creating all the time, so we find it hard to see how an education which imposed other people's constructions on to us has reduced our capacity to think clearly. We can know and regret that we never learned to swim or play the piano, but we find it very hard to see and therefore regret that we never learned to think clearly. Indeed, we find it very hard to see that there are, in every society, rules which forbid us not only from thinking clearly but from seeing that rules forbidding clear thinking are in force.

All social groups forbid certain topics to be discussed, and often the rule 'do not discuss' contains the rule, 'Do not be aware that this topic is never discussed.' Only an outsider can see that the first rule is operating.

Frank Reed, an American held hostage in Lebanon, described how, when he was allowed in captivity to talk with fellow hostages, they discussed endlessly how the Israelis were using force to gain their ends. When he returned to the USA he was amazed to find that criticizing Israel was taboo. He knew at first hand that the reason so many Arabs hate the USA is because they see the USA giving unqualified and unquestioning support to Israel. He had always believed that in the USA everything could be discussed openly, but now, as an outsider looking at the USA, he could see what many Americans failed to see: that they were forbidden to question whether the Palestinians might also have a cause.[14]

As an outsider I can see such rules operating in the USA, where few

Americans question the way their concepts of 'America' and 'God' prevent them from thinking clearly, and fewer, especially not the intelligentsia, see how the medical profession and the drug industry secure their profits and power by turning every aspect of human life into a medical problem.[15] Similarly, as an outsider, I can see how very difficult most English people find it to think clearly about the actual function of the Royal Family. They do not see how this charming soap opera is used to distract us from matters of real concern.

However, as Frank Reed found, the clearest outsider's view comes from being an outsider in your own country. I found this to be the case when I spent three months in Australia after being in the UK for twenty years. Some of that time I spent visiting parts of New South Wales which I had once known well.

West Wyalong, like Pine Creek in the Northern Territory, claims to be a 'gateway', West Wyalong to 'the West', and Pine Creek to Kakadu National Park. Whoever tried to imbue these sad and dreary places with some ersatz mystery and magic must have never come across Peter Sellars' satire on the 'gateway' themes in travelogues. Sellars described Balham in the grey suburbs of south London as the 'gateway to the South'.[16] What West Wyalong, Pine Creek and Balham have in common is not just that the traveller can go through them to some extraordinary and beautiful mysteries of nature (it is still possible to find such things in the south of England on the Downs and the cliffs), but that these towns show the failure to understand that when we reduce our life to nothing but meeting our physical needs and acquiring money and possessions we create a life which demeans and destroys us. We need food for ourselves as people as much as we need food for ourselves as bodies. To provide food for ourselves as people we need to use and develop our capacity for thought and imagination.

When as children we are deprived of food for our bodies, we grow up with a strong memory of the ache of hunger and an even stronger determination never to starve again, nor to let our children starve. The Australians of my generation who knew the hunger of the Depression years made this the purpose of their lives. By contrast, when as children we are deprived of food for ourselves as people, food which maintains our natural curiosity, enthusiasm, imagination and creativity, we grow up with a feeling of loss, but we do not know what this loss is. We feel sad, angry, resentful and envious, and we do not know why. Rather than find out, we deprive ourselves further, so that no matter what opportunity we have as adults to recover our curiosity, imagination, enthusiasm and creativity, we refuse to do so, and, worse, we deprive and dispossess our children just as we were deprived and dispossessed.

This happens to all people in all countries. It is a human tragedy.

To save ourselves from this tragedy we need to live in a place where the work necessary to feed ourselves and protect ourselves from the elements need not take most of our time, and where there is political freedom which allows us to think and explore and allows for individuality. These conditions could have been created in Australia, but Australians failed to do so. This is the Australian tragedy.

From West Wyalong I drove along the Western and Newell Highways to Forbes on the Lachlan River. These roads, raised above the level of the plains which stretch to the horizon, broken only by some low hills, are marked by flood signs. I remembered being taught at school that the explorer Oxley had travelled down the Lachlan only to be stopped by swamps which he hoped were evidence that there was an inland sea which created a fertile centre to the continent, just as the Mississippi and its tributaries created a fertile centre to North America. Oxley turned back, and when next he came there the cycle of flood and drought had moved on, and the barren watercourses showed him that there was no inland sea.

I had thought that the swamps which had stopped Oxley had been further to the west, and I wondered how a flood plain could be mistaken for a sea since such a plain would contain trees and a sea would not. I wondered where I could find answers to my questions, and by great good fortune the first person I engaged in conversation in Forbes proved to be a local historian.

I was right. The swamps which stopped Oxley had been further to the west in the Lake Cargeligo area. Yes, the trees should have told him that this was no inland sea, but the early explorers and settlers, not understanding that the Australian continent was so very old, and wanting to find an inland waterway, misread what they saw, often seeing what they wanted to see.

The explorers and settlers did not understand the function and importance of trees. They cut them down, not just to build houses and fences and to keep themselves fed and warm, but because they cluttered the landscape. Perhaps clearing the land created for the settlers the illusion that they controlled the land. However, no human being can possess the land, for the land is part of a system far bigger than we can easily comprehend. With the trees gone, the underground water levels rose, pushing the salts contained in the rocks and clay upwards to the surface and rendering the soil too infertile to produce crops or grass to sustain animals. Oxley's swamp is now a salt waste.

'The settlers didn't understand about the soil,' the historian explained. 'They thought it was like England where there's many inches of top soil. Here the top soil is very thin – an inch if that – and underneath is clay. The settlers brought their tools from England. They harrowed the ground, turned up the clay, and the soil disappeared.'

We went on talking about the implications of this lack of understanding of the land, and the historian told me how he had known hunger as a child in the Depression and how he had wondered why his father did not get a job. He had not understood that there was no work to be had. As he got older he tried to understand the political and economic forces which dominated Australia, but whose bases were far away, and the politicians and academics whose solutions to problems bore little relation to the realities, but he felt that he did not have the education to do so.

Moreover, he said, 'It's not a good idea to think too deeply about these things.'

I had often heard people use these very words, but they were talking of their inner world of thoughts and feelings, a world where they feared to tread. He was talking of social, political and economic matters, our common, shared, external reality in which we have our physical existence and which we must try to understand if we are to survive and prosper.

So I asked, 'What would happen to you if you thought too deeply?'

'People would think I was –' he put his forefinger to his forehead and turned it, the sign that a person is 'not right in the head', that is, mad.

'How would people show you that they thought that?'

'They would shun me. They wouldn't want to have anything to do with me. There are topics which you mustn't discuss. You can have an intelligent conversation about cricket. You can have an intelligent conversation about alcohol. You can have an intelligent conversation about sport. But you can't have a conversation about intelligence.'

It was obvious that he did think deeply, but that he had kept these thoughts to himself. He described the economic and political disasters which had overtaken the farmers in the area, and told me how the suicide rate among the farmers had risen by eight percent. 'They blame themselves for their failure. They feel they've brought disgrace on the family's good name. Having a good name is the only thing that matters here. They don't understand that it's not their fault that they went bankrupt.' (If we are forbidden to think, we can never work out how responsibility should be allocated. Church and State protect themselves by teaching us to blame ourselves.)

Often in our conversation he alluded to something he was thinking about most deeply. He had been brought up in unquestioning obedience to a simple Christianity of rewards and punishments, but his life had shown him that morality and metaphysics were more complex than that. He was trying to arrive at a metaphysical belief which made sense, and he wondered about the possibilities of reincarnation and of parallel universes different in time. Various events, including his vivid dreams which 'I'm not intelligent enough to create' made him wonder about other realities. He had one friend who, when no one else was around, would discuss dreams with him, but otherwise he had to keep these conjectures to himself.

We talked of how weak governments of every country are, for they are influenced by international cartels, vast, impersonal and unchallengeable in their power. 'There's a monster in control but no one can ever get to see this monster. All you can see is the people who work for the monster, and none of them can make decisions. Australians won't talk about this. They just say, Don't think, and don't complain. If you do think, they say you're not right in the head, and if you think and say that things aren't right, they call you a Commie. No one knows what a Commie is, but if you complain, you're a Commie.'

When I returned to Sydney I met another Australian man, the same generation as the historian, but a scientist and academician. He told me, 'Australians aren't interested in philosophy or morality. It's part of the macho image – not being interested in the broader questions. In England they're interested in broader questions but not here. You wouldn't have been able to do what you have done in Australia. Whenever I read something to do with philosophy I think, There's no one here I can discuss that with.'

The education which the historian, the scientist and I had received in Australian schools had been very regimented, organized around learning 'facts', being obedient and passing examinations. I had imagined that Australian education had changed in the way that British education had changed, with emphasis on the children's sense of discovery, imagination and creativity. But I was wrong. Australian education was summed up for me by a lecturer in a university education department. 'We are not taught to think. We are taught content, not process.'

As a child I loved poetry, but I could never express and explore that love. In school we had to learn poems to recite, and, as senior students specializing in the study of English, to analyse prescribed poems in the prescribed ways. When I mentioned to the English mistress that I was intrigued and excited by a poem I had just discovered, *The Waste Land*, she told me not to read it as I would not understand it. But is that not the point of poetry – its mysterious echoes which, because you do not understand them, lead you on? Attitudes to poetry in Australia have not changed.

John Forbes, one of Australia's most prominently published poets, has directed most of his time and passion to verse since he was 11 years old . . . 'I do it because I like it and would not do anything else. I'm not saying that the poems mightn't be profound, but so what? . . . It still surprises me, stuns me that people don't like poetry. They want to know what it means, but meaning has a terrible effect on people. People should read poetry for pleasure first, then let the meaning come. People are educated in Australia not to like poetry. The education system is like a giant series of inoculations. If you're not cured of poetry at secondary school, then you go to university. If you're not cured of poetry there, you can become an academic (something Forbes had the chance to do but is thankful he decided against) or a poet. If you become a poet, then you're like antibodies in the community because by that time you're so weird in the head, you don't have any money, you don't own a Celica and you don't offer an attractive proposition. They say, 'Look, there's Kevin, he's a poet, don't do it.'[17]

Margaret Coombs has written two outstanding novels, *Regards to the Czar*[18] and *The Best Man for This Sort of Thing*.[19] She had got in touch with me because she deals in her fiction with the same themes that I write about. We met for lunch in Sydney where she told me how, by writing as she does, she puts her head above the parapet and there are many people ready to shoot at her.

Margaret Coombs has found, as I have, that many people react with considerable hostility to any link being made between childhood experience and adult life. Writers like Margaret Coombs and Fay Weldon, who refuse to write about women with the traditional sentimentality, encounter much criticism and misunderstanding. In Australia, as in every country, there are professionals and academics who believe that only they have the intelligence to understand and the right to comment on life and literature. Within every profession each member is expected to hold the 'correct views'. This is why the scientist had said to me, 'You wouldn't have been able to do what you have done in Australia.' But in living there are no experts, and all of us are entitled to comment on our experience of life.

However, in a country where argument is conducted not so much by criticizing ideas as by attacking the person putting forward the ideas,[20] it is dangerous, as many people have found, to put forward any unpopular ideas. I shall never forget the vilification heaped on my friend and colleague Alex Carey when he publicly opposed Australia's part in the Vietnam War.

Literature is about truth, the writer's own truth. If you do not write about your own truth, if you lie, omit or distort your own truth, then what you write, no matter how cleverly expressed, is not literature. When you write about your own truth you cannot be wrong.

The population of Australia may have grown by several millions since I have lived in England and become multicultural in a way which was unimaginable when I was a child, but the old sport of cutting down tall poppies and intimidating those who might be considering becoming tall is alive and well. As ever, Australians who wish to think for themselves live in danger.

People who wish to think for themselves and who live in totalitarian countries know that they are in prison and in danger. When we live in a 'democracy' where we are always being told that we are free, it is much harder to see the prison and the danger.

The only thing that gives me hope that the human race might have the wit not just to avoid extinction as the climate changes but also to preserve that which is unique and best about us, our capacity for self-reflection, freedom and creativity, is that, despite the inhibiting and destructive education which most of us receive, despite the pervasive power of the Church, State and international cartels, a few people manage to keep safe within themselves their own truth, to value their own truth, and to have the courage to speak it. Vaclav Havel managed to do this. So, too, did a young child whose name I do not know but whose voice I heard on the BBC radio religious programme *Pause for Thought* (which should actually be called 'Believe, Don't Question'). Some children had been asked to talk about God and the environment. Their words had been recorded and a medley of their little voices was presented, each in turn speaking dutifully about how grateful they were to God for making such a beautiful world and creating them, and how they hoped and prayed that God would look after them and the world. Then, in the midst of these charming statements, slipped in, no doubt, by some BBC subversive, a child's voice said, 'I think that God relies on us to look after the world for Him. We shouldn't rely on Him to look after us.'[21] That is, we should be responsible for ourselves.

Love and Understanding

When I listed what I think is unique and best about our species – our capacity for self-reflection, freedom and creativity – I did not include love. Animal lovers would say that animals can love, if not humans, then their offspring. They may well be right, but, more importantly, I did not include love because 'love' is a much misused word, loaded with confusion and sentimentality. Like the ancient Greeks, we should have different words for all the tasks we make 'love' do, or, at least, different words for 'I love ice cream', 'I love you so do what I want', and that gentle, strong, boundless, secure, fearless, joy, contentment, bliss of being. Only to this last experience would I give the word 'love'.

Love such as this, true love as I called it earlier, contains no fear or hate.

If we fear what we love, then to protect ourselves from what we fear we put up a barrier, and behind that barrier love, once confident and secure, falters and fades. As small children we loved our parents with a love which was confident and secure, but when our parents, in order to make us obedient, made us fear them, our love disappeared and was replaced by guilt which, in our confusion, we thought was love.

Nor can love live with hate. Oscar Wilde, writing from his prison cell to Lord Alfred Douglas, the cause of his downfall, explained why:

> In you Hate was always stronger than Love. Your hatred of your father was of such a stature that it entirely outstripped, o'erthrew, and overshadowed your love of me . . . You did not realize that there is no room for both passions in the same soul. They cannot live together in that fair carven house. Love is fed by the imagination, by which we become wiser than we know, better than we feel, nobler than we are: by which we can see Life as a whole: by which, and by which alone, we can understand others in their real as in their ideal relations. Only that which is fine, and finely conceived, can feed Love. But anything will feed Hate.[22]

The hate which drives out love may be, as in Lord Alfred Douglas's case, of another person. Or it may be the hate which feeds the need for revenge against a group. Or it may be the hate which the lover feels for some aspect of the beloved.

I have often heard someone remark, 'I love so and so but I don't like him,' and each time I have thought, 'How stupid!' If we really love a person, we love all of that person. If a person we love does something which aggravates us, then we should take responsibility for our own aggravation and decide whether we should rightly defend ourselves ('I'll ask him not to phone me after 11 p.m.') or whether we are being selfish and unaware ('It must be something important for him to phone so late'). If we refuse to take responsibility for our own aggravation but instead push the responsibility back on to the person and blame him, we no longer love that person in his totality, as he is. The more we do this, the more rapidly the bit of the person we do love shrinks, until what we are feeling is not love but a fondness for a few attributes which exist separately from the real person. Moreover, the object of our affection and criticism is aware of this shrinkage, and knows that he is not loved. This is why the children of critical parents believe, and rightly so, that they are not loved.

Children who believe that they are not loved have great difficulty in becoming the person that they know themselves to be. To realize ourselves as we are, we need around us people who are prepared to realize us in the same way. This realization of the other person, seeing and accepting the other person as he is and is becoming, is the process of seeing the other person as an *equal*. There may be great disparities in age or position or wealth, but the equality lies in the recognition that we are all equally here, trying as best we can to endure and surmount the human condition. Where we see others as not being our equals, we cannot love them, though we may parade sentimentality as love. If we see them as our superiors, we fear them for they have the power to injure us, and fear drives out love. If we see them as our inferiors, we have put a barrier between them and us, a barrier which love will not cross. On the day Benazir Bhutto was deposed, someone who was reported to know her well said in a BBC interview that it was impossible to work *with* Benazir but only *for* her. Whether this was so I do not know, but working alongside psychiatrists in the NHS I had plenty of experience of men who had no concept of working with but understood only working for. In the teams they headed, misunderstanding and ill-feeling abounded, for while the psychiatrists were, on the whole, pleasant, well-meaning men, they did not possess the intellectual and experiential stature which would make their team members respect them and be glad to work for them. Nor did the psychiatrists have the wisdom to see the power of influence which is available when others see us as an approachable equal.

These psychiatrists felt compelled to maintain their position of authority partly because that is the way their profession is organized, and partly because they felt too unsure about themselves to risk treating others as equals and letting them approach. They did not accept and love themselves, so they feared that if others saw them without the trappings of office they would reject them, and so, keeping others at a distance, they did not get to know their team members and could never come to love them. Thus it is that we cannot love other people if we do not love ourselves.

We cannot love ourselves if we do not understand ourselves, and if we do not understand ourselves, we cannot understand others. Our understanding of ourselves is our own truth, our only certainty and solidity in a world of uncertainty. Only from this certainty and solidity can we try to venture into the uncertainties of another person's world of meaning.

Understanding another person is more than feeling sympathy or even empathy. To understand others we need to understand how we all operate as meaning-creating creatures, how we each experience ourselves and our world.

The understanding which we should seek is not the reductive and pejorative 'understanding' which most professionals create in order to feel good about themselves. Reducing human experience to an explanation in terms of a biochemical change or a 'stimulus-response' or a 'cognitive dysfunction' demeans us all, including those psychiatrists and psychologists who speak of their patients in such patronizing, judgemental terms. (The reason that some doctors oppose letting patients having access to their own case notes is because they do not want their patients to discover and be hurt and sickened by the way many doctors speak and write about patients.)

Nor should we seek an understanding which aims to reveal the other person as trapped, static, no more than his history or physiology. Psychoanalysts have specialized in this, describing other people as being no more than the outcome of their childhood experiences. In a television programme about amateur astronomers who, though not professionally trained, make a significant contribution to their science, one man talked of his passion for finding out what was unknown.[23] As he spoke, he clasped the long tube of his telescope to his body. It was a scene ripe for a Freudian interpretation – the phallic symbol, the child's curiosity about the primal scene – but such an interpretation would simply trap and negate this man. No doubt in his childhood he had become aware that there were secrets to which he was not privy. What is important is that he did not remain a little boy with his face pressed against the closed door of his parents' bedroom, or whatever it was from which he was shut out, but that he took this experience, shaped it, and used it intelligently, creatively, to give his life a meaning and purpose which was not just for him alone but for the good of mankind.

All of us suffer horrors in childhood, and our task is to use our intelligence and creativity to turn those experiences into something with which we can live and progress. We need people around us who will impose on us, not an 'understanding' which inhibits and cripples us, but an understanding which sees our infinite capacity to create and progress.

Thus, when someone says to me, 'My mother was depressed. Does that mean I will be?' I say, 'It's not compulsory. But you're free to think of it as being compulsory if you want to.' When a journalist phones me to ask whether a freed hostage will suffer nightmares, I point out that that new disease, Post-Traumatic Stress Disorder, is not compulsory for those who suffer major disasters, and that nightmares are not evil indications of a shattered mind but part of the natural, healing process of mastering difficult, painful experiences and extracting from them a fruitful and compatible meaning.

To find an understanding which aims to liberate us rather than imprison us, we have to make the major intellectual effort of listening and actually hearing another person's construction of meaning instead of just hearing echoes of our own. We have to discover the other person's set of values, and take them seriously. This is not easy to do, for we are so well trained in seeing and respecting only our own set of values.

In every country, in every society, groups of people live side by side and completely misunderstand one another, with much consequent suffering. Sometimes members of one or both sides try to find a scheme for reconciliation but soon discover that goodwill is not enough, and, in fact, such attempts at reconciliation can actually make matters worse. The understanding which is required is far more complex than just meaning well.

This is the situation which has existed in Australia between the original inhabitants, the Aborigines, and the descendants of those Europeans who came, first as convicts and soldiers, then as settlers and gold-seekers, and, after the Second World War, as seekers after a better life. In recent years some of these seekers have come from countries directly north of Australia, so, rather than use the common term 'white Australians', I shall speak of 'European Australians', who are descended principally, as I am, from the English, Irish, Scots and Welsh. This is the group which largely defines Australian culture.

In the culture which the Europeans established, there are many sources of pride, but perhaps the greatest source of pride is in how hard European Australians work. All European Australians work harder than anyone else in the world. Even those European Australians who have never done a day's work in their lives work harder than anyone else. This is their main complaint about the Aborigines. As a taxi driver in Townsville said to me, 'The trouble with Aborigines is that they won't work. A few of them work and they do real well, but the others – if they don't learn to work this generation, it's make or break for them.'

My first port of call when I visited Australia was Darwin, in the Northern Territory, where I was to lecture at the university and visit my ex-husband and his wife Sally. On the first day, Ted showed me around Darwin and his office where he told me about his mixed nationality staff, including his Aboriginal secretary. She was, he said, good at her job and an excellent typist. The problem she presented for him was that on two or three days in most weeks she did not arrive for work. If he questioned her as to whether she had been sick, she would just look at him silently. He knew that if, when she was getting ready for work, one of the tribal elders told her she should do something for him, she had to obey. Even on those days when she came to work she did not always stay at her desk. Instead, with no explanation to anyone, she would go downstairs into the mall where she would drift, peering into shops, not buying, just looking, and then, silently, return to work.

Not long after Ted had told me this, he, Sally and I set out to visit Lichfield Park, a huge area now a National Park, south-west of Darwin. We drove south on the Stuart Highway, turned west through the tiny township of Batchelor and on, mile after mile, over a red dirt road, past endless vistas of gaunt trees, outcrops of rocks, of red and brown fantastically shaped termite mounds, and clumps of spindly grasses.

The terrain is deceptive. The sky meeting the jagged hills in the west was that shade of blue which suggests that the sea lies beyond those hills, but an eager climber would find at the top of the hills a further vista of trees, rocks, and escarpments, and a sky still suggesting that beyond the further hill was the sea. In fact the sea was some three hundred miles away.

We turned south on a road marked to Florence Falls. The terrain did not change, even when more signs of human endeavour became apparent, wooden fences and signposts denoting a car park and a path to the falls. Ted stayed in the car while Sally and I made our way along the path.

We could hear a continuous sound, different from the endless buzzing of the locusts, but the path scraped through the bush was the only alteration in the sights we had seen in all the miles we had travelled. Ahead of us was a wooden platform, and it was not until we were at its edge, where a railing held us safe, that we could see the sudden deep gash in the escarpment side, down which a thread of silver water fell. This was the continuous sound which we had heard.

We followed the path down a precipitous side of rocks and dirt and wildly angled plants to a deep pool at the base of the falls. There were people picnicking and swimming there, but we went on, up the other side and around the top through the sparse, dry bush, following the path back to the car.

The heat was intense and dangerous. We had drunk some water before we set out, and again on our return to the car. In this country dehydration can be sudden and deadly.

We drove back to the road and on through endless variations of trees, rocks, anthills until, miles later, we came to the turn-off for Wangi Falls. Here a gentler incline had been turned into a car park and expansive tree-scattered paddocks with tables and fireplaces for picnics. Beyond the paddocks was a pool whose deep brown waters stretched across to a high, jagged cliff face down which two streams of water bent, split, shattered and fell. Sally and I swam slowly and silently across the huge pool to where we could brace ourselves against the rocks and let the waters of the falls spill like a shower of icy rain on our heads and shoulders.

It was a pool which imposed silence and meditation. As I swam slowly or floated in its gentle impassivity, I thought about the Aboriginal girl for whom the demands of work were not the be-all and end-all of her existence.

I remembered how Ted had told me how their elder son, Chris, wanting to get money to travel, had worked as a grass cutter during the day and as a barman at night. Neither Ted nor I were surprised at Chris's industry, any more than we are surprised at how hard our son Edward works. It would have been surprising, and shaming, if our children had not worked. We had always worked, and our parents and grandparents had always worked. Work is what we *do*. It is our means of survival and our pride.

Work is something more than survival and pride. It occurred to me as I meditated in the deep pool below the Wangi Falls that work is the means by which the people of my society knit together their internal and external realities. This knitting together is essential if we are to survive as persons.

If we ignore our internal reality and attend only to external reality, our actions become just reactions to the events around us. We live in the present, not remembering the past and not planning the future. We may daydream and tell ourselves stories, but these stories relate only to action and not to thought and feeling. There are many people who live like this, but their lives cannot be said to be satisfactory, for even if they avoid conflict with the law, they form no lasting relationships, since relationships require a past and a future and the imagination of empathy.

If we ignore our external reality and attend only to our internal reality, we may people our internal reality with fantastic visions of the past, present and future, but external reality trips us up, and, since in our external reality people exist, we fail to form relationships.

So our task is to be aware of and knit together internal and external reality. We do this by engaging in a process whereby we create something within us which we can put in a form that we can take and put outside us, in our external reality. Out there, that which we have created interacts with aspects of our external reality to create something new, some aspect of which we can then take back inside us to be used in other internal creative activity. The cycle is continuous.

Thus, in work, we create within ourselves some formulation, organization and planning. Usually the formulation comes from our observation of external reality ('the lawn needs mowing') and our knowledge of the past ('I know how to use the lawn mower'). The organization and planning involve the future ('It should take no more than an hour. I'll do it in the cool of the evening').

When we begin working we are taking the formulation, organization and planning out of our internal reality and putting it in our external reality. If it fits exactly, we internally experience satisfaction and a boost to our self-confidence and self-esteem. If it fits slightly less than exactly, we modify our internal formulation ('Next time I'll remember that it takes more than an hour to mow the lawn'). If it doesn't fit at all, we have to make radical changes to our internal formulation ('I'll have to pay someone to mow the lawn').

This way of knitting together our internal and external realities is traditional in our society. We encourage and reward young children for undertaking work-like activities. Wealthy people who do not need to work to survive strive to show that they are virtuous by working as directors of companies, or working for charity. The Royal Family, we are told, works very hard.

But work is not the only way in which we can knit together our two realities. We can do this in art and music, where we try to create in external reality our internal vision. We can do this in science and mathematics, where we create internally our theories and test them externally. We can do this in story-telling, where internally we create a past and a future in order to explain our present. We can keep our story inside us, or we can present it to others in one of the multitude of story-telling forms.

Or we can simply look, hear, touch, taste and smell. Our bodies occupy both realities and our organs of perception are tuned to both our realities, and so we can use them to knit together our two realities. The line of demarcation between our internal and external reality is not our skin. Our internal reality spreads over the world, incorporating this person and that object, while external reality invades our body, becoming the pain above my eyebrows, the ache in my bones, the buzzing in my ears.

Harassed by too many demands that we should pay attention to our external reality, or drawn into the troubled thoughts of our internal reality, we can resolve to escape from both by looking at the natural world about us and, by absorbing its sights, sounds and smells we can put together the formulations we have created about our natural world and the spectacle it presents to us. Our formulation usually involves how we see our place in the natural world, and the time we spend in contemplation of the natural world usually affirms a positive, accepted, contented, place for us.

The Japanese, according to Takeo Doi, 'sometimes have feelings of superiority toward Westerners who in their eyes cannot easily become one with nature.'[24] The Japanese have not observed how the Aborigines too not only have this capacity to become one with nature but have used it as their means of survival in a land which exists and will exist for ever in a state of indifference to human beings.

How can human beings, so weak and puny, survive in a vast and barren land? When the American settlers went west into the wilderness we now call 'the West', they took with them not only the skills developed in Europe and on the east coast of America, but a religion which permits a personal God. They defied the impersonal, unchanging vastness of their new home by believing in a God who watched over their every move, making a personal assessment of their virtues and vices, and rewarding and punishing them appropriately. The idea of a personal God protected them from being overwhelmed by the contrast between their puniness and the immensity of the plains and mountains.

Their predecessors, the Indians, knew better than to believe in the rewards and punishments of a personal God in a land where the rewards may be unexpectedly easy (a readily captured buffalo) and the punishments inordinately harsh (an all-encompassing blizzard). Like the Aborigines, they saw that the best way to survive in an inhospitable vastness was to people it with spirits and so become one with it.

To people a landscape with spirits who recognize and respond to us we need to create stories, and this is what the Aborigines did. They created the stories of the Dreamtime, and the bush they looked upon ceased to be alien and became theirs. They created in their internal reality stories to explain the past and predict the future. They put these internal creations out into their external reality by telling their stories to others and locating the scenes of these stories in the variations of the harsh landscape around them. Such landscapes created for them a mental map of a landscape whose subtle variations create confusion for the traveller, and this mental map enlarged and modified the stories.

The only way of remembering the maps and the stories was for the Aborigines to go and look at the places in their stories, retelling the stories as they went, thus locating themselves in time and space, and knitting together their internal and external reality. The stories, too, defined the relationships among people and allowed them to make the appropriate internal and external responses to one another. To gaze upon their natural surroundings and to tell the stories of those surroundings was not merely the means of survival as a person but was their outstanding virtue.

For the Aborigine to go walkabout is as virtuous as it is for us to work.

Not that we understand this. For us, work is the supreme virtue. We may gaze at nature and feel comforted, but we prefer to engage in all kinds of activity (which may, at best, be pointless and futile, and, at worst, destructive), rather than contemplate the possibility that we work, not just so that we can eat, but so that we know ourselves to be human. This is why many people become depressed when they lose their job or retire.

Most people learn to work because work is their only livelihood. The Aborigines, living in their tribal ways, had to work at hunting and gathering their food and building shelter and equipment. But, according to all accounts, they never made work the most important activity in their lives. Story-telling, being and living their roles in the stories, was the most important. The earth was their bountiful mother, meeting all their needs so long as they stayed at one with her. The earth and themselves were one subject. They knew the earth as themselves, not as the other, the stranger. They knew the earth personally, as a person like themselves, not as an object which can be used and abused.

A curious feature of human knowing is the way in which everything we encounter we can know in two ways, subjectively and objectively.

In subjective knowing we feel a direct apprehension of the subject of our knowing. This may be in the sense of becoming one with that subject, as when we lose our own sense of self in meditation, or when we join with another person in love, or when we lose ourselves in the sights and sounds of natural beauty, or in works of art. Or it may be when we make that leap of imagination called empathy where we are conscious both of how we feel and of how the subject of our imaginative leap feels. Such a subject may be another person, or it may be an animal or some feature of inanimate matter on to which we have projected human characteristics with which we can feel empathy.

In objective knowing we separate ourselves from the object of our knowing. Such an object has a relationship to us in that we see it as something we can use to meet our needs, but we are in no way subservient to or even mindful of the needs and the point of view of the object. The object is there, and we are here, and we share a relationship only of time and place.

Both forms of knowing are essential to our survival. To live effectively we need to use both forms of knowing, and to know that we use both forms. We get into difficulties when we try to use one form of knowing to the exclusion of the other, and when we tell ourselves that one of the forms of knowing is the only way to know.

We cannot operate and survive using only one of the forms of knowing. The Aborigines made and discarded tools. They may have apologized to their fellow creatures for killing them, but they still used objective knowing to trap and kill these animals.

Within the hierarchy of the tribe, those in power could use their underlings as objects. Sally, whose work brings her into close contact with tribal Aborigines, once remarked that the tribal Aborigine men treat their dogs better than they treat their women. Similarly, the European Australians, with their fascination with work, an occupation which requires objective knowing, still required subjective knowing in their relationships with other people. It was when the Aborigines and the European Australians exalted one way of knowing over the other that they each got into difficulties.

All human beings seem to have great difficulty in understanding that other people see things differently, and, even when they do see this, tolerating other people's perceptions. Most Aborigines have had little tolerance and understanding of the European Australians' fascination with work, while the European Australians have had no tolerance and understanding of the Aborigines' lack of interest in work. Of course the basic reason we do not want to recognize the existence and rightness of another person's perceptions is that this throws our own into doubt, and shows that what we see is merely our constructions and not solid reality. For our own safety we say that our perceptions are true, and that those who do not agree with us are mad and bad. Since we refuse to acknowledge that we construct the reality which we see, we lose our ability to distinguish and value appropriately objective and subjective knowledge.

The Aborigines regarded their capacity for subjective knowing as something special, something which marked them out as special people and made them superior to European Australians. Perhaps before the European Australians came they did not hold their subjective knowing in such special regard, but as the European Australians attacked and humiliated them they had to find some way of maintaining their pride, and this could only be by some special attribute which they saw that they alone could possess. This they found in their capacity for subjective knowing.

In this affirmation of their relationship to their land, the Aborigines reaffirmed their faith in their own worth and pride and knowledge. This knowledge of the land and its inhabitants they had acquired over the centuries, and only a very small part – mainly their ability to read the tracks of all animals, including the human animal – they revealed to the European Australians. Probably, initially, tracking was the only part of the Aboriginal knowledge which European Australians would value and use, but now, when there are many European Australians who value the Aborigines and want to share their lives, many Aborigines, especially those who have learned this special knowledge, want to keep such knowledge secret.

I have been told about researchers who, having been allowed by an Aboriginal tribe to live with them, and having shown genuine concern for and unity with the members of the tribe, have been allowed to learn some of the secrets, but only on the understanding that the researchers do not reveal any of the secrets to the outside world. Loyal researchers keep their promise, and Ph.D.s remain unfinished and books unwritten. This may be a blessing in a world awash with books, but we can still ask why the Aborigines demand such secrecy.

It is always sensible, when we are weak and in the power of people who do not have our interests at heart, to keep secret as much information about ourselves as we can. Then the people who have power over us cannot use this knowledge to harm us further. The Aborigines know only too well what it feels like to be the butt of the European-Australian cruel humour.

There is a further reason, and that has to do with magic. Magic is a mixture of subjective and objective knowing, and is used by all cultures at all times. The objective knowing involves observation of and action upon people and things, that is, the practice of science. The subjective knowing goes beyond using this observation and action to ameliorate suffering and/or to gain some advantage, but instead claims a special knowledge and power which allow the possessor to claim to have control over aspects of the world which do not ordinarily lend themselves to human control. We claim this special knowledge and power when we feel we can convince ourselves and others that we do possess such knowledge and power (the ability to do magic), when we want to impress others and build up our own self-esteem, and when we wish to deny that we are but puny mortals trying to survive in a vast, dangerous and unpredictable world. Magic is an elaborate form of whistling in the dark.

The Aborigines had good reason to keep secret what they valued most about their society. It is only recently that some European Australians have begun to appreciate the achievements of Aboriginal society. The archaeologist Josephine Flood wrote:

> It is in the creativity of the spirit, rather than material goods, that Aboriginal society excelled. Society was so organized that there was ample leisure time. Prehistoric Australians had more leisure to devote to matters of the mind – art, ceremonial, music, dance and myth – than did but a few Western artists until recent times. The achievements of early Australians are constantly underestimated by the Europeans who judge a society solely by its material possessions.[25]

Unfortunately, the combination of the Aborigines' secrecy and their cruel treatment at the hands of the European Australians[26] combined to prevent the Aborigines from learning about the European Australians, while the European Australians despised the Aborigines too much to even try to understand them.

To understand another person we have to understand how that person knits together his internal and external reality. We have to understand how that person perceives his world and how his society and other societies perceive him. All these perceptions must be treated with respect. We need to understand and to respect the functions of both objective and subjective knowing.

Reflection is a combination of objective and subjective knowing. What a pity it is not an Australian tradition! We need to make reflection a universal tradition.

When Only the Best Is All That We Want

By September 1989, I had reached the stage with this book where I had realized that it was going to be a long book, a Major Work! Then one day I opened the *Guardian* and found that Merillee Harper had put the essence of what I wanted to say in one small cartoon.[27]

This is our choice. We can go on as we always have, not thinking clearly, relying on our hope that somehow, by some magical means, it will all come right in the end. Or we can take what we have and recycle or rearrange it with careful, clear thought and create, out of what we have already got, all that we want. We can, as we have always done, hand responsibility for ourselves over to other people and institutions, and hope that they will look after us, or we can accept responsibility for ourselves.

The first choice does not even give us security, much less what we want. The second choice is full of uncertainty, but when we take responsibility for ourselves, knowing ourselves and one another, we can work out what matters most to us, and order our priorities. We accept that we can never return to the original bliss, but, more important, we can leave this world having enjoyed much of what we wanted. What matter that the relationships we had in the past were unsatisfactory and painful? *Now* we shall enjoy friendship and love. What matter that we missed out on so much? *Now* we shall make the most of our time. The only regret we can now afford ourselves is that those generations that went before us wasted their opportunities.

If, thousands of years ago, we had realized that we needed to understand what we did to one another and why, we would not have been able to eradicate from our lives death and the loss of love, but we would have been able to find ways of supporting one another in times of suffering, because we would have been kinder to and more tolerant of one another. We would have turned our intelligence to unravelling the complex network of human interactions and the effects of human interactions, and today would have developed a science of psychology as profound and complex as that of nuclear physics: not a science understood by an elite few, but one understood by everybody; a science not separate from everyday life, but one which is an integral part of how we live, informing our choices and offering consolation for our failures and defeats.

But we did not do this. Instead, our gift of intelligence was squandered, spilled on battlefields and drained away in poverty and enslavement. Precious little was used to increase our understanding, enthusiasm and joy. Most of what was used went to create an increasingly cruel world, while the planet on which we depend was plundered and destroyed. We consoled ourselves with myths which promised us eternal life but in fact trapped us in a sorry round of misunderstandings, punishments, disappointments and suffering. We looked to hero leaders to save us, and failed to see that they were no different from us.

Occasionally I read of tribes who treat their children kindly, who do not punish them, but listen to them with understanding and empathy. The pygmies of Africa and some Indian tribes in Brazil are reported to live with wisdom, but will not do so for long, because the trees are coming down and their home is being destroyed, all in the cause of 'progress'. Only evil flourishes, and not the green bay tree.

If, thousands of years ago, we had decided to use our intelligence to understand ourselves, we would not have looked for explanations as to why we do what we do by fantasizing about demons or spirits or genes, but we would have asked, 'Why do we hurt one another so?' and found answers based on the assumption that human beings are precious and need to be cherished, for all we have is one another. We would have looked not to some mythical Power to save us, but to ourselves, knowing we are part of everything that exists, and that our capacity to be an individual, while at the same time being joined to everyone and everything, gives us great power, a power which we have very rarely used to our benefit, a power which the Church and State have exploited to set one group in enmity against another.

If, thousands of years ago, we had decided to use our intelligence to understand ourselves, our history would have been entirely different. We might not have ever discovered the wonders of the motor car, and we certainly would not have discovered the terrors of nuclear weapons. We would probably have been fewer, but then many fewer would have died on battlefield or in childbirth or in hunger. We would have developed the arts beyond anything we can even imagine now, and all of us would be artists. Our arts would have been informed by tragedy, because tragedy would still be part of our lives, but we would not see tragedy as a punishment for wickedness or a deficit requiring compensation. We would not ignore or blindly try to ameliorate the sufferings of those around us, but we would unashamedly and unabashedly come together in the 'eternal reciprocity of tears'.

If, thousands of years ago, we had decided to use our intelligence to understand ourselves, we would have understood our wanting everything and have dealt with it, not by denial and blind grasping, but by turning 'everything' from the demand for immediate gratification into enlightened self-interest. We would have understood and taught our children that we should practise kindness, tolerance and sharing, not because this will assure our place in heaven or because they are the Great Virtues, but because a society where all the people practise kindness, tolerance and sharing is a pleasant place to live. It is in our own interests that we be kind, tolerant and share with others. We would have understood and taught our children that, since our life is limited, we have to make choices and order priorities, and, since we cannot have everything, we should focus on having the best. We would have understood and taught our children that a close and loving relationship gives more peace and joy and satisfaction than luxury and wealth, and that the capacity to live in the present and feel joined to and enthused by a vision of nature or a work or art gives more of a sense of being alive and excited and satisfied than the power of exploiting other people. We would have understood and taught our children that only by being responsible for ourselves can we be responsible for other people. We would have understood and taught our children that self-sacrifice is waste and that revenge, except in terms of mutual merriment, is futile.

If, thousands of years ago, we had decided to use our intelligence to understand ourselves, how very different our lives would have been!

Soon our lives will be very different. As the trees disappear, the rain turns acid, the temperature increases and the waters rise, our lives will change, but not in the ways we wish. Our chances of getting everything will get less and less.

We do have a little time. Perhaps, even at this late stage, we could decide to do what we should have done thousands of years ago. Let us use our intelligence.

Notes

Preface

1. Robin Morgan, *The Demon Lover: The Sexuality of Terrorism* (Methuen, London, 1989), p. 144.

2. Reports of respectable engineering, electrical and electronic firms supplying equipment intended for use in torture appear regularly in the British press. John Sweeney, writing in the *Observer* on 13 January 1991, described an electronic torture chamber, installed by a British company, Electronic Intelligence, inside the headquarters of the Special Branch of Dubai. 'Its purpose was to terrify prisoners without leaving signs of physical harm. To this end, a special cell was constructed, fitted with a terrifyingly loud sound system and a white noise generator designed to pulse sound at a frequency which will ultimately destroy the human body, 11 hertz. Synchronized with the white noise generator was a strobe light, also set at 11 hertz. The combined effect would be to reduce anyone inside the cell to a screaming, helpless supplicant within moments.'

3. Linda Valins, 'Conflict from an intimate problem', *Independent*, 30 August 1988, from her book *Vaginismus: Understanding and Overcoming the Blocks to Intercourse* (Ashgrove Press, UK, and Viking Penguin, USA, 1990).

4. Colin Wheeler, 'Is my daughter's life worth living?' *Independent*, 30 August 1988.

5. Quoted by Michael Foot in his article on the persecution of Salman Rushdie. He wrote:

> The great persisting threat to our world derives from this pursuit of absolute victory. Once it was Hitler's creed, and once it was Stalin's, and once it was called the Dulles doctrine, and once it came near to being adopted by President Reagan launching fundamentalist anathemas against the evil empire. It is too soon to say that all these perils have passed, but on the intercontinental stage they have been miraculously reduced, with mankind able to breathe again – as they did when the crusaders and their enemies became exhausted by their mad expeditions or when Catholic and Protestant reached their 16th century compromise.
>
> How strident or absurd or indeed wicked were the fundamentalist voices of those times, the Khomeinis and the Akhtars, who denounced any movement towards detente or rapprochement as blasphemy or treachery or godlessness. How much wiser and braver were the Montaignes, the Jonathan Swifts, the Voltaires, the Salman Rushdies who knew that if such insanities were to be stopped, they must be mocked in the name of a common human decency with a claim to take precedence over any religion. Montaigne's books were put on the Papal Index; Swift was accused, on the highest regal or ecclesiastical authority, of defaming all religions; many of Voltaire's volumes were actually burnt.
>
> So Salman Rushdie keeps good company. He is a great artist, even if, like Swift or Voltaire, he does not possess all the virtues too. But no shield

against religious intolerance can always prevail, as Voltaire himself explained in his epitaph on the Saint Zapata.
(*Guardian*, 13 March 1989.)

6. An oversimplified way of looking at the relationship between the first kind of intelligence (roughly, IQ) and the second kind of intelligence (Wisdom Quotient, WQ) could be set out as follows:

IQ HIGH	good at understanding	trying to do good	powerful
		can be useful	cruel
			very dangerous
	persecuted	can be dangerous	
MEDIUM	Fair at understanding	means well	supporting power and cruelty
		can be used	
	persecuted		
LOW	simple understanding	caring but confused, prejudiced and dogmatic	not understanding
	frustrated		used by others
			destructive
WQ	HIGH	MEDIUM	LOW

People with a high IQ and WQ have a good understanding of themselves and other people and the world they live in. Unless they are very careful, they are persecuted.

People with a medium IQ and a high WQ have a fair understanding of themselves and other people. Unless they are careful, they are persecuted.

People with a low IQ and a high WQ (quite common among people with learning difficulties, since they have not had their minds cluttered with 'expert' theories) have a very simple and direct understanding of the people around them, but, as they cannot marry this understanding to more intellectual matters, and since they are often treated with disregard by the 'normal' people around them, they are often hurt and frustrated.

People with a high IQ and a medium WQ try to do good, and this can be useful and effective, but if they are convinced that they know what is best for other people, they become dangerous.

People with a medium IQ and a medium WQ mean well, but they do not see issues clearly and can be used by those with a medium IQ and WQ and those with a high IQ and low WQ.

People with a low IQ and medium WQ can be very caring, but they are also likely to be confused, prejudiced and dogmatic.

People with a high IQ and a low WQ are powerful and cruel, very danger-ous people.

People with a medium IQ and a low WQ are also dangerous, for they sup-port power and cruelty.

People with a low IQ and a low WQ have little understanding of what goes on around them. So they are thoughtlessly destructive and are easily led and used by those with a high or medium IQ and low WQ.

Chapter 1. 'I Can Have Everything'

1. Alice Miller, *The Drama of the Gifted Child* (Faber, London, 1983), now published by Virago (London, 1988) under the title *The Drama of the Child*.

2. Dorothy Rowe, *Beyond Fear* (Fontana, London, 1987).

The greatest fear that we can ever know is that which we feel when our sense of self is threatened, as happens whenever we are treated as an object of no importance, or when the people on whom we depend abandon or reject us, or when we discover that we have got something important quite wrong, or that our life is going out of control. Then we can feel that our self is shat-tering or disappearing.

3. Dorothy Rowe, *Depression: The Way Out of Your Prison* (Routledge, Lon-don, 1983) and *Breaking the Bonds* (Fontana, London, 1991; first published in hardback as *The Depression Handbook*, Collins, London, 1990).

When we are unhappy, we might be suffering great misery, yet we still feel part of the world and close to other people. When we are depressed, we feel that we are cut off from other people by an invisible but impenetrable wall. When we are unhappy, we can still be a good friend to ourselves, and so we are kind to and look after ourselves. When we are depressed, we are unkind to and harshly critical of ourselves. Depression is a feeling of being in a prison where we are both the isolated prisoner and the cruel gaoler.

4. This is one of the themes of my book *Living with the Bomb* (Routledge, London, 1984). See also *Breaking the Bonds*.

5. Elizabeth's story is told in *The Successful Self* (Fontana, London, 1989), pp. 201ff.

Elizabeth had expected that her husband would reward her undoubted com-petence as a wife and mother by appreciating and thus rewarding her, and his failure to do this was one of the major factors in her losing confidence in herself and becoming depressed. Her husband would always thank her for a delicious meal, but he never attempted to understand her feelings, especially how she felt about the way he and his mother had treated her.

6. June's story is told in *The Successful Self*, op. cit. pp. 182ff.

When June lost confidence in herself and became depressed, her need to organize, plan and never act without great preparation and forethought increased. She decided that the way to deal with this was to act spontaneously, so she gave up her job and went to America.

7. T.S. Eliot, 'Burnt Norton' in *Four Quartets* (Faber, London, 1974).

8. In *The Courage to Live* (Fontana, London, 1991; first published in 1982 as *The Construction of Life and Death*), I have described how, when we in childhood discover that we shall die, we have to give death a meaning. Only two mean-ings are possible. Either death is the end of my existence, or it is a doorway to another life. Whichever meaning we choose determines what we see as the

purpose of our life. If we see death as the end of our identity, we have then to make the most of our life in order to feel that it is satisfactory. If we see death as a doorway to another life, we have to decide if there is a possibility that the next life could be better than this life and, if so, whether all people go there or only those who have been sufficiently good. A sense of justice usually leads to the belief that certain standards have to be met to qualify for this pleasant afterlife, and thus those people who believe in life after death have to live this life in terms of the next.

9. Kenneth Williams, quoted in the *Guardian*, 16 April 1988.

10. John Stonehouse, quoted in the *Guardian*, 13 April 1988.

11.

Violence in Aboriginal society took two forms – fighting between adults and infanticide. Violence between adults appears to have been an ever-present feature of Aboriginal life. Men were sometimes violent towards women, individuals of both sexes fought over real or imaginary grievances, as did whole bands or groups, and transgressors against customary laws were sometimes punished violently. It was widely believed in Aboriginal society that only the very young or the very old could die a natural death. If an adult died, the sorcery practised by a hostile group was held to be responsible and had to be revenged with a death. This aspect of reciprocity – of doing unto others what they do unto you – could escalate into a widening pattern of revenge killings which might continue for generations . . .

When bands were on the move and food was scarce, old people no longer able to care for themselves were sometimes reluctantly abandoned to die alone. It is possible that at times of scarcity the level of inter-group conflict could have increased as people fought for access to diminished resources . . .

All hunter-gatherer societies probably practised infanticide. Assessments of its incidence in Australia have varied from infrequently to nearly half of all live births. Deformed or sickly infants were often killed, as were one of twins. A child born too soon after its older brother or sister was unlikely to survive, for a mother would be hard-pressed to provide enough breast milk in the absence of substitute baby food. Furthermore she could not adequately fulfil her gathering role in the family economy if she were forced to carry two pre-toddlers with her on food-collecting expeditions.

(Tony Dingle, *Aboriginal Economy* (McPhee Gribble and Penguin, Fitzroy, Victoria), 1988, pp. 24–5.)

12. In her book *The Drama of the Gifted Child* (pp. 86–8), Alice Miller describes her observations of a young couple out walking with their two-year-old son. The couple had each bought an ice cream bar on a stick, but not one for their son who desperately wanted his own ice cream. His mother offered him a bite of hers, but each time he stretched his hand to hold the stick it was withdrawn. When he cried in frustration his parents laughed at him. The child's distress was immense.

Why were these parents, who in other ways were quite loving to their son, treating him with such contempt? Alice Miller concluded that they themselves had been treated with such contempt when they had been small and weak, and now, powerful, they vented on another small, weak person the contempt which they had once received. In later years, she foresaw, the boy will treat with contempt those whom he sees as weak.

13. I have described this process more fully in my books *Depression: The Way Out of Your Prison, Beyond Fear*, and *The Successful Self*.

14. Alice Miller, *Thou Shalt Not Be Aware* (Virago, London, 1988).

Here Alice Miller shows how the tradition of the child being sacrificed for the parent is a cornerstone of Judaic-Christian society, and how the child not only sacrifices himself but forgets that he has done so.

15. Joseph Needham, *Science and Civilization in China* (Cambridge University Press, Cambridge, 1956).

16. 'Joseph Needham FRS FBA in Conversation with Ronald Eyre', a Programme Enterprises Ltd production for Channel 4, 1988.

17. Lao Tsu, *Tao te Ching*, tr. Gia-Fu Feng and Jane English (Wildwood Press, London, 1974).

> Under heaven all can see beauty as beauty only because
> there is ugliness.
> All can know good as good only because there is evil.
>
> Therefore having and not having arise together.
> Difficult and easy complement each other.
> Long and short contrast each other;
> High and low rest upon each other;
> Front and back follow one another.

18. Peter Biddle, 'Hello Mummy', *Asylum*, vol. 3, no. 1 (1988).
19.
The study of the mind-brain-immune system interaction now has a name – psychoneuroimmunology. One of its chief proponents, Dr John Motl, director of the Centre for Stress Management in Fort Collins, Colorado, explained that the new important ingredient is the psychological or mind aspect and its initiatory role in the process. Hitherto, science was inclined to regard the brain as the primary source of consciousness and the mind as little more than a product of the brain's electro-chemical activity. However, Dr Motl says recent research on brain structure, in particular the work of the neurosurgeon, Wilder Penfield, and of E. Roy John has indicated the reverse: that the mind (or thought) could be interacting with the brain in much the same way as that of a programmer with a computer and that, 'as with most computer systems, the majority of the problems (and solutions) come from the software, not the hardware' . . .

Dr Motl is . . . particularly interested in the long-term effects of stress on the immune system and how people handle their stress. He does not believe cancer is caused wholly and solely by carcinogens: 'people have lived and worked around asbestos all their lives and never got cancer; people have smoked all their lives and never got cancer.' There has to be an internal process going on simultaneously.

'Something is going wrong, and it seems to go wrong when we don't allow the flow to occur between what happens in life and how we feel about it. Instead we tend to suppress. We would like to take action, or tell that person what we think of them, but that's not nice. There's clear data now that when people block emotions and feelings [these emotions and feelings] have to go somewhere, and studying the mechanism of the brain and central nervous system indicated very clearly the pathway taken.

'When stressful input comes into the brain, the limbic system becomes overloaded. Output from this system can follow two pathways: one to the motor part of the brain where we can physically act on the stress, and another to the speech centre where we can talk it out of the system. But if neither of these outlets are used, there's a downflow through the central nervous system into the immune system' . . .

All this could be depressing – one cannot always express one's aggression either verbally or physically – were it not for the fact that Dr Motl cites research that clearly indicates that not only does a positive attitude to stress have a beneficial effect on the immune system, but also mastery of stress actually strengthens it.

(Jillie Collings, 'In the mind's thrall', *Guardian*, 4 August 1988, in the series 'Life Forces', *Guardian*, 1987–9.)

Researchers studying *pain* have long been aware that there is no direct connection between the degree of injury and the degree of pain which is actually felt. Soldiers in the heat of battle can sustain major injuries and not be aware of the pain, while other people find quite minor injuries excruciatingly painful.

What researchers have now established is that across the neural pathways from the periphery of the body to the pain centres of the brain are connections which operate like gates and are now called just that. A gate can be closed, in which case the pain message does not get through; it can be partly open, in which case some of the message gets through; it can be wide open, and the message blasts through. The pain messages go both ways, from the seat of the injury to the brain, and from the brain to the injury. What closes, or partly closes the gates, is emotional states of peace, happiness and contentment. What opens the gates and holds them open are states of anxiety, stress and depression.

In treating people who suffer chronic, intractable pain, neurologists and psychologists teach the patients relaxation and stress management and help the person deal with depression and anxiety. These methods have considerable success, but only with those people who are prepared to take responsibility for themselves.

20. Bill Waterson, 'Calvin and Hobbes' (Sphere, London, 1988), p. 40.
21. George Armstrong, 'Enzo Ferrari: Making his marque', *Guardian*, 16 August 1988.
22. *The Courage to Live, op. cit.*
23. Riana Duncan in Sally Cline and Dale Spender, *Reflecting Men at Twice Their Natural Size* (Fontana, London, 1987).

Chapter 2. 'What's to Stop Me?'
1. David Smail, *Taking Care* (Dent, London, 1987), p. 11.
2. Robin Morgan, *The Demon Lover, op. cit.* p. 125.
3. *Breaking the Bonds, op. cit.* pp. 238–71.
4. In his book *The Emperor's New Mind* (Oxford University Press, Oxford,

1989), Roger Penrose examined the question why we perceive time moving forward, not backward, when, if the mind/brain operates by physical laws, such laws, being symmetric, should enable us to perceive time symmetrically, going backwards and forwards. He argues that the answer lies in quantum gravity which operated when the Big Bang occurred and time went forward but not backward.

Our perception of the forward motion of time is more than the functioning of a physical law.

The philosopher Immanuel Kant believed that the concept of time is a prior condition of our minds that affects our experience of the world, but this does not explain why different societies have had different concepts of time and have assigned different degrees of significance to the temporal aspect of phenomena. It is now coming to be realized that, instead of being a prior condition, our concept of time should be regarded as a consequence of our experience of the world, the result of a long evolution. The human mind has the power, apparently not possessed by animals, to construct the idea of time from our awareness of certain features characterizing the data of our experience. Although Kant threw no light on the origin of this power, he realized that it was a peculiarity of the human mind. In recent years it has become clear that all our mental abilities are potential capacities which we can only realize in practice by learning how to use them. For, whereas animals inherit particular patterns of sensory awareness, known as releasers because they automatically initiate certain types of action, humans have to learn to construct their patterns of awareness from their own experience. Consequently, our ideas of space and time, which according to Kant function as if they were releasers, must be regarded as mental constructs that have to be learned.

(G.W. Whitrow, *Time in History* (Oxford University Press, Oxford, 1988), p. 186.)

5. Leo Braudy, *The Frenzy of Renown* (Oxford University Press, Oxford, 1986), p. 10.

6. Ann Hocking, personal communication, 1988.

7. See *The Successful Self, op. cit.* pp. 123–5.

8. Joseph Needham, *Science and Civilization in China, op. cit.* vol. 2.

9. Karl Popper, lecture given to the World Congress of Philosophy, Brighton, 24 August 1988, reported in the *Guardian*, 29 August 1988.

10. Werner Heisenberg, *Physics and Philosophy* (Allen and Unwin, London, 1971).

11. Karl Popper, lecture (as above).

12.

Every scientist who turned to chaos early had a story to tell of discouragement or open hostility. Graduate students were warned that their careers could be jeopardized if they wrote theses in an untested discipline, in which their advisors had no expertise. A particle physicist, hearing about this new mathematics, might begin playing with it on his own, thinking that it was a beautiful thing, both beautiful and hard – but would feel that he could never tell his colleagues about it. Older professors felt they were suffering a kind of midlife crisis, gambling on a line of research that many of their colleagues were likely to misunderstand or resent . . .

Many mainstream scientists remained only dimly aware of the emerging science. Some, particularly traditional fluid dynamicists, actively resented it. At first, the claims made on behalf of chaos sounded wild and unscientific. And chaos relied on mathematics that seemed unconventional and difficult.

(James Gleick, *Chaos: Making a New Science* (Cardinal, London, 1988), pp. 38, 39.)

13. Martin Walker, 'Vanishing sea threatens ecological disaster', *Guardian*, 18 April 1988.

14. William Millinship, 'Russia: Go green or die', *Observer*, 16 July 1989.

15. Vicky Rippere, 'Behavioural treatment of depression in historical perspective', in S. Rachman (ed.), *Contributions to Medical Psychology*, vol. 2 (Pergamon Press, Oxford and New York, 1980), pp. 31–54.

16.

Arnold Mandell, the San Diego psychiatrist and dynamicist [asked]: 'Is it possible that mathematical pathology, i.e., chaos, is health? And that mathematical health, which is the predictability and differentiability of this kind of structure, is a disease?' . . . 'When you reach equilibrium in biology you're dead,' he said. 'If I ask you whether your brain is an equilibrium system, all I have to ask you to do is ask you not to think of elephants for a few minutes, and you *know* it isn't an equilibrium system.'

To Mandell, the discoveries of chaos dictate a shift in clinical approaches to treating psychiatric disorders. By any objective measure, the modern business of 'psychopharmacology' – the use of drugs to treat everything from anxiety and insomnia to schizophrenia itself – has to be judged a failure. Few patients, if any, are cured. The most violent manifestations of mental illness can be controlled, but with what long-term consequences, no one knows. Mandell offered his colleagues a chilling assessment of the most commonly used drugs. Phenothiazines, prescribed for schizophrenics, make the fundamental disorder worse. Tricyclic antidepressants 'increase the rate of mood cycling, leading to long-term increases in numbers of relapsing psychopathologic episodes,' and so on. Only lithium has any real medical success, Mandell said, and only for some disorders.

As he saw it, the problem was conceptual. Traditional methods for treating this 'most unstable, dynamic, infinite-dimensional machine' were linear and reductionist. 'The underlying paradigm remains: one gene ‹ra› one peptide ‹ra› one enzyme ‹ra› one neurotransmitter ‹ra› one receptor ‹ra› one animal behaviour ‹ra› one clinical syndrome ‹ra› one drug ‹ra› one clinical rating scale. It dominates almost all research and treatment in psychopharmacology. More than 50 transmitters, thousands of cell types, complex electromagnetic phenomonology, and continuous instability based on autonomous activity at all levels, from proteins to the electroencephalogram – and still the brain is thought of as a chemical point-to-point switchboard.' To someone exposed to the world of nonlinear dynamics the response could only be: How naive.

(James Gleick, *Chaos: Making a New Science, op. cit.* pp. 298–9.)

17. Cystic fibrosis is 'an uncommon hereditary defect of numerous glands,

369

including the mucous glands of the bronchi, the sweat glands, and the digestive glands. It is a recessive character – both parents carry the abnormal gene without showing the signs of the disease and there is a 4:1 chance that a child of the marriage will inherit the gene from both parents and develop cystic fibrosis.'

Peter Wingate, *The Penguin Medical Encyclopaedia* (Penguin, London, 1989).

18. See *Breaking the Bonds, op. cit.* pp. 325–368.

The American Association for the Advancement of Science Conference in February, 1990, was told:

Mental illnesses are proving more stubborn to molecular analysis than the first results over recent years suggested.

Dr Kenneth Kidd of Yale University told the meeting that the discovery three years ago of a genetic marker on chromosome 11 linked to the development of manic depression in a large extended family has failed to stand up. 'The possibility of a single marker for manic depression has turned out to be too optimistic,' he said . . . 'If there are two or three major genes involved we should be able to identify them, but if there are many minor ones we may never find them' . . .

And even if reliable linkages are found in mental illnesses, Dr Kidd said that researchers were only just at the borderline of knowing what to do with such controversial findings. 'Genes are clearly involved in predisposing people to develop mental illnesses, but there are other important factors. One of a pair of identical twins can develop mental illness and the other not.'

(Nigel Williams, 'Setback to genetic depression theory', *Guardian*, 19 February 1990.)

The genetic case for schizophrenia rests almost entirely upon twin and adoption studies . . . The most important and oft quoted of the twin studies, that of Kallmann . . . reported concordance rates of 86 and 15 percent for monozygotic and dizygotic twins, respectively. Yet it emerged, after Kallmann's death, that a variety of arbitrary statistical and diagnostic correction factors had masked original rates of 50 and 6 percent . . . Kallmann was deeply committed both to a biological psychiatry and to eugenics, and . . . he was a firm believer in a genetic model long before carrying out his twin research. The ways in which he dealt with two crucial variables in which he was interested, diagnosis and zygosity, both far from objective assessments, render even Kallmann's 50 and 6 percent most doubtful, especially as he did not take even the elementary precaution of obtaining the services of a disinterested assessor . . .

In the past decade it has been the Danish adoption studies which have been widely cited as definitive evidence of a major genetic component in schizophrenia. Yet several careful critiques seriously caution acceptance of such enthusiasm . . . They conclude that the weaknesses are so obvious that it is difficult to understand how distinguished scientists could have regarded them as eliminating all the artefacts which beset family and twin studies of nature and nurture.

(Richard Marshall, 'The role of ideology in the individualization of distress', *The Psychologist*, February 1988, p. 67.)

19. Such elitism is shown in Aristotle's views on economic thought. J.K. Galbraith in *A History of Economics* (Hamish Hamilton, London, 1987, p. 11) wrote:

As was true in Athens and in Greek cities generally, because slaves did the work, labour had a derogatory aspect that helped to exclude it from scholarly examination. The ethical justification of slavery and the terms of the treatment of slaves became, instead, the interesting questions, as in this defence of the institution by Aristotle: 'The lower sort are by nature slaves, and it is better for them as for all inferiors that they should be under the rule of a master . . . Indeed the use made of slaves and of tame animals is not very different.'

Galbraith went on in a footnote:

Aristotle adds, 'It is clear, then, that some men are by nature free, and others slaves, and that for these latter slavery is both expedient and right.' He was, it may be observed, equally certain as regards women. 'Again, the male is by nature superior, and the female inferior; and the one rules, and the other is ruled; this principle, of necessity, extends to all mankind.' Returning to lecture in a modern university or to receive an honorary degree, Aristotle would be accorded a somewhat qualified welcome.

Galbraith was writing in the USA. In the UK Aristotle would be accorded a warm welcome by the right-wing economists who flourish here.

20. 'View from the bottom', *Psychiatric Bulletin*, 14, 1990, p. 454.

21. *Ibid.* p. 453.

22. Alleen Ballantyne, 'Cancer patient shuttled round for treatment', *Guardian*, 19 August 1988.

23. Christopher Hill, *History and the Present* (South Place Ethical Society, London, 1989), p. 26.

24. For a fuller discussion of how we create our world of meaning, see the first three chapters of my *Choosing Not Losing* (Fontana, London, 1988).

25. J. Mark G. Williams, *The Psychological Treatment of Depression* (Croom Helm, London, 1986), p. 1.

26. Dagobert D. Runes (ed.), *The Dictionary of Philosophy* (Routledge, London, 1945).

27. Martin Herbert, *Caring for Your Children: A Practical Guide* (Basil Blackwell, Oxford, 1985), p. 28.

28. J. Mark G. Williams, *op. cit.*, p. 85.

29. *Ibid.* pp. 36, 111.

30. *Ibid.* p. 113.

31. *Ibid.* p. 119.

32. A.T. Beck, A.J. Shaw, B.F. Rush and G. Emery, *Cognitive Therapy of Depression* (Wiley, New York, 1979).

Beck *et al.* list as one of the objections a patient may have to cognitive therapy as: 'Cognitive therapy is concerned with mundane things in life and not with the serious problems that make me depressed.' They advise, 'The patient has to understand that cognitive therapy concentrates on concrete incidents because it is easy to get lost in rhetoric and metaphysical ideas . . . Many of these philosophical issues (Who am I? Where am I going? What is existence all about?) may appear irrelevant, but if they are important to the patients, they should be discussed eventually.' Just how the therapist should do this is not revealed. Beck *et al.* do not discuss death, loss or religion.

Gary Emery in his *Getting Un-Depressed* (Touchstone, New York, 1988) does talk about the death of a loved one by describing 'grief reaction' and advising, 'Your overall goal is normalization of your life so that you can get on with living as happily and productively as possible.' He gives as an example Mildred Lane 'who couldn't get over her depression until she came to terms with her grief over her husband's death. They'd been married for forty-two years. In normal reaction you reconcile the loss of an important part of your past with the need to move on without that person. Most people get through this painful process. Others, who hold certain beliefs that turn grief into depression, don't. In Mildred's case her beliefs were related to helplessness. She found comfort simply in talking about her irrational ideas, such as her anger at her husband for dying. What finally helped Mildred was concluding that her husband wasn't completely gone because he's left an important part of him with her. With realization that he would want her to get on with her life and not get bogged down in depression, she became more self-reliant.'(p. 232)

Presumably the important part of himself that her husband had left her was not his fortune or some bodily relic but her memory of him. Surely imputing to her internal representation of her husband the wish that she got on with her life is just as irrational, or rational, as getting angry with this internal representation?

All the families, friends and lovers who feature in the vignettes given by cognitive therapists in their books respond predictably and benignly once the patients abandon their irrational cognitions in favour of the ones which the therapist regards as rational. This always amazes me, because all the depressed people I have known have families, friends and lovers who behave like people, that is, they can be cantankerous and vindictive, especially when they want to punish the depressed person for the bad times which they have had to endure, and, even when they are at their most benign and cooperative, when faced with change they are unpredictable.

Cognitive therapists, like psychiatrists and psychoanalysts, prefer to ignore the complexity of our social, political and economic environment from which we can never detach ourselves.

33. J.K. Galbraith, *A History of Economics, op. cit.* p. 1.

34. Andrew T. Scull, *Museums of Madness* (Penguin, Harmondsworth, 1982).

35. The profession of psychology has flourished due to two world wars. Up to the First World War, officers in the British army came from the upper classes, but the death of so many officers in the trenches led to an urgent need to find young men from the lower classes who had the intelligence and aptitude to be army officers. This led psychologists to develop their theories of intelligence and the tests to go with them. In the Second World War, intelligence and aptitude testing was the major activity of psychologists. The welfare of children caught up in that war became an issue, and some important work was done in looking at how small children formed affectional bonds with the people who cared for them and what happened to children who had no opportunity to form such bonds. However, after the war this research was interpreted to mean that any mother who went out to work was putting her child at risk. This was just the message that the then government wanted, since

men returning from the war expected to take over the jobs which women had done during the war. In times of full employment, as in the sixties, psychological theories and research about the child-parent bond no longer stressed the importance of a mother staying at home. However, once unemployment became an issue, research started to appear showing the wide range of problems that women would incur if they insisted on working and competing with men. At the same time there was research which purported to show that unemployment had no deleterious physical or psychological effects.

36. Fiona Buckland, 1990.

37.

Inhumanity apart, in the area of political short-sightedness, the South African Government must score top marks for alienating the very people upon whom it will soon be dependent: its neighbourhood states and, inside South Africa, a generation of disillusioned and brutalized black children who, one day, will produce its future government. Since the 1986 State of Emergency more than 8,000 children have been detained. Most are never charged. The South African Detainees' Support estimate that only 25 percent of detainees are brought to court and fewer than 5 percent convicted. Under the 1983 Child Care Act, no child under 18 may go to prison. A submission to the courts last year stating that Parliament could not have intended that the State President, in exercising powers under the Public Safety Act, could permit the arrest of young children was thrown out. The court held that the State President had such power. Children are given no special protection under the Emergency regulations. Since the 1976 Soweto uprising, black children have been at the forefront of the apartheid conflict and the government's efforts to weaken their increasing politicization have grabbed headlines. The effects on children in the frontline states who have, along with other civilians, been specific targets in South Africa's strategy of destabilization on its borders have been less well reported . . . The effects on children of apartheid's war for survival is the subject of a documentary made by Toni Strasburg in which the children speak for themselves. Some are in refugee camps, some in hospitals, some in special emotional rehabilitation centres and some fending for themselves in the streets. Thousands are orphans – their parents killed, kidnapped or simply lost. Many have lost limbs to land mines. Others talk of seeing their parents shot or hacked to death. One child speaks of being forced to shoot people, another of turning his gun on his captors and killing them before running away. Two South African children tell of solitary confinement, electric shock torture and being shut in a refrigerator for half an hour at a time . . . Concerning the children who have survived, Toni Strasburg echoes the view of Mozambican Education Minister, Graca Machel: 'If you brutalize children, there's not much chance of reclaiming them. They're probably like that for life and these are the children who are going to run governments and become engineers and scientists. What kind of people will they be?'

(Wendy Woods, 'In front of the children', *Guardian*, 2 January 1989. Toni Strasburg's film, *Chain of Tears*, was broadcast on Channel 4, 3 January 1989.)

Andrew Dawes, a psychologist at Cape Town University, has been studying the effects of political violence on children. He wrote:

In South Africa, following teargassing and beating of school children by security forces, games of 'comrades vs boere' (police) are frequent. A plastic gun is often referred to as an A.K.47 and the targets of aggression are commonly 'boere' or white politicians. In families of political activists with whom I have worked clinically, children are sometimes named after political leaders in the African National Congress. This way of naming the child is a political act and is instrumental in constructing the child's political subjectivity from birth. In the homes of these political activists politics is central and the child is continually exposed to a powerful language of struggle, heroism and of course polarized orientations to the state and its agents. In this situation political role models are personal and it is likely they will be a powerful source of identification for their children . . .

Young political detainees in South Africa have reported that their political resolve has been strengthened by imprisonment. Prison cells have often become sites of political education particularly during times of mass arrests. Anger at the states coupled with heightened group solidarity under such conditions seems to increase political identification . . .

Beyond short-term reactions, children who have good family or community support are not likely, as a rule, to show clinical disturbance. This is however dependent on the type and duration of the stress and as those take on more serious proportions, clinical disturbance can result . . . One of the reasons that more children are apparently not damaged in large numbers by political violence, might be that this adversity is given a positive meaning by the community. It transforms people from 'victims' to 'fighters' as a means of building community resilience and binding them to a political cause. A related reason for the apparently low 'damage rate' . . . is that after a time, political violence is no longer exceptional but a normal backdrop to society. It is one of those things with which one has to cope and despite periodic mayhem, ordinary life goes on.

('The effects of political violence on children: a consideration of South African and related studies', *International Journal of Psychology*, 25, 1990, pp. 24–7.)

38. See note 19, Chapter 1.

Jacob Empson describes how dreaming probably 'has a positive function in the learning process' in *Sleep and Dreaming* (Faber, London, 1989).

39. *The Successful Self*, *op. cit.* pp. 60–70.

40. For a fuller discussion of this see *Beyond Fear*, *op. cit.*

41. Jessica Hobby Catto, 'What befalls the planet befalls all of us', *Guardian*, 31 July 1989.

42. Garry Trudeau, *Doonesbury*, Weekend *Guardian*, 24 February 1990.

43. Posy Simmonds, 'Seven Bounden Duties', *Guardian*, 4 March 1988.

44. By 'the State' I mean not just the elected government but all the people who wield power, even though they might not necessarily support the elected government. In Britain many of these people form a group called the Establishment. Writing about the Establishment, Richard Norton-Taylor said:

The word was first used in print by Henry Fairlie, political columnist of the *Spectator* (in 1955). Describing the cover-up over the defection of Burgess and Maclean, Fairlie wrote: 'What I call the Establishment in this country is even more powerful than ever before. By the Establishment I do not mean only the centres of official power though they are certainly part of it – but rather the whole matrix of official and social relations within which power is exercised.

The Establishment is normally taken to mean those who enjoy power and influence at the national level, people with shared values – and a shared assumption that they matter.

A significant part of the Establishment is the Civil Service. Successive prime ministers and cabinet ministers have tried, usually in vain, to limit the power of the Civil Service, not least Mrs Thatcher. Richard Norton-Taylor wrote:

The higher reaches of the Civil Service, the Whitehall mandarinate, have been the very heart of the Establishment for most of this century. Senior civil servants have decided who should be on the list of the Great and the Good – an index of existing and potential members of the Establishment – and which of them should be appointed to commissions, quangos, and sundry public bodies. (The Public Appointments Unit, which holds a central list of about 5,000 men and women who have expressed an interest in these posts, is run by civil servants.)

To its critics, the senior Civil Service is a cosy, protected elite, an oligarchy that perpetuates itself through the secret deliberations of the Senior Appointments Selection Committee, where the mandarins choose their successors . . . To its defenders, the Civil Service remains the repository of settled values in an uncertain world. The mandarin tries to promote consensus through consultations with different groups in society. He (women are few and far between in this world) is concerned about the common good, and represents the common ground. He believes in self-restraint, impartiality ('equality of misery' is often said to be one of the Treasury's guiding principles), incorruptibility, recruitment through fair and open competition . . . [Under Mrs Thatcher] the mandarins might have been forced to change their culture, to adopt more managerial skills and imbibe more business culture. But for the moment, the structure of the Whitehall establishment remains in place, together with their trademarks – above all – official secrecy – which happens to coincide with Mrs Thatcher's.

(*Guardian*, 13 September 1989.)

For all the apparent power of the elected government and the Establishment, 'He that pays the piper calls the tune,' and the people who decide what piper will be paid are the men heading the huge financial institutions which create and control the wealth of each country. These financial institutions are international, and so the effects of power which we as individuals feel arise from decisions made, not at Westminster, but in the financial centres of Tokyo and New York. Thus a Minister of Health might wish to reduce the number of deaths caused by nicotine, but will be unable to carry out any effective measure to eradicate smoking because such actions would reduce the profits of the tobacco industry. The Labour Party, out of office, might devote much time and effort developing a policy aimed at reducing spending on the military and its armaments, but once in office they will find themselves in conflict with the most wealthy and influential of the financial institutions, the armament manufacturers who supply not just arms but the sophisticated instruments of torture to all sides involved in conflict. The international armaments industry has a strong base in Britain, and any elected British government, Conservative, Labour or Green, is dependent on it to help balance imports against exports.

Our elected parliamentary system gives us the illusion that we live in a democracy. But here, at least, it is possible for a person of limited financial means to take part in this system and be elected to high office. In the USA only multimillionaires with multimillionaire friends can afford to play this game.

Paddy Hillyard and Janie Percy-Smith, in their book *The Coercive State* (Fontana, London, 1988), wrote:

> No one in Britain today lives beyond the reach of the state. In its numerous different guises it intervenes in all our lives. For some the state provides employment – in nationalized industries, the National Health Service and civil service; for others it regulates the conditions of their employment, through factory inspectors, wages councils and industrial tribunals. The state both 'gives' cash in the shape of social security payments, tax allowances, educational grants and subsidies to industry, and takes it away through taxation, rates and fines. The state selectively recognizes and meets certain needs, for example, education, health care and housing. It regulates the environment, through building and planning regulations and pollution controls. The state is a disseminator of information through government publications, official statements, 'leaks' and the education system and has power to control the flow of information from other sources such as newspapers, radio and television. In the guise of government the state determines policy; in Parliament it formally legislates for it; through the civil service, local authorities and a range of other public and private bodies, policy is implemented. Those who break the laws of the state are judged and sentenced in the courts, and through the penal system they are punished. The state defends its territorial integrity using armed forces and internally maintains itself through police and security services.(p. 13.)

They conclude their study by saying:

> Throughout this book the picture we have tried to present is of a country which is divided and ruled. There is a small minority with both wealth and political power; those who work enjoy a reasonable standard of living, who form part of the 'property and share-owning democracy'; and those with no money and no political power either. It is this latter group, the poorest and most vulnerable, who are subject particularly to state coercion. The fact that the state's coercive powers have increased at the same time as economic recession has deepened and unemployment increased is no coincidence. It is much harder to convince those who live on the margins of society that they have a stake in the present system and therefore have no cause to protest . . .
>
> Instead of a liberal democratic society we have described a society where classification, surveillance, control and punishment are the dominant features. For many people, securing the basic necessities of life like a roof over their head or money to buy food is dependent on giving the state increasing amounts of personal information. Giving 'wrong' infor-

mation – unacceptable information – can result in the withholding of benefits or offers of housing. Alternatively, it can be used as a means of coercing claimants into altering their behaviour – moral, social, economic and, in some cases, political. At the same time, many more people have been pulled into the criminal justice net and subjected to a range of restrictions and punishments . . .

The coercive aspects of the state will not be eradicated by petty reforms. It will not be enough to make the police more accountable, to pass a freedom of information act, to change the electoral system or to abolish means-tested benefits. These features of the contemporary state, although not instituted in line with some grand master plan, are not accidental either. They have developed piecemeal fashion as those with political and economic power have sought to retain their control in the face of threats – real and imagined – from ordinary people. At times, when their position has felt relatively secure, they have been prepared to loosen the reins slightly and we have seen the passing of progressive legislation and the enlargement of personal liberty. At other times, especially during periods of economic recession, measures are instituted which have the effect of not only reducing the standard of living for ordinary people but also reducing their personal liberties. The loss of rights and liberties associated with liberal democracy is important, if for no other reason than because, without them, political dissent and opposition become more difficult and dangerous.(pp. 320–23.)

Chapter 3. *'You Can't Have Everything'* – Society

1. Robert van de Weyer, 'A landslide for heretics?', *Guardian*, 22 July 1989.
2. Adrian Love, BBC Radio 2.
3. Robert van de Weyer, 'A landslide for heretics?', *op. cit*. For a fuller account see Robert van de Weyer's book *The Call to Heresy*, (Lamp Press, London, 1989).
4. George Steiner, *The Death of Tragedy* (Faber, London, 1974).
5. Aldous Huxley, *Brave New World* (Chatto & Windus, London, 1932), p. 259.
6. *Ibid*. p. 20.
7.

This type of intellectual conceit, which manifests itself in a truculent incomprehension of anything which might be described as artistically new or different, is a persistent feature of the English literary scene. You could detect it in the pronouncements of the late Miss Marghanita Laski on the contemporary novel, you can detect it in the editorials of the *Literary Review*, in the young people who seek to explain critical theory to the readers of the Sunday newspapers. Increasingly it can be decried in the newspaper attacks on 'intellectuals', on querulous writers who decline to support Mrs Thatcher, on pinkish film makers who persist in depicting Britain as an 'authoritarian rat-hole' to use Hanif Kureishi's phrase. On the face of it these assaults on the type of writer who signs an advertisement in the *Guardian* look like a political quarrel, the unconsidered reaction of the Right to woolly-minded liberalism, but the disagreement runs deeper than this. It is a symptom of the much broader dislike of 'cleverness', however displayed or expressed, which has been a feature of English cultural life for decades.

There is nothing very new in this peevish belittling of intellect. Always in England if you had the type of brain that was capable of understanding T.S. Eliot's poetry or Kant's logic, you could be sure of finding large numbers of people who would hate you violently for that dexterity.

(D.J.Taylor, *A Vain Conceit* (Bloomsbury, London, 1989), quoted in the *Guardian*, 15 September 1989.)

8. Robert Ornstein and Paul Erlich, *New World, New Mind* (Doubleday, New York, 1989).

9. Robert Ornstein interview in *USA Today*, 25 January 1989.

10. To assess probabilities with some degree of accuracy, we need to have access to information and a preference for scepticism over gullibility. Despite the lack of sound scientific evidence for the existence of phenomena which are called 'paranormal', many people still believe in precognition, telepathy, clairvoyance, psychokinesis and, most of all, astrology.

Christopher French is a psychologist who has looked at the differences between those who believe in the paranormal and those who do not. He calls these two groups the sheep and the goats. He wrote:

It is possible that cognitive biases within our information processing systems lead to misinterpretation of certain kinds of situation which may be wrongly perceived by the observer as only being interpretable in terms of psi (the paranormal) where in fact normal physical and psychological explanations may be quite adequate . . .

Langer presented a series of studies demonstrating what she called the 'illusion of control', i.e., a tendency for subjects to perceive a random process as being potentially under their control. This tendency is increased if the situation seems to incorporate elements of skill. For example, subjects rate their chances of success in a raffle as higher if they picked their own raffle ticket rather than having one allocated at random even though the objective probabilities are identical. Ayeroff and Abelson explored the implications of this theory with respect to perceived success of an ESP (extrasensory perception) task. They found that factors which seemed to imply that skill was involved in the task, such as a warm-up session and allowing the subjects to choose the cards to be used, increased the perception by the subjects that they were performing at higher than chance levels, even though in fact they were not . . . Blackmore and Troscianko found that sheep (were) more subject to the illusion of control even on tasks which did not overtly involve psi . . .

People are notoriously poor at estimating probabilities. For example, if asked, 'How many people would you need at a party to have a 50:50 chance that two of them have the same birthday (ignoring the year)?', most people are surprised to learn that the answer is 23. It follows that if people do not appreciate how likely a particular event is on a chance basis alone (e.g., a precognitive dream 'coming true'), they may be reluctant to accept an explanation which says that it was just a coincidence and prefer a paranormal explanation. Blackmore and Troscianko presented subjects with various probability estimation problems and found that sheep generally performed worse than goats, sometimes significantly so

. . . Alcock and Otis produced evidence suggesting that sheep were less able to think critically and were more dogmatic than goats . . . A number of studies have been reported which suggest that believers may be more prone to distort evidence to support their viewpoint than nonbelievers . . .

One is reminded of an incident involving James Randi who has done a great deal to debunk the likes of Uri Geller by showing that he can do all the same stunts by skilful conjuring. At one of his performances, as he revealed the techniques used by Geller to achieve his effects, an enraged member of the audience stood up and shouted, 'You're a fraud!' Randi calmly replied that, yes, of course he was a fraud, and that his intention was to reveal how Geller performs his stunts fraudulently. 'No, no. I don't mean that!' replied the man. 'You've really got psychic powers and you're pretending that you haven't!'

Another situation which is commonly misinterpreted as involving paranormal powers, but in fact does not, is the demonstration of population stereotypes. If a group of subjects are told that a number, say, between one and ten is to be telepathically transmitted to them and that they are to write down the first number that comes into their minds, their responses will be far from randomly distributed. In fact, '7' will be by far the most popular response regardless of the number that the 'sender' had in mind. Similar effects are found using other types of target (e.g., simple line drawings). Marks and Kammann present convincing evidence for the existence of such population stereotypes and for the claim that stage psychics such as Geller exploit such effects. Grimmer and White confirmed Marks and Kammann's results.

In his own study of how the sheep and the goats assessed the probability of the presence of ESP, Christopher French included a debriefing session in which he explained to the research subjects what had actually gone on in the experiment. He found that some of the sheep then revised their probabilities that ESP had actually occurred (after all, they were psychology students) but, 'It should be noted that throughout all stages of assessment, including the debriefing, the high-belief group rated the demonstration more highly than the low-belief group in terms of the probability that it did involve ESP.' ('Belief in the paranormal: do sheep and goats process information differently?' Paper given at the Annual Conference of the British Psychological Society, 1990.)

Just how reluctant we are to assess probabilities is shown in the study of twins adopted and brought up entirely separately. Our media often carry stories about such twins who, meeting as adults, are amazed to find that they have many features of their lives in common. Such phenomena is seized upon by those who wish to show that nature always triumphs over nurture. However, each item on the list of similarities is not subjected to a test of probability.

Suppose twin boys, adopted at birth, growing up without knowledge of the other, meet on their thirtieth birthday. They discover that they are both Catholics, they have each married a woman called Mary, they have named their children Teresa and Kevin, and they are each passionately interested in football. What are the differences in probabilities if

a) one had been adopted by a working-class family in Liverpool and one by a working-class family in Belfast?

b) one had been adopted by an upper-middle-class family in Basingstoke and one by a Mormon family in Salt Lake City?

See John Allen Paulos, *Innumeracy* (Penguin, Harmondsworth, 1990).

11. *Back to the Edge*, 'Everyman' series, BBC TV, 1989.

12. Joe La Fatch's story is told in *Breaking the Bonds*, pp. 290–2.

13.

Freedom may be breaking out in the rest of the world, but the US government is doing all it can to fence in Texas bass fisherman Dan Snow and Akron-area Vietnam veterans John Myers and Don Mills. While East Germans travel freely through what was once the Berlin Wall, Snow's sitting at home in Kingwood, Texas, facing up to 50 years in prison and a $250,000 fine for arranging fishing trips to Cuba. In Akron, Myers and Mills have been warned that they could be fined $50,000 and sent to prison for 10 years if they keep arranging return trips to Vietnam for their fellow veterans.

Today a House subcommittee will discuss legislation stripping President Bush of the authority to impose travel restrictions authorized under the Trading with the Enemy Act, which gives a president authority to impose sanctions, including travel sanctions, on countries hostile to US interests.

Snow doesn't expect a quick passage of the legislation, sponsored by Rep. Howard Berman, D-Calif. Rep. Tom Sawyer, D-Akron, who has helped Mills and Myers, is a co-sponsor . . .

Travel to Cuba is even more restricted than to Vietnam. Individuals may go to Vietnam, but it's against the law to arrange group visits, even if, like Mills and Myers, trip sponsors aren't trying to make a profit. Travel to Cuba is strictly limited to family visits, government business, newsgathering and research . . .

So far [Mills and Myers] have arranged for more than 200 veterans to return to Vietnam. One of them is Joseph La Fatch, 41, of Akron, who's scheduled to testify today. La Fatch said he returned home from Vietnam in 1967 with a Purple Heart, shrapnel in his right arm and right leg and a festering hatred for the Vietnamese. The Army paratrooper was injured and six friends were killed in a grenade attack. When he returned in 1988, he noticed scars on his Vietnamese guide and thought, 'This guy looks like a soldier.' It turned out, La Fatch said, that the guide had been injured in an American attack similar to the Vietnamese assault on La Fatch and his friends. The trip provided an opportunity for him to replace the images he had of Vietnam as a hostile place with images of a timeless, peaceful, rural place. 'It's not the bogeyman any more,' La Fatch said. 'It's just another place.'

(William Hershey, 'Panel considers ban on power to restrict travel', *Beacon Journal*, 13 March 1990.)

In a letter to me in September 1990, Joe said, 'Our Akron Chapter is being audited by the Internal Revenue Service, a branch of the US Treasury! Probably just a coincidence, eh?'

14. David Hearst, writing about the educational reforms in Northern Ireland, began with a story which illustrates how the rigidly divided educational system produces some remarkable depths of ignorance:

During the long hot summer of 1986, when Loyalist opposition to the Anglo-Irish Agreement meant a riot at least every Saturday night, a local journalist found himself outside an Orange Hall in the border town of Keady. The main street was cut off by a line of RUC Land Rovers and the Apprentice Boys of Derry were trying to hammer, stone and burn their way through.

Suddenly, the door of the hall opened and a hand emerged to pull the reporter inside. He thought his last hour had come, but instead he was hauled in front of a big mural, depicting the drowning of the Protestants by Catholics in the River Bann in 1641.

'That's what the lot of them did to us, and it's true because it was painted from a photograph.'

With history lessons like these, who needs a national curriculum?

David Hearst went on:

The second main plank of the reforms is the introduction of Education for Mutual Understanding and Cultural Heritage as themes in a curriculum on which every pupil will be tested. What these lofty phrases actually mean in practice has yet to be clearly defined.

Their clearest application is in the subject of history. While many head-teachers in the state sector would vociferously challenge the assertion that they run 'Protestant' schools, a Protestant education is fairly easy to define. Traditionally, it avoids any serious mention of Irish history, or even geography. Events in the far reaches of the pink map of the British Empire would be more familiar to them than events down the road.

The historian's point is not that each community has a profound ignorance of the rival's history, but of its own as well. The truth of William of Orange's relationship with the Pope of his day is unaddressed, while the subject itself is abandoned to folklore and gable end murals.

The need to redress the balance of the history curriculum, which has traditionally stopped at 1921 and avoids all mention of events since 1969, speaks for itself. But the change poses large problems for the teacher. No teaching materials on the Troubles exist and, according to the body responsible for assessing the subject, the Northern Ireland Schools Examination and Assessment Council, any thought of how to assess 'education for mutual understanding' is at the moment very premature.

The largest teachers' union, the Ulster Teachers' Union, supports any measure to improve mutual understanding, but says: 'Teachers are now legally required to assume a role which others – successive governments, politicians, churches and community leaders – have attempted with little success.'

Unlike in Britain, the Government is prepared to throw money at the problem. An extra £83 million on a budget which is set at nearly £1 billion is to be made available for the reforms. But teachers will still be beset by most of the problems experienced in enforcing the common curriculum and GCSE, as well as having to cope with the added dimension of local attitudes, which are fundamentally politically inspired.

As one teachers put it: 'If you are born, educated, work, marry into,

Notes

die and are buried in one community, what chance has a school got to change you?'
(*Guardian*, 20 February 1990.)

15. Project Censored, Sonoma State University, California, USA, is:

an annual national media research project with an innovative approach which hopes to improve print and broadcast journalism. The basic question is whether the news media provide the public with all the information it needs to make informed decisions. If not, it is suggested that much citizen alienation from public life and citizen apathy may be explained by a lack of reliable and usable information on critical issues.
Criteria for 'Censored' Stories
1. The story must concern a subject that should be known by a majority of the people but has not received sufficient coverage and exposure by the major news media. While the story may not have been 'censored' in the traditional sense of the word, it may have been overlooked, ignored, or under-reported by the news media.
2. The amount of coverage the story received must be minimal (determined in part through the *New York Times Index*, the *Los Angeles Times Index*, the *Magazine Index*, the *Newspaper Index*, the *Reader's Guide to Periodicals*, etc.)
3. The potential effects of a story must be of major significance, affecting a large number of people, as opposed to being of a minor concern affecting just a few people.
(Project Censored pamphlet.)
16. *Guardian*, 15 June 1989.
17.
Efforts to clean up continue three years after the Chernobyl nuclear disaster and threaten to bankrupt the Soviet republic of Byelorussia, according to the official newsagency Tass. It reported this week that the clean-up operations after the world's worst nuclear accident had failed to eliminate the dangerous effects of nuclear radiation across a third of the republic, and that another 100,000 people would have to relocated. Tass put the cost of the proposed removal at more than 10 billion roubles (almost £10 billion), roughly equal to Byelorussia's annual budget.
'If clean-up operations are carried out by the republic on its own, Byelorussia's economic and social development will grind to a halt for several years,' Mr Vladimir Yevtukh, the chairman of the republic's Chernobyl commission, told Tass . . .
At least 100,000 people were evacuated from the Ukraine and Byelorussia immediately after the explosion and fire at Chernobyl on 26 April, 1986, which killed 31 people and sent clouds of radioactive material across Europe. Local residents have accused officials of dragging their feet in the cleaning and relocation operations and of minimizing the effects of the accident. Doctors, they say, have been ordered not to blame Chernobyl for a regional upsurge in cancer and other illnesses, thereby limiting government liability and special pensions.
(*Guardian*, 23 August 1989.)

18.

Workers at the Three Mile Island nuclear plant near Harrisburg, PA, have found two marks that could be cracks in the bottom of the reactor vessel. The discovery of such cracks in the five-inch-thick carbon steel vessel would indicate that the accident in March, 1979 was much more serious than previously believed. Nuclear plants are not built to cope with the failure of the reactor vessel. Evidence of the seriousness of the accident has grown since the clean-up began. More extensive melting of the nuclear core has become more obvious after workers opened the vessel. There has been no conclusive evidence that the accident threatened to proceed to the next step, with the molten core escaping from the vessel. But researchers said last week that the marks, which have been observed with a black and white video camera, might not be in the vessel itself, but in metal from the core that melted and then resolidified. Another possibility, they said, is that the stainless steel liner of the vessel, which is about a quarter of an inch thick, could have cracked . . .

A spokesman for the utility, Douglas Bedell, said, 'There is no indication of its in any way having lost its integrity. There is no sign of leakage. We consider it a low probability that the vessel itself is engaged with cracking.'

(*New York Times*, 6 August 1989.)

19. *Time*, 23 July 1990.

20. *International Herald Tribune*, 25 July 1990.

21. David Ross, 'Electric Secrets', *Index on Censorship*, vol. 18, nos. 6 & 7, 1989, p. 47.

22. *International Herald Tribune*, op. cit.

23. Hermann Hatzfeldt, 'Damaging Trees, Damaging Truths', *Index on Censorship*, Ibid. pp. 52–6.

24. *The Courage to Live*, op. cit., is concerned with the metaphysical myths we create in order to explain the nature of death and the purpose of life, and with the effects of these myths.

25. F.W. Farrar, *Eric, or Little by Little* (London, 1858, reissued by Hamish Hamilton, London, 1971). This is the story of a boy who, too morally weak to be good, slid into sin and died.

26. Heinrich Hoffman, *Struwwelpeter* (Leipzig, 1845). A collection of cautionary tales, including 'The great, long-legg'd scissorman' who visits little thumbsuckers:

> And cuts their thumbs clean off – and then
> You know, they never grow again.

27. See Alice Miller, *For Your Own Good* (Virago, London, 1988) and Morton Schatzman, *Soul Murder* (Penguin, London, 1973).

28. Maureen Dowd, 'On the Gary Cooper Rescue Mission', *Independent*, 17 September 1988.

29. Christopher Hill, *History and the Present*, op. cit. pp. 22, 24, 26.

30. Eric Jacobs and Robert Worcester, *We British* (Weidenfeld & Nicolson, London, 1990), pp. 19–20, 77–84.

31.

In Britain today, one family in seven is headed by a single parent. According to the Office of Population Censuses and Surveys, the number of one-parent families grew from 562,000 to 916,000 in the decade between 1971 and 1981, and since then the figure has increased to over one million. This means that in Britain and Northern Ireland there are almost two million children living in the care of one parent, and in Scotland alone 153,000 children live in 93,000 one-parent families.

(Liz McNeill Taylor, *Bringing Up Children on Your Own* (Fontana, London, 1985), p. 15.

32. Simon Hoggart, *Observer*, 7 July 1989.

Lee Atwater died of a brain tumour in March, 1991. Andrew Stephen wrote, 'I, like everybody else who knew him, found myself deeply sad at his passing, admiring his courage in his illness and moved by his Christian repentance near his end for the wrongdoings he had committed to put Bush into the White House.' *Observer*, 31 March 1991.

Chapter 4. 'You Can't Have Everything' – Parents

1. Ogden Nash, 'Family Court', *Verses from 1929 On*, 1959.

2. Adewale Maja-Pearce, 'A witness to poetic injustice', *Guardian*, 2 September 1989.

3. Jo Brans, *Mother, I Have Something to Tell You* (Doubleday, New York, 1987), p. 16.

4. Edward Blishen, 'A comedy of uncles', *Guardian*, 24 December 1988.

5. E.M.W. Tillyard, *The Elizabethan World Picture* (Chatto & Windus, London, 1943).

6. George Weidenfeld, 'Here's to the Brits', *Guardian*, 11 February 1989.

7.

Quite a number of people emerged with no credit at all from the Salman Rushdie affair, but I doubt if you could find a more disgusting spectacle than the response of Mr Peregrine Worsthorne in the *Sunday Telegraph*.

'Salman Rushdie's apology may well reduce the danger to his life. But it won't remove it, and it is ironic that someone who was only recently inveighing against Mrs Thatcher for having created a police state should be compelled to rely on that same police state to save his life . . .'

It is difficult to believe that this was written while a man was going in fear of his life. But it was all of a piece with accounts of 'little Salman, lost in his humourless self-importance as the great writer': the fact that a man had been condemned to death was considerably less important than the fact that the establishment had got a liberal intellectual within its sights and was avid to let him have it with both barrels.

(D.J. Taylor, *A Vain Conceit* (Bloomsbury, London, 1989), quoted in the *Guardian*, 14 September 1989.)

Fay Weldon was one of the writers who spoke out clearly and strongly in the defence of freedom of speech. Because she has recognized her *wanting everything*, she knows that she cannot proceed with *getting everything* unless she has the freedom to think and say what she believes, and that she cannot have this freedom unless other people have it as well. Fay is brave. After I had watched her speaking on television I phoned her and said, 'Do be careful.' I did not want her to be blown up by a bomb. She said, 'I've got to die sometime.'

8. Neil Ascherson, 'In praise of revolutions', *Observer*, 16 July 1989.

9. Richard von Weizsäcker, *Time*, 28 August 1989.
10. Anna Mitgutsch, *Punishment*, tr. Lisel Mueller (Virago, London, 1988), p. 87.
11.
In Third World countries 14 million children die every year of preventable diseases and malnutrition (I). A total of 8 million children are abandoned because their parents can't support them (II) and another 150 million work full time – often in appalling conditions (III).
    I. *State of the World's Children*, United Nations Children's Fund, 1982. II. *Children Worldwide*, vol. 14, International Catholic Bureau. III. *All Work and No Play: Child Labour Today*, Trades Union Congress in conjunction with the UK committee for the United Nations Children's Fund.
    (Sue Shaw, 'How to Help Children', *New Internationalist*, April 1989.)

The estimate of 150 million children working full time does not include:

rural work, farm work, housework, care of younger siblings, water hauling and fuel gathering, and not counting bonded labour, prostitution, domestic servitude, and hidden-economy sweatshop labour.
(Robin Morgan, *The Demon Lover* (Methuen, London, 1989), p. 309.)

Ninety thousand child soldiers under the age of 15 died in the Gulf War. Slaves are selling for £30 a piece in the Sudan . . . A working group is struggling in Geneva to wrap up ten years of drafting a convention on children's rights. Two hundred thousand children under the age of 15 are bearing arms, and one aim is to raise the age of recruitment to 18. Britain, which sent young naval recruits to the Falklands, is resisting this. The result could be provisions weaker than the Geneva conventions. The US has insisted that the cost of the new convention on children be borne by states which join them, instead of the UN's regular budget. This is likely to discourage the poorest developing countries which draft children into the army, permit bonded labour, and turn a blind eye to the sale of infants for adoption.
    (Iain Guest, 'Magna Carta for unkind mankind: Human rights forty years on', *Guardian*, 10 December 1988.)
12. The Department of Health reports that in the year ending March, 1989, 40,000 children were on the offical child abuse register. *Guardian*, 21 March 1990.
13. 'Farms are the deadliest places', *New York Times*, 26 September 1988.
14. Diana Elrington, 1989.
15. Margaret Coombs' story, *The Most Important Man in Narramundi*, captures the child's experience of bamboozlement:

My father was the most important man in Narramundi, or so I thought. He was the doctor. He saved people's lives.
    Dr McCarthy and Dr Mason were also doctors, but Dr McCarthy was an RC and a quack, and Dr Mason called his consulting room a 'surgery' even though he did not *do* surgery (which was cutting people up and taking things out of them), only gave anaesthetics for Dr Diamond, my father, who did. Dr McCarthy went to church every Sunday and Dr Mason collected books. My father, on the other hand, quoted poetry:

'Woe unto you, scribes and Pharisees, hypocrites!' he would often say, 'for ye pay tithe of mint and anise and cummin, and have omitted the weightier matters of law, judgement, mercy and faith.'

These particular lines were a reference to the fact that going to church was a poor substitute for *being* good and collecting books was a poor substitute for *reading* them. It was not until twenty years later that I happened to discover that the verse had an ending my father invariably overlooked: 'these ought ye to have done,' it went on, 'and not leave the other undone'.

My father was very much inclined to leave the other undone, but this was something I was required to *admire* in him at the time. I accepted the view that Dr Mason and Dr McCarthy were foolish 'hypocrites' whereas my father *was* good and *had* read everything and knew the Bible practically off by heart. (Or at least the Old Testament and the best parts of the New – the Bible petered out towards the end and the books of Revelation were absolute twaddle.) He said the Bible contained some of the greatest poetry ever written, though read as philosophy it was rubbish. I didn't know quite what he meant by that, but I was sure from the way he said it that it was far better to contain great poetry than not to be rubbish when read as philosophy, even though 'philosophy' (he frequently told me) meant 'love of wisdom', from the Greek, and wisdom meant something even better than knowledge. What was wrong with people who went to church every Sunday was that they could not see that the Bible was great poetry and so they read it as philosophy *if* they read it at all. (Very few of them did.)

Poetry, as far as I could tell, was words put together in ways that ordinary people could not understand. Shakespeare and Milton were poetry, as well as the Bible. Great poetry was the most beautiful thing in the world but people could only *see* the beauty of it if they were as clever and good as my father. My *mother* could not see that it was beautiful. Whenever he quoted poetry at her, which was often, she would say to him

'Oh, for goodness sake, Isaac, come down to earth!'

Or

'Oh, for goodness sake, don't speak to me in riddles, Isaac! What do you *mean*?' Or

'That's all very well, but we have to live in this world, Isaac. You can't go on living in a world of your own all your life!'

But he could.

My father's favourite quotation from the Bible was:

'The Lord seeth not as man seeth; for man looketh on the outward appearance but the Lord looketh on the heart.'

This meant that no matter how well you behaved, it was no good if your heart wasn't in it. (Though my mother was always enjoining me to *behave yourself!* – as if that were enough!) I wondered what you were supposed to do if your heart *wasn't* in it. I tried to behave, and to hide the badness in my heart even from myself. I was glad that the Lord did not actually exist. It was puzzling to me that although so much of the beautiful poetry my father quoted at me with such approval was about the Lord and God and Heaven and Hell and things like that, the Lord and God and Heaven and Hell and such did not actually exist. It was only misguided fools who imagined that God and Heaven and so on existed.

I lived with my father and mother (and my two big brothers when they weren't away at boarding school) in a big old house in River Street with a swimming pool in the backyard. It was *not* the biggest house in town. Several families lived in larger houses with larger swimming pools. However, Mr Hoddle was only the manager of the brewery, and the Ingrams just ran a butter factory, and the Maloufs were Lebanese and their wealth came from the drapery store and the dry cleaning plant, and the Cunninghams were grocers and wine and spirit merchants, and it was Gilchrist's clothes-horse of a wife who had the money.

The biggest house of all in Narramundi was actually on a hill overlooking the town. It was owned by the Lenehans. The Lenehans were RCs of Irish extraction and were patients of Dr McCarthy. They owned the biggest store in Market Street – a real department store two stories high – as well as two hotels and a picture theatre and a lot of other property; but they kept themselves aloof from the town and conducted their social life amongst the wealthy farmers and graziers, and were always travelling back and forth to Sydney and appearing in the social pages of the *Herald*. The Lenehans themselves did not do any sort of work. They just owned *things*. 'Parasites', my father sometimes called them. Also 'rogues' and 'vermin'.

'He who trusteth in riches shall fail,' he would say whenever their name was mentioned.

But the Lenehans never showed any sign of failing. They simply went on being RCs of Irish extraction and patients of Dr McCarthy and growing richer and richer and appearing more and more frequently in the pages of the *Herald*. They did not even *behave* well, so you could easily imagine the parlous states of their hearts. They clearly weren't the sort of people likely to be able to see the value and beauty of poetry.

Which was a pity in a way. Because it meant that they had no way of knowing that the Lord (who did not exist) would see that their soul was wanting, and that they would not go to Heaven (which did not exist) when they died.

Still,

'Virtue is its own reward,' said my mother.

Though my father said that Virtue did not wish for a reward.

It was a consequence of being 'simply not interested in money' that my father owned the biggest car in the town. He had gone to Sydney to buy 'a reliable car' and had come home with a brand new Buick.

'I got it because they say it's got the best *engine*,' he explained, gesturing at a sheaf of advertising brochures on the dashboard. And his face was shining as he eagerly showed off this gadget and that.

'And look at the size of the back seat!' he said. It meant he'd be able to use the car as an ambulance in emergencies – there was room for a patient to lie down.

All the same, my mother flew into a terrible rage, saying over and over again that we couldn't afford it and asking what would become of it on the dirt roads around Narramundi.

'Anyway, if you were going to spend all that money, Isaac, why didn't you buy a nice *English* car?' she wailed. '*A Buick*! It's so vulgar! What will people think?'

'People can think what they like,' he scoffed. 'I don't give a damn what they think!'

But he did.

My first day at school was a day I longed for as, later, I longed for marriage. I expected it would magically change my life from misery to joy. My mother was sick, so it was my father who was to take me there. I could hardly wait.

But a patient arrived – an 'emergency' – just as we were about to leave, and my father had to drop everything (me) and attend to her, and that made us late. And as my father led me up the concrete path between the straight-edged garden beds, I noticed a glob of his Fix-a-line hair emulsion smeared on the sleeve of his coat. It looked (I was sure that people would think) like a large glob of snot. My heart sank with dismay. I glanced in fear at the doorway and saw a blurred image of a tall, too-neat, blonde-haired woman peering down at us from the top of a short flight of steps. The woman must have caught my father's eye because my father jerked his head up at her and gave a sheepish smile and simultaneously raised his hand to his hat and tripped on the bottom step. My dismay deepened. I was sure that my father was much, much better at heart than this perfect-looking woman could be, but somehow the glob of Fix-a-line and his tripping on the step . . .

'So this is Helen, is it?' asked the too-neat, blonde-haired woman's thin crimson lips. Her thickly powdered face had a cold smile fixed on it.

'Miss Withers, may I present Miss Helen Diamond,' my father announced with a laugh in his voice as he fumbled for a packet of cigarettes.

I peeped at the woman's face again, and then stared down at the ground and wondered if Miss Withers could guess what my father really thought of her. *Incompetent fool!* I heard him say of her once. *Phoney! She makes me sick!*

'How do you do, *Miss* Diamond,' Miss Withers simpered, condescending to go along with my father's childish game. She bent down to me. 'I've already heard how much you're looking forward to school.' Then she paused, and straightened up, and looked at her watch, and said: 'Though we are half an hour late – even on our first day!' And then she looked straight at my father and added in a way that I knew was meant to make him feel foolish, 'Daddy will have to make sure to get you here before the bell rings in future, won't he?' She finished with a spiteful crimson smile.

I looked to my father for help, but he was engrossed in a hopeless battle to light his cigarette in the wind. I turned my attention to the Fix-a-line on his sleeve and gazed at it in silent misery until at last he gave up the struggle to light his cigarette, darted another sheepish glance at Miss Withers and then cast his eyes down at me again to avoid Miss Withers's mocking scrutiny.

'Well, all right then, Pixie?' he muttered, the unlit cigarette still jiggling between his lips. And as he took it out, he said: 'Off you go!' and then turned to Miss Withers with: 'Unfortunately, er, a confinement . . . I'm needed urgently . . .'

'I *quite* understand, Dr Diamond,' she said. 'I quite understand.' And then she smiled coldly again, and added, as she slowly and gracefully stooped to pick up the dead matches that my father had scattered carelessly on the steps: 'Helen will be perfectly all right with me. Won't you dear?'

There was clearly no choice of answer, so I did not give one. I stared down at my father's shoes, noticing that one of his laces was coming undone and longing for him to explain to Miss Withers that she made him sick. Why did he pretend to look *up* at her? Why did he *allow* her to look down on him? Why didn't he just *say* how much better than her he was?

All he did say, at last, to break the awkward silence, was: 'Well, goodbye. Be a good girl, Pixie. Chin up! Goodbye, Miss Withers.'

'Goodbye, Dr Diamond,' smirked Miss Withers.

'Goodbye, Daddy,' I squeaked.

I followed my father with my eyes as he made his escape, ineffectually puffing on his unlit cigarette and stumbling at the gate as his shoelace caught him up. I felt crushed and desolate as I watched the big cream car swerve away, the strips of chrome along its side glinting in the sun. How could my father leave me with this *fool*, this *phoney*? How could I protect him from this woman's contempt? If *Miss Withers* were dying, I wondered, would my father save *her* life? Or would he . . .

'Well, come *on*, child!' snapped Miss Withers. 'We haven't got all day!'

She grasped me firmly by the arm and hurried me down the dark, cold corridor.

(From *Regards to the Czar*, University of Queensland Press, St Lucia, 1988.)

16. Elizabeth F., 1988.

17. Edmund Gosse, *Father and Son* (Penguin, London, 1980), p. 65.

18. Martin Walker, *Guardian*, 4 July 1988.

19. W. Scully, *Punch* cartoon, 13 May 1988.

20. Alister Hardy, *The Spiritual Nature of Man* (Clarendon Press, Oxford, 1979). Two contributors to Hardy's research said:

'The phenomenon invariably occurs out of doors, more often than not when I am alone, although it has occurred when I have been in the company of others. It is generally prefaced by a general feeling of gladness to be alive. I am never aware of how long this feeling persists but after a period I am conscious of an awakening of my senses. Everything becomes suddenly more clearly defined, sights, sounds and smells take on a whole new meaning. I become aware of the goodness of everything. Then, as though a light was switched off, everything becomes still, and I actually feel as though I am part of the scene around me.' (p. 35)

'I have become steadily more convinced that "There's a Divinity which shapes our ends, rough hew them how we will," and experiences such as these confirm and strengthen this view.

'In my early twenties . . . in Wales, I went for a walk one evening alone. The path led up to a very narrow precipice walk along the hill's edge, and while I was there . . . the setting sun blazed out turning the whole world crimson and gold, there was a gust of wind, and I felt as if I had been swept into the very heart of all that glory and colour, taken over by something outside myself of which I was yet a part.

'The same thing happened on my first visit to Chartres Cathedral. It was when I turned and saw the blue west windows hung like jewels on velvet . . . Again I was part of some creative force outside myself, so I could not move, and found myself shaking with the force of my emotional response.

'It does not necessarily take great scenic views or great art or great architecture to induce such a state. About 14 years ago when life was difficult and I was in a state of near despair one evening, the quality of the sunlight seemed to change, and this time, though the scenic beauty around was magnificent, it was the colour and patterning of a common weed's tiny clustered flowers which I found I was seeing for the first time, and in the contemplation of which I was again swung into that wider vision and participation.' (p. 72)

21. Psalm 51:5.
22. *Today*, 29 December 1988.
23. Anna Mitgutsch, *Punishment*, op. cit. p. 99.
24. Edmund Gosse, *Father and Son*, op. cit. p. 55.
25. *Ibid*. p. 57, 168.
26. *Ibid*. p. 150.
27. Ed Vulliamy, 'March ends in battle at Westminster', *Guardian*, 29 May 1989.
28.

Sports betting is not even the largest, or fastest growing, type of American gambling. Christiansen/Cummings Associates in New York City, a consulting firm to the gaming industry, figures that all kinds of wagering (except friendly bets between individuals) have increased a thumping 57% in the past five years. Casinos took in more than half of all bets, or $164 billion; sports gambling was a distant second with a $28 billion take, up 57% from 1983. Although impressive, that increase was dwarfed by a 98% jump in the coins clinked into slot machines, a 103% rise in legal bookmaking and a 228% leap in money wagered in cardrooms.

Even those figures understate the spread of gambling fever. The biggest jump is in gambling that state and local governments not merely tolerate but also promote. By next January, lotteries will be operating in 32 states and the District of Columbia; in 1964 only one state, New Hampshire, had a lottery . . . Legal gambling also prompts more illegal wagering. It was once thought that lotteries and other state run betting ventures would pull money away from ghetto numbers game, horse-parlours operating behind candy-store fronts and the like. But the illegal games usually flourish alongside the legal ones and sometimes even piggyback them. One example, the Chicago numbers operators have adopted the state's winning number in their own daily drawings . . . If there is one opinion on which both the gambling experts and ordinary bettors are in unanimous agreement, it is that state-sponsored gambling has been behind the huge increases in all types of wagering, legal and illegal.

'Gambling has been part of every known society,' says Dr Eric Plaut, vice chairman of the department of psychiatry and behavioural sciences at Northwestern University Medical School, Evanston, Ill. 'What has changed in the past decade is that it is now publicly endorsed. Since the government has got into the business of being an operator of gambling itself, it has given (betting) an imprimatur . . .'

Some experts credit modern technology with contributing to the gambling surge. Computers have made possible the instantaneous distribution of odds on any race or ball game anywhere in the country . . . 'The new technology makes gambling much more accessible,' says Richard Rosenthal, a Beverley Hills psychoanalyst who specializes in treating compulsive gamblers. 'It makes gambling much more addictive.'
(George J. Church, 'Why pick on Pete?', *Time*, 10 July 1989.)
29. *Guardian*, 10 August 1990.
30.

The concept of exactness is an ideal – a comforting mental fantasy; in the objective world there is, as far as we know, no exactness (i.e., no two things have been proved to be devoid of any difference between them) and in our observations of objective phenomena we can do no more than approach exactness. 'Although this may seem a paradox, all exact science is dominated by the idea of approximation . . . Every careful measurement in science is always given with the probable error, which is a technical term, conveying a precise meaning.' (Bertrand Russell, *The Scientific Outlook*.)

The situation is analogous in the case of all our knowledge of objective phenomena. Every statement we make about things is analysable down to an attempt to place these things, in virtue of one or other of their qualities, in a category appropriate to the particular purpose we have in view at the time. Our simple classification of phenomena into 'tables', 'cheeses', etc., are thus similar in object and method to those scientists who, with the object of increasing our power to deal with the world, have arbitrarily divided up a large part of its phenomena into categories and have called these categories 'metal', 'arthropods', 'mammals', 'nerves', and so on. Even in these scientific categories there is no exactness; the mammals all differ in various respects; there are animals which fit so badly into any one category that there is argument as to where they belong. More important, it depends on the particular purpose in view into which category a particular phenomenon is placed, e.g., some chemical may be poison for one purpose and tonic for another, while killing may be murder for some purposes and war for others.

However, although these categories are not exact in conception – although they do not give us an accurate picture of the objective world – they are sufficiently differentiated to be of immense help in systematizing our knowledge. The naming of things and the placing of them in categories is thus a sort of simplification (inaccurate but useful all the same) of the extreme complexity of 'real' life. We can never understand this full complexity; as a rule we do not even need to. But we need to understand it to an extent which will help us to deal with it – to survive. We therefore simplify it.

Knowledge of Things is, however, according to our present classification, only part of our knowledge of the world. We also have to understand the laws which control these things. (There is, strictly speaking, no sharp division between knowledge of Things and knowledge of Laws, but I make the division – in the same way that all divisions are made – for the sake of convenience.) In other words, we have to know such facts as that water boils when we heat it enough, and that apples, and other things, fall to the ground when their support is withdrawn. These pieces of knowledge, when stated in a more precise form, are applications of 'laws' (in the scientific sense) in that they predict what will happen in certain circumstances. And in fact all such knowledge is of the same type, though the laws which it invokes vary greatly in the wideness of their application. The application of the law about boiling water is relatively restricted, while that of the law of gravitation is relatively general.

Such laws, however narrow in their application, are strictly speaking matters of probability, not of absolute certainty; for, in the objective world, the concept of absolute certainty is, like that of absolute exactness, an ideal only – a comforting fantasy. Though we can be absolutely certain of our own sensations, as I can be certain that I feel hot, we can never be absolutely certain – in the sense that there is no possible doubt – about anything outside our minds and sensations. I might, for instance, *feel* hot, but I cannot be logically certain that there is, in the objective world, an object emitting heat-rays which has caused my sensation. I may have a temperature, or I may have had some whisky; it is even possible that I am suffering from delusions and that the fire I see there is not really there at all.

(Rupert Crawshay-Williams, *The Comforts of Unreason* (Kegan Paul, Trench, Trubner and Co., Ltd, London, 1947), pp. 16–17.)

Chapter 5. 'Yes I Can' – Power

1. Emily in Andrew Bethell's television programme *Just an Inch Away* (Channel 4, September 25 1989).

Bethell arranged for four British youngsters, two black and two white, to stay with families in South Africa for a couple of weeks last spring. One of them at least, you felt, went out there a political innocent and came back a committed voter. The two white students, Scott and Emily, stayed with what by their English standards were comfortably off middle-class families in Johannesburg, with black servants in the kitchen and pools in the garden.

The two black students, Leonore and Charles, stayed with families in Soweto, where the only piped water is a tap in the yard, next to the shed with the lavatory. It was clear, from the bedroom Leonore was given, and the barrack-like hutments, that this was the more presentable part of Soweto. But none of the four British, nor the children of their white South African hosts, were spared the squalor and poverty of the other parts of the township – an experience from which all the young people emerged a bit shaken and very thoughtful.

The title of the documentary only makes sense when you hear a tearful Leonore on the soundtrack recounting her Soweto friend's experience of the loss of friends, killed in the violent repression of black protest 'just an inch away from her'. Scott was surprised by white hosts who were less racist than he expected, and by the lack of hostility to them as whites in the township. 'If I was in their position I wouldn't be so bloody friendly.' Leonore and Charles, who had never been involved in the anti-apartheid movement in Britain, confronted what that all too familiar phrase meant, and maybe Emily – the oldest of them – summed up the impact of the trip on the four students: 'Politics is not another subject. It is everything. It is your life.'

(*Guardian*, 26 September 1989.)

2. David Smail, *Taking Care* (Dent, London, 1987), p. 87.
3. *Yorkshire Post*, 5 September 1989.
4. David Smail, *op. cit.* pp. 115–16.
5. *Ibid.* pp. 116–21.

At a relatively coarse level of analysis, there are several almost standard ways – familiar, I would suggest, in most people's experience – in which the fundamentally baleful nature of our society is reflected in the manner in which parental power comes to be exerted over children. Without running to further volumes, I can do no more here than sketch some of them rather as caricatures.

At the bottom of the pyramid, the very base of the social hierarchy, many people are too drained and oppressed, too robbed of ability or initiative to feel that they can or want to do anything for their children but simply keep them quiet. In this kind of situation children are likely to be indulged, neglected, bullied or mistreated, handed over to 'experts' in the welfare services, and generally left to find their way through the system as best they can. Nobody will have the resources of time, money or personal concern to observe their talents or nurture their interests and abilities, though they may encounter a degree of formal (but, because over-stretched, highly undependable) support from official agencies. To avoid becoming nothing more than fodder for a depressed labour market or marginally useful for the consumption of mass-produced junk, the child in this position needs an almost miraculously lucky encounter with someone (most often an unusually strong and capable grandparent or aunt or uncle) who will through affection, wisdom and energy, open up for it a world of possibility and a realization of its own potentialities which would otherwise be missed. The only consolation to occupancy at this level of society, and it is indeed the smallest of mercies, is that tired neglect, though it generates the most dreadful waste, often avoids the malign distortion of growth which leads to such emotional pain in people who have been subjected to more positive abuses of power.

It is virtually impossible to occupy a precariously insecure position in the power hierarchy without the anxiety and hostility such a position occasions being reflected in family relations. People who, as it were, find themselves perched on a ledge a little way up the social pyramid – far enough to want to hang on to the small advantage gained but not far enough to be unaware of the unattractiveness of rock bottom – live particularly threatened lives, and it can be little surprise if they hedge their children round with all kinds of exhortations and prohibitions, keen for them to climb higher and anxious lest they drag the family back down to what they see as social ignominy. Here is to be found the much maligned 'petty bourgeoisie', renowned for its mean-spirited narrow-mindedness, envy and authoritarian moralism. But the values of generosity and liberalism make little sense to anyone having to cling to this perch, where the threat of economic power is probably felt at its most acute and life becomes an unrelenting pursuit of the always just-unattainable security, a panicky clinging to advantages gained and an angry contempt both for people who have silver spoons in their mouths and for those who have fallen into torpid resignation. The reality here is of economic survival and obedient subservience to power, and other values, other ways of perceiving the world become mere self-indulgence. Rigid conformity to narrow ideals and denial and repression of emotions, perceptions and values which do not meet them, resentful respect for authority and uncritical acceptance of established social institutions breed an atmosphere in which children are likely to find it hard to develop a firm sense of subjectivity, but will be moulded to occupancy of stereotyped social and sexual roles and will experience considerable anxiety and guilt when they find themselves departing from them. Self-deception and hypocrisy, emotional deprivation and defensiveness follow naturally from this kind of situation, which, not surprisingly, is one of the most psychologically mutilating in which one can find oneself.

It is in this stratum, and those close to it, that the course of development most typical of our society is perhaps most obviously to be found – the transformation of a lively and promising human infant, through a period of indoctrination, disillusion and rebellion, into an emotionally constricted, competitively hostile adult saturated in the values of commodity consumption, desperately conforming, anxiously pursuing an ever-receding 'happiness', bereft of any ability to criticize the society in which he or she is located, pathetically eager to enjoy those of its 'fruits' (consumer durables) which are within reach. This is the great, inertly stable backbone of our society, the guardian of its values and the target of the mass media, working tirelessly in the interests of others and blindly against its own, forced by the crushing vice of economic power into reproducing itself reliably and endlessly in its children.

At the upper end of this stratum, and extending into the managerial and professional strata, one finds family relations set in a rather less rigid context in which a degree of economic security allows room for, on the one hand, genuinely realizable ambition, and on the other economically riskable (though strictly one-dimensional) criticism of the *status quo*. Here, for example, managers may manage their children, organizing their experience (e.g., controlling which television programme may be watched) and to a lesser extent their social and educational environment in accordance with aims seen as desirable and attainable. The relatively greater degree of power available at this level makes in general for a rather more relaxed and less moralistic hedonism, but the culture is still likely to be highly materialistic in one form or another and the emphasis on child-rearing will probably be on the gaining of increased status, so that children will often experience strong pressure to achieve and 'succeed'. In the absence of crude economic threat (e.g. relative security of parental job tenure and provisions of pensions, etc.) the atmosphere is more often likely to be one of alienation rather than anxiety: the pursuit of comfort and satisfaction, the possibility of actually obtaining recurrent quiescence of the nervous system, may lead to a kind of flaccidity in values, an incipient sense of purposelessness and a desperation to realize purpose in 'relationships', which may in fact result in chaotic, manipulative and dishonest relations between parents. Children in this type of situation may be or feel emotionally distanced from their families, and their parents, intent on pursuing their own gratification, may simply buy their offsprings' upbringing from educationalists and 'experts' of one sort or another. Particularly in the families of middle-class intellectuals and academics children may be permitted or actually encouraged a kind of rebellion against conventional norms as long as they 'achieve' intellectually. In adolescents from this kind of background one can often encounter an intelligent criticism of their parents' apparently dishonest involvement in materialist values and lack of emotional commitment to anything very much, but idealism seems to give way all too soon to a learned indifference to people, a sort of profound disaffection which in the end simply reproduces a drifting indulgence in commodified relationships and embarkation on one of society's more comfortable bandwagons, propelled more by fashion than commitment.

It is only towards the apex of the social hierarchy that one comes across the most direct application of economic power within the family itself, i.e. the parental control of children through the straightforward manipulation of money-power. It is no doubt a blessing that for the vast majority of us institutions such as male primogeniture no longer exist to poison family relations, but even so it seems to me that we vastly underestimate the psychological consequences of inheritable wealth for those who actually stand in line to inherit it. This does not of course constitute a widespread social problem, but it does throw into relief the way that power may be socially exerted and reflected in individuals' personal lives and relations. I cannot claim that my knowledge of people in this position is extensive, but it has struck me as interesting how often those I have come across – i.e. people who have wealthy parents and who profit or stand to profit by the relationship – seem simply to have failed to grow up. For such people as this, however advanced in years themselves, the parental shadow seems to fall heavily over them, in such a way that emotionally and socially they remain perpetual adolescents – angrily dependent, sulkily rebellious, rather unstable and changeable in their personal relationships, apparently vocationally paralysed, i.e., dilettantish and unable to strike out for themselves in any independent direction. However firm our intentions, very few of us manage to be disinterested, and it is extremely difficult for even the most affectionate parent not to wield unconscious power over a son or daughter who stands to gain financially from the relationship. It is not the habit of psychologists to inquire closely into the financial background and circumstances of those whose 'behaviour' and 'attitudes' they are trying to understand. On the whole, I suspect, to do so would be far more enlightening than to pursue, for example, the much more common inquiries into sexual history.

6. In April, 1990, Bill Goodwin, a trainee journalist on the *Engineer* was fined £5,000 for refusing to disclose a source who volunteered some financial details about a company. In 1963 Reginald Foster, a *Daily Sketch* journalist, was sentenced to three months in prison for contempt of court after refusing to reveal sources at the Vassall spy tribunal.

7.

The Christian Science Church says its right to exist goes on trial this week when a jury determines if two church members are guilty of manslaughter for relying on prayer alone to heal their two-year-old son. During the trial, which opens today in Boston, the world headquarters of the Christian Science Church, the prosecution will argue that David and Ginger Twitchell's son, Robyn, who died almost four years ago might still be alive had his parents sought medical attention for his bowel obstruction. The Twitchell's attorney, Rikki Klieman, said she will argue that her clients, far from acting recklessly, sought a cure dictated by their deeply held beliefs.

There has been little concensus among courts around the country faced with similar cases. The US Supreme Court, with constitutional power to set nationwide rules on the issue, has refused to hear such cases.

John Kiernan, the special assistant district attorney, denied that the case was an attack on Christian Science or a repudiation of spiritual healing. He said it had nothing to do with freedom of religion. Religious 'practice is subject to regulation by the state. Belief is not,' Mr Kiernan said. He argued that an adult could choose to forgo conventional medical treatment but that a child was not in a position to make such a decision. Mr Kiernan will charge that by relying exclusively on Christian Science healing, the Twitchells acted with reckless disregard for the health of their son. The state, he said, had a duty to protect children.

(*Independent*, 17 April 1990.)

A Christian Science couple, David and Ginger Twitchell, convicted of manslaughter for choosing prayer over medicine to cure their son, were put on 10 years probation yesterday in Boston. – Reuter.

(*Guardian*, 7 July 1990.)

8. Hedrick Smith, *The Power Game* (Fontana, London, 1988), p. 76.

9. *Ibid*. p. 74.

10. *Ibid*. p. 1.

11. *Ibid*. p. 13.

12. Andrew Stephen, 'A hostage to prime time TV news values', *Observer*, 18 March 1990.

13. John Pilger, 'Distant voices of dissent', *Guardian*, 12 February 1990.

14. *Punch*, 23 May 1984.

15. J.E. Lovelock, *Gaia* (Oxford University Press, Oxford, 1989), pp. 11, 152.

16. *Ibid*., p. 152.

17. *Ibid*, p. 148.

We might wonder why Gaia should choose the human species as the purpose of Gaia's existence when the ant has lasted for so much longer and is so much more efficient.

John Ryle, reviewing *The Ants* by Bert Holldobler and Edward O. Wilson (Springer-Verlag, 1990), wrote:

> Ants are the most successful organisms in evolutionary history: there are over 8,000 species, distributed everywhere on Earth except the polar regions. In Peru, 43 different kinds of ant have been recorded in a single tree. Compared to this, primates are just a flash in the pan. Ants antedate us and will undoubtedly outlast us. There are a million times more of them: 10 million billion, it has been estimated, alive at any one time – a quarter of a million for every acre of land on the Earth's surface . . .
>
> Ants can eat us, but we cannot eat them with any pleasure. Unlike termites (which have a rich, oily taste something like pork scratchings), ants, with a tough outer layer of chitin and a nasty whiff of formic acid in their body tissues, are generally undigestible, except by other ants. Even anteaters prefer termites. Ants, furthermore, are resistant to hard radiation and, in the case of some species, industrial pollution; some can live in deserts; some can float; some can slow their metabolism down and survive underwater for days on end . . .
>
> Why are ants so successful? Instead of the endless competition of human societies, where social hierarchies are continually demolished and rebuilt, ants have the division of labour written into their physiology. The ant colony is an almost exclusively female society, with the males remaining in the nest only until the time of their fatal nuptial flight. Like other social insects, males mate once and die . . . Ants waste no time; and, as Holldobler and Wilson inform us sternly in a chapter heading, Ants Do Not Play. They fight – in defence of the colony, the breeding unit – but they do not have civil wars or revolutions.

(*Independent on Sunday*, 12 August 1990.)

18. Larry cartoon, *Guardian*, 19 April 1990.

19. 'Carping over the Catechism', *Time*, 19 April 1990.

20. Robin Morgan, *The Demon Lover* (Methuen, London, 1989), p. 56.

21. *Ibid.* p. 57.

22. Martha Crenshaw, *Terrorism, Legitimacy, and Power: The Consequences of Political Violence* (Wesleyan University Press, Middletown, Conn., 1983), p. 395, quoted in Robin Morgan, *op. cit.* p. 72.

23. Robin Morgan, *op. cit.* p. 63; Joseph Campbell, *The Hero with a Thousand Faces* (Princeton University Press, Princeton, N.J., 1968).

24. Charles A. Russell and Bowman H. Miller, 'Profile of a Terrorist', in *Perspectives in Terrorism*, ed. Lawrence Zelic Freedman and Yonah Alexander (Scholarly Resources, Inc, Wilmington, Del., 1983).

25. *Ibid.* p. 54.

26. *Ibid.* p. 55.

27. Fatima Mernissi, *Beyond the Veil: Male-Female Dynamics in Modern Muslim Society* (Indiana University Press, Bloomington, 1987), pp. xviii-xxii.

28. Robin Morgan, *op. cit.* pp. 63–5.

29. Quoted in Daniel Goleman, 'The Roots of Terrorism', *New York Times*, 2 September 1986, pp. C1, C8.

30. *Ibid.*

31. Wilfred Owen, 'Insensibility', *Collected Poems* (Chatto & Windus, London, 1963).

32. 'Deadly Remark', *Time*, 29 January 1990.

33. Anna Mitgutsch, *Punishment* (Virago, London, 1989), p. 89.

34. Ruth Rendell, *Make Death Love Me* (Arrow Books, London, 1988), p. 14.

35. *The Macquarie Dictionary* (Macquarie Library Pty Ltd, St Leonards, NSW, 1981), p. 1481.

36. *Ibid.*

37. W.L. Webb, 'The clocks go back in Cairo', *Guardian*, 31 March 1989.

38. Letter to the *Observer*, 12 March 1989.

39. Haider Reeve, 'Islam's reply to sedition', *Guardian*, 13 March 1989.

40. Ya Ding, 'Can hope survive?', *Guardian*, 15 July 1989.

41. Patric Searle, *Guardian*, 15 May 1988.

42. Quentin Crisp, *The Naked Civil Servant* (Fontana, London, 1988), p. 87.

43. David Smail, *op. cit.* p. 37.

44. Kirsty Milne, *Observer*, 15 May 1988.

45. *Punch*, 13 May 1989.

46. Edmund Gosse, *Father and Son, op. cit.*, p. 123.

47. Quentin Crisp, *op. cit.* p. 88.

48. Following the violence of the Leeds United supporters at Bournemouth (5 May 1990), Hugh McIlvanney wrote:

Perhaps neither the bungling at the Football League that contributed so much to the Bournemouth mayhem nor the less spectacular instances of rowdyism elsewhere last weekend should be seen as particularly relevant to the threat of major violence at the World Cup finals which are due to begin in Italy on 8 June. Yet the general alarm about where football is heading can only be deepened by the evidence that, in England and several other significant places, the game still has a blinkered reluctance to accept the full seriousness of the mess it is in.

Of course, there is an immediate obligation to emphasize that nothing – not even the accumulating achievements of Dutch hooligans – can obscure the uniqueness of English football's reputation in terms of the spread of ugliness at home or the virulence of the contagion so frequently exported to the Continent. Anyone seeking representative villainy need look no further than last week's principal wreckers, the supporters of Leeds United. Their record, stretching back to the storming of Paris at the European Cup Final of 1975, reads like the CV of Conan the Barbarian.

For such a crew, Bournemouth on a Bank Holiday weekend was like an old lady waiting to be mugged. The admission that warnings from the Dorset police about what was likely to happen never even reached the League's management committee, that the decision to reject police requests for the fixture to be rescheduled was taken at a lower level by 'a number of full-time officers', is staggering but perhaps not untypical of an organization which has its headquarters in Lytham St Anne's, an office in London and a chief executive who operates from his home in Nottingham.

The League's bumbling insularity, the way it has so often combined a pathetic lack of worldliness with incorrigible complacency, must call into question its right to go on playing such a central role in the running of

English football. Its main figures seem to be utterly incapable of realizing the the utter pointlessness of repeating the obvious truth that the sort of damage done in Bournemouth is not a purely football phenomenon, that something similar might have been perpetrated three decades back by the Mods and Rockers and other mobs at other stages of our history.

'Across the centuries,' wrote Geoffrey Pearson in *Hooligan: A History of Respectable Fear*, published in 1983, 'we have seen the same ritual of territorial dominance, trials of strength, gang fights, mockery against elders and authorities, and antagonism towards outsiders as typical focuses for youthful energy and aggressive mischief. Even under vastly different social conditions there are striking continuities between the violent interruptions to pre-industrial fairs and festivals, and the customary eruptions during modern Bank Holidays or the weekly carnival of misrule in contemporary football games – where the football rowdy, with his territorial edginess, mascots, emblems and choral arrangements in the rough music tradition, must seem like the incarnation of the unruly apprentice, or the late-Victorian Hooligan.'

All this is true but the argument for historical continuity simply underlines how crass the League was in refusing to recognize that football is the main focus of youthful aggression these days and that letting the notorious marauders from Leeds descend on the South Coast during a holiday meant that there would indeed be a carnival of misrule . . .

The Dutch have been hearing from one of their leading sociologists, Professor Andre van den Burg. He says that Calvinism is still as strong in the Netherlands as it was 200 years ago and suggests that its suppression of emotion and the outward show of feeling has much to do with the fact that 'the po-faced Dutch are renowned for sudden outbursts of violence, often quite out of proportion to their apparent cause.'

But it is Van den Burg's prognosis, with its application to soccer rowdyism as a whole, that is especially discouraging: 'Bringing in hordes of police to stop thugs from going on the rampage is like putting bandages on a boil to stop it erupting. You've got to tackle the root cause of the problem and, since it has been taking root over centuries, it will not be stopped overnight by police, politicians or even sociologists.'
(*Observer*, 13 May 1990.)

49. Jocelyn Taggart, 'England v Sardinia', *Weekend Guardian*, 7 April 1990.

50. Quoted by Emma Tennant, 'Kiss and tell', *Guardian*, 27 January 1983.

51. Uta Ranke-Heinemann, *Eunuchs for Heaven*, tr. John Brownjohn (André Deutsch, London, 1990).

52. Anthony Burgess, 'Church, sex, and the chaste pachyderm', *Observer*, 8 April 1990.

53. Landon Y. Jones Jr, 'Busted by the baby boom', *Time*, 29 January 1990.

54. Quoted by Adewale Maja-Pearce in 'The fierce voice of Africa's conscience', *Independent on Sunday*, 18 March 1990.

55. William Millinship ,'Millions threatened as fall-out from Chernobyl spreads', *Observer*, 22 March 1990.

56.
As the official report on the *Challenger* disaster pointed out, the booster seals were defective and there also 'was a serious flaw in the decision-

making process' at NASA. But the O-rings manufactured by the Thiokol Corporation always functioned adequately at temperatures above fifty degrees. They usually functioned at temperatures much lower than that, so nobody at the Florida launch site thought much of the 'low temperature enhanced probability' of booster seal erosion.

On 28 January, 1986, the date of the *Challenger* disaster, predawn temperatures dropped below freezing at Cape Canaveral. Thirty-mile winds created a wind chill factor in the teens. Ice formed in the water tanks containing antifreeze. Icicles clung to the rocket boosters. At the moment of blast-off, the temperature was thirty-eight degrees. People watching the launch were shivering.

The myth that you can escape the winter in Florida, which created Miami, was also what killed the astronauts.

(T.D. Allman, *Miami* (Atlantic Monthly Press, New York, 1987), p. 411.)

57. Phil Elmer-Dewitt, 'The ghost in the machine', *Time*, 29 January 1990.

58. Michael J. Reddy, 'The conduit metaphor – a case of frame conflict in our language about language' in *Metaphor and Thought*, ed. Andrew Ortony (Cambridge University Press, Cambridge, 1979), p. 287.

59. *Ibid*. p. 287.

60. *Ibid*. p. 290.

Examples

(1) Whenever you have a good *idea* practise *capturing it in words*.

(1) You have to *put* each *concept into words* very carefully.

(2) Try to *pack* more *thoughts into* fewer *words*.

(2) Insert those *ideas* elsewhere in the paragraph.

(3) Don't *force* your *meanings into* the wrong words.

(3) The lines might rhyme, but *they are empty* of both *meaning* and *feeling*.

(4) Let me know if you *find* any good *ideas in* the *essay*.

(4) That *remark* is completely *impenetrable*.

61. *Ibid*. p. 291.

Examples

(1) Put those *thoughts* down on paper before you *lose* them.

(1) Mary *poured out* all the *sorrow* she had been holding in for so long.

(2) That *concept* has been *floating around* for ages.

(2) You'll *find* better *ideas* than that in the library.

(3) Her delicate *emotions went right over* his head.

(3) How many different *concepts* can you *get into your head* in one evening?

62. *Ibid*. p. 292–3.

63. *Ibid*. p. 295, 296.

64. Simon Winchester, 'Dream has died for an old communist', *Guardian*, 17 April 1990.

65. David Hirst, 'Loneliness of a trapped tyrant', *Guardian*, 8 June 1990.

66. Colin Hughes, 'Children miss out on American dream', *Independent*, 20 March 1990.

67. David Smail, *op. cit*. pp. 151, 152.

68. Issues concerning power and the therapist are discussed in *Breaking the Bonds*, chapter 23, *The Successful Self*, Chapter 8; Jeffrey Masson, *Against Therapy* (Fontana, London, 1989), and *Final Analysis* (Fontana, London, 1991); and David Smail, *Taking Care, op. cit.*

Chapter 6. 'Yes I Can' – Greed and Envy

1. Ed Janoff, aged nine.
2. Charles Peattie and Russell Taylor *Alex II* (Penguin, London, 1989).
3. Brenda Polan, 'The slight fantastic', *Guardian*, 15 September 1988.

In the gangs of the inner city of Los Angeles 'Most gang leaders are in their late teens and early 20s, but kids as young as ten or eleven readily join. They are called wanna-bes and are looked on even by cops as apprentices in the trade.'
Time, 18 June 1990.

4. John Sweeney, 'Honest fool who bared his soul', *Observer*, 23 July 1989.
5. Cotham cartoon, *Punch*, 16 May 1984.
6. *Wall Street*, Twentieth Century Fox Corporation, 1987.
7. 'Alex', *Independent*, 11 August 1988.
8. Editorial: 'Irony turns to base metal', *Guardian*, 30 April 1988.
9. 'Wogan', BBC TV, 28 April 1988.
10. Gibbard, *Guardian*, 12 July 1989.
11.

In the December issue of *Clinical Psychology Forum* (no. 24, p. 50) there is a notice which announces that, from the new year on, membership fees for the Clinical Division will be increased by 50 percent.

I have no quarrel with the decision of the Division Committee to raise the membership subscriptions as a result of financial difficulties. But I cannot help becoming sad and dismayed by the effort of the Honorary Treasurer to justify this increase in terms of the cliché, 'value for money'.

What does 'value for money' mean? What does it presuppose? What is the criterion of 'value'?

I think the phrase 'value for money' subtly evokes the notion of money being the most crucial criterion of all that we do. It implies the expectation of the least expenditure for the greatest return: it implies efficiency as the ultimate goal. What is 'money'? It is a system of power-bestowal: the power to purchase.

The more money a person has the more he or she can buy. The more a certain a sum of money can buy, the more valuable it is. Value for money: the power of the market-place.

Arguments, debates and disagreements do not contribute to 'value for money' because they inevitably use up a lot of time, preventing speedy conclusions, hampering actions or implementation of plans, thus reducing efficiency. The tacit assumption is that we are employed to produce, to compete, to achieve: not to discuss, to ask questions, to doubt. Philosophy is the activity most at odds with the mentality of 'value for money' and so, not surprisingly, it is the prime target for cuts in higher education. It would be natural to conclude, following this type of thinking, that the most efficient, technologically sophisticated and monolithic power hierarchy is the best guarantee for 'value for money'.

Chin K. Li, *Clinical Psychology Forum*, no. 27, June, 1990.)

12. Address to the General Assembly of the Church of Scotland in Edinburgh, 21 May, 1988, reported in the *Observer*, 22 May 1988.
13. *Guardian*, 20 June 1989.

Notes

14. 'Panorama', BBC1, 20 June 1989.

The Government has admitted the widening gulf in living standards between the rich and the poor has been masked for two years by a statistical mistake. Official figures, showing that the incomes of the poorest households rose twice as fast as the national average, have been repeatedly used by Mrs Thatcher and other senior members of her Government to justify tax cuts and economic liberalization, on the grounds that they proved that wealth 'trickled down'.

Last week, the Social Security Secretary, Mr Tony Newton, acknowledged in a brief parliamentary written reply that the figures should have shown the opposite. Revised figures show that the incomes of the poorest 10 percent rose only at half the rate of the whole population, not double, as previously thought. But the findings went largely unnoticed, since they were published the day before the Commons rose for the Easter recess.

Mr Newton's statement, prompted by research by the independent Institute for Fiscal Studies and by statisticians at his own Department of Social Security, corrects statistics issued for the first time in 1988 measuring average household incomes.

(Tim Miles, 'Gap between rich and poor growing, Whitehall admits', *Observer*, 8 April 1990.)

15. *Observer*, 17 April 1988.
16. Kurier cartoon, *Observer*, 3 June 1990.
17. Judith Cutler, *Coming Second*, BBC Radio 4, 15 May 1990.
18. *Living with the Bomb: Can We Live without Enemies? op. cit.*
19. It was not just that the US Government tried to destroy the Sandinista Government and actively aided General Pinochet in destroying democracy in Chile but that what followed was great suffering and misery to the peoples of those countries.

Ana Saez spent the weekend waiting for her son, Michel Nash – waiting for his bullet-ridden body to be dug from a mass grave in the sun-baked waste of Chile's Atacama desert. In a bare church hall in the city of Iquique, 1,200 miles north of Santiago, her husband steadied her as she held her trembling face between her hands. 'It's been 17 years of impotence,' she said. 'Now at last we'll see his body, but I don't know if I can stand it.'

Michel Nash's fate, and that of some 30 others, is the focus of a drama which has horrified Chile, three months after it returned to democracy. For the first time, evidence of the human rights abuses under the former military regime of General Augusto Pinochet is filling the front pages and television screens – and could threaten the General's standing as army commander-in-chief.

One hundred miles north of Iquique is Pisagua, a tiny village on the edge of the world's driest desert . . . [It] is a natural jail. Bounded by the sea and desert, escape from here is impossible. It is a Chilean Devil's Island. General Pinochet knew this, and after his 1973 coup reopened a prison camp built by an earlier anti-Communist regime. Some 300 political prisoners and a few alleged drug traffickers were transported to one of the harshest of the post-coup camps.

Ernesto Montoya, now a human rights lawyer in Iquique, was held here for 10 months. 'We were crammed in groups of 35 into wooden cells measuring three yards by four,' he said. 'They tortured us with electricity, by hanging us by our wrists, and making us drag ourselves naked by our elbows up hillsides strewn with stones and glass.' The scars on his elbows are still there, and those of cigarette burns on his stomach. His foot is bent from trampling by guards. He was twice subjected to a mock firing squad.

He remembers the genuine executions. Michel Nash, a young Communist and conscript who refused to take part in post-coup operations, and five others were the first taken out and shot – allegedly for trying to escape . . . Other victims disappeared after their releases were announced by the military, or are believed to have died under torture . . . For years, it was suspected that the dead and disappeared were buried near the camp. Last year, the Catholic Church's human rights office in Santiago, the Solidarity Vicariate, made contact with a doctor who witnessed one of the executions when taken there to confirm the death. Last week, a Vicariate lawyer applied for a search order. Secretly, to avoid detection by police and soldiers, they began digging . . . By Saturday . . . 20 bodies had been removed. They were blindfolded, wrapped in potato sacks and pierced by bullet holes. The grave is 11 yards long . . . The shootings took place alongside. As the 28 volunteers dig, the stench of decay issues from the pick-axe holes. At the white-fronted morgue, relatives like Ana Saez and her husband await the arrival of the corpses. Periodically, they are called in to identify them.

There has been no response from General Pinochet or the army . . . It is an open secret that similar killings took place throughout the country after the coup. The Solidarity Vicariate knows of some 700 such deaths.

(Malcolm Coad, 'Victims return from the dead to haunt General Pinochet', *Guardian*, 11 June 1990.)

20. The Savings and Loan scandal is the biggest to ever hit the USA. When President Reagan lifted the regulations which limited the activities of the Savings and Loan industry, long the means by which millions of Americans saved and acquired their own homes, he neglected to revise the obligation of the Federal Government to underwrite loans by S&Ls. Accordingly, many greedy financiers saw the opportunity to make a great deal of money by moving into the S&L business and lending money to themselves and to people and organizations who were not likely to repay their debts. The Government was required to meet these debts, and in 1989 President Bush was forced to set up the Resolution Trust Corporation to meet its obligations.

The cost of the S&L bailout seems to keep on rising uncontrollably. Since the President signed the cleanup law amid loud fanfare exactly one year ago, the price has grown from a White House projection of $166 billion over 10 years to what some experts fear could be a $1 trillion bill spread over 30 years as the Government shuts down nearly half the entire thrift industry. The White House's own current forecast projects a cleanup cost of at least $500 billion over the next 40 years. That includes $160 billion to be used mainly to pay insured depositors at shuttered thrifts plus some

$340 billion of interest on the government bonds that will finance the bailout . . . While the bailout has protected depositors at hundreds of failed thrifts, it has also hobbled surviving institutions, hurt real estate values, infuriated taxpayers and stirred doubts that the Government can really bring the S&L mess under control.

(*Time*, 13 August 1990.)

The financiers who made money out of the S&Ls seem not to have realized that, even if they are not prosecuted for their activities, they, as taxpayers, have to meet the cost of their depredations.

21.

Compensation claims for money misappropriated by solicitors more than doubled last year, says a Law Society report. Total claims increased from £6.7 million in 1988 to £14.6 million. Six solicitors described as 'extraordinary defaulters' together accounted for more than £7 million.

The biggest defaulter, Hugh Simmonds, a failed Conservative parliamentary candidate, defrauded clients and others of more than £3.8 million. A former speechwriter for Mrs Thatcher and ex-mayor of Beaconsfield, he gassed himself in 1988 on the day that the society was to begin to examine his books.

(Clare Dyer, *Guardian*, 7 June 1990.)

22.

When Ossie Ardiles returns to Swindon this weekend, he will find it different from the town he left two weeks ago. He went on holiday to his home near Buenos Aires, triumphant after his club had won a place among the elite of English football for the first time in English history. But yesterday, the fans who had cheered their side to victory at Wembley in the play-off for promotion to the First Division were disillusioned, hurt and angry. Scandal and the Football League's decisive action against the club mean that it will not be the great clubs such as Liverpool which Swindon will host at their modest ground next season, but the likes of Crewe Alexandra of the Third Division.

There is worse to come. Ardiles, the hero of Argentina, Tottenham Hotspur and most recently this Wiltshire town, may yet be cast in the role of the alleged villain. Like his predecessor, Lou Macari, and the football club's former chairman, Brian Hillier, he, too, may be charged by the Football League in relation to illegal payments made to the players in his first year as manager of the club.

Mr Hillier and Mr Macari face criminal trials. On Tuesday they will be charged with tax fraud relating to the club. Vincent Farrer, the club's former accountant, will be charged with forgery. Other Swindon players, directors and officials may soon be charged by the Football League with other financial irregularities.

Some fans have taken the dimmest view of what they see as betrayal by the men who guided the club. Mr Hillier is under police protection and is facing pressure to move house. Mr Macari has been advised not to appear personally in court lest he be attacked by the crowd of what were once his most loyal supporters.

(Simon Garfield and David Rowan, 'Fans pay the penalty for Swindon's foul', *Independent on Sunday*, 10 June 1990.)

23. Psalm 2:8, 9.
24. Psalm 1:1, 3.
25. Luke 12:15, 20, 23, 31.
26.

The past quarter of a century has seen 'a revolution in smoking behavior,' declared C. Everett Koop, the current Surgeon General. 'In the 1940s and '50s smoking was chic; now, increasingly, it is shunned.' But, he continued, tobacco is still 'the single most important preventable cause of death, responsible for 1 out of every 6 deaths in the US.'

The most disturbing news in the 679-page report was the assertion that smoking has exacted a heavier toll in death and disease than had previously been thought. Among the findings:

Tobacco claims 390,000 lives a year, 90,000 more than earlier estimates. Two-thirds of those deaths result from cardiovascular disease, lung cancer and chronic respiratory ailments like emphysema. The average male smoker is 22 times as likely to die from lung cancer as is a non-smoker, double the previous risk estimate. For the first time the Government has concluded that smoking is a major cause of stroke, accounting for 26,500 deaths a year. Half of all strokes in people under 65 stem from smoking.

While the incidence of lung cancer has been levelling off in men, it has been rising in women. The report cites the American Cancer Society's estimate that lung cancer has surpassed breast cancer as the second leading cause of death among women. 'Women took up smoking in large numbers about three decades after men did so,' explained Koop. 'We envision the catastrophic epidemic of lung cancer that is likely to occur among women in the coming years.'

(*Time*, 23 January 1989.)

While cigarettes fall out of fashion in most of Western Europe and the US, the rest of the world continues to smoke more and more. Britons smoked 94.5 billion cigarettes last year, equivalent to 1,680 per head. But that marks a 27 percent fall since 1970. In 1972, more than half of all men were smokers. Now the proportion is below 35 percent. The pattern has been repeated in many other developed countries like France, Japan and the Netherlands.

But that fall has been more than offset by an increase in cigarette consumption in the rest of the world. Global cigarette production is likely to hit 5.2 trillion (5.2 million million), up by almost a fifth since the beginning of the decade. China's population of over 1 billion have increased cigarette consumption by more than 10 percent a year, and other developing countries are increasing their smoking by about 2 percent a year.

(Ben Laurance, 'Third World's smoke signals', *Guardian*, 12 July 1989.)

27.

In 1949 UK residents made 1.7 million visits abroad. In 1986 the figure had risen to 25 million. Two million Britons a year now travel to parts of the world classified as a high health risk. Recent research shows that 40 percent of British holidaymakers arrive home with an infection or an illness.

Last October, in response to this problem, the London Hospital for

Tropical Diseases decided to branch out from cures to prevention and opened a Travel Clinic . . . [It] is one of 20 such clinics up and down the country. The clinics offer advice, immunization, and goods such as mosquito nets and AIDS protection kits. The St Pancras clinic recently added a telephone Healthline with recorded information about health care for specific destinations. Dr Ron Behrens, who runs the unit, is exasperated with the lack of adequate health warnings given by the travel industry.

'They should have the same rule for selling travel as they do for selling cigarettes. The brochures should say, There are serious illnesses in this area which can cause death and disability, and it is important that you seek medical information and protect yourself. If people get the message put across in strong enough ways they will either decide not to go or do something about it.'

A survey of patients visiting the hospital for advice prior to travelling last summer (and therefore an enlightened sector of the population) showed that one in four did not know that malaria was spread by mosquitoes. This was an alarming finding, to say the least, particularly as a virtual malaria epidemic is sweeping the world. In the 1970s there were only 100 cases of malaria in Britain, of which less than a third were Falciparum – the strain of the disease which can be fatal. In January of this year there were 51 cases of Falciparum at the Tropical Diseases Hospital alone. The epidemic is largely the result of mosquito resistance to the anti-malarial drug chloroquine . . .

Though malaria is the biggest worry, the most widespread tropical diseases are gastro-intestinal, principally diarrhoea and vomiting caused by eating tainted food and water. Even in the Mediterranean, the risk of contracting diarrhoea is 20 times greater than in more northern parts of Europe. More serious illnesses contracted from food and water, such as typhoid, cholera and hepatitis, continue to be a problem. Although there is an effective typhoid vaccine, several hundred travellers return with the disease every year.

(Helen Fielding, 'Clinical lore of the jungle', *Independent on Sunday*, 17 June 1990.)

28. Martyn Turner cartoon, *New Internationalist*, July 1990.

29. Walter Swartz, *Guardian*, 20 June 1988.

30. Martin Walker, 'Deadly drug-dealing fashion in shoes', *Guardian*, 19 May 1990.

31. Matthew 25:29.

Jesus gave this warning after telling the parable of the talents, where the servant who invested the money which his master had given him was praised, while the servant who had kept it safe by burying it in the ground was cast 'into outer darkness' where 'there shall be weeping and gnashing of teeth'. The poor, so many Christians down the centuries have believed, are poor because they are wicked and incompetent.

32. Hugh O'Shaughnessy, 'UN's World Bank condemned for immoral profits', *Observer*, 22 March 1990.

33. Victoria Brittain, 'Why is Africa hungry?' *Weekend Guardian*, 21 October 1989.

34.

On a summer day an air-conditioned luxury bus wends its way along Portugal's southern coast. Impeccably dressed in custom-tailored silk, Mobutu Sese Seko, President of Zaire, peers intently through a window, surveying the crystal-blue sea, fashionable resorts and luxuriant vineyards. 'Halt!' he orders. The man who rules 35 million of the world's poorest people has found himself another property to buy in the Algarve.

When Portugal caught Mobutu's fancy in 1984 he started regularly jetting into Lisbon and touring the countryside with swarms of friends and retainers. In a single month he spent over three million dollars on Portuguese investments including a 15-acre beach resort and a plantation of orchards and vineyards in the far north. He hosted convivial dinners for his friends – including Portugal's President and Prime Minister – entertaining them with his encyclopaedic knowledge of gastronomy, wine and 'beautiful things'.

More recently Mobutu has begun conducting official business from the ancient village of Roquebrune near Monte Carlo. Last October, French police obligingly sealed off the road to his beachfront property for a succession of official guests including US Africa policy chief Herman Cohen, Angolan and South African foreign ministers, US Congresspeople and Israeli investors. During Zaire's critically important negotiations with the World Bank and the International Monetary Fund (IMF), even Zairean government officials flew to Roquebrune to brief their president. Mobutu's long-time friend Adnan Khashoggi, the Saudi billionaire arms merchant who has been charged in the US with helping Ferdinand and Imelda Marcos loot the Philippines, has a conveniently located home nearby.

When Mobutu tires of Europe, luxury homes await him in Zairean province. Up to four months a year he lives at his family's ancestral village of Gbadolite near the Central African Republic border. He lengthened the Gbadolite airport runway a few years ago, offically for 'security reasons' but actually so the supersonic Concorde he charters from Air France can land here.

Critics peg Mobutu's fortune at five billion dollars. Mobutu himself insists it totals 'less than $50 million', but confidential financial reports suggest that Mobutu receives almost $100 million a year directly from his government to spend as he sees fit. This is more than the Government spends on education, health and other social services combined.

Foreign friends helped Mobutu become a millionaire almost 30 years ago. His first few million dollars came from the US Central Intelligence Agency and from a United Nations peacekeeping force in the early 1960s. By the mid-1970s, the CIA alone had paid Mobutu more than $150, according to Roger Morris, a former aide to Henry Kissinger . . .

The real culprits are the foreign powers, and especially the US, which has kept Mobutu in power for 25 years. He has served their interests by making Zaire the most important staging ground for Western military intervention in Central and Southern Africa. Secret files of the IMF and World Bank are full of reports on corruption at the top in Zaire and suffering at the bottom.

These records describe how much of the money lent to Zaire by multi-lateral institutions and Western governments over the past quarter-century was squandered or siphoned off. Despite their secret knowledge, these same institutions persist in demanding that Zaire pays off its foreign debt of eight billion dollars by accepting economic austerity pro-grammes. This would involve further cutting an already disastrously underfunded public sector and hit the poor hardest.

The West has economic as well as military interests in Zaire. In the early years of Mobutu's regime investors from the US and other Western nations profited enormously from a multi-billion-dollar investment and construction boom funded by foreign loans. Foreign investment ground to a virtual halt after the near collapse of the Zairean economy in the mid-1970s. But the loans which paid for that investment remain to be paid.

(Steve Askin, 'Zaire's den of thieves', *New Internationalist*, June 1990, pp. 18,19.)

35. *Ibid*. p. 19.

36. *Ibid*. p.19.

37.

The statistics released by the Home Office show that 1,081,000 offences were reported in England and Wales in the first three months of this year. The sharpest rises were in burglary (up 18 percent), theft (16 percent) and criminal damage (12 percent). These three categories account for 94 percent of reported crime . . .

Academics tend to prefer the social and economic explanations for ris-ing crime. Professor Jock Young, head of criminolgy at Middlesex Poly-technic, said that the figures were not a blip but part of a clear underlying rise in crime committed by people who felt unfairly deprived.

(Emma Campbell, *Independent on Sunday*, 1 July 1990.)

38. Donald Trelford, 'Mr Khashoggi's day in court', *Observer*, 8 April 1990.

39. Peter Hillmore, *Observer*, 1 April 1990.

40. *Observer*, 1 July 1990.

41. Martin Walker, 'Full fathom five the coral suffocates from fishing lines and phosphates', *Guardian*, 6 March 1990.

42.

In the past four years, about 1,000 people died in major disasters . . .

Bradford, 11 May, 1985. Fifty-six fans were killed in a football stand blaze at Valley Parade. The Popperwell Report said that the disaster could have been prevented. The Health and Safety Executive, West Yorkshire county council, the fire brigade and Bradford City football club were all aware of the fire hazard caused by years of accumulated rubbish. Nothing was done to eliminate it.

Manchester Airport, 25 August, 1985. Fifty-five people died in a burn-ing British Airtours charter jet as it prepared for take-off. The inquiry said economic pressures for more seating had impeded escape from the aircraft. Among the 31 safety recommendations was change to materials used in the construction of seats – 48 of the 55 victims were killed by smoke and toxic gases.

Zeebrugge Ferry, 6 March, 1987. The P&O ferry *Spirit of Free Enterprise* capsized, with the loss of 188 lives, as a result of its bow doors being left open. The Sheen inquiry found that the ferry company was 'infected with sloppiness from top to bottom'. The master, chief officer and assistant boatswain were directly responsible for the 'errors of omission' which led to the tragedy. But the underlying and cardinal faults had to be laid at the management door. Managers failed to consider safety on its ships, did not listen to masters' complaints.

Glanrhyd, 19 October, 1987. Four people died when a train plunged into a flooded Welsh river. BR accepted liability and an inquest jury returned a verdict of unlawful killing. The Welsh Water Authority issued a rare Red 2 flood warning and BR's own control centre at Swindon telexed Swansea station warning it would be 'probably imprudent' to allow the train to depart. An hour later it slipped into the swollen river.

Kings Cross, 18 November, 1987. Thirty-one were killed when a fireball engulfed the Underground station's ticket hall. The Fennell inquiry said London Underground senior management had 'narrow horizons and a dangerous, blinkered self-sufficiency' and were unwilling to take advice from safety officers. Safety officers were described as voices in the wilderness – for year after year they reported poor electrical wiring in escalator rooms, but no action taken. Staff were unsupervised, untrained and ill-equipped, the report said. Outbreaks of fire in the Tube stations were regarded as inevitable by a management which strictly monitored financial matters, but not safety.

Piper Alpha, 6 July, 1988. An explosion on the North Sea oil rig claimed 167 lives. The inquiry was told that fire-fighting equipment had been 'virtually useless' for months before the disaster. Several safety audits were carried out following an earlier explosion in 1984, but the owners, Occidental, never released the findings. A lack of life jackets and portable fire extinguishers in the emergency muster area, and the role of the rig's support ship during the rescue operation, were also criticized.

Clapham, 12 December, 1988. Thirty-five people were killed in a triple train crash. An inquiry heard that the disaster had been 'wholly avoidable'. BR was criticized for failing to check that proper safety procedures were carried out. Technicians were criticized for defective workmanship on vital signalling equipment, lack of checks on work and a lack of proper testing. Excessive overtime – with many signalmen working seven days a week for months – was a factor.

Lockerbie, 21 December, 1988. All 259 passengers and crew aboard a Pan Am jumbo bound for New York were killed by a bomb in Britain's worst air tragedy. Calls for tighter airport security followed.

Kegworth, 8 January, 1989. Forty-seven people died when a British Midland 737 crashed while attempting an emergency landing. The air accidents investigation branch interim report did not explain why the crew shut down the sound right engine, when it was the left engine that was disintegrating.

Purley, 4 March, 1989. Five people were killed and 87 injured. A BR internal inquiry blames the driver for going through a red light.

Glasgow, 6 March, 1989. Two people are killed and 40 injured as two suburban trains collide. British Rail pointed to human error in handling signal warning systems. The number of drivers passing red lights had doubled to about 800 a year since 1979.

Hillsborough, 15 April, 1989. Ninety-five football fans died in the crush at Sheffield Wednesday's ground. The Taylor report blamed the failure of police control. Senior officers did not even visit the ground before approving the crowd control plan. The club was criticized for the lack of rescue and medical equipment, and inadequate signposting to steer latecomers away from the full terraces.

('Corners cut on the road to disaster', *Guardian*, 22 August 1989.)

Fresh evidence from the investigation into the Lockerbie bombing indicates that the suitcase containing the bomb was allowed on the doomed Pan Am flight because of a failure to match baggage to passengers. Within the last week detectives have established that only one item of luggage, pierced together from the wreckage after one-and-a-half years of painstaking forensic work, cannot now be positively linked with a passenger from Flight 103. That item is the Samsonite suitcase which held the bomb.'

(John Merritt, 'Baggage clue points blame at Pan Am', *Observer*, 1 July 1990.)

Major disasters could often be prevented if people learned from past mistakes rather than just blamed accidents on human error, Dr Deborah Lucas, a safety expert, [said]. 'Inquiries into major accidents repeatedly emphasize that the disasters were preventable.' What was needed, she said, was for management to improve their company's 'safety culture'.

After the sinking of the *Herald of Free Enterprise* in 1987, previous incidents of ferries leaving Zeebrugge with their bow doors open had come to light, said Dr Lucas, of Human Reliability Associates, near Wigan, Manchester. There were also numerous fires on escalators in the London Underground before the King's Cross fire the same year. Signal failures were recorded by British Rail before the Clapham Junction train crash in 1988, and there were crushes, non-fatal, of football fans before the 1989 Hillsborough disaster.

'In each of these cases it was argued that the earlier incidents should have helped to prevent the later disasters,' she said. It was important to learn lessons from accidents and near misses, to emphasize safety, to allot funds for safety measures, and to have a proper perspective on human error and its prevention.

(*Guardian*, 22 August 1990.)

Chapter 7. 'Yes I Can' – Responsibility and Selfishness

1. James Gleick, *Chaos*, op. cit. p. 8.
2. Václav Havel, *Letters to Olga*, tr. Paul Wilson (Faber, London, 1990), pp. 321, 322.
3. *Ibid.* p. 323.
4. *Ibid.* p. 147.
5. *Ibid.* p. 268.

I feel that there is more than mere intellectual quibbles preventing me from professing faith in a personal God. Behind those 'quibbles' lies something deeper: I have not had the mystical experience of a genuine, personal revelation, that supremely important 'last drop'. No doubt I could simply substitute the word 'God' for my 'something' or my 'absolute horizon' but that would hardly be responsible. I am trying to describe the matter as precisely as I can, as it appears to me and as I feel it; in other words, I don't wish to feign certainty where none exists. I admit to an affinity for Christian sentiment and I'm glad it's recognizable; nevertheless, one must be extremely cautious in such matters and weigh one's words well (as a matter of fact the archbishop of Prague himself once told me this when we were discussing the matter). There are many other aspects to a faith in the Christian God, such as a belief in the divinity of Christ, in the Immaculate Conception of the Virgin Mary, etc. – and I take all that too seriously to pass off as belief various more or less figurative acceptances of those things. (p. 269.)

6. David Rieff reviewing Richard Nixon's autobiography *In the Arena* (Simon and Shuster, New York, 1990) wrote:

Things get off to a rather grim start with the book's epigraph, which is taken from Theodore Roosevelt. 'It is not the critic who counts,' wrote the burly architect of America's first imperial golden age, 'not the man who points out where the strong man stumbles . . . the credit belongs to the man who is actually in the arena.' This is second-rate Roosevelt, of course, but it is vintage Nixon. As usual, a translation is required. What this passage actually means is: 'The liberal press did me in and I was a great fellow.'

There is nothing new about this line, and, for all the publishers' claim that Nixon has something different to say about his presidency and about Watergate, not much that is new in this book. About his fall, Nixon offers his standard justification. He acknowledges that he should have paid more attention to what his staff was up to, and, in the managerial newspeak he has always favoured, declares: 'I should have focused on the issue immediately, dug out the truth on top priority basis, fired everyone involved, and taken the political heat.' In other words, damage control. Once this ritual *mea culpa* is out of the way, Nixon is free to say what he really thinks. 'Watergate,' he writes, 'was not a morality play . . . but rather a political struggle.' In other words, everybody does that in politics.

(*Independent on Sunday*, 22 July 1990.)

7. *Time*, 18 June 1990.

8. Quoted in *Child Pornography* by Tim Tate (Methuen, London, 1990), p. 106.

9. Fiona Buckland, 1990.

10. Igor Stravinsky and Robert Craft, *Dialogues and a Diary* (Faber, London, 1968).

11. Luke 12:48.

12. Nicky Harris in 'Nothing to Fear', produced by Brendan Hughes, DBA Television, Belfast, Channel 4, 24 March 1990.

13. Edmund Gosse, *Father and Son, op. cit.* pp. 136, 162.

14. Bryan McAllister, *Look, No Feet* (Victor Gollanz, London, 1987), p. 40.

15. D. Rowe, *Beyond Fear, op. cit.* pp. 215ff.
16. Lynn Barber, 'Captain Paranoia in the pulpit', *Independent on Sunday*, 3 June 1990.
17. *Beyond Fear, op. cit.* pp. 250ff.
18. Peter Nasmyth, 'Once a soldier', *Observer*, 22 April 1990.
19. Bryan McAllister, *op. cit.* p. 90
20. Paul Smith, 'Lord Linley hits the road again – and how!', *Daily Mail*, 4 May 1988.
21. Lynn Barber, *ibid.*
22. Geraldine Brooks, 'Tea and sympathy with Mrs Khomeini', *The Sunday Times*, 30 July 1989.
23. *Beyond Fear, ibid.* Chapter 10.
24. Alice Miller, *Thou Shalt Not Be Aware* (Virago, London, 1988).
25. Alice Miller, *The Untouched Key*, tr. Hildegarde and Hunter Hannum (Virago, London, 1990), p. 52.
26. *Beyond Fear, ibid.* Chapter 4.
27. *Guardian*, 27 February 1990.
28. *Guardian*, 8 March 1990.
29. Peter Beaumont, 'The demons on my roof – governor', *Observer*, 6 May 1990
30. *Time*, 16 July 1990.
31. *Observer*, 7 July 1990.
32. Nirad Chaudhuri, 'The grandeur of suffering which the West cannot understand', *Independent on Sunday*, 8 July 1990.
33. Hugo Young, *Margaret Thatcher, One Of Us* (Pan, London, 1990).
34. Andrew Gimson, 'Alderman Roberts as a role model for the nation', *Independent*, 6 May 1990.
35. Robert Woods, 'Aid monstrosities', *New Internationalist*, June 1990, p. 23.
36.
> Nobody told the villagers that eucalyptus doesn't burn well, and so is not good for cooking purposes; or that unless you spray DDT it gets so riddled by termites that building poles scatter white power on the heads of those living below before suddenly falling down; or that the tree leaches the soil, preventing almost anything from growing thereafter. (*Ibid.*)

When I was travelling in Israel, many Israelis showed me special attention when they discovered that I was Australian, for Australia had supplied them with the eucalyptus trees which had been so effective in draining the swamps infested with malaria-carrying mosquitoes. I hesitated to tell these Israelis that these eucalyptus may now be up to no good, especially now they were so large and flourishing. Moreover, I was very taken with my images of Jesus preaching under the gum trees in Capernaum and being baptized in a river indistinguishable from the green reaches of the Murrumbidgee.

37. *Ibid.* p. 24.
38. *Beyond Fear, op. cit.* Chapter 7.
39. On 28 April 1988, Channel 4 began a retrospective series on *World in Action*. The first was a programme by Granada Television which brought together Mick Jagger, who had just escaped prison for a drug offence, with

the then Home Secretary, the editor of *The Times*, and church leaders to discuss the generation gap.

40. Vaclav Havel, *Letters to Olga*, *op. cit.* p. 351.

Chapter 8. 'Yes I Can' – Martyrdom and Revenge

1. W.B. Yeats, 'Easter Rising 1916', *Collected Poems* (Macmillan, London, 1950).

2. Vaclav Havel, *Letters to Olga*, *op. cit.* p. 300.

3. Fiona Buckland, 1990.

4. *The Australian*, 4 October 1978.

5. Julie Flint, 'Palestinian recruits sing a battlesong to death and honour as training gets tougher', *Guardian*, 28 April 1988.

6. *Trotsky's Diary in Exile*, 4 April 1935 (Faber, London, 1959).

In her book *The Untouched Key* (tr. Hildegarde and Hunter Hannum, Virago, London, 1990, pp. 62–8), Alice Miller shows how a helping witness in childhood can be the determining factor in whether a cruelly treated child becomes a despot who turns his repressed feelings of helplessness against others, or an artist who speaks of his suffering through his work.

Stalin in his childhood had no protector.

The family of Stalin might have come out of Gorky's play *The Lower Depths*. It was brutally unhappy. They lived in grinding poverty, constantly in debt. Sometimes the neighbours would have pity on the struggling seamstress and her undernourished son; and their pity may have done more harm to Joseph than the beatings he received from his father. Sometimes poverty drove Ekaterina close to madness, and we hear of her wandering through the streets with her hair dishevelled, crying, praying, singing and muttering to herself. From an early age the boy knew what it was to live alone in the world.

According to Iremashvili, who knew the family well and was constantly in and out of the house, the father beat the son vengefully, with a kind of brooding, deliberate passion, without pleasure and without any sense of guilt or wrongdoing, for no other purpose than to provide himself with some excitement in an otherwise empty and purposeless existence. The result was inevitable. The boy learned to hate. Most of all he hated his father, but gradually this hatred expanded until it included all other fathers, all other men.

'I never saw him crying,' Iremashvili relates, and the statement has a ring of authenticity. The boy became hardened by his beatings, and became in the end terrifyingly indifferent to cruelty. His face and body were covered with bruises, but he was determined not to surrender. Somehow he would survive his father, but in order to survive it was necessary to become as brutal as his father . . .

Church was a consolation, for no one beat him in church, no one scorned him or had pity on him . . . His earliest ambition was to be a priest; and his mother looked forward to the time when she would be blessed by her son . . .

('The family of Joseph': Payne, *The Rise and Fall of Stalin*, p. 9.)

Stalin's left arm was shorter than his right and badly bent. Alice Miller points out that injuries to the left arm are common in children who are beaten by an adult using a weapon like a broomstick against the child.

By contrast, Charlie Chaplin's childhood was spent in great poverty, but he was always assured of his mother's love. She had to put him in an orphanage, but never failed to visit him. His films portrayed poverty and disaster but also love and tenderness. Stalin as a child was punished by a cruel tyrant and never knew why he was punished and when the punishment would occur. 'When a child's boundless powerlessness never finds sheltering arms, it will be transformed into harshness and mercilessness; when, in addition, it is spurred by a mother's ambition, it can result in a great career that introduces all the elements of the child's repressed misery into world history.'

David Hirst, writing about Saddam Hussein after he had invaded Kuwait in 1990, said:

> Saddam made of Iraq a family business in the most literal sense. It is hard to grasp its inner workings without looking at the social and moral climate of his youth. He was born into a poor peasant family in a region which had fallen on hard times. His childhood environment in his town of al-Ojja near Takrit, recalls an exile intimate with it, was 'full of evil'. His father died before he was born and his mother, 'renowned for her ugliness and vile tongue', took her third husband, Hassan Ibrahim – 'Hassan the Liar' as he was locally known. The stepfather took to extremes local Bedouin notions of a hardy upbringing, and for punishment the stepson was beaten with an asphalt-covered stick, forced to dance around to dodge the blows. Ibrahim used Saddam to steal, and the youth had a spell in a juvenile asylum. At school his idea of a practical joke was to make as if to embrace a dignified old Koran teacher and then insert a snake beneath his robes.
>
> His uncles were 'robbers and murderers', the exile said, and to 'kill more than one person at a time was a sign of courage'. Saddam's first murder, in his teens, was that of a shepherd from the nearby Ajil tribe. He had committed three more murders before he achieved national prominence in his attempt on the life of General Kassem in 1959. He was a natural to head the Ba'ath party's Khatt al-Hunain death squad, the first important rung on his ladder to absolute power.
>
> Ever since he attained it, an amazing range of security precautions by one of the world's most fearsome despotisms would never have been enough without the loyalty of the Takritis. Apart from the undreamt of spoils it has brought them, their loyalty has been based on two, sometimes contradictory, emotions: their fear of Saddam and the fear that, if he goes, they will go too in the most appalling bloodbath that Iraq, a traditionally violent land, has witnessed.
>
> (*Guardian*, 14 August 1990.)

When Saddam Hussein used chemical weapons against the Kurds, President Bush vetoed Congress's demand for sanctions against Iraq, and the British Government increased export quotas to Iraq. It was only when the wealth of the USA and Britain was threatened that George Bush and Margaret Thatcher found his actions 'unacceptable'.

7. J.M. Cohen and J.F. Phipps, *The Common Reader* (Rider, London, 1979), p. 63.

8. Luke 6:27–8.

9. 2 Thessalonians 1:7–9.

10. Donald W. Riddle, *The Martyrs: A Study in Social Control* (University of Chicago Press, Chicago, 1931).

11. *Ibid*. p.1 26

12. *Ibid*. p. 2

13. *Ibid*. p. 98

14. *Ibid*. pp. 109, 120, 121.

15. *Ibid*. pp. 180, 12.

16.

The role of penance ritual in the Christian church was to provide the Christian guilty of committing a heinous sin with a way of restoring the spiritual purity of the newly baptized. In its earliest form, as it first appeared in the second century, the process involved a formal petition to the bishop on the part of the sinner for entrance into the order of the penitents. For a period of time, which varied with the flagrancy of the violation, the penitent was excluded from communion and obliged to undertake a spiritually therapeutic regime of prayer, fasting, and the distribution of alms, and to avoid potentially compromising activities such as sex, business negotiations and public office . . . Even after the prescribed period of penance had elapsed and the penitent was once again allowed to attend mass, sex and the other potentially damaging pursuits remained off limits so as to protect the reconciled sinner from a fatal relapse . . .

As onerous as the *ordo poenitentiae* must have appeared to Christians obliged to enter it in expiation of a mortal sin, it proved a strong magnet for others who, while not guilty of any particular infraction, were attracted to the ascetic discipline that it involved . . .

The popularity of this *poenitantia spontanea* among lay men and women seems itself to have been a product of the inherent limitations of a penitential system . . . Because each Christian could apply for the cleansing effects of a public penance only once in a lifetime, it became a standard practice to postpone penance until the deathbed to minimize the occasion for relapse. While this may have proved the safest avenue in terms of the ultimate goal of salvation, such procrastination afforded little in the way of solace for anyone anxious about a lifelong accumulation of venial sins. Voluntary penance offered the conscientious Christian not only a way of avoiding many potentially sinful situations, but an opportunity to make a positive contribution to his or her own spiritual standing by means of a self-imposed ascetic discipline . . .

The ease with which a layperson could adopt a life of penance stood in marked contrast to the subsequent difficulty of resuming a normal secular life. Like the monks, the penitents were permanently bound to their professions . . . [The Church] councils repeatedly authorized bishops and priests to enforce the penitent's commitment with threats of anathema . . . Martyrdom was a perfect solution to the spiritual anxiety produced by an inflexible penitential system.

Notes

(Kenneth Baxter Wolf, *Christian Martyrs in Muslim Spain* (Cambridge University Press, Cambridge, 1988), pp. 108–12.)

17. Edmund Gosse, *Father and Son, op. cit.* p. 137.

18. Andrew Higgins, 'Self-sacrifice for socialism back in vogue in China', *Independent*, 4 November 1989.

19. Axel Munthe gave an amusing account of his success as a doctor to society women in Paris and Rome in his erstwhile best seller *The Story of San Michele* (John Murray, London, 1929).

20. Susie Orbach, *Hunger Strike* (Faber, London, 1988).

21. Cecil Woodham-Smith, *Florence Nightingale* (Constable, London, 1950).

22. Mary Carey, *Kissing the Rod*, ed. Germaine Greer, Jeslyn Medoff, Melinda Sansone and Susan Hastings (Virago, London, 1989).

23. Sudhir Kakar, *The Inner World* (Oxford University Press, Delhi, 1981), p. 66.

24. Fiona Buckland, 1990.

25. Oscar Wilde, writing under his assumed name of Sebastian Melmoth in 1904, quoted in *The International Thesaurus of Quotations* (Penguin, Harmondsworth, 1973), p. 389.

26. Fiona Buckland, 1990.

27. *Breaking the Bonds, op. cit.*, pp. 205–10.

28. Jane Walker, *Guardian*, 28 March 1990.

29. *King Lear*, Act I, scene iv.

30. The ninth century martyrs of Cordoba, Spain, were greatly criticized by many of the Christian community who lived in relative harmony with their Muslim rulers.

They accused the confessors of selfishness, being more concerned about their own salvation than about the fate of the Andalusian Christian community as a whole. Such audaciously suicidal behaviour, in their opinion, was motivated by pride, *initium omnis peccati*. It proved that the confessors were 'indiscreet and unwilling to suffer with the weaker Christians, striving instead to purchase the comfort of their own peace and tranquility in heaven with their blood.'

(Kenneth Baxter Wolf, *op. cit.* p. 116.)

31. *Breaking the Bonds, op. cit.*

32. Fiona Buckland, 1990.

33. *Strawberry Blonde*, Warner Brothers, 1941.

34. Tomas Borge, *Mi Venganza Personal*, tr. Jorge Calderon (*New Internationalist*).

Chris Brazier wrote:

After the Revolution Tomas Borge was to face the ultimate test of his own principles when he became Justice Minister and had to take responsibility for that very National Guard which had tortured him, his family and his comrades. One of the Sandinista's first acts as a government was to abolish the death penalty: members of the National Guard were instead imprisoned. But they were not locked up in the same prison system over which they had presided but one that was reformed absolutely. Prisoners began in secure jails but progressed through good behaviour into ever more open and humane environments until they ended up visiting their home at weekends and guarding themselves. The principle of rehabilitation which has been all but lost in the Western penal system here came back to life – the belief that for people to behave as humans they have to treated as humans.

(*New Internationalist*, August, 1990.)

35. Sheldon Kopp, *No Hidden Meanings* (Science and Behavior Books, Palo Alto, Ca., 1975), nos. 7 & 8.

Chapter 9. The Best Is Good Enough

1. Radio 2, March, 1990.
2. *Guardian*, 10 April 1990.
3. Vaclav Havel, *Letters to Olga*, *op. cit.* p. 243.
4. Diana Elrington, 1989.

When I asked Diana if she would draw a picture of a monkey with his paw in the monkey trap, she set about trying to find a picture or description of such a trap. Was it a woven basket? Or a gourd? Everyone she spoke to knew about the monkey trap, but her diligent searches in libraries found no mention of it. Was the monkey trap a universal myth?

Finally, her search being fruitless, she drew the picture shown here. A year later, having long ceased to search for an account of the monkey trap, Diana, whose reading interests are very wide, borrowed a biography from the local library called *Give Me Yesterday* by James Williams (Gwasg Gomer, 1971). Later she wrote to me about this book.

James Williams told of an old ships' painter he had met in 1917, and I quote, 'One of his best stories was about rounding the Horn. So cold it was that men's feet swelled to the size of pumpkins, and then beating up the coast of South America, they'd call at various ports doing quite a bit of coastal trading. Once when they were ashore they were shown by the natives how to catch monkeys. A coconut was opened, the aperture being large enough for a monkey to insert his paw. Then this was tethered by a knotted lanyard through the soft eye and pegged to the ground. A dollop of demerara was placed inside. And you retired to watch the event. Curiosity overcoming discretion, the monkeys would shin down from the trees to examine the nuts, then tentatively taste the sugar. And, alas! overcome by greed, would shove their hand inside, and clutch as much sugar as was possible. They were trapped, for the clenched paw full of sugar was too big to be withdrawn. You rushed out and held the animal by the scruff of the neck, then grimacing fearsomely you bit his paw hard. The old salt swore that the monkey would never bite you after that.!!!' So now we know. Or do we? (6 May 1990.)

5. John MacLachlan, 'Fighting alone in the valley of fear', *Observer*, 26 August 1990.
6. *Guardian*, 31 August 1990.
7. Lynn Barber, Interview with Nureyev, *Independent on Sunday*, 19 August 1990.
8. Personal communication, 1989.
9. Edmund Gosse, *Father and Son*, *op. cit.* p. 248.
10. Vaclav Havel, *op. cit.* pp. 367, 368.

In August, 1990, the major newspapers and magazines in the UK carried a series of large, glossy advertisements devoted solely to information about sugar. For instance, one such advertisement carried large, coloured pictures of a stick of sugar cane and a sugar beet, and a text which read:

> You're looking at two of Nature's sugar factories. And highly productive operations they are too. On the left, *Saccharum officinarum*, or sugar cane. On the right, *Beta vulgaris*, or sugar beet. They work every hour daylight sends, seven days a week . . .

and so on with more facts about sugar until:

> Of course, artificial sweeteners are also made in plants. But plants of a rather different kind. The question is, do you prefer your sweetener made from sodium saccaride, aspartic acid, aceto-acetic acid and phenylalanine? Or sunshine, air and water? Sugar. The more you know about it, the sweeter it tastes.

In tiny print on the black earth background to the beet are the words 'SILVER SPOON AND TATE AND LYLE'.
Radio Times, 25–31 August 1990.
11. Garry Trudeau, 'Doonesbury', *Guardian*, 17 August 1990.
12. Vaclav Havel, *op. cit.* pp. 352–4.
13. BBC Breakfast TV, 10 March 1990.
14. *Time*, 27 August 1990.
15. *Breaking the Bonds, op. cit.* pp. 327–69.
16. Peter Sellars ,'Balham – Gateway to the South', *The Best of Sellars* (Parlophone, Australia, 1957).
17. 'A.man who hasn't been cured of writing poetry', *Sunday Age*, 14 January 1990.
18. *op. cit.* (Queensland University Press, 1988).
19. Black Swan, Moorebank, NSW, 1990.
20. An outstanding example of how Australian politicians typically conduct discussions is that given by the Federal Treasurer, Paul Keating. John Pilger wrote:

> His descriptions of the Opposition and others opposed to his economic policies include the following: harlots, sleazebags, frauds, immoral cheats, boxheads, brain damaged, loopy crims, stupid foulmouthed grubs, pieces of criminal garbage, rustbuckets, scumbags, dimwits, dummies, perfumed gigolos, piss-ants, gutless spivs, stunned mullets, gouls and barnyard bullies. Inexplicably, Keating is described by his supporters as 'eloquent'.

(*A Secret Country*, Jonathan Cape, London, 1989.)
21. BBC Radio 2, 18 September 1989.
22. *The Letters of Oscar Wilde*, ed. Rupert Hart-Davis (Rupert Hart-Davis Ltd, 1962), Jan-March, 1897, p. 445.
23. 'Equinox: Earth Calling Basingstoke', Channel 4, 26 August 1990.
24. Takeo Doi, *The Anatomy of Self*, tr. Mark A. Harbison (Kodansha International Ltd, Tokyo, 1986), p. 155.

Yes, it's cherry blossom time in Japan and that's serious business for the nature-loving people of Tokyo. Only a few trees have blossomed so far but the first picnickers are already setting up. Last year saw a record

450,000 people descend on Tokyo's Ueno Park in a single day. That's more than 500 people per tree.

(*Guardian*, 23 March 1990.)

25. Josephine Flood, *Archaeology of the Dreamtime* (Collins, Sydney, 1983), p. 250.

26. Sally Morgan, *My Place* (Fremantle Arts Centre Press, Fremantle, 1986).

27. *Guardian*, 21 September 1989.

Index